Read **FASTER**

Read FASTER —

and Get More
from Your Reading

by **NILA BANTON SMITH**

Professor of Education
New York University

PRENTICE-HALL, INC.
Englewood Cliffs, N. J.

Library of Congress Catalog Card No.: 58-8990

Tenth Printing. . . . . . . *September, 1965*

PRINTED IN THE UNITED STATES OF AMERICA
75336—T

Contents

Reading · Tackling the Job · Vocabulary Development · Maintaining Your Skills · Maintaining Speed in Reading Easy Material for Main Ideas · Maintaining Speed in Skimming

ACKNOWLEDGMENT

Grateful acknowledgment is made to the following able instructors at The Reading Institute of New York University, who tested and successfully used the procedures described in this book in teaching adults to read better:

Harry L. Donahoe, Justin H. Miller, Harold H. Ferster, Donald S. Leeds, Irwin L. Joffe, Robert Chamberlain, Edward T. Clark, and James Devine.

Special acknowledgment is given to Justin H. Miller and James Devine for valuable assistance in helping to prepare testing questions which accompany several of the practice selections in the book.

Introduction

This book has one basic purpose—to help you read as well as you want to read. Regardless of your age or occupation or the kind of reading that you have to do, you *can* learn to read more rapidly and with better understanding.

But how?

There *is* a new art of reading. This new art has arisen in response to the deeply-felt need of adult Americans to read faster and better. In this book you will find explanations of the basic techniques in this new art of rapid, effective reading, together with selections to which you may apply these new techniques for practice. *If you follow the instructions faithfully and practice their application conscientiously, you can achieve whatever goals in reading efficiency you may desire.*

First Step in Reading Improvement

First, take an inventory of your present skills in reading.

When you begin any self-improvement course you should know where you are at the start and the progress you make as you go along. If you take a weight-reducing course, you weigh and measure at the beginning and at frequent intervals thereafter to find how much you are losing in pounds and girth. In a reading course you should measure frequently to find how much you are gaining in speed and comprehension.

Chapter 1 contains the *instructions and materials you need to find out where you stand in regard to these reading skills at the beginning of your work in this book.*

"Discovery"—What Is It?

The discovery discussed in Chapter 2 is that good readers read for ideas and take in several words at each glance, while poor readers read in short units, taking in only one, two, or three words at each pause of the eyes. So long as a person reads in this latter manner, he cannot pick up much speed. The larger thoughts are cut up into so many small units that it is hard to get the full meaning of a passage.

All of this is explained to you in Chapter 2, where you are given practice in stretching your own reading units. This chapter equips you with the *foundation for all the speed work* in the remainder of the book.

Do You Long to Read More Rapidly?

If speed is your chief objective you'll get a lot of satisfaction in working with Chapter 3. It is in this chapter that you really take off!

The title of the chapter is "Faster! Faster!" This title tells you straight from the shoulder that you should abandon your present rate of reading and take on a new tempo.

But you aren't simply given this instruction. You're told how to put yourself in the right physical setting for fast reading, how to set up a purpose for faster reading, what to do mentally in starting your speed reading program.

Then you are given an opportunity to apply these instructions in the selections provided for rapid reading practice.

A special feature which appears for the first time in this chapter is "Vocabulary Development." Increasing your vocabulary contributes to your speed and comprehension. So you will find *vocabulary helps* in this chapter, and in all the following chapters except the last two.

What Are Signposts in Reading?

There are words that tell you to keep on going straight ahead in your reading—that there will be more of the same thing. There are other words that warn you of a change in thought, that tell you to slow down, there's a sharp turn ahead. It's important for you to know *how to use these word signals*.

In Chapter 4 you will find out what these signposts are, and how to make the most of them in your reading.

What Is Meant by "Shopping Before You Read"?

You shop before you buy clothes, food, or a house. In other words, you *take a preview*. This same general technique applies to an article or book before you buy it, meaning "before you read it."

In Chapter 5 you will learn how to "Shop Before You Read." This is one of the most useful reading procedures you can acquire.

Sight-Seeing!

Everyone loves to sight-see. This is the basic reason why millions of dollars are spent every year in traveling.

Think of the last trip *you* took. What sights do you recall? No doubt a few outstanding ones. The lesser ones have faded.

In the chapter on "Sight-Seeing As You Read" you will learn how to find the outstanding thoughts quickly in printed material. You will learn *how to "spot" the main idea in paragraphs.*

When you have acquired this skill, you will be well on the road to becoming an expert reader.

Do You Grasp Details Readily?

Some of us have no trouble reading easy narrative material. Nowadays, however, most of us have to do much informative reading which is packed with numerous details. These can be confusing. We can't give equal attention to all of them, and often we end up not grasping any of them. Do you have this experience when reading detailed factual or technical material?

There are special techniques for *grasping details readily and reading difficult factual material faster* than you have been accustomed to do. You will learn how to "Mine for Details" in Chapter 7.

Do You Forget What You've Read?

Maybe you understand what you read while you are reading, but can't recall what you've read when you have finished. If you have this common trouble you need to "Wake Up Your Memory." And this can be done quite easily. You have a memory. You just need to learn how to use it while reading. You will find the *secrets of recalling what you read* in Chapter 8.

Patterns of Writing

There are patterns in tool-making, patterns in dressmaking, and patterns in writing.

Every author has some purpose in mind when he starts to write. Different purposes require different patterns of writing. Certain techniques are helpful in reading certain patterns. If you learn how to recognize the most common of these different patterns, and how to deal with each pattern, you will increase your reading competency.

You will learn *the most common patterns of writing, and how to read them*, under the chapter title "Riding Along with the Author."

What About Skimming?

Most people skim in a hit-or-miss fashion. This skill, however, has a potential for tremendous development. It is an art in itself and can be perfected to a high degree.

Skimming is based upon and makes use of all the other skills; consequently, it is the most complex of all. You'll be ready, though, to rise to *new horizons in your skimming techniques* when you reach Chapter 10.

How to Read a Newspaper

It is said that Americans pay $1,000,000,000 a year for the right to read and use a free press. What do you get for your share of this expenditure? A smattering of sports news, a moment of amusement with the comics, a hastily-gathered collection of headlines? This sums it up for many people who are not deriving all the benefit they should from their daily paper.

You can get more—and in less time. First, become aware of all the different types of information a good newspaper contains. Secondly, learn how to *find* what you want quickly. Then make a time-budget to distribute your reading to different departments in the time at your disposal.

By the time you reach Chapter 11 you will have no new skills to learn in order to read a newspaper more effectively. You will use all the skills you have developed up to that point. But you should know which skills to use for what kinds of newspaper content. Chapter 11 discusses this problem and gives you information concerning all of the other *newspaper-reading techniques*.

Do You Know When Writers Are Trying to Influence You?

Much of what you read these days has been written to influence you to accept a point of view or to take a certain action. Some people write to make you buy some article which yields profits to the seller. Others write to cause you to vote the way they want you to vote. Still others write to change your attitude toward some social, political, or religious problem. Or to get you to accept a different philosophy or to change your way of thinking about government or the affairs of life in general.

Like every other good American, you want to assert your privilege of making your own decisions; yet you may be unconsciously influenced by some of the things you read because you are not acquainted with propaganda techniques.

In Chapter 12 some of the common tricks used by writers of propaganda are described and illustrated. In this chapter *you will learn how to detect propaganda and how to analyze it*. After working with this material you should be keenly aware of planted text when you see it. You should know at once when a writer of an ad, article, or book is "working on you."

Are You Confused When Reading Legal Documents?

Do you have trouble reading your agreement for buying a car, your insurance policy, the lease for your apartment, or the deed for your home?

Do you get lost in the repetition of such terms as: "party of the first part," "party of the second part," "grant and demise," "thereof described by the parties hereto," "performing the covenants aforesaid," "hereinbefore mentioned," and so on?

Maybe because of lack of special reading skill and law vocabulary, you become frustrated by such papers and just sign them without reading them, to get the ordeal over with. Plenty of trouble and loss of money has resulted from such careless signing of legal documents.

If you are one of the thousands of people who are baffled by the special kind of reading required for an understanding of legal papers, then Chapter 13 will give you the help that you need. In this chapter *common legal terms are defined and explained*. Information is given in regard to *special reading skills needed in dealing with legal papers,* and provisions are made for applying these skills in reading samples of legal forms. This chapter should take the "bugaboo" out of your reading of legal documents. It may save you a lot of trouble and money besides.

Are You Planning to Have a Reading Improvement Program in Your Company?

Executives and personnel directors know the values of reading training for employees who have substantial amounts of reading to do. If you are an executive or a personnel or training director, you have heard and read about the effects of reading training in companies which have installed improvement programs. Increased production, savings in dollars and cents, and, on the human side, reduced tension, strain, and fatigue—these are the benefits most frequently mentioned.

Perhaps you are thoroughly "sold" on the idea of installing a reading program, but don't know how to go about doing this. There is a lot of quackery in this field, and many false claims, as is always the case in a new and rapidly growing development. You need guidance, careful, sound advice before spending your company's money for a reading improvement course or program.

In Chapter 14 you are given *suggestions for initiating reading improvement training with your personnel.* Qualifications of an instructor are discussed. Necessary materials and equipment are described. Procedures for setting up a program are outlined. Bases for estimating cost are given. This information is essential to you if you are planning to start a reading improvement program in your company office.

The Author's Wish For You

You have had a glimpse of what this book holds for you. Now let me speed you on your reading way with good wishes. I trust that you may achieve whatever goals you have set for yourself in becoming an expert reader.

Happy journey in reading improvement!

NILA BANTON SMITH

Read **FASTER**

Taking Inventory

How Do You Rate Yourself?

WHAT do you have to start with? That's the first thing to find out. You've been adding to or, more likely, depleting your stock of reading skills for the past one, two, three, or more decades. Without specific checking you probably have a general idea that you're a good reader, an average reader, or a poor reader.

Mr. H., a famous newspaper columnist, said to me when he came in: "I think I am a very good reader. I've never had any trouble at all in reading. But if I could learn to cover double the amount of material in the time at my disposal, this would just be a matter of plain efficiency. Mind you, though, this isn't because I'm a poor reader to start with. I'm an excellent reader already."

Miss G., a story reader at a moving-picture studio, said: "I read about fifty pages an hour. Isn't that pretty good?"

Professor R., a college teacher of English, told me with pride: "I can read a novel in one sitting. That's really pretty fast reading, isn't it?"

"I never finish a novel," complained Mrs. B. "I read too slowly to cover books, so I've given them up entirely. About all I can do is to follow the headlines in a newspaper. I must be the world's worst reader."

And so it is that we "grade" ourselves. These impressions, however, are too general to be a basis for making any precise judgment in regard to reading competency. Maybe you, like the columnist, have "never had any trouble in reading." Does that mean that you are an excellent reader as compared with highly-skilled adult readers who have learned the modern techniques of reading?

Even if you do read fifty pages an hour, how well do you get the thought out of what you read? As for the professor, was the book a thin volume with small pages printed in large type like Steinbeck's *Sweet Thursday?* Or was it a huge, compact volume printed in relatively small type such as *Not as a Stranger?* And how long was the "sitting"? Two hours? Six hours? Twelve hours?

Obviously there are many fallacies in attempting to grade oneself in reading. If you wish to find out exactly how well you read and how much improvement you achieve as you go along, then you must make more careful measurements than general impressions.

Measuring Your Reading Growth

Measuring your own growth in reading is comparable to measuring your child's physical growth. If you want to know how fast your child is growing, you periodically weigh him and measure his height. Then you make your comparisons in terms of exact units—pounds and inches. You must do the same sort of thing in evaluating your growth in reading.

Reading is not a "lump sum," as so many people seem to think. It is a very complex mental process involving many different skills. A horse uses one set of muscles when pulling a heavy load uphill and an entirely different set when trying to hold back that load on his way downhill. So it is with reading. We use different sets of skills when we read different kinds of material for different purposes. You will have opportunities to practice several of these different sets of skills as you work through this book.

Regardless of how varied the skills may be, there are always two fundamental skills which are in operation. Growth in reading is judged in terms of progress in these two basic skills as commonly as physical growth is judged in terms of height and weight. And like height and weight these two skills should grow together simultaneously and in relation to each other.

One of these basic skills is *speed*. It is the rate with which you can cover printed material through reading. The basic unit used in measuring speed is the number of words per minute. The abbreviation W.P.M. is written after the number indicating a score, as 275 W.P.M. The other basic skill which easily lends itself to measurement is understanding of what is read. This is *comprehension*. The terms *speed* and *comprehension* have special meanings in a reading-instruction vocabulary. You may as well right now become accustomed to these terms as used in this book.

The writer was one day amused when a gentleman came in with this complaint: "I want to talk with you about my wife. I'm very much worried. She's having a dreadful time with her apprehension."

He might have been told not to seek improvement of his wife's "apprehension" lest he have occasion to worry still more. But instead he was told to bring her in for a check-up of her speed and *comprehension.*

The average reader covers about 250 words per minute. Very good readers read 500 or 600 words per minute. Occasionally there is a person who reads at the phenomenal rate of 1,000 words per minute, or in rare instances even faster. However, ability to cover printed words rapidly is quite valueless unless the reader gathers meaning as his eyes travel over the lines of print.

Fortunately, these two basic skills, speed and comprehension, can be developed with guidance and practice. But they must increase together. Like height and weight in the growing child, comprehension must keep pace with speed in the reading growth of an adult. If you should increase your speed to 600 words per minute and drop your comprehension from 80 to 40 per cent, your speed would do you more harm than good. Therefore, in all the chapters in this book you will be asked to work on *both* speed and comprehension.

First you need to find out what your normal rate of speed is and also get some idea of how well you are comprehending. You can then use these first scores as a basis for comparison to see later on how much you have improved.

For checking purposes you are asked to read two selections. One is very easy, and you will read it simply for entertainment. The other is more difficult, and you will read it for the information it contains.

You'll have to time yourself in taking both of these tests, so get out a watch with a second hand. Note the hour and the minute that you begin to read each of the selections and jot this data down in the space provided. This test is given to check your present speed and comprehension in reading easy, narrative material.

Reading for Entertainment

Don't try to read fast for test purposes. Just read at your comfortable normal rate and for the purpose of enjoying the story.

Ready! Start!

Selection 1

BEGINNING TIME:_____
HR._____ MIN._____

The Great Molasses Flood[1]

From early Colonial days on, ships loaded with wooden hogsheads of thick, dark molasses came regularly from the West Indies to unload at Boston's wharves. Molasses took the place of sugar, which few colonists could afford, and it made Yankee rum. It was a keystone of Boston's prosperity and trade for almost three centuries—until January 15, 1919.

I was a reporter on the *Boston American* on that fateful day. The stories coming in over the wire were predicting, rightly, that on the morrow Nebraska would become the 36th state to vote dry, thus bringing nationwide Prohibition upon this country (and rendering great quantities of molasses virtually useless). But even before the news could be printed, the biggest molasses storage tank in all Boston burst and sent an angry deluge of the stuff rampaging through the old North End, tearing down the elevated railway, demolishing buildings, drowning and crushing 21 persons and dozens of horses, wreaking property damage of more than a million dollars.

For years the tank, a bulging giant 50 feet tall and 282 feet in girth, had loomed above the freight-loading depots, stables, and firehouse on Commercial Street, near Boston's inner harbor. Three days before, the pumps of tankers from Puerto Rico had filled it right up to the brim with 2,320,-000 gallons—14,000 tons—of molasses.

At five minutes to noon on that mild winter morning, a telephone rang in the molasses plant's office in the shadow of the tank. Superintendent William White picked up the receiver and heard his wife insist he join her

[1] Ralph Frye, "The Great Molasses Flood," *Reader's Digest*, August 1955, pp. 63-67.

uptown for lunch. White took a cursory look at the frowning tank, ignored the molasses sweating ominously through the riveted seams, and left—thus undoubtedly saving his life. But the busy market district was thronged with people destined to be less fortunate.

Along Commercial Street, new-fangled motor trucks and horse-team drays clattered on the cobblestones beneath the elevated railway. In the doorways of shops and brick dwellings across the street from the tank, residents were taking advantage of the warm weather to sun themselves. In stables of nearby draying companies, dozens of workhorses were placidly munching hay. Teamsters chatted over their lunch boxes on the freight-loading platforms. Mrs. Bridget Clougherty, 68, stood watching them from the doorway of her frame house at the corner of Copp's Hill and Commercial. Her big son Martin, a well-known boxer and referee, lay in his third-floor bedroom, sleeping soundly. The time was 12:41.

At this moment Patrolman Frank McManus was making a routine duty call at a police-signal box down the street. Suddenly he heard a "grinding, rumbling" noise. Looking up, he saw a dark sea of liquid gush from the bottom of the tank. He saw the big tank open out and fall apart, and a towering wall of molasses roll over the ground with a seething, hissing sound. Going 35 miles an hour with a push of 25 tons, it enveloped the fire station; then buildings began to collapse. McManus yelled for all the ambulances and policemen available.

At the same moment, the brakeman of a northbound train coming around the curve on the elevated yanked his emergency cord. "All I could see was molasses rushing toward me," the brakeman later said. The train stopped just as the elevated structure ahead sagged into the raging molasses below; the forward wheel trucks of the first car were lifted off the rails.

Mrs. Mary Musco, watching from the window of her house when the "explosion" came, saw the three-story Clougherty house rise from its foundations and "fly into the air," then disappear beneath the El in a caldron of floundering horses, people, jagged timbers, splintered wagons, huge crates of goods and—molasses. "I ran for help," Mrs. Musco said. "It was awful. People were running every which way all covered with molasses."

To many people the breaking of the tank came with a tearing sound, like the ripping of a huge sheet of paper. To a Navy gunner on a ship in the harbor it was like a succession of reports from an impossibly-enormous machine gun. The tearing sound was caused by the initial giving-away of the tank at its base; the machine-gun reports were rivets bursting upward from the bottom, like buttons popping off a vest.

Then the very steel of the plates themselves sundered and burst outward. One 400-square-foot section of steel weighing two and one half tons was catapulted 182 feet into North End Park. Another murderous ribbon of half-inch steel plate swept across Commercial Street, sheared through a tree-trunk-size steel El column like a knife through butter. A few hours later, boxer Martin Clougherty, bandaged like a mummy, was able to tell reporters: "I was asleep on the third floor, and I awoke in several feet of molasses. A little way from me I saw my sister. I struggled out from under the wreckage and pulled my sister onto a board. Then I began to look for my mother." But the roof had fallen on Mrs. Clougherty and crushed her.

Russel McLean, a commuter from Waverly, Mass., was on his way to North Station when the tank burst. The next thing he remembered he was lying in a doorway across the street with a young woman unconscious in his lap. "All around me horses and men were struggling in the thick molasses." One man, running from the onrushing molasses when it over-took him, landed sitting and was swept right out into the harbor. Crew-men of the Naval tug *U.S.S. Pawnee* picked him out of the water sticky and frightened, but unharmed.

We at the *Boston American* knew nothing of any of this at the time. I was on my way to lunch when a single alarm came in. Henry Daily, assistant city editor, called to me: "Ralph, take a look at this fire. Prob-ably nothing to it, but there are a lot of old firetraps down there."

I cut north to Commercial Street. At first there was no sign of trouble until, away up past Constitution Wharf, I saw it. What looked like a moving wall of volcanic lava filled the street and was moving relentlessly toward me. Everything it overtook—horses, automobiles, people—disap-peared. I telephoned Henry. "Where's the fire?" he said.

"Wait!" I yelled. "This is no fire. I don't know what it is. Shoot some cameramen and legmen down here fast. Listen—there seems to be an awful stink of molasses around here. Maybe molasses has something to do with it."

"Molasses?" Henry was outraged. When I got nearer I realized that this was the story of all stories. . . . Sailors, firemen, and policemen, wallowing thigh-deep in the wreckage, were coated from head to foot with molasses; it gave them a weird copper color.

The big old firehouse had been shoved off its foundation and stood with its tower canted at a crazy angle. Inside several firemen were still trapped. It took nearly four hours before their comrades freed the last of them—and discovered George Layhe dead at the foot of the sliding pole, with the firehouse piano and pool table piled on top of him.

Even in the shallow places the molasses was dangerous. It was worse than quicksand. It held your feet. Well-meaning bystanders waded in to help floundering victims and couldn't get out. Scores of persons trapped in the upper floors of buildings kept up a plea to be rescued. Fire lines were strung around the area, but the crowd pressed so hard against the ropes that some persons slipped into the goo. Ambulances manned by molasses-stained interns were continually carrying away victims.

One ambulance outfit of Red Cross girls arrived in Oxford-gray uniforms with shiny black puttees and pretty white shirtwaists. They were very beautiful and very earnest, and they plunged into the flood. When firemen dragged them out, swollen and tottering with the weight of molasses, they looked like loathsome creatures of the primordial slime.

By midafternoon the flood had settled. Hundreds of residents and curious spectators went slipping and slopping through the mess and tracked it all over the metropolitan district. The next day if you sat down in any public place or conveyance in the city of Boston, you stuck to the seat. Riders in streetcars and buses in Worcester, 44 miles away, found them smeared. There wasn't a telephone booth in Boston where the instrument didn't stick to your fingers.

Streams of water were played on the molasses to wash it into the sewers and the harbor. But ordinary fire hoses proved useless to dissolve the muck. Firemen discovered that salt water managed somehow to "cut" the molasses. Fireboats and pumping equipment were called into play. Police used huge hydraulic siphons to pump molasses out of flooded cellars. It was nearly a week before all of the bodies were recovered, and months before signs of the disaster disappeared.

The distillery owners tried to wash their hands of responsibility for the disaster, only to find this as sticky a task as the molasses itself. Accident-insurance underwriters, too, tried not to get stuck. "They do not believe," reported the Boston Globe, calmly, "that the aggregate claims will be very great, as the persons affected were for the most part of the wage-earning class."

The courts of Massachusetts took a different view. One hundred and nineteen separate damage suits were filed. Hearings, continued as late as 10 p.m. to give workmen a chance to be heard, consumed 309 days. Three thousand witnesses spoke more than six million words of testimony, filling 40,000 pages of court record.

The defendant distillers spent more than $50,000 on expert witnesses, built three tanks and blew them up in an effort to show the disaster had been caused by an "anarchist bomb." But when it was shown that the molasses tank had been built of thinner plates than were specified in the plans filed with the Boston Building Commission, the defense collapsed. In 1925 the company settled the suits out of court, for a total of more than one million dollars.

Cleaning up the mess took longer than the litigation. Men scraped and scrubbed and painted, but the taint of molasses persisted. It is said that even now, on humid days, a sickly sweetish aroma surrounds some of the older buildings of Boston's North End.

Began   *Finished*   No. words: 1500

No. seconds:

$$\frac{1500}{600} \times 60 = \underline{} \text{ W.P.M.}$$

Write your finishing time in the appropriate space in the form above. If you finished at 34 minutes and 10 seconds after 9, write 9:34:10 under *Finished*. Next, turn back to find your beginning time which you recorded when you started to read the article. Let us suppose that this was 28 minutes after 9. Then write 9:28 under *Began*. Subtracting the beginning time from the finishing time you have 6 minutes and 10 seconds.

Now use the formula given above in computing your reading rate. Divide 1500, the number of words in the selection, by the number of seconds that it took you to read the article. Multiply the answer by 60 to convert to minutes, and the answer will give you the number of words per minute that you read.

Following through with the example above: suppose it took you 6 minutes and 10 seconds to read the article. This would amount to 370 seconds. Dividing 1500 by 370 would give you 4.05. You would then multiply 4.05 by 60 and get 243. This would be the number of words per minute which you read and should be written in the space preceding W.P.M.

Compute your rate according to this procedure and record it in the appropriate space.

Checking Comprehension

Read each of the exercises below. Choose the answer which you think is correct. Write the corresponding letter in the appropriate answer space at the end of the exercises.

1. The article says that one of the uses to which the Colonists put molasses was (a) to pour it on their pancakes, (b) to make candy, (c) to mix with cattle feed, (d) to make Yankee rum.

2. The first person to call ambulances and policemen was (a) Mrs. Bridget Clougherty, (b) Superintendent White, (c) Patrolman Frank McManus, (d) Mrs. Mary Musco.

3. The tank contained about (a) 5,000,000 gallons, (b) 25,000 gallons, (c) 2,300,000 gallons.

4. The writer approached the scene of the disaster (a) because of his own curiosity, (b) because one of the editors of the *Boston American* asked him to do so, (c) hoping to offer some aid, (d) wanting to take pictures.

5. It can be correctly inferred that the time of day when the disaster occurred was (a) early morning, (b) midafternoon, (c) about noon, (d) late evening.

6. As far as clean-up work is concerned the statement least true is (a) the Fire Department helped greatly in the clean-up work, (b) the Police Department directed the activities, (c) the Red Cross was on hand, (d) the Navy helped.

7. The *Boston Globe* (a) declared that the fault lay with the distillers, (b) quoted the underwriters in their underestimation of contingent claims, (c) believed that the underwriters had overestimated the probable claims, (d) made no comments about this matter.

8. The cause of the disaster was traced to (a) the failure of the builders to adhere to specifications, (b) the Building Commission's standards, (c) an anarchist's bomb, (d) none of these.

9. The company finally settled the suits (a) with the state, (b) with the city of Boston, (c) in the Supreme Court, (d) out of court.

10. The cleaning up (a) lasted until after everyone immediately concerned with the flood was dead, (b) was a quick job, (c) lasted longer than the litigation, (d) is not yet completed.

Answers: 1)—, 2)—, 3)—, 4)—, 5)—, 6)—, 7)—, 8)—, 9)—, 10)—.

Check your answers with the Answer Key on page 374. Multiply the number of correct answers by 10. Record your score.

Rate: W.P.M. ____150____　　　Comprehension Score: ____70____

Reading for Information

The following test is provided for the purpose of checking your speed and comprehension in reading more difficult material. Read the article in your normal manner for obtaining its information.

Selection 2

BEGINNING TIME:_____
HR._____ MIN._____

Life on Other Planets[2]

Although climate is chiefly a matter of winds, ocean currents, sunshine, rains, and snow, it involves also the responses of plants and animals to these physical factors. Plants grow on the mountainsides and control the evaporation and contribute to the cloudiness. One industrious animal affects the weather by diverting the water courses, thereby producing lush vegetation in arid regions. Clearly life and climate interact on each other. If life had never appeared on the earth's surface, the local climates would have been different from those which have prevailed. And if the climate had everywhere been unchanging throughout geologic time, the variety of life we know—the millions of species—might not have come about; possibly the organisms would never have got their start in the dim Pre-Cambrian ooze. . . .

Let us consider the solar system and its climatic problems. The existence of life on Mars is still an open question although astronomers have for years rather uncritically assumed that the seasonal color changes on the surface must mean that life is present. An observer looking at the planet Earth from a moderate distance, say a scientist on the Moon, would also see our winters come and go. He should be able to locate the positions of the poles of the earth by watching the alternating color changes due to winter snowfall and summer melting in our northern and southern hemispheres. He would note that we have much water on the surface, in strong contrast to the small amount on Mars, where it is weakly recorded by the skin of hoarfrost in the polar caps. The color changes on the surface of the earth, visible to the observer on the Moon, could be quite independent of vegetable or other forms of life. Even in the absence of snow, the moisture on desert lowlands should produce color that would fade out with the drying up in the annual rainless season. Fog on a lifeless desert could produce a widespread color change. In other words, variations in the color of Mars do not necessarily mean that vegetation is present. The Martian problem is still open.

II

Some of the climatic changes on Mars can be readily deduced. The surface is relatively free of high elevations and certainly free of large bodies of water. Air and water currents must be relatively uncomplicated. The mass is low, and the air is rare even at the Martian surface. The inclination of the equator to the plane of the orbit is like that of the earth and consequently the seasonal phenomena are similar. The rotation of the planet is a little more than 24 terrestrial hours; the year is 1.9

[2] Harlow Shapley, "Life on Other Planets," *The Atlantic Monthly*, November 1953, pp. 29-32.

terrestrial years, and the months may be ignored because the two little moons are ineffective, both tidally and photometrically. We can predict the daily and annual meteorological changes from our own experience after making allowance for the low temperatures and the weak effects of air currents on the lowland elevations. The orbit of Mars has an eccentricity of 0.093, compared with 0.017 for the earth; and therefore the Martian temperature (and climate) will be somewhat affected by the fact that Mars is 26 million miles nearer the sun at perihelion than at aphelion—a change of 18 per cent in the distance. The perihelion effect on the earth's temperature and climate is relatively small, in comparison with the many other contributing factors to terrestrial climatic change, for the perihelion to aphelion difference in distance is only 3.4 per cent.

If we knew how life got started on our own planet, we could better guess whether the Martian conditions have been hostile or friendly to the origin of organisms. Certainly the mean temperature is painfully low, the atmosphere at the surface is rarer than on our highest mountaintops, and both oxygen and water vapor are scarce. Carbon dioxide has been detected and we all agree that argon, produced by the radioactivity of one of the isotopes of potassium, is almost certainly a constituent of the thin Martian atmosphere. The dominant gas presumably is nitrogen, which has not yet been recorded. Could it be detected without going to the planet? Dr. Rupert Wildt of Yale suggests that Martian aurorae may at some time be observed, and, if so, they would probably indicate the presence of a deep but low-density atmosphere composed mostly of nitrogen surrounding the dry, cool planet.

The Moon, of course, is lifeless, waterless, and essentially airless. Hydrogen, helium, nitrogen, and oxygen gases would all leak away from the surface of this small-mass satellite. The Moon might not permanently retain by gravitation even the inert argon, produced radioactively from Potassium 40. Very little of it could get to the surface in the absence of water erosion and volcanic action. The writer interpolates the suggestion, however, that the ever-impinging meteors, with their consequent explosions, would produce, throughout the three or more thousand million years that the Moon has been under meteoric bombardment, various gases, including some that are relatively so heavy that they would not easily escape from the surface. The meteoric impacts would also release from the surface some of the entrapped argon. The Moon must therefore have an atmosphere, but in quantity perhaps not many lungfuls and in character not very salubrious.

The cloud-shrouded surface of the planet Venus remains as yet something of a mystery. In general, the students of planetary atmospheres find little likelihood of life of the terrestrial sort on that planet, notwithstanding its earthlike mass and its fairly suitable location with respect to the sun. Is it covered with oceans of water? Does the rotation period permit an equable night and day alternation? Is the oxygen situation suitable for air-breathers? Some of the astrochemists have rather positive answers to some of the questions of this sort, but doubts still prevail and we must await improved technologies before we penetrate the shroud and agree on the living conditions on the planet Venus.

The other planets of the solar system are too hot or too cold, and they have other limitations. For example, Mercury is too hot on the sun side, too cold in the endless night of the hemisphere that is never exposed to the sun; and life of our sort would be impossible in Mercury's twilight zones because of the lack of atmosphere and water. Jupiter, Saturn, and the other distant planets, out in the icy cold that is inevitable so far from the sun, have poisonous atmospheres, heavy with methane and ammonia; and they have other hostile characteristics.

III

Climate is not the only important factor that determines the possibility of life on a planetary surface. The following are necessary for the origin and continuance of life:

1. Water, the practical solvent for living processes, must be available in liquid form.

2. The planet must have a suitable rotation period so that the nights do not overcool nor the days overheat.

3. The orbital eccentricity must be low to avoid excessive differences in the isolation as the planet moves from perihelion out to aphelion and back. Most cometary orbits would be lethal for organisms.

4. The chemical content of air, ocean, and land surface must be propitious, not perilously polluted with substances inimical to biological operations.

5. The controlling star must not be variable by more than 4 or 5 per cent; it must not be a double star, and of course must not be subject to catastrophic explosions like those of the novae.

6. Finally, life must get started, and it must establish a tenacious hold on the seas, shores, or inland.

Certainly many adjustments could be made by organisms on a planetary surface to physical conditions unlike those we experience, but the major requirements still stand. The most important requirement is, of course, that life must in some way get started.

Began	*Finished*	No. words:	1300

$$\frac{\quad\quad}{\text{No. seconds:}} \times 60 = \underline{\quad\quad} \text{ W.P.M.}$$

Compute your rate in the same way as described above, and record the number of words per minute in the appropriate space.

Checking Comprehension

Mark the letter of each correct answer in the appropriate answer space below the statements.

1. Climate (a) exists quite independent of plants, (b) exists quite independent of animals, (c) has no effect on life, (d) interacts with life.

2. Astronomers have assumed that there is life on Mars because (a) it has canals which they think men have excavated, (b) because Mars has a climate much like our own, (c) because of the color changes on Mars, (d) because Mars apparently has seasons.

3. The length of the Martian year is: (a) about half of our year, (b) about one and three fourths as long as our year, (c) about twice our year, (d) about three times our year.

4. Mars is 26 million miles nearer the sun (a) at aphelion, (b) at perihelion, (c) in the middle of a Martian year, (d) at the end of each axial revolution.

5. The dominant gas on Mars is probably (a) oxygen, (b) carbon dioxide, (c) argon, (d) nitrogen.

6. The moon has (a) a damp atmosphere, (b) no atmosphere, (c) an atmosphere highly limited in quantity, (d) an atmosphere heavily saturated with oxygen.

7. A planet which has a poisonous atmosphere is (a) Venus, (b) Mercury, (c) Jupiter, (d) Mars.

8. One of the conditions for life on a planet is that (a) the planet must revolve around its orbit every 12 months, (b) it must have seasons, (c) it must have a suitable rotation period to prevent extremes of heat and cold, (d) it must have high orbital eccentricity.

9. Another condition necessary for life on a planet is that (a) it must have a chemical content inimical to biological operations, (b) it must be lethal for organisms, (c) its chemical content must be propitious to life, (d) it must have catastrophic explosions.

10. The most important requirement for life is (a) that it be able to adjust to physical conditions different from ours, (b) that it be intelligent enough to survive, (c) it be strong enough physically to survive, (d) that it get started.

Answers: 1)—, 2)—, 3)—, 4)—, 5)—, 6)—, 7)—, 8)—, 9)—, 10)—.

See Answer Key on page 374. Allow 10 for each correct answer.

Rate: W.P.M. ———   Comprehension Score: ———

Using Your Test Scores

Now you have at least some idea of your speed and comprehension in reading easy narrative material and also in reading difficult material. These are your basic beginning scores. You will wish to refer to them frequently in making comparisons with successive scores that you achieve as you proceed through the book.

You may have found that your rates of reading easy material and of reading difficult material are about equal at this time, but they shouldn't be. As you work through this book you will be taught to "shift your gears" when you read different types of materials for different purposes. You will, however, need always to go back to these two sets of beginning scores to ascertain your gains.

Checking Your Physical Habits

Now you should do some informal checking of physical habits which may interfere with attempts to increase speed.

As you continue to read on this page, notice whether or not you point to words or follow the lines of print along with your fingers as you read. If so, break yourself of this habit. One way to do this is to hold the book or magazine with both hands, one on each side of the open pages. Your fingers, then, will not be free to point.

Note whether you move your head from side to side as you read. If so, nest your chin in one hand and hold it firmly. This will prevent your head from moving.

Watch yourself to see if you vocalize the words while reading silently. If your lips move as you read each word, then you are a vocalizer, and this will interfere seriously with your speed. Perhaps you do not actually say the words with your lips, but you may still vocalize to the extent that a slight movement of the muscles in the throat can be detected. If you find yourself vocalizing in either of these ways, place your fingers on your lips or the part of the throat which is moving. Whenever you feel the movement starting, stop it! You can break yourself of this habit by conscious and persistent attention.

Analyze your reading habits to see if you reread a great deal. Note how many times you go back to read a word, phrase, or sentence a second time. If you do not reread at all in pursuing nontechnical material, such as you find on this page, then all is well and good. If you frequently reread, then this is another habit which you must dispense with. When you feel the urge to reread, just proceed straight ahead. You'll probably be surprised to find that you didn't miss anything after all, and in the meantime you will have saved yourself a lot of time.

Perhaps you found that you do not have any of these habits to begin with. If you are free of them, so much the better. If you found that you do have some of them, then consciously break yourself of these practices. With undesirable physical habits cleared away, there is nothing to prevent you from increasing your reading speeds to any goals that you may set for yourself.

CHAPTER 2

Discovery

A Stick and a Drumhead

Back in 1879 there was a Frenchman by the name of Javal who became interested in investigating eye movements. He thought that, if he could ascertain exactly how the eye behaves when a person is reading, this would afford some insight into the mental activities that go on as reading takes place.

First he tried observing the eyes of people who were reading just by looking at them with his own naked eyes. But the eyes of the readers moved so fleetingly that Javal couldn't tell just what did take place. He then tried placing a mirror in front of the reader, watching the reader's eyes in the mirror. But this didn't work either. Finally Javal concluded that the movements of the eyes could not be detected accurately by another pair of naked eyes.

He continued to work on the problem for some time. His thought was that it might be possible to rig up some sort of contrivance which could be used in obtaining really objective evidence in regard to movements of the eyes. He consulted his friends, asking them to help him invent some way of checking the eye movements of a person reading. "Nonsense," said they. "Why bother about something that everybody already knows? The eyes have to look at each letter in every word as they move across a line of print. Otherwise, how could the reader tell one word from another?"

This theory had been accepted as a fact throughout the centuries. The whole methodology of teaching reading was based for many years on the assumption that a person looks at each separate letter as he reads. Hence children were always taught their ABC's as a first step in learning to read.

Javal, however, doubted that a person recognized printed sentences letter by letter, so he persisted in trying to figure out some method by which he could detect and record the movements of the eyes under reading conditions. At last he hit upon it—a stick and a drumhead!

In developing his experimental equipment, Javal first fashioned a cup of plaster of Paris which was to fit over the eyeball of the person reading. He made an aperture in the middle of the cup through which the page could be seen.

While the plaster of Paris was still damp and pliable, Javal inserted one end of a long, slender stick into the outer side of the cup. When the cup dried, of course the stick was securely rooted in the plaster of Paris.

Next, Javal smoked a drumhead as people sometimes prepare a piece of glass for use in looking at an eclipse of the sun. The smoke left a heavy black coating on the drumhead.

When this equipment was ready, Javal asked a man to sit close to the drumhead and read. The plaster of Paris cup was placed over one eye of the subject, and as he read the stick traced a design in the smoke on the drumhead.

What did this design reveal? That the eyes did not look at one letter at a time or even at one word at a time. Rather, they proceeded in a series of pauses and jerks, stopping only three or four times in covering an entire line. Thus it was that a startling discovery about reading was made, one that is the very foundation of modern speed reading—namely, that the good reader quickly moves his eyes along over the lines of print, grasping whole meaningful units at each glance, rather than stopping to scrutinize each letter or even each word.

Other investigators, stimulated by Javal's experiment, began to make studies of their own. Huey improved upon Javal's equipment by using an ivory cup on the eye. The ivory cup was lighter and more comfortable than the plaster of Paris cup. Others used still different kinds of experimental equipment. Finally a huge camera was devised which would actually take photographs of the eye movements. This camera was designed by a professor who devoted full time for a year to its perfection, and it cost $6,000.

When using this camera, a bead of mercury was placed on the eyelid of the reader. If you have ever dropped a thermometer and broken its glass you have seen that little beads of mercury, almost as light as air and as round as balls, rolled about here and there in response to the slightest movement. Because of these properties, mercury was a highly satisfactory medium for this experimental work with eye movements. Furthermore, rays of light were reflected from these bright mercury beads. These rays were photographed as they were reflected on the lines of print while the reader was in the act of reading.

Once this thoroughly scientific procedure for detecting and recording eye movements had been developed, hundreds of studies were made with all kinds of readers at various age levels. Voluminous evidence piled up, showing beyond the shadow of a doubt that there were decided differences between the way poor readers read and the way excellent readers pursue the printed page. These studies revealed that the poor reader perceives just one word or perhaps a part of a word at a time, while the excellent reader takes in an entire group of words at a glance.

The plate[1] on page 19 is a composite photographic reproduction of the eye movements of eight different adults as each one read the same line of print.

The vertical lines represent the points at which the eyes rested as they moved across the line. These are called *fixation pauses*. It is during these fixation pauses that the eyes "pick up" the content. We do not "read" while the eyes are moving from one fixation point to another. The movements are just waste motion in so far as actual reading is concerned, but they are necessary in conveying the vision to another point on the line where the eyes again pause "to do some reading." During the fixation pauses the eyes of the good reader perceive two or three words on both sides of the pause; that is, the pause is in the middle of the cluster of symbols which the reader perceives. The width of this portion of a sentence which the eyes perceive at one glance is called the *span of recognition*.

The number at the top of each vertical line represents the order in which the fixations took place. For example, the numbers 1, 2, 3 above the vertical marks in the first line indicate that the reader

[1] Guy Thomas Buswell, *How Adults Read*. Supp. Educ. Monograph, Univ. of Chicago, 1937.

Subject

655 After the war he gave the Negro a little house on

582 After the war he gave the Negro a little house on

790 After the war he gave the Negro a little house on

455 After the war he gave the Negro a little house on

491 After the war he gave the Negro a little house on

427 After the war he gave the Negro a little house on

747 After the war he gave the Negro a little house on

846 After the war he gave the Negro a little house on

paused three times in reading this line and that the pauses occurred in the numerical order. The figure under each vertical line represents the length of time the fixation endured in sixteenths of a second. For example, the reader's first fixation in the first line of the diagram lasted $\%_{16}$ of a second.

Now that the symbols in the diagram have been explained, we should consider the larger implications of this photographic reproduction.

Subject 655 was the most skillful of the readers whose eye movements were photographed. This adult made only three fixations in covering the line. These were in exact order straight across the line and were of about the same duration. The first fixation lasted $\%_{16}$ of a second; the second $\%_{16}$ of a second; and the third $\%_{16}$ of a second. The pauses became somewhat shorter as he got under way with his reading. His total reading time for the line was only $2\%_{16}$ or $1\text{-}\%_{16}$ of a second.

Subject 582 was also a very good reader. His eyes paused only four times in passing across the line, in the right order. He was not able, however, to take in quite so much at one glance as Subject 655, and therefore he required more time to read the line. His first pause endured for $1\%_{16}$ or 1 full second; his second pause for $1\%_{16}$ of a second. His total reading time amounted to $4\%_{16}$ or $2\text{-}1\%_{16}$ of a second as compared to $1\text{-}\%_{16}$ of a second for Subject 655.

In the photographic representation of the other subjects on the page, each succeeding diagram represents a less competent reader.

The eye movements of the poorest reader, Subject 846, are represented in the diagram at the bottom of the page. This reader made 20 fixations while reading the line, as compared with 3 fixations made by Subject 655. His total reading time for the line was $16\%_{16}$, or $10\text{-}\%_{16}$ seconds as compared with $1\text{-}\%_{16}$ of a second for the first reader.

Furthermore, this Subject 846 did not proceed regularly across the page as did Subject 655. He made his first fixation on the g in *gave;* then he swept his eyes backward and made his second fixation on the r in *after*. Then he proceeded ahead with his third fixation which centered between the t and h in *the*. His next eye movement was a regressive one, and his third pause took hold at the point of t in *after*.

In similarly studying his other fixations you will note about 7 times as many fixations as those of Subject 655. Besides, he took about ten times as much time to read the line as did Subject 655, and he made several backward or regressive movements instead of proceeding straight ahead.

The fundamental difference between the good and poor readers whose eye movements are shown in these photographic representations is that the good readers grasped a large, meaningful unit of thought at each fixation; whereas the poor readers fixated each time upon a single letter or a small group of letters which had little or no meaning in itself. These latter subjects were frequently forced to go back over the line to figure out what the text was saying.

The Fallacy of Treating Symptoms

Following these scientific studies of eye movements, instructors in some quarters began striving to train people to change their eye movements. For a time, this was considered the chief panacea for slow reading.

The writer recalls watching Dr. R., a psychiatrist, while under instruction designed to increase his reading speed. Since Dr. R.'s professional field was developing so rapidly that it was impossible for him to do all the necessary reading and also take care of his patients, he had applied at a reading laboratory. He was told over and over again that he "must widen his eye span" and was put through the routine of exercises designed to "increase his span." He sat in a tense position, clutching a book and straining every effort to widen his eye span. His eyelids were opened wide, and his eyes were fairly bulging out of their sockets. He soon became fatigued and remarked, "Well, I think I forced a pretty good span. The only trouble is, I was concentrating so hard on making my eyes work right that I don't know what I was reading about."

There you have in a nutshell the fallacy of striving to change the physical movement of the eyes only. When a patient is ill, the doctor takes his temperature and his pulse. If the temperature is high and the pulse rapid, he sees these as symptoms of the degree of illness. However, he looks for the cause of the illness and treats that rather than the symptoms.

So with reading. The eye movements are simply symptoms of the mental processes which a person uses while reading. The eyes are the servants of the mind and do its bidding in reading, just as the hands do the bidding of the mind when you tell them to "shell those peas rapidly and get it over with."

So don't make the mistake of concentrating on the mechanics of changing your eye span to accomplish faster and better reading. In other words, don't try to treat the symptom; work on the fundamental mental process itself.

Read for Ideas

The great value of investigations in eye movements is the picture they furnish of the different ways the mind works in perceiving reading symbols. They tell us that the mind of the poor reader loafs along, picking up very small units at a time, while the eyes of the excellent reader race over the lines, gathering an entire meaningful idea at each glance.

Cultivating the habit of reading for ideas not only increases speed, but it also increases understanding. A person who reads one word at a time thinks in terms of the meanings of these separate words and thus he "can't see the woods for the trees." The synthesis of important meanings is lost in any meticulous perception of the meanings of separate words or small units.

The first and most important instruction is *Read for ideas!* If you can cultivate the habit of rapidly picking up one complete thought unit after another, the eye movements will take care of themselves.

Try yourself out. Read each of the sentences below. As you go along determine which pattern you are using. Have your mind bid your eyes to pause at each slanting line and "take in" the meaning in so far as you can see on each side of the line. The pattern which you feel most comfortable in using is no doubt the one which best represents your own habits.

Poor

Many/adults/are/now/suffering/from/habits/which/became/ fixed/during/the/early/stages/in/which/they/were/learning/to/ read.

Average

Many/adults are/now suffering/from habits/which became/fixed during/the early stages/in which/they were/learning/to read.

Good

Many adults/are now suffering from habits/which became fixed during the early stages/in which they were/learning to read.

Even though you find you are reading according to the third pattern, there is still room for improvement. Everyone can with practice learn to pick up longer thought units.

Several short selections are provided on the following pages for your use in learning to read in increasingly longer units of meaning.

You are not asked to time yourself in doing these exercises. The first step in your reading improvement program is to get yourself into the habit of taking in large groups of words at a glance. Therefore, in these exercises concentrate on just one thing—your intake of increasingly longer units of meanings.

To ascertain whether you are getting the meaning as you lengthen the span of words that you perceive at a glance, checks of comprehension are provided. These checks are based largely on your ability to grasp meanings in increasingly longer word groups.

Selection 1

Move your eyes down from top to bottom as you read these columns. Follow the vertical line straight down without moving your eyes either to the right or left. Try to grasp the full meaning of each group of words as you impel your eyes down through the center of each list of phrases.[2]

Here is	This profit	Our best	If any
an idea	is entirely	knowledge	young man
for every	aside from	is that which	will get
young man	the money	we absorb	this thought
who works	that changes	as a result	well rooted
for a living.	hands	of work.	in his mind
The worker	in the	It is	he will
gets the	transaction.	part of us.	increase
biggest profit	It is	We do not	his chances
out of	the profit	forget it.	for recognition
any job	of increased	It is ours	and promotion
that is	ability.	to command.	100 per cent.
well done.			

Checking Comprehension

Write the letter which appears before the correct answer in the blank spaces below. Follow this same procedure in taking all the other comprehension tests throughout this book.

1. This article is directed primarily to (a) old men, (b) middle-aged men, (c) young men, (d) all men.

2. The worker gets the greatest profit out of (a) increases in salary, (b) promotions, (c) investments in the company, (d) any job well done.

2 *Reader's Digest,* August 1955, p. 133, quoted from *The William Feather Magazine.* (Rearranged.)

3. The profit of increased ability (a) includes money that changes hands in the transaction, (b) includes money earned by promotions, (c) is entirely aside from the money that changes hands in the transaction, (4) is concerned only with the money that changes hands in the transaction.

4. Our best knowledge is that which (a) we get in college courses, (b) absorb as a result of work, (c) learn through self-study, (d) pick up from others who possess the "know-how."

5. Chances for recognition and promotion can be increased 100 per cent by (a) cultivating someone who will give you a "pull," (b) asking for a raise, (c) doing something spectacular, (d) realizing that increased ability resulting from the job is one's most important asset.

Answers: 1)——, 2)——, 3)——, 4)——, 5)——.

Check your answers with the Answer Key, page 374. Allow yourself a score of 20 for each correct answer.

Comprehension Score:————

Selection 2

These thought units are longer than those in the preceding exercise. Use the same technique in reading these units as suggested for Selection 1.

Pushbutton Rain[3]

For many years
drought-stricken farmers
have sought relief
by praying
for rain.
Now they are
beginning to answer
their own prayers.
With aluminum pipe
the average farmer
can have rain
if and when
he wants it.

Of course,
it will be
much easier
for some farmers
than for others.
The important thing
is to have
an accommodating creek,
river, strong well,
or some other
convenient source
from which water
can be obtained.

The farmer will hook
up a pump
with a long pipe
and put that water
where it will
do the most good.
He will no longer
have to look
toward the clouds
and wistfully hope
for the heavens
to spill out
their moisture.

[3] Ross L. Holman, "Pushbutton Rain," *Science Digest,* August 1955, p. 61. (Rearranged and adapted.)

Checking Comprehension (Selection 2, page 24)

1. This article concerns the farmer's problem of obtaining (a) seed, (b) better fertilizer, (c) top-grade soil, (d) water.

2. The method with which a farmer may now obtain water when he wants it is by (a) running it to his fields with a pipe, (b) "seeding" clouds to make rain, (c) praying for rain, (d) using water from large dams built by the government.

3. The factor that will largely determine each farmer's ease or difficulty in obtaining water will be (a) the shape of his fields, (b) the altitude of his fields, (c) the availability of a source of water, (d) the ease or difficulty of digging drainage ditches.

4. Water will be made to flow through the pipes by means of (a) gravity, (b) a pump, (c) siphons, (d) the force of the water flowing downhill.

5. From now on, farmers will no longer have to worry about (a) poor crops, (b) low prices, (c) drought, (d) insects.

Answers: 1)__, 2)__, 3)__, 4)__, 5)__.

Check your answers with the Answer Key, page 374. Allow yourself a score of 20 for each correct answer.

Comprehension Score:———————

Checking Comprehension (Selection 3, page 26)

1. The custom of shaking hands is (a) purely American (b) practiced in most parts of the world, (c) a New-World custom, (d) mainly a custom of English-speaking countries.

2. In England and Holland shaking hands is (a) considered an affront, (b) done daily with each employee, (c) reserved for introductions, (d) done on every conceivable occasion.

3. In Italy, Turkey, and Greece (a) everyone shakes hands everywhere, (b) people never shake hands, (c) a firm grip is the custom, (d) people shake hands only at introductions.

4. In many countries, an American who normally uses a firm grip may find it wise to (a) refrain from handshaking, (b) not change his habit at all, (c) wait until the other party offers to shake hands, (d) ease off his grip.

5. In the Orient, shaking hands is (a) done in imitation of American ways, (b) more widespread than in the United States, (c) reserved for special occasions, (d) something to beware of.

Answers: 1)__, 2)__, 3)__, 4)__, 5)__.

Selection 3

On Shaking Hands[4]

Shaking hands
is an old custom
in almost every part
of the world.
In feudal times
it was the symbol
of homage and fealty.
Today the glad hand
is an exchange
between equals,
but there are shades
of variation in its use.
In Holland and England
the handshake
is reserved for introductions.

In France and Portugal
employers shake hands daily
with each employee.
In Italy, Turkey, and Greece,
everyone shakes hands everywhere
—in street, cafe, office, home—
on meeting and leaving
his friends.
The American who is
proud of his firm grip,
and normally uses
an energetic one,
may find it wise
to ease off
in many countries.

In the Middle East,
for example,
the proper handshake
is just a gentle pressure.
And in the Orient, beware of
personal contact,
including shaking hands.
Holding the arm
or tapping the shoulder
is an affront.
Instead, practice a bow
and you'll have
as firm a grip
on the situation
as is required.

4 "On Shaking Hands," *Holiday*, September 1955, p. 93.

Selection 4

Don't Get Seasick[5]

A century ago
Sir Henry Bessemer
built an English Channel steamer
in which the cabins
were hung on brackets.
Through a mechanism
which was manipulated
by a crew member
when the water was rough,
the cabins would swing
so as to offset
the uncomfortable roll
of the little vessel.

Since then, engineers
have tried out scores
of ingenious arrangements
intended to free travelers
aboard sea-going vessels
and other conveyances
from the usual hazard
of motion sickness.
They have eliminated
numerous jolts and twists
but not motion sickness.
Fortunately, engineers are not
the only ones concerned
with this problem.

The traveler of today
has no occasion
to fear motion illness,
for in recent years
active chemical investigators
have found useful drugs
that make the passenger
immune to the unpleasantness
which he otherwise
would feel in his stomach.
Outstanding among these drugs
is one called Bonamine,
a unique long-acting
antimotion sickness compound.

[5] Milton Liebman, *Mechanics Illustrated*, April 1954, p. 76.

Check your answers with the Answer Key on page 374. Allow yourself a score of 20 for each correct answer.

Comprehension Score: —————

Checking Comprehension (Selection 4, page 27)

1. Sir Henry Bessemer tried to eliminate seasickness by (a) preventing ships from rolling, (b) using drugs, (c) allowing the cabins to swing, (d) increasing the speed of the ship.

2. Since Bessemer's time, engineers have (a) given up the attempts to prevent motion sickness, (b) continued to work out ingenious arrangements, (c) succeeded in their attempts to prevent passengers from getting motion sickness, (d) not given any more thought to the problem.

3. Through the years, attempts to keep parts of ships from moving have resulted in (a) the elimination of numerous jolts and twists, but not motion sickness, (b) the elimination of motion sickness, (c) no improvement because of theoretical impossibility of cutting down motion in a moving conveyance, (d) failure because of the expense involved.

4. People who travel today (a) face the same hazards of motion sickness as travelers faced years ago, (b) are better off only because they grow used to motion, (c) are more subject to motion sickness than people were years ago, (d) have no occasion to fear motion sickness.

5. Today's improved protection against motion sickness is largely the result of (a) the success of engineers in reducing motion, (b) the development of antimotion drugs, (c) the greater size and speed of modern ships and planes, (d) the fact that modern diet has made us more resistant to motion sickness.

Answers: 1)——, 2)——, 3)——, 4)——, 5)——.

Check your answers with the Answer Key on page 374. Allow yourself a score of 20 for each correct answer.

Comprehension Score: —————

Selection 5

Mark this selection into phrases yourself. Divide the sentences so that, as often as possible, each meaningful unit is four or five words long. Then read the selection, trying to grasp each one of these long, meaningful phrases at a glance.

Vanishing American Sounds[6]

The other afternoon when the house was temporarily quiet, I found myself remembering the sounds of my childhood.

Missing now is the sound of carpet-sweeper and broom, of eggs being beaten with a fork in a platter, of suds being squeezed through wet cloth, with an occasional rib-rub on the scrub board, the slow tick-tock of the grandfather's clock at the foot of the stairs.

In summer, the lop-lop-lop of the ceiling fan, the gentle creak of the porch swing. Or the sound of ice being shaved in the kitchen. From the street came the clip-clop of the vegetable man's horse, the ding-dong of his bell, the wonderful high call of the strawberry man walking along the sidewalk.

Rhythmic sounds, comforting sounds—a relaxing fabric of sound for a child to read against or dream against.

Today's children are under constant bombardment of noises. Clocks don't tick-tock any more; they hum endlessly. Instead of the broom there is the whine of the vacuum cleaner. Instead of the fork against the egg platter, there is the higher whine of the mixer. Instead of the gentle creak of the porch swing, the roar of the power lawn mower. Instead of the rocking chair and soft talk, the blare of television or radio on full blast. Outside, in the place of the clip-clop or the strawberry call, we have the jet plane, the squeal and roar of a teen-ager's car.

No, houses don't sound the same as they used to.

No comprehension check is given for this exercise. Since you were asked to mark the selection into meaningful units before you read it, you are no doubt so familiar with the meaning that a check of comprehension would be valueless.

Selection 6

Read this entire selection without marking it into meaningful word groups. Try to grasp a sizable unit of meaning with each glance as you read across the lines of print. Force yourself to take in as large an "eyeful" of meaning as possible at each fixation pause. You will be given a comprehension check at the end of the selection.

Nebraska's Fabulous Fishworm Farmer[7]

Meet Pete Scheidt, of McCook, Nebraska, the one farmer in America today without a gripe, subsidy, or worry to his name, with one exception.

[6] Marguerite Johnston, *Reader's Digest*, August 1955, p. 85. (Quoted from the *Houston Post*.)

[7] Pearl P. Puckett, *The American Mercury*, June 1954, pp. 23-24.

"Doggone it!" Pete grumbles every day of his life. "I ain't had time to go fishin' only once in two years."

Pete didn't really intend to get into the big farming business. It just caught up with him in an accidental sort of way. All Pete asked of life was just something to tinker around with after he'd retired from the railroad in 1951. "If you would live longer and happier, get a hobby," he'd read over and over again in a hobby magazine, and so Pete was in quest of his fountain of youth and happiness with a hobby—when it happened.

One Spring morning a little red wriggler stuck his head out of the soft warm earth in Pete's back yard and smiled at Pete. Pete smiled back, and then it struck him like a bolt from the blue!

That very morning Pete started digging pits, then digging worms to fill them. He calculated he had close to 20,000 big red wrigglers to start with. A female worm lays 100 to 120 eggs a year, and each egg, which looks like a small brown seed, hatches five little wrigglers—so that's exactly how big business caught up with Pete.

The first year he sold more than 140,000 worms wholesale at $4.20 per box of 12-pint cartons. Each pint contained 60 to 70 worms. And he retailed thousands of worms at 60 cents a pint, or approximately one cent per worm.

To get all the eggs possible, Pete keeps 150,000 breeder worms in boxes in his hatchery. Every six weeks they are transferred to new boxes, and the eggs are deposited in hatchery boxes made especially for that purpose. Pete's hatchery is a frame building on the rear of his lot, with hundreds of clean sunny south windows across the entire front of the structure. The hatchery is immaculate, and a heater is kept burning night and day at the right temperature to raise worms. Each box is watered with care and regularity. Under normal conditions maintained in the hatchery, Pete has a box of eggs hatching every 30 days, and in this way he is able to select one-year-old worms for his breeding stock.

Pete has had to hire a lot of help, too, because his worm pits are a little out of the ordinary. Each pit is lined with a soft mulch of leaves, barnyard fertilizer, and then alfalfa "leavings."

Last spring he started something new. He bought fifty old white-enamel washing-machine tubs, something that a dealer had had to take in on trade and intended to junk. Each tub was placed in a pit, and grape vines were planted around each pit to run arbors over the tubs. This will, as Pete says, "kill two birds with one stone": keep his worms from cooking in summer heat and produce the finest grapes known. The soil is extremely rich, and the worms act more or less as cultivators in keeping it stirred up deep down in the pits.

Not long ago a young chemical engineer from Sun Valley saw Pete's sign along Highway 6 and stopped in to find out about fishworm farming. Before he left, he bought 100,000 worms.

Pete ships worms all over America today, and he just can't keep up with the demand. In fact, it requires more than one man to count and box them for shipment. The worms are sent parcel post. He lines waxed-paper pint cartons with peat moss, puts in his worms and adds just enough water; then punches holes in the lid so that the worms can breathe.

Counting worms for his shipments is the hardest part of the business, because it is necessary to dig your hands down into the warm mulch, and the worms move very fast. Let a little light in, and they swarm over to the dark side of the box quick and slippery.

"Takes me exactly 13 days to count out 96 boxes," Pete says. "So I bring my radio out here to make the job more pleasant."

Pete is possibly the largest fishworm farmer in the world today, as orders pour in from the 48 states and Canada. He has pits all over his yard with more than 100,000 worms per pit. Pete believes that the reason there aren't more fishworm farmers in America today is because it's a squeamish business and time consuming; then, too, the big resorts and fellows who love to fish would rather pay one cent a piece for their worms than stop and dig them.

Pete doesn't have to worry about subsidies, overproduction, or embargoes. He quotes his own prices, and so far there hasn't been any ceiling placed on worms or worm eggs. Fishworm farming is pretty big business. It can be handled on a small acreage, and a million worms a year at approximately one cent each adds up to a five-figure income.

Checking Comprehension

Write the letter which appears before the correct answer in the appropriate answer space following each statement.

1. Pete Scheidt got into the business of raising worms through his search for (a) a hobby, (b) a means of obtaining a modest living without too much work, (c) a means of making a lot of money quickly, (d) a means of getting rid of some worms which had been tearing up his land.

2. Pete raises his worms in (a) the soft, warm soil in his barnyard, (b) in one of his fields, (c) in pits lined with special materials, (d) in black soil in his garden.

3. Pete obtains most of his worms by (a) searching for them, (b) paying boys to find them for him, (c) getting them from people who want to get rid of them, (d) breeding them himself.

4. Pete's idea of "killing two birds with one stone" involves (a) getting rid of worms on the neighbors' land when he sells them, (b) raising grapes near the breeding soil, (c) fertilizing neighbors' gardens with worms he is raising, (d) raising vegetables in the breeding soil.

5. The young chemical engineer who visited Pete Scheidt (a) bought a lot of worms, (b) wrote a paper on worm breeding, (c) gave Pete valuable advice on the chemistry of soils, (d) set up another farm next to Pete's.

6. The market for Pete's worms (a) extends all over the United States and Canada, (b) is local, (c) has to be kept to a small area because worms would die if shipped a long distance, (d) is kept in the United States by laws which prohibit shipment of worms over national borders.

7. Pete has found that the demand for his worms (a) has fallen off lately, (b) was not good when he began his business but has improved, (c) is so great he can't keep up with it, (d) would be better if he did not have so much competition.

8. The most difficult job that Pete Scheidt faces in his work is (a) breeding the worms, (b) counting them for shipment, (c) hiring help, (d) finding customers.

9. Pete gives some reasons for the fact that there are not more fishworm farmers in America. One of these reasons is that (a) it is a squeamish business, (b) it is difficult to raise worms efficiently, (c) the market is not large enough for additional producers, (d) raising worms requires too much hired help.

10. One of the many advantages that Pete Scheidt's farm has over more conventional farms is that (a) his machinery lasts longer, (b) he can do all the work himself, (c) he does not need to water his crop, (d) he is free of governmental regulation.

Answers: 1)—, 2)—, 3)—, 4)—, 5)—, 6)—, 7)—, 8)—, 9)—, 10)—.

See Answer Key, page 374. Allow yourself a score of 10 for each correct answer.

Comprehension Score: —————

Follow-Up Suggestions

You have now learned one of the basic secrets of rapid, meaningful reading—that of grasping large thought units at each glance. If you wish to read fast you must gulp—not nibble!

There are three avenues open to you for further development of your ability to grasp sizable meaningful units at each momentary pause of your eyes.

1. You are given opportunity to practice this technique throughout the remainder of this book. Many other skills will be developed, but each new skill will be added to this basic skill, and each one will be founded upon the assumption that you are continually striving to improve your ability to grasp larger thought units at each glance.

2. You should try to apply this technique in all your outside reading, as well as while working with this book. Whenever you have to read something in connection with your work, consciously look for wide groups of words, each of which expresses a significant idea. Do the same thing when you read casually from a newspaper, magazine, or novel. In other words, apply the technique continuously in *all* the reading you do.

3. In addition to the two suggestions above, set aside a definite time for practice each evening. Devote from fifteen to thirty minutes regularly to practice reading in increasingly larger thought units. You may use any material you have at hand. It is advisable, however, to begin practicing with easy material such as that used in this chapter, then gradually to work with more difficult material.

CHAPTER 3

Faster! Faster!

An amusing story is told about Puccini, the great Italian composer. One day he dashed out of his flat in Milan, fifteen minutes late for an appointment. As he rushed up the street he encountered an organ-grinder who was drowsily turning the crank of his organ under the spell of the warm Italian sunshine. The disturbing thing to Puccini was that the aria which the grinder was so indolently reproducing was one from his own *Madame Butterfly*.

Puccini, deeply irritated by the agonizingly slow movement of his masterpiece, cried out impatiently, "Heavens, man, faster, faster!" without slackening his pace. As he ran, however, he momentarily attempted to set a tempo by waving his right hand rapidly back and forth in true maestro fashion.

The next week Puccini again met this same organ-grinder. This time he was grinding out *Madame Butterfly* in the rapid, sprightly tempo which Puccini's hand had indicated. Even more surprising, however, was the sign suspended from the grinder's neck: "Pupil of Puccini."

For you who would speed your reading, this story holds more than passing amusement at the organ-grinder's capitalizing on his brief contact with the great master. Maybe you, too, have fallen into the habit of "grinding out the tune" in a slow tempo when you read. Perhaps you need to be startled out of your lethargy by having someone shout at you, "Heavens, man, faster, faster!"

Working for Speed

You have learned in the preceding chapter that the rapid reader's eyes move fleetingly across the lines, pausing briefly two or three times on each line and picking up an "eyeful" of words at each pause. Speed is achieved by increasing the rapidity of the eye movements, decreasing the length of the pause, and taking in a large number of words during each pause.

While these are the mechanics of eye movements, you have been warned that it is the mind which controls the reading process, and better eye movements are but a reflection of increased mental tempo in absorbing the meaning from printed symbols. So, first of all, set your mind to take in long, meaningful units, with fleeting eye pauses that gather in everything within the range of vision. Don't point, don't say the words with your lips, and don't move your head. Free your mind from all bodily accompaniments. Let it race ahead unimpeded.

Now that you know what to do, make up your mind that you must practice. A person learns to type rapidly and accurately by practicing; he learns to play the piano excellently by practicing; he learns to skate skillfully by practicing. So it is with reading. As a busy man or woman you must definitely resolve to tackle your reading improvement in the same way that you would tackle skill improvement in any other area. Desire, determination, practice—these are the basic ingredients in your recipe for reading improvement. Once you've put yourself in the frame of mind to work, you've made a good start.

Choose the right physical setting for this practice. Don't start your improvement program in the midst of a busy office where phones are ringing, employees are asking questions, and people are coming and going. And don't start it in the living room at home where television is shouting out attention-arresting phrases and the children are playing cops and robbers. You probably can withstand such distractions when you become a highly proficient reader. But to start with, go into a room by yourself—and close the door! Shut out the distractions.

Once you are in a room free from distractions, look for a chair which isn't too comfortable. Your period of reading practice is no time to loll on a chaise lounge or to recline on soft pillows in a bed. You have a job to do. You are about to sharpen one of your most important tools. With the importance of your new job in mind, find a straight-backed chair. Seat yourself so that you know you have a spine, square your shoulders, and go to work.

At this stage in your program, you should practice on easy material. Practice with difficult material will come later on. Easy material will serve you best while you are breaking the old tempo and establishing new habits. Consequently, each of the selections which follow in this chapter will be very easy—so easy that you'll dare to "let go" and sweep your eyes across the lines with a speed you've never tried before. As you are about to begin each of the selections, set your own purpose for reading it. A strong purpose helps to pull your eyes rapidly along over the lines, and it gives you something to tie to in gathering meanings as you go along.

So when you are ready to read, make up your mind just why you want to read that particular selection. Just to follow the plot of the narrative? To get some ideas that might be useful to you? To find out what happened in a current event? Whatever the reason, phrase it concisely and keep it uppermost in your mind throughout the reading of the selection. Your purpose is the pilot light which guides you over the sea of print with a well-filled dragnet of ideas at the end of the journey. It is a magnet which attracts useful information to satisfy your business and pleasure needs.

Above all, force your speed! Consciously push your eyes across the line as fast as you can make them go and still know what you are reading about. Across, back, across, back, across, back, in rapid, rhythmic sweeps! Make those eyes leap over each line. They are your servants. You can control them. Don't let them loaf along in the old lazy way.

Practicing and Checking

Now see if you can apply all the things you've learned while reading the next selection. It is about banks, a topic in which all people are interested.

After seating yourself in the right physical setting, look at the title. What specific information do you think will be presented in regard to banks? For what purpose would you like to read this article? To obtain general information about the differences between the banks of "Yesterday" and "Now"? To find out if differences between old and new banking procedures have parallels in your own business? To get additional insights into changes in banking procedures which might be beneficial to you in making greater use of the bank in furthering your own business interests? Or what?

Whatever your purpose, phrase it concisely and keep it uppermost in your mind throughout the reading of the article.

Resolutely determine to read *fast, faster than you've ever read before.*

Jot down the beginning time on an even minute.

Ready! Go!

Selection 1

BEGINNING TIME:_____

HR._____ MIN._____

Banks—Yesterday and Now[1]

Time was—and not so many years ago, either—when the average citizen took a pretty dim view of banks and banking. That this was so, it should be said, was to no small extent the fault of banks and bankers themselves. Banks used to be—and a few still are—grim and forbidding structures, where business was conducted in a sort of genteel gloom, atmospherically and personally. Behind the little barred windows were, more often than not, elderly gentlemen whose cordiality—and that may be an over-generous word to apply—reflected the size of the customer's account, and nothing less than a few hundred thousand on deposit could have inspired the suggestion of a smile. As for the officers and junior members of the firm—well, the man on the street rarely saw them and perhaps even more rarely thought seriously of speaking to them in a business way.

Now, that appraisal may be a bit too harsh. And yet the average bank for many years was, to the average citizen, an awesome if necessary instrument for the transacting of business—usually big business. But somewhere in the past quarter century—perhaps in the wake of the depression —banks began to grow human, even pleasant, and started to woo the little man, the man who had been in awe of banks and bankers. It is possible that this movement began in medium-sized towns, or in small towns where people know each other by their first names, and spread to big towns. At any rate, the results have been spectacular.

The movement to "humanize" banks, of course, received a big push during the war, when more and more women were employed to do work

1 *New York Times,* February 17, 1954, p. 30.

previously performed by men. Also more and more "little people" found themselves in need of personal loans, as taxes became heavier and as the institution of installment buying broke down the previously long-held concept that there was something almost morally wrong about being in debt. All sorts of people began to discover that the intelligent use of credit could be extremely helpful—and this idea was encouraged to grow by forward-looking banks that saw a great future in aiding large numbers of small depositors and borrowers to meet their financial problems.

Today's banks present a picture startlingly different from that offered by the banks of yesterday. For the most part their officers are accessible and are known to a surprisingly large number of small depositors whom even vice-presidents can call by their first names. Some banks even have women—not unattractive, either—as personal loan interviewers. And, of course, at many cashier's windows—most of which are now bar-less—pretty young women greet the customer with a smile regardless of the size of his account. Banks today make personal loans that few, if any, banks perhaps a quarter of a century ago would have considered. For example, not long ago a young man moved to a large city to embark on a new job and appealed to a bank for help in obtaining funds sufficient to move his family to the new location, some distance from his former home. He had no collateral—only a bright future and a creditable past. One bank did turn down his petition—in a friendly way—but another studied his problem and decided to invest in his future. He got the loan. In a not-too-distant past he'd have been regarded as a poor risk by any bank.

In view of the public's increasing acceptance of banks and bankers as friendly counselors, it is indeed surprising to discover that banks feel it necessary to embark on an elaborate public relations program to make people more conscious of their place in the community and the national scene. It may well be that the role of banks in keeping the nation's financial arteries functioning properly is not as well understood by the public as it might be. But in most communities today's banks and bankers have "sold" themselves and their services at the local level. It may be that the local banker has not yet established himself as firmly as a source of help and counsel as has the family doctor, and it may be also that by the nature of his services he never will, but he is making rapid strides in that direction.

Began   *Finished*   No. words: 735

$$\frac{\quad\quad}{\text{No. seconds:}} \times 60 = \underline{\quad\quad} \text{ W.P.M.}$$

Checking Comprehension

1. The author believes that the unfriendly atmosphere in banks of many years ago was due to (a) economic pressures of the times,

(b) hostility of customers toward banks, (c) the attitudes of bankers and people who worked in the banks, (d) the physical structure of bank buildings.

2. The bank of many years ago paid the bulk of its attention to (a) businessmen, (b) large depositors, (c) small depositors, (d) none of the above.

3. Which of the following was not stated as a cause of the bank's more "human" policies of recent years: (a) business growth, (b) increased installment buying, (c) employment of women in banks, (d) increased needs of "little people."

4. The author believes that the movement to "humanize" banks may have begun in (a) large cities, where more banks are located, (b) all over the country, (c) small and medium-sized towns, (d) Federal Reserve banks.

5. During the war, banks saw new possibilities in (a) accounts of war industries, (b) only large accounts, (c) manufacturers' accounts, (d) large numbers of small depositors and borrowers.

6. One common example of banks' friendlier attitude is (a) smaller-sized banks, (b) more-expensive decorations, (c) better-dressed employees, (d) greater accessibility to officers.

7. The example of the young man's loan was intended to show that (a) banks must be careful when making loans, (b) banks will now make loans that they would not have made years ago, (c) there is no set policy on loans, (d) people now need more money than they did in times past.

8. The author feels that bankers are approaching the role of (a) businessmen, (b) lawyers, (c) brokers, (d) doctors.

9. Perhaps the present public-relations program of banks is necessary because (a) banks want to drain off surplus earnings, (b) they want to complete a planned program, (c) they are sorry for poor people, (d) people do not understand the role of the banks in keeping the nation's financial arteries functioning properly.

10. It is probable that today's banks have sold themselves at local levels (a) to big business, (b) in most communities, (c) in a few towns, (d) in a few large cities.

Answers: 1)—, 2)—, 3)—, 4)—, 5)—, 6)—, 7)—, 8)—, 9)—, 10)—.

Check your answer with the Answer Key on page 375. Multiply the total correct items by 10.

Rate: W.P.M. ———   Comprehension Score: ———

Selection 2

Set yourself a purpose for reading this article, and try to read it even faster than you read the first one.

BEGINNING TIME:_____
HR._____ MIN._____

Why Do They Move?[2]

The Population Reference Bureau says that about 3 per cent of the nation's population move from one state to another each year. Many more persons undoubtedly move intrastate; the Institute of Life Insurance estimates that this year 31,000,000 people will pull up stakes and move to other homes. It is difficult to see why this is so. If moving one's household from one home to another in the same city, or from one city to another, were as simple as changing a pair of shoes, those figures pertaining to Americans on the move would not be surprising. But moving, and especially long-distance moving, is an incredibly complex, uncomfortable, unsettling, wearisome, expensive and distasteful operation.

Here in City A, for example, are old friends and neighbors, old haunts—familiar faces, familiar schools, familiar church, comfortable if not plush house—and firmly fixed habits. There in City B, are neighbors of as yet undetermined humors, new surroundings and perhaps customs; strange schools and—at first glance—gimlet-eyed teachers, a church with perhaps different hymnbooks (very unsettling) to say nothing of a wholly strange order of worship. And high on the list of painful adjustments is the necessity of forming new habits, of finding new restaurants, perhaps changing one's mode of transportation. And then there is the little matter of the new house.

The matter of the new house appears on the agenda early in any moving operation. The lady of the (old) house says that the new house must be larger, nearer to stores, nearer to schools, with a large yard, with fireplaces, a sunny kitchen, etc., etc. And the head of the (old) house finds himself saddled not only with the task of adjusting himself to new associates in what may be a totally strange place but also with the responsibility of finding a new house answering the foregoing description. If he is wise, the head of the (old) house will somehow turn the important (and time-consuming) business of discovering a new house to the distaff side so that in the event matters turn out poorly he, and not she, can say, "Well, I didn't think much of the house in the first place, but I didn't like to say so."

But no matter what, the new house will be a problem. Even the most careful inspection of a house does not prepare one fully for living in it.

2 *New York Times*, March 15, 1954, p. 24.

Inspection before moving in does not prepare one for the discovery that the movers with their van load of furniture—and what looks more worn and frazzled than worn furniture being carted across a pavement, from truck to house, in the cold light of day?—and a small army of painters have arrived at the new house at the same time. Inspection before moving does not prepare one for the discovery that the previous occupants have decamped with all but three window shades, leaving the new residents and all their dusty furniture and their undisguised misery fully exposed to curious eyes.

Inspection does not disclose that, although one may come from a place where trash, ashes, and garbage were picked up twice a week, here at the new house trash is picked up once every two weeks on one day, ashes on another day, and garbage on still another. Or that the paper boy's aim at the new house is worse than a certain lad's aim at the old. Or that the new house's windows rattle alarmingly even in a light breeze. Or that there are fewer shelves in the kitchen than one had supposed. Or that one of the garage doors—a heavy, heavy door—is about to fall off.

But there is the new house—and its larger yard, just as the lady of the (old) house wanted it. With more grass to cut. A nice, big hedge to trim. Lots of trees to shed their leaves in season. And a lot of neighbors, who, as yet, do not appear to be the type eager to share any of their belongings with newcomers who have no shades on their windows and appear to be, for all the world, a bunch of gypsies with a heap of broken-down or at least badly-bent furniture. The new house will be all right some day, but when the movers have gone and the door is closed (stickily), the old house looks pretty good, wherever it was.

| *Began* | *Finished* | No. words: | 680 |

$$\frac{\quad\quad}{\text{No. seconds:}} \times 60 = \underline{\quad\quad} \text{ W.P.M.}$$

_____	_____

Checking Comprehension

1. The author seems to believe that moving is an operation (a) as simple as changing shoes, (b) much easier than it used to be, (c) not at all expensive nowadays, (d) complex and distasteful.

2. According to the Population Reference Bureau, the percentage of people that move from one state to another each year is (a) one per cent, (b) three per cent, (c) five per cent, (d) seven per cent.

3. *Not* mentioned as one of the adjustments which must be made in a new neighborhood is (a) finding new restaurants, (b) forming new habits, (c) attending another church, (d) finding suitable stores.

4. It is suggested that the head of the (old) house (a) find a new

house himself, (b) leave the choice to his wife, (c) have the family do it together, (d) depend upon a real estate agent.

5. It is likely that the lady of the house will want a new house that is (a) larger and more conveniently located than the old one, (b) a duplicate of the old one, (c) more conveniently located but smaller in order to require less work, (d) one having one floor only so that she won't have to climb stairs.

6. The author seems to believe that the difficulties of getting settled in a new home (a) can be practically eliminated by careful planning, (b) will take care of themselves, (c) are so numerous that it is no use trying to cope with them, (d) will arise no matter what.

7. Furniture being moved from a truck to a house looks (a) good to the neighbors, (b) the way it looked in the old house, (c) worn and frazzled, (d) suitable for the old home but not for the new one.

8. The previous occupants of the new house were said to have taken (a) the lawnmower, (b) all Venetian blinds, (c) all but three window shades, (d) a screendoor.

9. At the new house, pick-up service of trash, ashes, and garbage may be (a) more frequent than at the old, (b) less frequent than at the old, (c) same as at the old, (d) nonexistent.

10. The new neighbors seem to be (a) very friendly, (b) destructive, (c) helpful, (d) not eager to share their belongings.

Answers: 1)—, 2)—, 3)—, 4)—, 5)—, 6)—, 7)—, 8)—, 9)—, 10)—.

See Answer Key, page 375. Allow 10 for each correct answer.

Rate: W.P.M. ———   Comprehension Score: ———

Selection 3

See if you can beat all your records so far in covering this with high speed and increased comprehension.

BEGINNING TIME:————
HR.———— MIN.————

Wizard of the Vegetable Patch[3]

It all started with "the carrot job." The Campbell Soup Company wanted a drastically remodeled carrot, one with no yellow in its core, and uniform in size and shape. The company found that pale-yellow cubes

[3] Frank J. Taylor, *Reader's Digest*, July 1954. (Reprinted from *Town Journal*, July 1954.)

among deep-orange cubes in vegetable soup cut down eye appeal and that odd-shaped carrots left too much waste when they went through the dicing machines. They asked the C. C. Morse Seed Company what could be done about it.

For centuries carrots had matured with yellow cores and in assorted shapes. Changing their growing habits called for horticultural magic. So Lester Morse, head of the firm, sent for a ruddy-cheeked young Scot, Frank G. Cuthbertson, who had bred flowers but had never tried to restyle a vegetable to order.

He tackled the job, and over the years his efforts have burgeoned into a widespread vegetable-remodeling drive. In three decades Cuthbertson and his team of hybridizers have redone so many truck crops that it is almost impossible to sit down to dinner without enjoying at least one of his restyled vegetables. Last year the American Seed Trade Association honored him with a medallion for "outstanding contributions to horticulture."

The carrot job back in the '20's confronted Cuthbertson and his colleague, Walter Nixon, with unique obstacles. To breed a strain with orange cores, they first had to find one carrot with orange "blood," the seedman's term for a trait. To find that one carrot they grew thousands.

To get a peek at the cores without checking the carrots' further growth they plugged each root with a small glass tube. Whenever the plug revealed a darker-than-usual core they replanted the carrot, put a marker beside it and waited patiently until the plant bore seed. Then they planted again, repeating the tedious hunt for a darker-cored carrot.

Eight years and thousands of carrots later Cuthbertson had ten carrots with no trace of yellow in their cores. Furthermore, their size was just what the soup makers wanted. Today progeny from those ten carrots produce enough seed annually to plant 100,000 acres.

Home gardeners, canners, and produce merchants wanted a beet that was red all the way through and would resist mildew. So Cuthbertson and Nixon induced beets to give up the characteristic pink rings in their flesh, then grew a generation in fields of mildewed beets. The plants that defied mildew became the parent stock for a mildew-resistant strain known as Morse's Detroit Dark Red. This year U. S. seed growers will produce 300,000 pounds of seed of this made-to-order beet.

But gardeners who grow beets for the greens as well as for the roots were still unsatisfied. So the Morse team built a red-fleshed beet with many tender leaves, called Green-Top Bunching. Now everybody in the beet patch is happy.

Ironically, after the seed of a restyled vegetable is introduced to growers and gardeners, any competitor can grow seed. Most of them do, sometimes giving the variety another name. The vegetable designer takes his reward in prestige among seedsmen and commercial growers.

Born in Scotland, Frank Cuthbertson came to San Francisco in 1911 with 20 borrowed dollars in his pocket. His first job, at $2.50 a day, was "roguing"—pulling out the off-foliage plants on the Morse farm.

With the eye of a perfectionist, the young Scot rogued so mercilessly that he made a shambles of the company's sweet-pea fields. His ruthlessness paid off. Before long the seed of Morse sweet peas was selling for four times the previous price. (The Cuthbertson sweet pea is now famous.) Impressed, Morse offered Cuthbertson an interest in the firm, merged in 1930 with the Ferry Seed Company. Today Cuthbertson is executive vice-president of Ferry-Morse and boss of all the concern's seed-growing farms.

Sometimes a Cuthbertson made-to-order vegetable launches an entirely new appetite. In the 1920's, when a team started to work on broccoli, it was called "sprouting calabrese" and eaten mainly in Italian homes. Instead of its present-day large head it produced small buds which sprouted on many stems along the stalks; they were tasty but very difficult to pick. Frozen-food processors wanted a variety that bore the buds in clusters, like those of cauliflower—a vegetable easy to harvest and pack.

Cuthbertson planted broccoli by the acre. His fieldmen went down the rows, whacking out all plants except the few that showed a tendency to develop "umbrella heads." Repeating this season after season, nine years later they had narrowed their selections down to a new-style broccoli that delighted growers and packers. Pickers could harvest the umbrella heads with one sweep of a knife; at the processing tables cutters easily sliced off the stem, broke up the head and left the clusters of buds ready for packing. In the rapidly developing frozen-food trade the new broccoli grew from nothing in 1939 to 89 million pounds last year. Broccoli now ranks among the frozen-vegetable Big Four, along with peas, limas and snap beans.

"We made broccoli an American vegetable that has almost pushed spinach off the frozen-food table," says Cuthbertson, his eyes sparkling. "Now I guess we'll have to do something about spinach."

Correcting a vegetable's bad habits sometimes takes ten or more plant generations. Canners, for instance, wanted the curve bred out of stringless snap beans. Straight beans would go through their cutting machines 25 per cent faster than the naturally curved bean. The Cuthbertson team launched their bean-straightening project in 1941; 12 years later they delivered Blue Lake FM-1, a bean without a curve; it met canners' specifications exactly.

As the frozen-food business boomed, lima beans became a problem vegetable. About one per cent of the beans had thick skins, through which the flesh showed in a bluish color. These are known as "blue beans" or "oyster beans." They are just as edible as other limas, but the processors reported, "Frozen foods sell on appearance, and if the housewife sees one blue bean in the pot she is unhappy."

Getting rid of that one blue bean is about the most exasperating project that Cuthbertson and his team have tackled. They started by planting the seeds from a single vine free of blue beans. The offspring of this plant were carefully scrutinized by fieldmen who, on hands and knees, opened pods on every vine. If a single bean looked blue the plant was yanked out. Each year of this tedious roguing unearths fewer throwbacks. Shortly Cuthbertson expects to have a strain free of blue beans. It is a worthwhile search; packers freeze and ship 100 million pounds of limas each season.

In this amazing modernization program nearly every vegetable presents a different problem. Growers wanted a corn that would mature in the Pacific Northwest, which isn't corn country because the nights are too cold. By 1950 Johnny McCabe, who is the corn expert on Cuthbertson's team, had a hybrid that could take the cold nights and whose kernels remained sweet and soft even after the stalks dried. That same year John Moran, the tomato man, came up with the heavy-yield deep-red tomato for which canners had been praying.

A partial list of the commercial vegetables restyled under Cuthbertson's direction during the last three decades includes more than 70 varieties of 14 vegetables. Cuthbertson contends that no vegetable is so good that it cannot be made better. "Vegetables are like autos," he says. "They become obsolete—but there is no used-vegetable market."

Began	*Finished*	No. words:	1260
			$\dfrac{\quad}{\text{No. seconds:}} \times 60 = \underline{\qquad}$ W.P.M.

Checking Comprehension

Select the correct answer for each statement and write the corresponding letter in the appropriate answer space.

1. Cuthbertson did his "carrot job" because (a) he had a special interest in experimenting with vegetables, (b) Morse Company wanted him to develop a carrot that had a taste flavor which more people would enjoy, (c) Walter Nixon wanted him to develop a carrot that could be raised in poor soil, (d) Campbell Soup Company wanted carrots that had more eye appeal.

2. The process of producing carrots with orange cores involved (a) coloring carrot roots with a dye, then using the seeds from these carrots to produce others, (b) searching the world over for a patch of orange-cored carrots, then producing seeds from these carrots, (c) plugging the roots of carrots until a darker-than-usual one was found, then replanting the seed from such carrots, (d) calling upon

home gardeners to search for a carrot with "orange blood," then reproducing it.

3. The problem with the snap bean was that (a) it was too big, (b) it was too small, (c) it was the wrong color, (d) it was curved.

4. A "blue bean" is undesirable because (a) its food value is good, but its taste is bad, (b) its appearance hurts sales, (c) it is unfit for human consumption, (d) it cannot be quick-frozen.

5. A special corn was needed which could take cold nights in (a) the Northwest, (b) the Southwest, (c) the Northeast, (d) the Southeast.

6. Cuthbertson's restyling of one vegetable created a new appetite in Americans for (a) string beans, (b) beets, (c) spinach, (d) broccoli.

7. When a grower develops a new vegetable he (a) patents it, (b) allows others to produce it on a royalty basis, (c) protects it by a "gentleman's agreement" with other companies, (d) does nothing to prevent competitors from growing the seed.

8. An industry that caused lima beans to become a problem vegetable was (a) canning business, (b) frozen-food business, (c) development of super-markets, (d) advertising.

9. Mr. Cuthbertson rose from the position of "roguing" to that of (a) director of research, (b) president, (c) executive vice-president, (d) salaried employee doing experimental work.

10. Mr. Cuthbertson contends that the need for more improved vegetables will (a) end soon, (b) end when all vegetables are grown to suit packers' specifications, (c) never end, (d) grow less as processing improves.

Answers: 1)——, 2)——, 3)——, 4)——, 5)——, 6)——, 7)——, 8)——, 9)——, 10)——.

See Answer Key, page 375.

Rate: W.P.M. ————   Comprehension Score: ————

Vocabulary Study

A knowledge of word meanings will contribute much to your improvement in reading. If you cannot pronounce an unfamiliar word, or if you do not know the meaning of a word, you are apt to stop and pause over that word, thus interrupting your flow of speed. Your comprehension is hampered also by lack of a specific word meaning. Misunderstanding or ignoring even one word may change the import of a sentence or paragraph or of an entire selection.

Since vocabulary is important in reading growth, you are given some practice in vocabulary building in this chapter and in the successive chapters of this book.

The words presented in the vocabulary section of each chapter will be taken from the given selections. Follow carefully the instructions which accompany each vocabulary section, and check your work with the appropriate Answer Key. If you make mistakes in some of the exercises, study the word list and its definitions again, to see if you can find why you made each mistake.

Here is a list of words taken from the selections which you have just read, with their definitions. Study the words and their definitions. Then read the following sentences, and for each one select from the word list the word which best completes the meaning. Write that word in the blank space. You may have to add *ing* to some of the words.

abrasion	wearing away in shreds
burgeon	to put forth buds, to sprout
decrepit	worn out
agenda	memoranda of things to be done
prestige	power to command admiration
obsolete	gone out of use
horticulture	art of growing fruits, vegetables, etc.
paradox	an idea opposed to common sense
hybrid	offspring of specially-selected species
congeals	changes from a liquid to a solid
derelict	neglectful, not attended to
engrossing	monopolizing all attention
primordial	first in order of time, primitive
progeny	offspring
irony	humor which implies the opposite of what is meant
intrastate	not outside the state
concept	a thought, opinion, or idea
distaff	woman's authority or domain
collateral	something of equal value
disintegrate	to destroy the wholeness of

1. The prestige of the Roman Empire was rapidly ⸺.
2. With sufficient ⸺, a large loan may be negotiated.
3. The old gardener still maintains his interest in ⸺.
4. Quill pens are no longer used. They are ⸺.
5. A mother skunk and her numerous ⸺ ambled serenely from the garden.

6. Asian affairs are scheduled for discussion on this week's ————.
7. To be ———— in so important a duty is dangerous to security.
8. Bob and his father were in disagreement with the ————
side of the family.
9. The house, a ———— structure, had broken windows, sagging
shutters, and missing shingles.
10. The plant wizard becomes very busy when buds ———— in
the springtime.

Check your answers with those given in the Answer Key on page
375. Allow yourself 10 for each correct answer.

Vocabulary Score: ————

Follow-Up Practice

You have had some experience in trying to increase your speed.
You should avail yourself of much more practice, however, than that
afforded in the three selections which you have just covered.

Using materials of your own selection. Now begin your speeded
reading practice in earnest. This practice should be of two types:
(1) general informal practice throughout the day; and (2) specific
practice within stated periods of time.

Your general informal practice will consist of forcing yourself to
read faster everything that you have to read all day long. Try the
same techniques that you used in reading the articles in this chapter
on *everything* you read. Regardless of whether you are reading
memos or ads that are piled up on your desk, news items, magazine
articles, or chapters in books, push your eyes along as fast as you can
make them go, and speed up your mental process of absorbing
meanings rapidly.

You have to work at this business of increasing speed. Nothing
short of continuous and abundant practice will develop the new
rapid reading habits which you wish to acquire. So jolt yourself
out of the old complacency and force yourself to read faster every
time you have or can make an opportunity to read. Take in whole
meaningful groups of words at each fleeting glance.

You won't be able to read technical material so rapidly as nontechnical material, so while you are breaking old habits and establishing new ones try to devote the bulk of your reading practice to
subjects of general interest and material which is easy. Don't shy

away from any technical reading that you have to do, however. If this is a must in your daily program, apply the same speed-reading techniques to this that you do to reading easy material. Try to read even technical material at a higher tempo.

Don't let a low comprehension score slow you down at this stage. Keep right on pushing yourself to a high speed. Let yourself go, whether or not you are getting the meaning of every sentence. The important thing at this time is to accustom yourself to a new tempo.

Of course if you continue to do badly with comprehension after, let us say, ten different sittings of practice, then for a time you should devote more attention to this phase of your improvement. You will be given a great deal of help on comprehension in the remaining chapters of this book. With the aid of the additional techniques suggested, your comprehension should keep pace with your speed improvement, once your new speed habits become established.

If during your speed practice you meet a word which you cannot pronounce or for which you do not know the meaning, skip over it for the time being. After you have finished your speed reading, go back over the selection, pick out any such words, and look them up in the dictionary. There is no surer way of building your reading vocabulary.

CHAPTER 4

Heeding

the Signposts

A STORY is told of Rollo, the illiterate mountain boy who received a letter one day and asked the postman to read it to him. "Can't you read the writing?" asked the postman. "No," replied Rollo. "I have trouble with words. I can get along a lot better with numbers. When I see the signposts I can tell how fur to but not whur to." Surely signposts were not of much use to Rollo. And signposts aren't of much use to any of us, even though we can read the "whur to" words, unless we watch for them and make use of them.

Ordinarily when you are driving in unfamiliar territory, you keep yourself on the alert for road signs. You have a definite destination, and you are acutely aware of the fact that the quickest and surest way to reach this destination is to heed the signs which tell you when to turn left, when to turn right, and when to go straight ahead. If you become preoccupied with other thoughts and fail to note the signposts as you roll complacently along, you will later on find that you are on the wrong road. Then time and gasoline and driving energy are all wasted as you retrace the route to the very important sign which you should have observed in the first place.

Printways are similar to trailways in that they, too, are posted with signs which aid the reader in finding his way quickly and surely to his reading destination. If the reader ignores these signs, he, like the motorist, is apt to find it necessary to retrace his steps.

The signposts in reading warn you when to go straight ahead, and when to make a sharp turn. If you pay attention to these signposts, you can read much more intelligently and much more rapidly. They warn you what to expect, and thus you are prepared to anticipate the meaning and to adjust quickly to change in the printed stream of thought.

What are these signposts? Usually they are words; occasionally they are phrases. There are two distinct groups.

Go-Ahead Signals

One group of direction words tells you to go ahead with speed. These words assure you that there will be no turns, or bends, or obstacles in your printed pathway. They indicate that there will be more and more ideas added which carry forward the same course of thought.

Some of the most commonly used sign words in this group are *and, more, moreover, more than that, furthermore, also, likewise.*

And is the most common of all of the go-ahead words. It connects ideas of equal importance, or ideas which occur in a certain order. Notice how *and* signals you to go ahead in the sentence below—to read more and more equivalent ideas.

Mr. Jennings was angry and guilty and apologetic and harassed all at the same time.

The three *ands* in this sentence tell you to race right along, that you will find more and similar ideas about Mr. Jennings.

More, moreover, more than that, furthermore, indicate that there is something to be added on the same subject and that the thought will be carried forward in the same direction.

Also literally signifies "all in the same manner." *Likewise* means "in like manner." Both of these words are used to join ideas which have a sameness in the whole, and therefore they tell you that there will be a continuance in the same thought direction.

Underline the direction words or phrases in the paragraphs below, which signal you to go straight ahead. At each one, stop and think about its function in the sentence. Ask yourself, "Does this word *really* warn me that the discussion is going to run along in the same tenor—that there will be no change in the course of thought?"

They reported the usual number of hunting accidents this year. They also reported that mistaking men for game came third in all causes of wounds. More than that, they painted a picture of the type of man who usually commits this most inexcusable of hunting accidents. Furthermore, they stated flatly that this type of person ought to stay out of the woods and view television for his recreational diversion.

Hugh Watson, operator of a substation of the City Power and Light Company, was closing the windows against a sudden gust of rain and wind. Suddenly his lights flickered and went out. The next thing he knew his entire station was dead. Likewise the radio. Likewise the telephone.

Did you note that *furthermore* and *likewise* in the paragraphs above told you to continue right on, that there would be more of the same thing?

There are go-ahead words which belong in a slightly different classification from the ones discussed above, because they have a more specific function to perform. These are words such as *thus, so, and so, therefore, consequently,* and *accordingly.* These words give you a go-ahead signal in so far as the stream of thought is concerned, but they mark the beginning of a more weighty idea—an idea which may be a summary or a consequence of ideas previously presented. While these words signal you to continue without change in thought, they also tell you that something is coming which is of significance—which, indeed, may be the "heart" of the paragraph. Therefore, when you see such words, you think, "I must pay special attention to this sentence. It may summarize the whole paragraph for me."

Note the specific function of these more commanding go-ahead words in the paragraphs below.

One phase of sociology deals with social amelioration. If we know the influences which made any human condition what we find it to be, we can, with scientific precision, point out the influences that must be brought to bear upon that condition to improve it. Thus we have the science called practical or applied sociology.

The world is now reduced to a state of little better than moral anarchy. Consequently, nothing but renewed ideals and good government can bring the people back to the use of their sober senses.

Another group of go-ahead words is even more decisive. They signal you to continue, but they tell you also that you are about to come to a stopping place. They announce that the author has developed all the ideas he intends to use in the discussion and is about to sum up the entire set of ideas, or draw the conclusion. Some of the words and phrases which give you these warnings are *as a result, finally, concluding,* and *in conclusion.*

When you encounter one of these words or phrases, alert yourself for a sudden termination of the flow of thought. You are about to reach the end.

Read the examples below. Note the direction words that warn you of a stopping place and heed these words!

A college girl reports that she has a fear of eyes. She admits that this is unreasonable, yet she cannot look anyone directly in the eyes without experiencing panic. The phrase "fear looking out of her eyes" runs through her thoughts constantly. As a result of this condition, her social relationships and academic achievements are approaching ruin.

The monthly figures are based on a combination of techniques. In some cases, samples are used; sample data are received from banks and from retail outlets, for example. In other areas, where little current information is available, straight-line extension of past trends is used. Finally, estimates are made, based solely on trends in somewhat related credit series.

The double-wedding-ring ceremony, although an old one, continues to be very popular. Jewelers state, however, that it is the rule rather than the exception that the groom discards his ring after a few years. Women wear theirs as long as they live. One firm states that less than one per cent of wedding rings sold to bridegrooms have been made to wear. Conclusion: women are much more sentimental about wedding rings than men.

Turn back to the beginning of this chapter. Underline all the go-ahead words which you can find in the discussions from the beginning of the chapter up to this point. You will of course omit the examples in which you have already underlined the go-ahead words.

Turn-About Signals

The words we have discussed so far are the leading-on words which warn that the stream of thought is flowing straight ahead. In opposition to these go-ahead words another group serves to turn the thought sharply in a different direction.

The most common of these adversative words is *but*. Literature is filled with laments of writers concerning the effect of this word *but*. As an example, here is a quotation from Samuel Daniel, the English poet:

Oh, now comes that bitter word—*but*, which makes all nothing that was said before, that smooths and wounds, that strikes and dashes more than flat denial, or a plain disgrace.

If all readers would heed every warning which this little word *but* signals to them, they would read with much greater ease and more decisive understanding.

Read the quotation below. Keep yourself alert for the word *but*. Note how this one word is the harbinger of a complete change in thought.

Life is like a beautiful and winding lane, on either side bright flowers, beautiful butterflies, and tempting fruits, which we scarcely pause to admire or taste, so eager are we to hasten to an opening which we imagine will be more beautiful still. But by degrees, as we advance, the trees grow bleak, the flowers and butterflies fail, the fruits disappear, and we find we have arrived—to read a desert waste.—*G. A. Sala*

There are other words and phrases which also negate preceding statements with equal effectiveness. Some of these words are *yet, nevertheless, otherwise, although, despite, in spite of, not, on the contrary, however, notwithstanding, rather* and sometimes *still*. When used to divert the current of thought, these words usually occur either at the beginning of a new sentence or in the middle of a two-clause sentence.

When you come upon such words, prepare yourself for an abrupt change. These deflectors tell you to stop going ahead and to change your course to the opposite direction, since the author is about to usher in an idea adverse to those that you have been reading. Don't go jogging along past these signposts on a straight-ahead road. When a signpost says "Sharp Turn," adjust to the change of course which the author is about to take. Travel with the author, and you'll reach your destination more quickly and more accurately.

Read the sentences and paragraphs below. Underline the deflecting words and phrases. Note the effect which these words have on the direction in which the thought is flowing.

Addison was not a good speaker, yet he was an admirable writer.

He has acted an unworthy part; nevertheless, I will be a friend to him as far as I can.

She was glad in a way; still, she felt unhappy.

Treat kindly every miserable truth that knocks at your door. Otherwise you will some day fail to recognize Truth Himself when He comes in rags.—*Austin O'Halley*

Because of the variability in dyes from color to color, the ratings can give only an indication of the likelihood of getting desired results under a particular set of circumstances. For example, it is probable that if you select a brand which was rated as good for wool, and if you follow the correct procedures, you'll get good results. However, since an overall rating of "good" represents a composite of individual color ratings, there is always a possibility that your selection of color may be one of the less satisfactory shades of a generally good brand.[1]

You decide to reduce. And so you set your jaw as you hurry off to the grocery to lay in a supply of lettuce, asparagus, lamb chops and tomato juice. But even as you vow that *this* time you are going to stick with it until you get down to the desired weight, you hear your subconscious whispering to you, "You won't do it. You know you won't. You've tried it before and you never stayed with it."

He who says much says but little in proportion to his thoughts. He selects that language which conveys his ideas in the most explicit and direct manner. He tries to compress as much thought as possible in a few words. On the contrary, the man who talks everlastingly and promiscuously, who seems to have an exhaustless magazine of sound, crowds so many words into his thoughts that he always obscures and very frequently conceals them.—*Washington Irving*

Now turn back to the beginning of the chapter and underline all turn-about words that you can find in the discussion, studying the effect which each such word has on the flow of thought.

Checking Your Awareness of Direction Words

Read the following selection. Underline all the direction words which you think influence the flow of thought one way or the other.

[1] "Household Dyes," *Consumer Reports*, August 1951, p. 359.

Selection 1

Traveling in Summer[2]

It isn't the mere joy of speeding "on spinning rubber shoes" along the broad highways, nor the fellowship of the road, that completes the satisfaction of eating up the landscape in the good old summer days.

Rather is it the glorious sense of freedom, and the peace and quiet, and the invigorating tonic of good fresh air in the great outdoors.

Not on the dusty highroad but in the shaded by-lanes and in the cool woods where we lunch or set our camp—that's where we find our Eden.

Sailing has its thrills, tramping and fishing their own enticements, and golf links have a lure that few can resist.

But when, after a long day's run, we have turned our car into a bosky dell, and settled ourselves down for our own camp meal and bed under the whispering pines by the side of a mountain stream, we are a-tingle and full-tuned to a sense of joy in living that our golfer friend seldom finds, even though he reaches the nineteenth hole. Not that I discount his enjoyment of this sport. There is a world of satisfaction in playing a round in par. On the other hand, the honorable and ancient games may yield only sorrow and vexation of spirit. Therefore golf is not all pleasure.

But here in the enfolding shadows of night, as the sparks fly upward from our own campfire, there is no trouble. We shuffled off the coil of trouble when we left the noisy streets of town. Moreover, here there are no flashing, blinding lights, no crashing trolley cars, no nerve-wracking sounds of any kind. Consequently we have peace and rest, and a few hours of quiet communing with the real, simple things in the midst of which we humans used to live—long, long ago.

And so it's nice to get back there. There we find the oldest fellowship of life, the fellowship that Thoreau, John Burroughs, Muir, Jefferies, Hudson and other sons of nature found—the finest and most enduring fellowship on earth.

And it is all within easy reach today. Our car, "be it ever so humble," will get us there and back. Could the fabled magic carpet of Arabian tales afford us greater pleasure than a trip in the country with our jalopy?

Now that you have underlined the direction words in the selection above, write these two headings on a piece of paper:

Go-Ahead Words   Turn-About Words

Copy each of the words you underlined under the appropriate heading.

Then turn to the Answer Key on page 375 and check your work.

[2] W. D. Moffat, "The Open Letter," *The Mentor,* August 1926, p. 68.

This will give you an indication as to whether or not you are fully aware of direction words and their function in reading.

Heeding Signals in Timed Selections

As a result of the study and practice which you have had thus far, you should be ready to heed signals as one means of increasing both your speed and comprehension.

Two selections are provided for your use in timed practice. Read them as rapidly as you can. Jot down your beginning and ending times in the appropriate blank spaces. Speed forward without restraint as long as the go-ahead signals flash out their message to you, *but* take heed when you see a turn-about word and adjust quickly to anticipate a change.

Selection 2

BEGINNING TIME:———————
HR.——————— MIN.———————

The Spirit of Paper Making[3]

For 1,800 years my spirit has gone from land to land, from continent to continent, from China to Turkestan and to Arabia, thence to Spain, Italy, and France; thereafter to Germany, England, and Sweden—and finally to the great new country on the western side of the Atlantic.

And I have everywhere worked with the substances men were familiar with and the tools they knew how to handle. So it was that a hundred years after I made paper from the mulberry tree I taught my own people of the Flowery Kingdom how to make even a stronger and better paper from rags of cotton and flax, and also a cheap paper from the straw of the rice plant.

And it was from rags that the craftsmen of Arabia and of Europe and of America learned to make paper, and for 1,700 years but little paper was made of aught else—and no better paper has ever been made than was made in those days.

Yet a man with much labor and sweat could make only a little pile of sheets a day.

Learning was carried throughout every land, but books were dear and hard to get, and mostly kept in the temples by the priests who wrote the

[3] Royal S. Kellog, "Paper Making, From Papyrus to the Printed Page," *The Mentor*, September 1925, pp. 21-26.

words therein by hand or mayhap printed a page at a time from shapes cut into a block of wood.

A better way must be had if there were to be more books, so one day when I found a man in Germany named Gutenberg, who had more sense than most, I told him that many centuries before, in faraway China, printing had been done with single types each representing a character so that, by making many of these types, they could be put together quickly in the form of words for the page of a book and then set again for another page. This man had much skill with his hands as well as with his head. He printed a sacred book and thereafter there was so much printing that more paper must be had.

Next I caused a Dutchman to make a great vat in which was a heavy wheel with sharp edges, turned by water power so that fibers could be beaten up quickly and more men kept busy with the frames and screens.

Then did I cause a Frenchman, Robert by name, to make a great wire screen moving over pulleys so that the water would fall through the screen and leave the fibers on it, after which the wet sheet was run over hot iron cylinders and dried quickly.

This was the beginning of paper making as people know it today and was during the period of my twenty-second rejuvenation.

And men made new machines for the types so that there was much printing of books and the things called "newspapers," unknown to my people.

But not for long was there enough paper even when it was made by machines, because there could not be found enough rags of cotton and linen. So men did try many strange substances—even grass and leaves and straw and seaweed and stalks of many plants—but with little success for most.

And when I was unable to solve the problem did the spirit of the great Confucius come to me once more during the Moon of the Harvest and say: "Ts'ai Lun, as thou first went to the tree, go thou again, but this time take not the bark, for it is not enough. Take thou the solid wood itself. Hold blocks of it firmly against a turning stone with water thereon so that it is ground finely and yet most of the fibers left unbroken.

"This when washed and screened as thou knowest how to do will give thee much paper-making material—not so good as rags, but cheap and plentiful so that men may have newspapers and papers of divers other kinds."

Thus again spoke the great Confucius. And it was even so. There arose paper mills in the forests and along the streams where there was much falling water to turn the stones, and ten men were making paper where there was one before. Great rolls of paper came from them ready for the other machines that held the little types.

And then men put the forms of the types on great cylinders and turned them even faster so that thousands of books and newspapers were printed where there was one before.

And there were schools; and all the children learned to read and write.

And then other men made a wondrous machine that set more of the little types than seven could do, so that there were more books and newspapers and magazines than ever before; and more paper was used in other ways, so there was not enough paper until more mills with bigger machines were built.

And merchants took much space in the newspapers and magazines to tell of their wares, and trade was greatly increased thereby.

And all manner of business was done by means of papers, and paper was used in the place of other substances for many purposes.

And then the printing machines were made bigger and swifter, so that twoscore thousand newspapers might be printed in an hour; and the paper machines were made still bigger and swifter, so that one machine might make enough paper in a day to cover four hundred acres of land.

And people began to say again that there was not enough wood to make paper and something else must be found or there would be no more paper.

And then the foresters arose and said that there might be wood enough if men were to grow more trees, so that there would always be plenty of paper.

All-wise Ho-Ti spoke truly when he said that a kingdom of knowledge is greater than a kingdom of arms.

And I shall carry out his charge as long as the world endures, for I am the Spirit of Paper Making.

Began	*Finished*	No. words:	1130

$$\frac{}{} \times 60 = \underline{} \text{ W.P.M.}$$

No. seconds:

Checking Comprehension

Read each of the paragraphs below. Choose the answer which you think is correct. Write the corresponding letter in the appropriate answer space at the end of the exercise.

1. The spirit of paper-making has traversed the earth for a period of (a) 1000 years, (b) 2300 years, (c) 1800 years, (d) 400 years.

2. The earliest paper makers in the "Flowering Kingdom" made paper from the mulberry tree, from cotton and flax, and a cheap paper from (a) hide of animals, (b) plastics, (c) poppy leaves, (d) straw of the rice plant.

3. The chief ingredient used in paper-making for 1700 years was: (a) wood, (b) rags, (c) straw, (d) a combination of wood and straw.

4. Paper mills arose in forests when it was discovered that good

paper could be made of (a) solid wood, (b) bark, (c) leaves, (d) roots.

5. An invention which brought about a great demand for more paper was (a) a machine for running off newspapers quickly, (b) steam engines which made it possible to transport wood pulp great distances, (c) typesetting by Gutenberg, (d) a glue which would hold rag fibers together.

6. A Dutchman's contribution to the manufacture of paper was (a) a newsprint machine which would turn off large sheets of newspapers, (b) a large water-power wheel with sharp edges which would beat the fibers up quickly, (c) a pulp digester which would cook the fibers, (d) a machine for sizing paper.

7. A Frenchman by the name of Robert invented (a) a method of making pulp, (b) straps to guide the pulp as it rolls over cylinders, (c) a reel for winding paper as it comes from the cylinders, (d) a wire screen moving over the pulleys so that water would fall through the screen and leave the fibers on it.

8. An advance in typesetting which gave an impetus to the production of more printed material was (a) making better type, (b) putting forms of types on cylinders that turn rapidly, (c) training compositors to work more rapidly, (d) a machine which increased the production of the type itself.

9. As bigger and better machines were made for typesetting and for manufacture of paper, there was not enough wood to supply the demand, so it was suggested (a) that some way be found to manufacture synthetic wood, (b) that certain chemicals be combined with straw to make paper, (c) that more trees be grown specifically for paper-making, (d) that a search be made for some entirely new paper-making substance.

10. The statement that most closely sums up the gist of this selection is (a) There is an increasing need for paper, (b) Paper-making is an ancient art, (c) There has been a strong relationship between invention and paper-making, (d) The spirit of paper-making always has been and always will be an inspiration and stimulation to many, (e) The fact that paper today has reached its peak in both production and quality in response to man's resourcefulness in meeting the demands that civilization has placed upon him is not to be interpreted to mean that the spirit of paper-making will not continue to guide man to further achievements, (f) The spirit of paper-making has had far-reaching influences in civilization, noticeably in the realms of education and business, chiefly because it has been the outstanding means of distributing knowledge throughout the world.

Answers: 1)—, 2)—, 3)—, 4)—, 5)—, 6)—, 7)—, 8)—, 9)—, 10)—.

Check your answers with the Answer Key on page 375. Multiply the number of correct answers by 10.

Rate: W.P.M. ————————   Comprehension Score: ————————

Selection 3
_____

BEGINNING TIME:————————
HR.———————— MIN.————————

How to Negotiate for a House[4]

A great many houses are not advertised by the owners, but are listed with brokers (realtors, agents). The broker's commission is usually 5% of the sale price; consequently, elimination of this fee by giving priority inspection to owner-advertised houses may be a justified first step.

But don't ignore broker-advertised houses. If the broker is a man of intelligence, tact, and integrity he can be well worth his fee. The problem is to find a good one. The chances are best with brokers whose advertising copy is matter-of-fact and moderate in tone. If the agent turns out to be unpleasant, take a quick look at a couple of his listings and pass on.

While you are sorting out the brokers you will be seeing houses and getting a preliminary idea of values. Also, in active neighborhoods, you are likely to meet a number of brokers who are at least not impossible. Moreover, you may be fortunate enough to find one who is both frank and expert in his judgment of houses—but it does not follow that he will be the one through whom you finally buy, for chance plays as great a part in realty transactions as merit and good intentions.

If you have seen a property through a broker or by direct contact with the owner and you are later inadvertently taken to it by another broker, you should immediately so state, and not enter the house with the second broker. Otherwise, if you should later buy the house, you may find yourself involved in a lawsuit.

Factors which sometimes play a part in bidding include the length of time the property has been on the market, and when the present owner acquired it. If he bought it and made improvements in the Thirties or early Forties he can sell relatively cheap and still make a whopping profit. On the contrary, the recent buyer, builder, or improver, having paid top prices, must get a top price in turn if he is not to lose. A property which lingers on the market may sometimes be acquired advantageously by a buyer who comes along just when the owner decides he can't get his price and decides to come down to a more reasonable level. It is advisable,

[4] *Consumer Reports,* October 1952, pp. 468-471.

nevertheless, to let the property rest a while longer and investigate to check whether price was the only reason for its failure to move.

In deciding how much you can afford to pay, one rule of thumb is that the total price should not exceed double your annual income. If followed rigorously in the present market, this simply means that few low-income families can own their homes. It is true enough, however, that you should be especially cautious in buying if your income is under say $5,000 a year, or if it is precarious for any reason. And if you have lived in apartments all your life, don't be taken in by the monthly charges quoted in the developers' ads as "covering everything, just like rent." Although these charges do cover interest and amortization or mortgage, real estate taxes, and insurance, there are also heat, electricity, maintenance and repairs, water taxes, special assessments, and other costs, which may come to another 40% and likewise must be paid for—just like rent. Furthermore, if your move is from the city to suburbs, there is the not-inconsiderable cost of commutation and the possibility that you will need another car.

When you find a house in which you are really interested, an offhand estimate of market value is not good enough. You should appraise it yourself, if you feel competent to do so, or get it appraised.

You can get a direct appraisal of the property's value by hiring a professional appraiser but, unless he is both competent and disinterested, his findings may not be very helpful. Be especially careful in a small town, where bank officials and directors, realtors, assessors, and tax collectors, the probate judge, and realty-minded lawyers are all likely to be good friends. You go to the bank for an appraisal and the bank sends out or recommends a man. Neither the bank nor the appraiser will deliberately set out to rob you, of course, but the bank may prefer to see you buy the house for one of a number of reasons—the broker or the owner may be a friend or a director, the bank may want to make a loan, it may favor an active market on general principles, or it may have any of a dozen equally cogent reasons. Appraisal being an art, not a science, there is a normal latitude of perhaps plus or minus 5%. Therefore, if the appraiser is acting in the interest of the bank, the 5% is apt to be minus; if he has reasons for wanting the house sold, it may chance to be plus. The difference—say $2,000 on a $20,000 property—is no slight one.

When a property needs repairs or remodeling, some brokers transform themselves into architects or builders and glibly quote the cost of heating plants, plumbing, masonry, and "streamlined" kitchens. Such estimates are usually a fraction of actual cost. Not many brokers will tell you anything worth listening to about building costs, or any other technical matter. If you are seriously interested in a house that needs extensive remodeling or repair work before it comes up to your standards, call in a builder or contractor and get a firm bid on the cost of the job. Do this before you make any bid, otherwise you may be unpleasantly shocked at how much more the house costs than the amount you thought you were paying for it.

When the difference between bid and asked prices is small but both parties stand firm, the broker can sometimes save the deal by reducing his commission. Before resorting to this final and painful expedient he may enlarge on the possible consequences to him: loss of license, expulsion from his trade association, ostracism, etc. Despite his story these penalties are almost always imaginary; the broker's colleagues will do the same thing when they have to.

Began   *Finished*   No. words: 1260

$$\frac{}{} \times 60 = \underline{\qquad} \text{ W.P.M.}$$

_____   _____   No. seconds:

Checking Comprehension

Select the correct answers and write the appropriate letters in the answer space below.

1. The broker's fee is justified because (a) of his knowledge of houses and property, (b) of his ability to secure houses more cheaply, (c) many houses are for sale which are not advertised, (d) the legal aspect of the situation requires a broker.

2. In regard to broker advertisements, you are advised to accept (a) nothing of what is claimed, (b) everything except that which pertains to future improvements, (c) that which is moderate and matter-of-fact, (d) only that which you would like to believe.

3. In negotiating for a house, you are advised (a) not to consult more than one broker in regard to houses, (b) to sort out your brokers as they show you houses, (c) to consult two reliable brokers as a general rule, (d) to make a visit to the house you may want to buy before consulting any broker at all.

4. Not mentioned in the article as significant in the bidding is (a) the length of time the house has been on the market, (b) when the improvements were made, (c) the financial status of the seller, (d) when the house was purchased by the present owner.

5. The total price in regard to the buyer's income should (a) be less than double his annual income, (b) not exceed double his annual income, (c) be approximately three times his annual income, (d) not necessarily be a major consideration.

6. If the owner of a property which has been lingering on the market comes down to a lower price you are advised (a) to buy it at once before he changes his mind, (b) ask him to sell at a still lower price, (c) disregard the deal entirely, (d) let the matter rest while you investigate to find out if the price was the only reason why the property hadn't been sold previously.

7. Appraisals should be made by (a) yourself, if you feel competent, (b) an appraiser, not necessarily professional, who is connected with the bank but who doesn't know the broker, (c) professional appraisers recommended by both the broker and the bank, (d) a friend who has bought a house.

8. The writer claims that appraising is (a) a science, (b) an art, (c) an inexact science, (d) a combination of art and science.

9. If repairs and remodeling are to be made, the best course to pursue is to (a) consult the owners about the cost, (b) have the real estate man give you an estimate, (c) figure out yourself about how much it would cost, (d) call in a contractor to give a bid.

10. The consequences which the broker tells you may befall him when he offers to reduce his commission in order to make a sale should cause you (a) not to accept his reduction, (b) to worry over the consequences to the broker, (c) to take his story of penalties lightly because they are almost always imaginary, (d) to give him a substantial tip.

Answers: 1)—, 2)—, 3)—, 4)—, 5)—, 6)—, 7)—, 8)—, 9)—, 10)—.

See Answer Key, page 376.

Rate: W.P.M. ————   Comprehension Score: ————

Vocabulary Study

The following sentences were taken from the selections you just read. Below each sentence you will find three words within parentheses. Underline one of these three words which the author might have used in place of the italicized word in the sentence. Refer to a dictionary if necessary.

1. Paper-making underwent a *rejuvenation* after the invention of the printing press.
(regression, retrograde, reinvigoration)

2. *Craftsmen* from Arabia made paper out of rags.
(artists, artisans, laborers)

3. Men use wood for newspapers and papers of *divers* other kinds.
(scattered, diverse, several)

4. If the broker is a man of intelligence, tact, and *integrity* he can be well worth his fee.
(honesty, expediency, ascendancy)

5. Neither the bank nor the appraiser will deliberately set out to rob you, but the bank may prefer to see you buy the house for any of a dozen *cogent* reasons.

(vexing, inadvertent, convincing)

6. When a property needs repairs or remodeling, some brokers transform themselves into architects or builders and *glibly* quote the cost of heating plants, plumbing, masonry, and "streamlined" kitchens.

(flippantly, sarcastically, insidiously)

7. Before resorting to a final and painful *expedient* the broker may enlarge on the possible consequences to himself.

(appraisal, resource, privilege)

8. The broker may say that he faces expulsion from his trade association, *ostracism*, and financial ruin.

(rejuvenation, exclusion, conversion)

9. Your broker will tell you he is subject to penalties, but his *colleagues* will under pressure do the same thing.

(competitors, associates, probationers)

10. It is true enough that you should be especially cautious in buying if your income is under, say, $5,000 a year, or if it is *precarious* for any reason.

(inconsiderable, insecure, irreparable)

Check your answers with those given in the Answer Key on page 376. Allow yourself 10 for each correct answer.

Vocabulary Score: —————

Follow-Up Practice

Continue forcing your speed in all the reading you do, both in connection with your daily activities and during your specific practice periods. In all this reading, be sure to note the signposts. Now that you are sensitive to the signpost words, let them mean something to you. When you encounter a go-ahead sign, be assured that the course of thought will proceed in the same manner, that more will be said in the same tenor, and that you may continue full speed ahead with no change in thought. On the other hand, when a turnabout word or phrase pops up, be prepared to change your course of thinking, but continue your speed without loss in comprehension.

CHAPTER 5

Shop Before You Read

Why Shop Before You Read?

BEFORE you buy a car you shop. You look over the various makes and "size up" their appearances, special features, colors, promise of performance, price, etc. Similarly, you should shop before you select an article to read; that is, take a preview. A book, chapter, or article has certain prominent characteristics, just as a car or a suit has outstanding features. If you briefly study these characteristics before you read, your survey may be as valuable to you as your general "sizing up" of a car or suit before you buy it.

In some cases the preview will provide you with all the information you desire, and you won't find it necessary to read the selection at all. In other cases the preview will "whet your appetite," increase your interest, and strengthen your motive for reading. In these latter cases, when you actually do begin to read you will find that your pre-reading insight has paved the way for speedier and more comprehensive coverage of the printed page.

How to Shop

The first step in making a preview is to study the title. The title holds a world of information, for it gives you a quick cue as to what the topic of discussion is. It may be a deciding factor in determining whether or not you want to read the selection. If you decide that you do want to read it, then you have advance information and can read in terms of the promise that the title holds out to you.

Next, glance through the material to see if subheadings are used. If so, a quick survey of them will be valuable to you. You should consider each one for the information it gives or implies. These subheadings reveal to you the trend of discourse in the article as a whole. There will be occasions in which a preview of these subtitles will tell you all you want to know. At other times they will serve as interest leads to reading the difficult sections and as door-openers to better understanding of the text.

If any visual aids are furnished, study them for their significance. Look at illustrations carefully. They will aid your comprehension by giving you a vivid mental picture of the people, things, and locale dealt with. If maps are provided, study them. Your reading will be more meaningful if you have precise geographical locations in mind. If graphs and charts are provided, study these before you read the article. They will give you a quick grasp of relationships and proportions among data discussed in the text.

Next examine the length of the paragraphs. Turn the pages quickly and find out if most of the paragraphs are short, medium, or long. Remember, each paragraph is a thought unit, and a single idea is developed in each. If there are many short paragraphs, this is a fairly reliable indication that the article will include many ideas but will not be heavy with details. On the other hand, if the paragraphs are long, there will be fewer ideas, but each main idea will be expanded by numerous details. On the whole, this material will be more difficult to read.

Finally, make an estimate of how long it will take you to read the article. Count the words in several lines to ascertain the average number of words per line. Then multiply this number by the number of lines in the article. Once you have estimated the total number of words, decide how long it ought to take you to read it. Don't be easy with yourself. Set as short a time limit as you think you can possibly meet. Then live up to it!

Applying Preview Techniques
to a Selection

After you have previewed the following selection, you will be given a test to enable you to find out how much information you have gleaned as the result of your rapid survey.

Gathering information from title and subheads. Examine the title of the selection that follows on page 69. What does it tell you?

Obviously it tells you that the selection is about an adventure in canoes which took place in Labrador.

Glance at the first subtitle. What additional information does that give you? Since it is "Million-Paddle-Stroke Journey," you now know that the adventurers must have traveled by canoe and that it must have been a long journey.

Skim on to the second subheading: "Rails Soon Will Split Wilderness." You now know that the trip was through a wilderness where there were no railroads as yet.

Glance at the next subheading. From this you gather that the adventurers built fires to warm themselves or to cook, and that at times they had difficulty finding a beach wide enough for a fire to be built.

Now skim on in search of the next subheading. It tells you that the adventurers, accompanied by guides, journeyed to some place so seldom traveled that even the guides were unfamiliar with the route.

Now glance at the subheading "Few Eyes Have Seen Unknown Falls." This gives you the idea that seeing Unknown Falls was something very special—perhaps the goal of the whole adventure.

Move your eyes rapidly on to later subheadings. What do they tell you about the source and kind of food? What was another sight they saw? What did it resemble? What hardship did they encounter? What exciting experience did they have?

Noting lengths of paragraphs. Since the paragraphs are comparatively short, there won't be too much detail; therefore you will be able to move right along in your reading.

Testing yourself. If you should take a test to find out how much you know about this article without having read it, you would probably be surprised to discover the amount of information you have gained simply by making a preview. Turn to page 75 and see how many of the statements you can complete.

BEGINNING TIME:——————
HR.——————— MIN.———————

Labrador Canoe Adventure[1]

Two Indians ran dark hands and eyes over our twin aluminum canoes lying outside a warehouse in Burnt Creek, northern Quebec mining camp.

Prospectors, geologists, and drillers strolling by in their iron-reddened clothing expressed doubts about the unfamiliar metal craft. One hairy giant muttered something about "tin-can-oes."

. . . Despite pessimistic comment, we were confident the little canoes could carry us from the Quebec border across hundreds of miles of Labrador wilderness to Atlantic tidewater. It could be disastrous if they let us down! . . .

"Mathieu say the first jagged rock will gash 'em," interpreted John Michelin, one of our trapper guides.

"Well, they weathered a rough test last summer running the Susquehanna River," we pointed out, reassuring ourselves as well as the guides. "We'll go ahead as planned. They'll do better than you think."

By journey's end the 18-foot Gruman aluminum craft were scratched and dented, but watertight and sound. And—final vindication—our guides wanted to buy them.

Million-Paddle-Stroke Journey

In five weeks we paddled 578 miles on waters of Labrador's Hamilton River, trudged 61 miles over portages and up lookout hills, and navigated 150 fateful yards by raft. From height of land to sea level, each of us dipped a quarter of a million paddle strokes.

We embarked near the heart of the vast peninsula of Labrador-northern Quebec (Ungava). End of our water trail was North West River, trapper's town on Lake Melville, tidal arm of the Atlantic.

A chief objective was North America's next-to-greatest waterfall, the seldom-seen Grand Falls of the Hamilton, a stupendous cataract 245 feet high. Niagara, by its huge volume, alone surpasses it.

We traveled the interior of the land where Europeans probably made their first landfall in the New World. Yet the tides of history have largely swept by this corner of North America. Explorers recoiled from Labrador's barren, arctic coast. The wooded inland, far more pleasing and habitable, still is rarely visited.

1 Andrew Brown and Ralph Gray, *The National Geographic*, July 1951, pp. 85-99.

In Labrador's wilderness the dense spruce forest marches north, like an immense army, to the edge of subarctic barrens. Myriad lakes break its ranks; also stretches of spongy muskeg and the scars of forest fires. Water laces the country everywhere—twisting rivers, lakes great and small, and grassy marsh.

Moss takes the place of soil. Gray or yellowish caribou moss, really a lichen, covers drier ground with its fluffy mat. Crossing moss-quilted bog and boulder fields, every step is a gamble.

Rails Soon Will Split Wilderness

The Hamilton, Labrador's mightiest river, gathers its flood from this bewildering tangle. Long the domain of snowshoe and canoe, its western sources soon will echo to locomotive whistles and the clatter of cars on rails.

For the upper Hamilton basin encompasses part of a vast, newly-explored iron deposit that straddles the Quebec-Labrador border region. Track-laying has been begun on a 360-mile railroad to carry the ore from semibarren hills of Labrador and Ungava to the Gulf of St. Lawrence, whence ships will bear it to the market.

It was early summer, 1950, when we set out to see and picture Hamilton River wilds. At Montreal we picked up our trapper guides, John and Leslie Michelin, distant cousins. They had come from North West River, Labrador, by plane. . . .

On a Sunday afternoon we launched our canoes and slipped away into the silent wastes. John Michelin, our head guide, took the helm and Andrew Brown the forward paddle of bright-red *Loon*, Leslie Michelin the stern and Ralph Gray the bow of sky-blue *Trout*. . . .

On Monday, after 25 miles of paddling down Dyke Lake, we clambered up Fault Hill. A mighty sweep of country lay revealed. Long ridges banded the gently rolling land. Lakes filled nearly every depression. Higher hills thrust up bare crowns, overtopping the spruce and fir forest that reached, green and untouched, to the horizon. In silence we gazed out upon the haunting scene.

Beach Barely Wide Enough for a Fire

Skimming down the swift Ashuanipi River next evening, our wool shirts beaded by a steady drizzle, we searched for a campsite.

"We'll try here," John called out at last, indicating a narrow, rocky beach at the foot of a 40-foot sandy bluff.

Our paddles swung the canoes in toward shore. Ralph and Andy jumped out and tied the craft to boulders.

"We'll pitch the tent on top of the bank, I 'low," said Leslie. "It's a good job we've got this beach to unload on, and for our fire."

It took fancy stepping to move around, after the fire was blazing and all the supper things were strewn along that skimpy shore. To pass the fire we had to climb the bank or wade the brimming river. . . .

Long after the sky was black we pulled ourselves up the steep slope to the tent. Cobblestones dislodged by our feet rolled out of sight and plunked into the inky Ashuanipi.

The following day was better. The rain let up and the clouds parted briefly. Toward evening we navigated our first bad rapid. A tossing run of white water—the icing on any canoeing cake—tumbled us into Sandgirt Lake at sunset. . . .

Route Unknown Even to Guides

The all-water route between Sandgirt Lake and Unknown Falls was as new to our guides as to us.

Caching most of our outfit on an island, we ascended the Atikonak and were caught up in a battle with racing current and wind-lashed lakes.

Often we seemed to ride a watery treadmill; no matter how hard we dug at the stream, trees on shore crawled astern in slow motion.

John and Leslie never spoke of a river's current; it was always "tide." "There's less tide behind that island," they'd say, or "We'll have fair tide today."

Three miles up the Atikonak we reached a wild rapid. Here, and at a rough place a few miles above, we had to track the canoes through. . . .

Six days out, we reached the upper end of Gabbro Lake and couldn't find the inlet. . . .

After miles of futile searching for an inflowing river, we ran out of water at the head of the bay. No channel there! Next day we found the inlet—a broad stream, at that—not two miles from where we had read the compass! Moral? If you won't believe your maps and compass, stay home.

In Ossokmanuan Lake we got lost twice more, pushing to the heads of dead-end leads. . . .

Beyond "Ossok's" island-girt midsection we knew by the map we were drawing close to Unknown Falls, though the exact route was uncertain. But when we detected the first slow eddies of Unknown River slipping blackly out of Ossokmanuan, each of us felt his pulse step up a few beats.

Few Eyes Have Seen Unknown Falls

Unknown Falls were not completely unknown, but even on latest maps Unknown River's course is only a dotted line.

Prior to 1929, only three parties had fought their way to Unknown Falls. Each group saw one pair of falls and departed, unaware that another existed. . . .

Drifting down Unknown River, we were alert for surprises. Below a heavy rapid the stream swept the flanks of a high hill we had sighted from Ossokmanuan Lake.

We moored our canoes and climbed up a nearly vertical slope through incredibly tangled woods to the barren summit. The country unrolled like a map.

Ghostly wreaths of vapor marking Unknown Falls lay 10 airline miles away, just beyond a fine-looking lake Watkins had identified as "Lake E." The falls were twice that far off by the river's roundabout course. . . .

Modern Packing Allowed Varied Diet

The wetter the weather, the bigger our fires—and the more Lucullan our repasts!

We did our buying for the trip on the premise that a wilderness menu can list something more than a tiresome succession of beans, pork, hardtack, and pemmican. We wanted good food, but had to keep the total weight down because of the canoe's limited capacity.

So our grub stores featured solid foods of high nutritive value. We stocked up liberally on canned meats—boned chicken, bacon, ham, Spam, corned beef and tuna. There was plenty of sugar and peanut butter—but not enough jam. We slathered jam on everything from cereal and biscuits to crackers and cake.

Dates and raisins, dried prunes and apricots were our fruits. We never could serve enough mashed potatoes (we just added the powdered tuber to hot milk or water) to satisfy the guides. Favorites also were hot bouillon from cubes, and vegetable stew (dehydrated) mixed either with ham or chicken.

For grain foods we took oatmeal, rice, corn meal, and flour mixes—pancake, biscuit, and cake. Cake mix, too, was in short supply before the trip was half done. . . .

Butter and dried eggs came in cans; we had powdered whole milk and tinned evaporated milk. Tea and powdered coffee rounded out the list of staples.

Not far below Lake E, past two more rapids, we came into an expansion at whose foot plumes of vapor hung above tossing breakers. There was the thunder of falling water. We had reached Unknown Falls! . . .

Upper Cataract Resembles Victoria Falls

The majestic Upper Unknown Falls suggested to us a lesser Victoria Falls; in half a dozen spouts the river tumbled 90 feet over an escarpment into a wild gorge running nearly at right angles to the face of the falls.

An island divided the cataract into two sections. The western fall was the greater. . . .

A half hour later we stood in admiration of the right-bank Lower Falls. Funneled into a single channel, the river fell more than 100 feet, straight and sheer. Spray billowed up from the foot. Swirling mists dimmed the caldron from which the stream, a mass of foam, surged down a sheer-walled canyon. . . .

That night we stumbled into camp long after sunset. Heaping plates of hot chicken and vegetables (from dehydrated stock) revived our strength.

Next morning we canoed across the river to the western shore and bushwhacked to the left-bank side of the Upper Falls, a race of frothing water. Eddying mists alternately obscured and revealed the snowy face of its two 90-foot chutes.

The sun still shone bright, so we hustled downriver, jumping brooks and striding across burned-over lands.

The map showed a tributary flowing into Unknown River from the west, above the left-bank Lower Falls. Anticipating that the stream might be too deep to wade, we had brought with us an ax and some rope to build a raft. We could not have portaged the canoe five miles across that rough country.

Sure enough, the tributary soon blocked our way. It was a moat between us and the fourth Unknown Falls. . . .

Raft River Imposes a Barrier

Fortunately, the tributary—which we dubbed Raft River—flowed with slackened current through a pool just before dropping into Unknown River.

John and Leslie cut six or eight dead trees and bound the trim logs together.

"Looks O.K.," said Ralph, but when he and Leslie stepped aboard, the raft sank to the bottom! The men quickly cut and tied another layer of logs.

We poled to the head of the pool. Away from shore even 12-foot poles failed to touch bottom. Leslie, viewing our flimsy vessel askance, volunteered to stay behind. Ralph and Andy were determined to cross. John thought the voyage worth a try.

Leslie cut two paddles. They were heavy, awkward, and narrow, but better than poles that wouldn't reach bottom.

Pushing off into the welter of the in-flowing rapid, we caught the current. At first, the heavy raft scarcely responded to our paddle thrusts.

"Let's go back and start higher up," John shouted, glancing at the approaching crest of the outlet rapid.

"We're all right now," Andy said, as the raft lurched heavily toward shore. We landed halfway down the pool.

It was a short walk to the left-bank lower Falls. Here again an islet split the flood into two thunderous sluiceways. This chute was more broken up than the others. The creamy spate of water surged with terrifying force through the corkscrew canyon that received it.

We returned to our jerry-built raft, stepped aboard, and shoved off. Suddenly one of John's legs dropped through the logs right up to his thigh.

"Paddle back!" he called out. "I'm stuck. We'll go over the rapid!"

With a frantic tug, John retrieved his leg, but a moment later Andy's foot slipped through. The raft was loosening up. Grunting with the effort, we leaned to paddles and poles—and presently the eddy caught us. We swung safely in to shore.

Leslie helped us to relax with a cup of hot tea.

Well, we thought, our persistence paid off, despite the chance taken. We were the first, we were quite sure, ever to reach and photograph both pairs of Unknown Falls in summer.

Below its two foaming steps down from the plateau, Unknown River is unnavigable to its junction with Hamilton River below Grand Falls and Bowdoin Canyon.

So we had to retrace our route to Sandgirt Lake.

Stalking a Stag Caribou

We set backs and shoulders against Unknown River rapids to reach Ossokmanuan Lake again. Threading islands just below the lake, we heard a loud whisper from Andy: "Look there, on the beach! A caribou!"

A magnificent stag with a spreading rack of antlers was browsing on willows at the water's edge. John ordered us to paddle quietly. We might slip close enough for a picture.

We were 100 yards from the caribou when he came stiffly to the alert, nose lifted to sniff the air. He cantered up the beach, toward John and Andy. But out of camera range the animal took alarm, shook his antlers and plunged into the woods.

The second rapid below Gabbro Lake, scene of tough tracking on the upstream leg, gave us a thrilling run on the way back to Sandgirt. . .

Wave crests around visible boulders, or below submerged ones, stayed in place. We twisted through, facing each hazard as we met it. Responding to John's steering, *Loon* slipped past one rock on the left, barely grazed two more on the right.

A hard bump over a shoal at the bottom, and the rapid was behind us! *Trout* followed close on our heels. "A good run!" observed Andy. John's face, now relaxed, was wreathed in smiles.

Began   *Finished*   No. words:

$$2333 \times 60 = \rule{2cm}{0.4pt} \text{ W.P.M.}$$

No. seconds:

_____   _____

Preview Test

Complete the statements below by writing in the missing words.

1. This is an adventure story which took place in _____.
2. The men who took the trip were accompanied by _____.
3. They traveled in _____.
4. This was called a "_____-paddle-stroke journey."
5. The word which you supplied in the phrase above indicated to you that it was a _____ trip.
6. The country was unsettled. It was a _____.
7. Much of this country was unknown even to the _____.
8. Sometimes they had difficulty in finding a landing place wide enough to build a _____.
9. The falls called "Unknown Falls" had been seen by only a _____ people.
10. The food of the adventurers allowed _____ diet.
11. The Upper Cataract which they saw resembled _____.
12. They ran into a river that was a barrier to them. They named it

    _____ _____.

13. There must have been wild game in the wilderness, for among other thrills they stalked a _____ _____.
14. The article will probably be fairly easy reading, since the paragraphs are _____.

Correct your answers by referring to the article itself.

Did you realize that you could get so much information by simply previewing an article and not taking time actually to read it?

Reading the article. Perhaps you have become sufficiently interested in the adventure of these two men so that you would like to find out more about the experiences they had. Try reading the article as fast as you can just for entertainment. Jot down your beginning and ending times and compute your rate as usual. Then take the test.

Checking Comprehension

Write the letter which indicates the correct answer for each statement in the appropriate space at the end of the test.

1. When People in Burnt Creek saw the men's canoes, this is how they felt about the possibility of the canoes' carrying the men on

their trip: (a) confident, (b) hopeful, (c) assured, (d) pessimistic.

2. The land in which the adventurers travelled (a) had been inhabited at one time, (b) was partially cultivated, (c) had been settled by iron miners, (d) was a rarely-visited wilderness.

3. The upper Hamilton basin encompasses (a) some old iron-ore pits, (b) newly-discovered uranium mines, (c) newly-explored iron deposit, (d) abandoned silver mines.

4. When the men were ready to sleep, they (a) crawled into sleeping bags, (b) pitched tents, (c) looked for an abandoned hut, (d) lay down under a thick pine tree.

5. On their trip from Sandgirt Lake to Unknown Falls, the men (a) found smooth sailing, (b) had to walk most of the way, (c) encountered a racing current and wind-lashed lakes, (d) were attacked by wild animals.

6. The diet of the travelers included (a) meat, vegetables, cereals, fruits, milk, and butter, (b) meat, vegetables, and cereals only, (c) meat and fruits only, (d) meat, milk, bread, and butter only.

7. Unknown Falls are divided by (a) a mountain, (b) an island, (c) a boulder, (d) a canyon.

8. These men were the first to (a) build a bridge over Unknown Falls, (b) see all of the cataracts, (c) photograph all of the cataracts, (d) visit Unknown Falls on foot.

9. When they tried to photograph the caribou it (a) stayed long enough for a picture, (b) charged at them, (c) reared up on his hind legs, (d) plunged into the woods.

10. On their way back from Unknown Falls, the men encountered (a) stiff winds, (b) boulders in the rapids, (c) logs in the rapids, (d) heavy fog.

Answers: 1)—, 2)—, 3)—, 4)—, 5)—, 6)—, 7)—, 8)—, 9)—, 10)—.

Check your answers with the Answer Key on page 376. Allow yourself 10 for each correct answer. Record your score below:

Rate: W.P.M. ——————   Comprehension Score: ——————

Making the preview. In making your preview of the following article, read all the instructions below, then carry them out from memory. Jot down your beginning and ending time for the preview. You should be able to do this preview in just a few seconds. After completing it, take the short true-false test following the article.

1. Glance at the title to find out the topic discussed.

2. Now quickly read the subheadings and abstract as much information as you can from them.
3. Jot down your finishing time.
4. Take the previous test.

Time of beginning preview Min— Sec—
Time of ending preview — —
Total time for preview — —

Reading the article. After you have completed the preview and taken your preview test, read the article, under timed conditions, for the purpose of finding more information about the topic mentioned in each subheading.

Selection 2

BEGINNING TIME:_____
HR._____ MIN._____

Today on the Delaware, Penn's Glorious River[2]

Trickling from mountain spring and duck pond, the Delaware grows—as the Nation has grown—from small beginnings to a mighty role in our busy industrial world.

Latest act in the drama of the river is the rise of one of the world's greatest steelworks, 3800 acres of vast, towering structures, amid the somewhat surprised artists, writers, and farmers of Pennsylvania's placid Bucks County.

In today's closely interconnected world, a mountain in Venezuela and deepening holes in Minnesota can cause a steel plant to spring from broccoli fields on the Delaware. For the Venezuelan mountain is mostly iron ore, and the holes are the rust-red pits where power shovels are nearing the bottom of the richest United States iron ranges.

To meet the South American ore, steelmakers turn to the Delaware, wide, deep, majestic bearer of burdens in its lower reaches. "A glorious river," William Penn, the founder of Philadelphia, called it.

Might Have Been Called the Hudson

Seeking a passage to the Orient, Henry Hudson probed the river's broad bay in 1609. Shoals turned back his *Half Moon,* and he sailed on north; otherwise the Delaware instead of the Hudson might bear his name.

[2] Albert W. Atwood, *The National Geographic Magazine,* July 1952, pp. 1-40.

Such lordly streams later determined the location of many of our major cities. Rivers like the Hudson and Delaware, which met the simple needs of early settlers, are equally essential to the teeming millions of today. . . .

River Born as Puny Twins

Both branches of the Delaware begin humbly, a few miles apart, on the western slopes of New York's Catskill Mountains.

A spring on a hill near the resort town of Stamford gives rise to the west branch.

Outside Grand Gorge, in a small marshy pond close to a creamery, the east branch is born. Although so insignificant here, it is potentially fecund enough 40 miles to the south to warrant thirsty New York City spending more than a hundred million dollars to impound and tap its waters. . . .

For some 60 miles the two branches parallel each other, zigzagging along from 8 to 15 miles apart. They come together at Hancock, New York, to form the Delaware. Both branches and the main stream as far south as Trenton, New Jersey, have an almost primitive, unspoiled beauty early recognized by the artist George Inness and the naturalist John Burroughs. . . .

Canals Carried the Region's Coal

On a trip down the Delaware, abandoned ditches show that canals once figured importantly in the life of the New York-Pennsylvania-New Jersey region. When anthracite coal was discovered in the Pennsylvania hills, canals were built to carry it to the market in New York and Philadelphia.

At Minisink Ford, New York, one of the first bridges erected by John A. Roebling, designer of the Brooklyn Bridge, is still in active use after 103 years of service.

As a pedestrian, I crossed this suspension bridge for two cents to Lackawaxen, Pennsylvania. If I had ridden a bicycle, it would have cost five cents; and if I had driven my car, twenty-five.

Originally, the bridge was an aqueduct carrying coal-bearing canal boats across the river on their way from the Pennsylvania coal fields at Honesdale to Kingston, New York. Roebling built it so well that, after railroads ended the usefulness of the Delaware and Hudson Canal, the bed of the aqueduct was simply changed to a roadway, now used by automobiles. . . .

Shrewd Tom Penn Gets a Bargain

Downriver I came to the first sizable cities—Easton, Pennsylvania and adjacent Phillipsburg, New Jersey—at what the Indians described as the "forks" of the Delaware. At Easton the Lehigh River joins the larger stream.

Treaties with the Delaware Indians were made at the "Place of the Forks," some of them in Easton's First Reformed Church, still standing after several remodelings.

Near-by landmarks commemorate the notorious "Walking Purchase" of 1737. The Indians promised Thomas Penn as much land as a man could walk in a day and a half and felt tricked when a trained walker did 66½ instead of an expected 40 miles. . . .

Art Colonies Take Over Canal District

In 1900 Philadelphia artists began to settle in and around New Hope, Pennsylvania, 15 miles above Trenton, attracted by the canal, old stone houses, inns, and abandoned gristmills. The little village was then a quiet out-of-the-way backwater.

The canal ceased to operate in 1931, but the remnants of towpath, locks, and aqueducts still make excellent subjects for painting and the right setting for art schools and coffee houses. . . .

Today New Hope is a tourist town and summer resort as well as an art colony. This is partly because of the Bucks County Playhouse, which occupies an old mill. Lillian Gish was playing when I visited it, with "Alice in Wonderland" next on the bill.

Other summer playhouses may have as good bills, but this is the only one I know where a waterfall must be turned off before each performance, for there is a large and noisy one directly outside the theatre. . . .

Washington's Christmas Surprise Party

Not only school children but many adults suppose that Washington crossed at Trenton. Actually the crossing took place eight miles above Trenton. Pennsylvania and New Jersey State parks now mark the points of embarkation and landing. In roaring contrast to Washington's flat-bottomed boats is a Navy jet-propulsion experiment station a few miles east of the New Jersey park.

At the site of the crossing the river is only 1,000 feet wide. But one gets a thrill standing where the boats put off on their perilous journey, and it looks a long way to row through floating ice. . . .

"Trenton Makes, the World Takes"

It is a curious fact, not generally realized, that Washington as Commander in Chief spent a fourth of his time in New Jersey and moved his army across the state four times.

To this day, indeed, New Jersey is the most traveled state in the Union, being the natural corridor between the first and third largest cities. Benjamin Franklin described it as a cider barrel tapped at both ends. Cross-roads of the Middle Atlantic States, it is crisscrossed by 13 major rail-roads and has more track per square mile than any other state.

On the main line of through travel across New Jersey stands Trenton, its capital, and each day 170 passenger trains cross the Pennsylvania Railroad bridge which spans the Delaware at this point.

Millions of passengers see a sign that reads, "Trenton Makes, the World Takes," appropriate because Trenton is among the most highly indus-trialized of American cities. Despite this fact, it has been singularly fortunate in being able to retain as park three miles of river frontage. In this riverside park are the Capitol Building and other state buildings. Several persons deserve credit for saving Trenton's water front, Governor Woodrow Wilson among them.

Nearby is the historic section of the city, with its old churches, its tablets and monuments, as well as banks, stores, and hotels. Perhaps the most striking relic is the Old Barracks, built for troops in the French and Indian War and later occupied by Washington's forces and by the British and Hessians who opposed him.

New Jersey is such a small state that no legislator can live more than 100 miles from Trenton or require more than three hours to reach it by rail or automobile. . . .

At Trenton the River Changes Its Character

Although the so-called "Falls" at Trenton are merely rapids, the city is on the fall line, that geological boundary where rivers pass from rocky formations to softer soils. Close to the fall line there has developed a north-west south-east axis of travel and trade, from New York through Trenton, Philadelphia, Wilmington, Baltimore, Washington, Richmond, and on through the Carolinas to Georgia.

In a number of cases ocean-going vessels can navigate rivers below the fall line, while even a canoe has difficulty above it. The Delaware Valley levels off at Trenton into a low coastal plain, and the river itself becomes an inlet of the sea, gradually widening into an estuary and merging into the broad expanse of Delaware Bay.

Thus the bay and lower river form a long, continuous navigable chan-nel for cheap water transportation. But more than half a billion cubic yards of sand, gravel, and rock had to be dredged from the river during the past 35 years to maintain deep draft to Philadelphia.

Further dredging between Trenton and Philadelphia will create, in effect, a single port of harbor which will include many cities and towns. Among them, besides Trenton itself, are Bordentown, Burlington, Cam-den, and Paulsboro in New Jersey; Bristol, Philadelphia, and Chester in Pennsylvania; and Wilmington in Delaware. . . .

Philadelphia's "Scituation" Grows

William Penn planned and built the original city at the junction of the Delaware and Schuylkill Rivers. "The Scituation," he wrote, "is a Neck of Land Between two Navigable Rivers . . . whereby it has two Fronts upon the Water. . . ." Since then the city has spread out from an area 2 miles square until it now covers 135 square miles.

Some 50 years ago Henry James, novelist and essayist, wrote of Philadelphia's "admirable comprehensive flatness," of the "absence of the note of the perpetual perpendicular, the New York, the Chicago note."

Philadelphia's great abundance of flat land has resulted in a natural spreading out of population and industry alike. Thousands of workmen live near the plants where they work, in single two-story row houses, many owned by occupants, rather than in tall, rented apartments, as in New York.

Although Philadelphia was the largest seaport in the country for about a century and is now the second largest in terms of tonnage of water-borne commerce, there is very little feeling of the sea about it, no tang of salt air. A person may live in Philadelphia all his life and not even know it is a seaport.

This is natural because the city is 101 miles from the ocean. Yet 17,635 vessels arrived at and cleared from the Port of Philadelphia area in 1951, bound from and to most of the ports of the world.

$500,000 Willed for a Street

The Philadelphia water front is well worth a visit. When you get within a couple of blocks of the river, you suddenly and abruptly leave department stores and ordinary office buildings behind and come upon customs brokers, marine insurance companies, stevedoring companies, and dealers in marine and ship supplies.

Stephen Girard, early merchant, philanthropist, merchant, and banker, and founder of Girard College, dreamed of a tree-lined boulevard along the water front but did not live to see it. He left the income from a $500,000 trust fund "to lay out, regulate, curb, light, and pave a passage or street, fronting on the Delaware River, to be called Delaware Avenue."

And there it is, Delaware Avenue, not tree-lined but a fine long, broad water-front thoroughfare.

Philadelphia is not a regular passenger port like New York, but it handles a great variety and volume of merchandise. Far overtopping everything else in imports is petroleum, although large quantities of iron ore, to be greatly increased in the future, and sugar and molasses, with lesser amounts of honey and syrup, are brought in. The chief exports are manufactured goods and grain.

The Delaware has always been one of America's chief shipbuilding centers, and during the two World Wars it was a veritable American

Clyde. The Sun Shipbuilding and Dry Dock Company at Chester, Pennsylvania, built some 40 percent of all United States tankers in World War II.

This company and the New York Shipbuilding Corporation at Camden, New Jersey, directly across the river from Philadelphia, together with the Philadelphia Navy Yard, are the principle builders and refitters of ships in that area, although there are several other concerns which build smaller vessels. The New York Shipbuilding Corporation occupies nearly a mile of water front in Camden.

Six major oil companies, including two with headquarters in Philadelphia, are spending several hundred million dollars to expand and modernize their refining capacities on both sides of the river at and below Philadelphia.

An oil tanker may seem an unromantic foundation on which to build a great port, but the modern world moves on oil, and Philadelphia is becoming one of the world's foremost refining centers.

No crude oil is produced near this city, but it can be brought in from the Gulf area, South America, and the Near East, and refined products shipped away, by cheap water transportation.

Began   *Finished*   No. words: $\dfrac{1900}{\rule{2cm}{0.4pt}} \times 60 =$ _____ W.P.M.

_____   _____   No. seconds:

Preview Test

1. This article is a description of a _____.
2. Would you think from the title that the article will deal largely with the history of the river, or its present? _____
3. A famous colonial statesman is associated with this river in the title of the article. His name was _____.
4. The Delaware might have been called another name. What name? _____
5. The Delaware begins as _____ small rivers.
6. In former years coal was carried in these regions over _____.
7. Who got a shrewd bargain in connection with some deal that had to do with the Delaware? _____
8. What group of people have taken over one of the old canal districts? _____ _____.
9. What great American general carried on activities in connection with the Delaware? _____
10. What town on the Delaware is mentioned as one that makes many things that the rest of the world takes? _____
11. Where does the river change its character? At _____.

12. A street discussed in the article is unique in that someone willed a sum of money for its betterment. The amount willed for the street was ———.

Correct your answers by referring to the article.

Now read the article as fast as you can to find out more about the Delaware River. Time yourself and take the comprehension test as usual.

Checking Comprehension

Write the letter of each correct answer in the answer space below.

1. The new steel mills on the Delaware get ore from (a) Canada, (b) the Mesabi range, (c) Brazil, (d) Venezuela and Minnesota.

2. An early explorer who probably would have sailed up the Delaware had it not been for shoals was (a) Magellan, (b) De Soto, (c) Henry Hudson, (d) Balboa.

3. The two branches of the Delaware as well as the main stream as far as Trenton lie in country which is (a) highly industrialized, (b) monotonous and uninteresting, (c) wet and marshy, (d) almost primitive in its unspoiled beauty.

4. John A. Roebling was famous for building (a) skyscrapers, (b) canals, (c) bridges, (d) factories.

5. The Indians thought that Penn tricked them in a real estate deal by employing (a) an experienced broker, (b) a trained walker, (c) a good lawyer, (d) an Indian scout.

6. When the canal ceased to operate at New Hope, the town (a) died out entirely, (b) became an industrial center, (c) became a community center for farmers, (d) became a tourist town and summer resort.

7. Washington crossed the Delaware at (a) Wilmington, (b) Trenton, (c) 8 miles above Trenton, (d) Philadelphia.

8. The most traveled state in America is (a) New Jersey, (b) Delaware, (c) New York, (d) Pennsylvania.

9. Ocean-going vessels can in time navigate all the way to the fall line of the river. This fall line is at (a) Philadelphia, (b) Trenton, (c) Camden, (d) Bristol.

10. Philadelphia doesn't have the usual characteristics of a (a) large city, (b) industrial center, (c) city of fame in colonial days, (d) a seaport.

Answers: 1)—, 2)—, 3)—, 4)—, 5)—, 6)—, 7)—, 8)—, 9)—, 10)—.

Check your answers with the Answer Key on page 376. Allow yourself 10 for each correct answer.

Rate: W.P.M. ———   Comprehension Score: ———

Vocabulary Study

Here is a list of words taken from the selections you have just read. In the sentences that follow, one word, or sometimes a pair of words synonymous with a word in the list, has been italicized. Write in the blank space the word that can be substituted without changing the meaning of the sentence.

bushwhack	estuary	lichen	wraith
myriad	vulnerable	vindication	spate
chute	shoals	encompass	escarpment
muskeg	fecund	bend	veritable
tributary	domain	portage	pessimistic

1. At one point in their journey the canoeists were troubled with *shallow water.* ———

2. The rocks were covered with a *parasitic plant.* ———

3. The birds in the forest were *innumerable.* ———

4. Australia's most *fruitful* producer is the rabbit. ———

5. The men had to *cut away* the bushes. ———

6. What does the suspect offer as *justification* for his action? ———

7. It will take seventy-five rods of fence to *surround* the plot of ground. ———

8. The wisp of fog which arose from the lake was like a *specter.* ———

9. An inclined *trough* of water came rushing down from a higher level. ———

10. There was a sharp *deviation* in the stream just beyond the rapids. ———

11. The wide lower part of the *tidal river* had salty water in it. ———

12. A caribou is *capable of receiving injuries* when hunters are around. ———

13. The men climbed to the top of a *steep slope*. ―――――

14. The canoeists were victims of a *sudden, violent rainstorm*.

15. The story the men told about the height of the falls was a *genuine* fact. ―――――

16. As the men walked on one of the islands their feet sank deep in a kind of *swamp-moss*. ―――――

17. Unknown River is a *branch* of the Hamilton River. ―――――

18. Hamilton River has long been the *province* of snowshoers and canoeists. ―――――

19. Natives took a *gloomy* view of the canoeists' proposed trip.

20. The men carried their canoes across the *land* between two rivers. ―――――

See page 376 for answers. Allow 5 for each correct answer.

Vocabulary Score: ―――――

Follow-Up Practice

Applying Preview Techniques in Your Regular Reading

Continue to practice during definite periods each evening. Try taking a preview of everything you read, both materials which you read informally as a part of your work or recreation, and materials which you read during your regular practice periods.

Concisely, these are the characteristics which you will need to observe in making your initial surveys:

1. Title
2. Subheadings
3. Visual aids
4. Length of paragraphs
5. Number of words (to make your time-of-reading estimate)

CHAPTER 6

Sight-Seeing

As You Read

Taking an Excursion

SUPPOSE you are a stranger in New York and you decide to take a sight-seeing trip on one of the excursion boats that encircles the Island of Manhattan. As you glide past the shores of the magic city in the misty haze of a sultry August afternoon, perhaps all you see is a mass of buildings. "Huge, gray boxes piled one upon the other," you say to yourself.

Then the voice of the guide breaks into your reverie.

"Now, folks, look right between the low, yellow building on your left and the red building with a flat roof on your right, and you'll see a dark gray building with a spire on top that towers above everything else on the Island. This is the Empire State Building, the tallest building in the world. It has 102 stories above the street and two stories below ground. It houses 25,000 tenants."

Suddenly, as the guide talks, one building in this previously nondescript mass stands out as something significant. All the other buildings still remain just a heap of piled-up gray boxes as far as you're concerned, their only function being to furnish background for this one momentous piece of architecture. The sameness of the view has now been broken.

You sail on past another segment of water front. Suddenly one of the dozens of piers which you scarcely noticed before leaps out with color, shape and meaning.

The guide is saying, "Look at this light-green pier which is more modernistic in shape than the others. This is the world's most unusual pier. It was recently built by the city and leased to the Grace Line. It has a roof parking area for 250 cars, and a huge storage basement entirely below the water surface."

As the guide talks, Pier 57 becomes the most important edifice on the landscape, and you keep thinking about it as the boat moves on.

"Now, look between that brown building with the tower and the gray one with the water tank on top," shouts the guide. "You'll see a wide and tall cream-colored building with a flat roof. This is the Whitehall Building where the Weather Bureau is located. The equipment is on that roof. Mr. Christie, the head of the Bureau, may be up there right now, studying the weather."

Once more one building stands out in the vista in front of you as being more important at the moment than all of the others.

And so the trip continues. As you pass each section of the shoreline the guide points out one feature as having some special significance. The dreary sameness disappears, and the aggregate of gray structures which you saw at first becomes colorful and meaningful and interesting.

An excursion in reading is very much like a trip around Manhattan. The successive sections of buildings may be likened to the consecutive paragraphs which you pass as you read an article or chapter. At a glance they all look alike, but if you examine them you will find one thought in each paragraph which will stand out above all the others. And the details in the paragraph fall into line to add information and interest, just as the information the guide told you about the Weather Bureau contributed to your interest in the cream-colored structure in which this Bureau is housed. In pointing out a building the guide told you one thing about it which made it distinctive. This was the main idea in his oral paragraph. Then he continued, giving you facts of lesser importance about the building. These lesser facts were the details in his paragraph. The details expanded upon the main idea, but they would have been quite

meaningless without the one important sentence in which he identified the building and told the single thing for which it is most
famous.

You should learn to use the sight-seeing technique as you read,
grasping the one significant idea in each paragraph and letting the
details fall into line. The chief difference between a sight-seeing trip
around Manhattan and your own sight-seeing trips in reading is that
you'll have no guide along while you're reading to point out the
most significant thing in each paragraph. That you must do for
yourself.

The Art of Reading Paragraphs

Perhaps no one technique will aid you more in improving your
reading ability than learning to read paragraphs effectually. Every
selection is made up of paragraphs. Each paragraph is a unit of
thought. Quickly grasping the essence of each of these thought units
enables you to cover reading materials rapidly and, at the same time,
to get the most important ideas which the author is expressing. In
a paragraph there is one point of fundamental importance, and the
details revolve around this hub idea, expanding upon it.

When you toss a pebble into a pool of water, you immediately perceive a circular ripple at the spot where the pebble came into contact
with the water. Then other concentric circles appear, one after the
other until there is an entire set of circular ripples. So it is with a
paragraph. Figuratively speaking, the author tosses one main idea
into a paragraph which sets all the other ideas in motion. It is your
job to learn how to find this pivotal idea, swiftly and surely.

In much of the reading that you do you won't care to take time
to consider all of the details. You will be satisfied if you can speedily
glean the main ideas in the selection. Expertness in "spotting" the
basic thought in each paragraph is the skill that you need to
cultivate.

On the other hand, some selections will be of such significance to
you that you will want to read and consider the minor ideas carefully.
Then you will find that locating the main idea in each paragraph is
of major importance because the central thought provides you with
a core around which you can organize the details. In Chapter Seven
you will be shown how to use the "main idea" technique as a starting
point in factual reading. In the meantime, whether you are doing

cursory reading for the purpose of gathering the larger ideas, or whether you are doing detailed reading for exact information, you will find it to your advantage to acquire the technique of reading paragraphs. In order to do this you must develop a systematic approach to paragraph reading rather than just following along one sentence after the other without effort or thought in regard to paragraph organization.

The position of the key sentence in a paragraph varies. Often the germ idea appears in the first sentence. If so, this is a convenience to the reader because he doesn't have to search through the entire paragraph for the central thought. At other times, the important idea occurs in the middle, at the end, or somewhere else in the paragraph. Because of the variance in the location of the key sentence within a paragraph, position is not a reliable guide in finding the main idea. You must learn surer ways of locating the one basic thought.

The first thing to do is to develop a new attitude toward paragraph reading—the attitude of thinking of each paragraph as a unit. As you encounter a new paragraph, view it as if it were all the reading material you had before you at the moment. Decide what is the *one* important idea this paragraph has to impart. Ask yourself two things:

1. What is the basic thing, place, condition, or person discussed in this paragraph?
2. What does this thing, place, condition, or person do, or what is done to it, or what property does it have, or what condition is it in, which makes it worth while for the author to write about it?

Keep these questions in mind while studying the paragraph below. See if you can locate the main idea with certainty.

The calcium cycle is one of the most interesting cycles of nature. The ocean contains vast quantities of calcium salts in solution. These are withdrawn by living creatures and built into coral reefs and the shells of mollusks and are precipitated in other ways. In the course of geologic time, deposits of calcium carbonate laid down in the ocean become lifted up from limestone strata in mountain ranges. These formations are then attached by atmospheric and organic acids and slowly dissolved and carried back into the sea from which they came. Sometimes great caves are left behind as a result of this process and many secondary calcite and aragonite formations come into existence.[1]

[1] W. Scott Lewis, "Cycles in Nature," *Hobbies*, August 1947, p. 138.

1. What is the basic topic discussed in this paragraph?
2. What special property does it have?
3. At what position in this paragraph did you find the key sentence?

If you analyzed this paragraph correctly, you will have concluded that the main topic is "the calcium cycle," and that the special property which the calcium cycle possesses is that it "is one of the most interesting cycles of nature." All the remaining sentences in the paragraph are subordinate details which tell how the calcium cycle is interesting. In this particular paragraph, then, the main idea is contained in the first sentence.

See if you can quickly find the main idea in the paragraph below.

A fraction over two minutes is all that it takes to run the Kentucky Derby at Churchill Downs in Louisville. But the Derby packs more excitement into these two minutes than any other sporting event in the country. The Derby Day "Run for the Roses" dates back to 1875 when a little red horse named Aristides came in first. There were 12,000 spectators on hand then. More than 100,000 attend now, and millions more watch or listen with breathless interest on TV and radio. The build-up of excitement increases year by year.

1. What is the basic subject of discussion in this paragraph?
2. What makes this subject distinctive?
3. In what position in the paragraph do you find this information?
4. What is the function of all of the other sentences in the paragraph as related to this topic sentence?

If you were right in your analysis, you decided that "the Derby" is the basic subject of discussion and that the distinctive thing about it is that it "packs more excitement into these two minutes than any other sporting event in the country." This information which expresses the main idea appears in the second sentence of the paragraph. All the other sentences are related to the subject of the Derby and expand upon this main idea, but no one of them is nearly so important or inclusive as the topic sentence, which really holds the essence of the entire cluster of thoughts expressed in the paragraph.

See if you can "spot" the key sentence in this paragraph:

We're intrigued by an ingenious device Chock Full O'Nuts Corp. used during the World Series. During the Series time, salesmen for Chock Full O'Nuts coffee were particularly welcomed by the grocers they visited. Reason: the salesmen carried portable radios tuned to catch the latest scores.

Check the most important idea:

(a) The writer was intrigued by an ingenious device.
(b) Salesmen for Chock Full O'Nuts were welcomed by grocers during the Series time.
(c) Salesmen carried portable radios tuned to catch the latest scores.

Number (c) is the most important idea in the paragraph. The first sentence merely tells us that there was an ingenious device; the second sentence tells us that the salesmen were particularly welcomed by grocers during Series time. Both of these sentences alert us to read on and find out what this ingenious device was which caused salesmen to be welcomed during Series time. The heart of the paragraph is found in the last sentence, which tells us what the device was and what it did. The big idea in the whole paragraph is that "salesmen carried portable radios tuned to catch the latest scores."

So far you have been studying paragraphs for the purpose of learning how to locate the main idea. You probably read very slowly during this initial work. Don't worry if you slow down while learning this new technique. Soon you will unconsciously include looking for the main idea in a paragraph as an integral part of your new streamlined reading ability. Then the skill-building in paragraph analysis which you are now doing will function significantly in increasing both your speed and comprehension.

Practice in Finding the Main Idea in a Paragraph

Exercise 1

As the next step in your skill-building program try to find the main idea in the paragraphs below. See also if you can pick up a little more speed as you apply this technique.

1. Find the noun or noun phrase that names the basic subject with which each paragraph is concerned.

2. Find the group of words that tells what this subject does, what it could or should do, what it is, what it has, or what happens to it which is sufficiently important to justify a written paragraph about it.

3. Try to read each paragraph a little faster than the one before as you apply this technique.

PARAGRAPH 1

The Far West states continue to be the most rapidly growing region in the nation, with an undiminished flow of migrants from all other regions. The population gain is more than twice as great as that of the rest of the nation. The whole economic structure of the Far West has expanded and continues to expand enormously. This is necessary both to serve the needs and to tap the labor and capital resources of the constant flow of newcomers to its labor force.[2]

Select the key idea:

a) The Far West states continue to be the most rapidly-growing region in the nation.
b) The population gain is more than twice as great as that of the rest of the nation.
c) The whole economic structure of the West continues to expand enormously.
d) This is necessary to serve the needs of the constant flow of newcomers.

PARAGRAPH 2

Most hunters have pet peeves. Jacob's pet peeve was that he detested the cat and all its wild cousins, such as the cougar, the panther, and the lynx. With unscientific zeal he threw the sneaky coyote into the same category. He stalked coyotes through the Blue Mountains of Oregon with a fanatical passion, but to no avail. They outsmarted him at every turn. He could never get them within shooting range to put a bullet through their pesky carcasses. "That's the cat of it," he would say.[3]

Select the sentence which is the "heart" of this paragraph:

a) Most hunters have pet peeves.
b) Jacob's pet peeve was that he detested the cat and all its wild cousins.
c) He stalked coyotes through the Blue Mountains of Oregon.
d) He could never get them in shooting range.

PARAGRAPH 3

Among engineers and plant operators there's a lot of talk about today's heavy oils—they're not what they used to be. Some of this is just old-fashioned griping, but we also find more than a grain of fact. Heavy oils *have* been made less easy to use. This is due to changes in refining meth-

---

[2] "People Begin to Pour in," *Sales Management*, November 10, 1954, p. 106.
[3] Mike Revise, "They Tried It Before," *Field and Stream*, May 1954, p. 40.

ods. The newer methods aimed at improving yield and quality of gasoline, and light fuel oils have affected the by-product heavy oils and caused them to be less easy to use than the straight-run residuals of years past. So you see there is some substance back of all this talk.[4]

Select the sentence which completely and concisely sums up the information in this paragraph:

a) There's a lot of talk about today's heavy oils.
b) Some of this is just old-fashioned griping, but we also find more than a grain of fact.
c) Heavy oils *have* been made less easy to use.
d) So you see there is some substance back of all this talk.

Check your work by referring to the Answer Key on page 376.

Speeded Practice in Finding the Main Idea

Exercise 2

Now you have had enough practice in finding the main idea to be ready for some time pressure while applying this technique. In working with the following five paragraphs, try to find the main idea and at the same time apply the speed-reading procedures which you learned in Chapter Three.

1. Jot down the time at which you begin reading.
2. Note the time you finished in exact minutes and seconds. Subtract your beginning time from your finishing time and record your answer in minutes and seconds.
3. Check the sentence in the list of choices which you believe represents the "heart" of each paragraph.

PARAGRAPH 1

BEGINNING TIME:_____
HR._____ MIN._____ SEC._____

From the earliest days the conviction has been growing among the people and their leaders that the state must be responsible for seeing that its citizens have a certain quantum of education. That the state has this responsibility is shown by the state constitutions, the hundreds of school statutes in each state, and the scores of decisons of local, state,

---

[4] A. J. Weber, "You Need to Know How and Why Study Fowls up Fuel-Oil Systems," *Power*, September 1954, p. 109.

and federal courts. In brief, education has come to be universally regarded as a state function. The assumption of educational control by the state is not fortuitous; state control has come because of the early and ever growing belief that education is the buttress of a democratic government and cannot, therefore, be left too much to the whims of any individual or of any community. In a democracy the people cannot be permitted to remain ignorant although some of them might desire that status.[5]

ENDING TIME_____
HR._____ MIN._____ SEC._____

a) The conviction has been growing that the state should be responsible for education.
b) Education has come to be universally regarded as a state function.
c) The assumption of educational control by the state is not fortuitous.
d) In a democracy people cannot be permitted to remain ignorant.

PARAGRAPH 2

BEGINNING TIME:_____
HR._____ MIN._____ SEC._____

The business meeting of any board may be handled efficiently and expeditiously if it is carefully planned in advance. One excellent guarantee that the business will be thus handled is to see in advance that a definite routine, or order of business, is established. An order of business saves time and gives greater assurance that no item of business will be forgotten during the meeting. Such order of business should be made a part of the rules and regulations of the board. Another guarantee to an efficient and expeditious conduct of the board's business is to formulate ahead of the meeting a definite parliamentary procedure to follow. The more important phases of this procedure also should be made a part of the rules and regulations of the board. While the permanent pattern of fundamental procedures can be established in the rules and regulations, fresh planning will be necessary for each new meeting.[6]

ENDING TIME:_____
HR._____ MIN._____ SEC._____

a) An order of business saves time during the meeting.
b) Parliamentary procedure should be made a part of the rules and regulations of the board.

[5] Ward G. Reeder, *Public School Administration*. Macmillan, 1941, p. 55.
[6] *Ibid.*, p. 95.

c) The business meeting of any board may be handled expeditiously if it is carefully planned in advance.

d) One excellent guarantee that the business will be handled is to see in advance that a definite routine is established.

PARAGRAPH 3

BEGINNING TIME:_____

HR._____ MIN._____ SEC._____

Ideas are elastic and flexible. They reach out beyond ordinary bounds and barriers. You have no right to take the sword and cross the bounds of other nations and enforce on them laws or institutions they are unwilling to receive. But there is no limit to the sphere of ideas. Your thoughts and feelings, the whole world lies open to them. You have the right to send your ideas into any latitude, and to give them sweep around the earth, to the mind of every human being.—*Henry Ward Beecher*

ENDING TIME:_____

HR._____ MIN._____ SEC._____

a) Ideas are elastic and flexible.

b) They reach out beyond ordinary bounds and barriers.

c) There is no limit to the sphere of ideas.

d) You have the right to send your ideas into any latitude and to give them sweep around the earth.

PARAGRAPH 4

BEGINNING TIME:_____

HR._____ MIN._____ SEC._____

Advice and reprehension require the utmost delicacy; painful truths should be delivered in the softest terms and expressed no farther than is necessary to produce their due effect. A courteous man will mix what is conciliating with what is offensive; praise with censure; deference and respect with the authority of admonition, so far as can be done in consistence with probity and honor. The mind revolts against all censorian power which displays pride or pleasure in finding fault; but advice, divested of harshness and yet retaining the honest warmth of truth, is like honey just round the brim of a vessel full of wormwood. Even this, however, is sometimes insufficient to conceal the bitterness of the draught.—*James Gates Percival*

ENDING TIME:_____

HR._____ MIN._____ SEC._____

a) The mind revolts against all censorian power which displays pride or power in finding fault.

b) Painful truths should be delivered in the softest terms.

c) Even careful handling is sometimes insufficient to conceal the bitterness of the draught.

d) Advice and reprehension require the utmost delicacy.

PARAGRAPH 5

BEGINNING TIME:————————
HR.———— MIN.———— SEC.————

A young woman working at a very modest salary in a New York office wanted some good imitation pearls. When Christmas came and she was given a $25 check by her employer, she decided to go to a good store and spend the whole sum on a string of beads. A new clerk helped her pick out some nice-looking pearls. She loved them, wore them constantly to work. One day, on the subway, the string broke and pearls flew in every direction. Kind passengers helped her pick up the beads, and she tied them in her handkerchief until she could take them to the jewelers to be restrung. She explained she had bought the string there a couple of years before. When she went to get the beads, she had the surprise of her life. She was ushered into the manager's office. The new clerk two years before had sold this woman a $2,500 necklace for $25.[7]

ENDING TIME:————————
HR.———— MIN.———— SEC.————

a) A young woman working at a very modest salary wanted some good imitation pearls.

b) When Christmas came and she was given a $25 check she decided to spend the whole sum on beads.

c) She was ushered into the manager's office.

d) The clerk two years before had sold this woman a $2,500 necklace for $25.

Checking Speed

Compute the time it took you to read each paragraph. Add the items of time for the five paragraphs and record your total reading time below.

Total Time

————————

No. Words: 660

—— × 60 = ———— W.P.M.

No. seconds:

[7] Artemisia B. Bryson, "A String of Necklace," *Hobbies,* August 1947, p. 42.

Checking Comprehension

Check your accuracy in finding the main idea in each of the paragraphs by referring to the Answer Key on page 376. You may allow a score of 5 for each correct answer. Multiply 20 by the number of answers you had correct. This will be your Comprehension Score.

Rate: W.P.M. _____   Comprehension Score: _____

What About Exceptions?

"This paragraph doesn't have any main idea in it" is the first comment an instructor hears when he begins to teach the technique of finding the main idea in a paragraph. It is true that occasionally you will run across a paragraph in which one "hub" idea is not stated. This, however, is the exception rather than the rule.

Furthermore there *are* techniques which can be employed in dealing with the unusual types of paragraphs.

The simplest of the exceptions is the paragraph which is made up of just one sentence, such as:

The broken-hearted scientist fell ill under the strain, and died shortly afterward with the laughter of the scientific world ringing in his ears.[8]

In such cases the reader who is searching for main ideas, should gather up the one basic import of the paragraph. The basic idea in this case is that the scientist died shortly. Scientist is the subject, and the thing that happened to him was that he died shortly.

Another type of paragraph which is more puzzling than the one-sentence paragraph is the type which enumerates several items of equal importance. For example:

The Old Testament speaks familiarly of fishhooks, and compares a woman's eyes to fish pools. The paintings on Egyptian tombs show fishermen at work using dragnets, hooks, and lines, and also bronze harpoons. The Red Sea, the Nile, and the artificial lakes gave employment to a host of dark-skinned fishermen, and supplied sea food for all the tribes of Egypt. For the trick of drying and curing fish—something not evolved in Europe until the fourteenth century—was known to these remarkable narrow-headed Africans some six thousand years ago.[9]

[8] Leon Augustus Hausman, "The Famous Fossil Hoax," *The Mentor,* February 1922, p. 42.
[9] John D. Whiting, "Fishing and Fisher-Folk," *The Mentor,* July 1923, p. 3.

Since all the ideas in this paragraph are of about equal significance, the most expedient thing for the reader to do is to formulate his own topic sentence. It might be shaped up something like this: "Fishing was practiced in Egypt six thousand years ago."

Another exception is the type of paragraph which has two ideas of considerable weight, when it is difficult to tell which is more important.

What the whole undertaking revealed to me most was the interest there is in the history of paper-making and watermarking. I have been so absorbed with these subjects since my experimenting in paper-making that I am writing a book, in two volumes, on the history of paper.[10]

Which sentence expresses the more important thought? The writer states that the most important outcome of his experience was the development of an interest in paper-making and watermarking. It is equally important that he is now writing two volumes on the history of paper. Instead of trying to decide which of these two thoughts is the main idea, it would be better to consider them together and sum them up in some such fashion as this: Because of the great interest which he developed in the history of paper-making, he is now writing a two-volume book on the subject.

Occasionally one will run across a paragraph that is just a mass of details with seemingly no outstanding idea in it. Such a paragraph is usually sandwiched in between two other paragraphs that do have main ideas. So waste no time puzzling. Forge ahead with those paragraphs that do have something important to say.

Applying Paragraph Techniques in Reading an Entire Selection

Read the next selection as rapidly as you can. Apply the techniques you have already learned for rapid reading and direction words. In addition, try to locate the main idea in each paragraph as you go along. Pass the details lightly, but try to absorb the main idea. If you encounter a paragraph which doesn't seem to contain a basic idea, use the appropriate techniques discussed on the preceding pages.

Time yourself, and take the comprehension test after the reading.

[10] Dard Hunter, "A Maker of One-Man Books," *The Mentor*, March 1922, p. 31.

Selection 1

BEGINNING TIME:_____

HR._____ MIN._____ SEC._____

Music And Life[11]

Life begins and ends with music. It envelopes and permeates the world we live in. Land, water, and sky are full of elemental music of many kinds and degrees of intensity. The wind sings through the responsive leaves and plays on the harp strings of the waving reeds by the rivers; birds pour forth their lyric tunes to charm the waking morn; and the ocean waves swell in rhythmic chorus as if at the command of a master conductor.

The potency of music has been acknowledged in all ages and by all races. And it was so from the beginning of time. It is said that long, long ago Orpheus charmed all things animate and inanimate with the strains of his lyre. He even went down to Pluto's domain, Hades, and coaxed back the soul of his dead and lost love Eurydice with his music. And everyone knows of the Sirens who bewitched sailors with their songs in the Grecian Isles, and the Lorelei maiden on the rock above the Rhine.

Good and Bad Music

This suggests the thought, often stated, that good music ennobles and bad music degrades. It semes clear to me, however, that there is only one kind of music, and that is GOOD music. When music can be called bad, it ceases to be music. It simply becomes rhythmic noise. I do not think that music, in itself, produces good or bad effects, but rather that it enhances and intensifies existing ideas and instincts, good or bad. To a man in love, music may deepen the feeling of romance; a man suffering from melancholia may have his sorrows dyed a shade deeper; a warrior may have a heightened feeling of war fever. In this connection music may be compared to HASHEESH. That powerful drug produces good or bad dreams in keeping with the mental condition and environment of the drug-taker. In a room furnished in good taste, he dreams of things beautiful, but in ghastly surroundings he dreams frightful dreams. That alluring composition, HUMORESQUE, to a religious man may mean devotional ecstasy; to the frivolous, a sensuous dance. I have even been told that some highway robbers once were heard whistling it before they started on a daring escapade.

Music Is Relative

I do not think that there is such a thing as ABSOLUTE religious or sacred music. What is true of other things in life is true of music. It is

[11] Fritz Kreisler, *The Mentor*, December 1921, pp. 5-12.

relative. What is true in art today may be deemed quite untrue by the next generation. Take, for example, the musical consonance and discord once recognized as essential elements in music. Modern composers and musicians do not recognize the old order of things. The Gregorian chant has been associated in Christian nations with religion for hundreds of years, so it invokes within us religious feeling. In a non-Christian land the same chant might rouse martial sentiment, if it had been used there for that purpose TRADITIONALLY. Play the Gregorian chant to an Australian bushman and it may not affect him devotionally at all—but a certain crude melody of his own will; at the same time, his wild music may inspire feelings of a quite different nature in others in a different environment.

The same is true of the music of different musical instruments. The horn has been associated with the chase. When we think of the chase we instinctively think of the horn. The guitar is associated with romance—a gondola under the Rialto in Venice, or a young man under a window in Seville. Nowadays, we associate war with trumpet and drum—the instruments of fire and fury. But in ancient Greece the bards were wont to lash the country into feverish martial activities by singing and playing on the lyre. The Gaelic bards did the same. Now, the lyre is to us an instrument of tender tones and romantic feeling.

During the exciting days of the French Revolution the singing of the Marseillaise was thought more dangerous by those in power than incendiary speeches or weapons of war. It inspired people to make sacrifices, it roused them to fight and to die fighting. I am certain that, in a country that knows nothing about the French Revolution or of this great song of France, the Marseillaise could be effectively used for religious revival.

Art, then, is influenced by environment, education, and association of ideas. Art, like love, is a state of mind and heart, and the art of music more so than other arts. The arts of poetry, painting, and sculpture have tangible forms. But music is formless—it is all feeling. For that reason it is the more dynamic, and produces a deeper emotional effect.

Music Helps and Heals

A beneficial act, like healing, is quite often accomplished by the art of music. The world is destined to hear more and more of this practical side of music. I shall not be surprised if a book on musical therapeutics, written by a scientist, shall have, before long, a place on the shelves of the medical libraries of the world. In the ancient scriptures of the Hindus, the Christians, the Egyptians, and the Chinese, there are references to the healing power of music. Thus we read in the Bible: "When the evil spirit from God was upon Saul, then David took an harp, and played with his hand. So Saul was refreshed, and was well, and the evil spirit departed from him."

My father was a physician, and I studied medicine for about two years—so I know a little about medical science. I do not think it is unscientific to say that, in certain instances, music can be effectively used as a healing agency. Scientists have just begun to investigate this matter. Healing is largely a normal adjustment of the malajusted molecules of the body. Recently a case was brought to my notice. A young lady was sick with high fever in her home on a ranch in one of the western states of the Union. The doctor's home was far away and he could not be summoned readily. A friend asked the mother to give her daughter a "music cure." A certain record was played on the phonograph a few times. The young lady's temperature came down, and, I am informed, she was soon on her way to recovery. A case has been cited recently of a young woman, suffering from sleeping sickness, who was brought to consciousness and health through the ministration of music. . . .

The effect of music not only upon the ill, but also upon the insane, has been noted and considered by physicians. For my own part, I believe in the soothing, comforting, and healing effect of music. We all know how thought affects the human body. An embarrassing remark causes a rush of blood to a woman's face, and she blushes. If you look at something sour your mouth waters, or if at something tragic, tears rise in your eyes. Think of your absent beloved and your body and mind ache with the bitter pangs of separation. Happy thoughts make the body buoyant, and melancholy thoughts depress it. If the mind is "low," if the nerves are weak, the power sent to the muscles is diminished. Now every musical note is a living thought current. If electrical waves in air can carry a wireless message over thousands of miles, a musical wave may also find a response in the physical and mental being. The musical waves no doubt act and react on our nervous system. And surely they do adjust or maladjust, disturb or harmonize, the atoms and IONS of our natures.

I found my musical ear of value in war service. I soon got accustomed to the sound of deadly missiles—in fact, I quickly began to make observations of their peculiarities. My ear, accustomed to differentiate sounds of all kinds, had noted a remarkable discrepancy in the whine produced by different shells as they passed overhead, some sounding shrill, with a rising cadence, and others rather dull, with a falling cadence. Every shell describes in its course a parabolic line, with the first half of the curve ascending, and the second one descending. Apparently, in the first half of its curve, while ascending, the shell produced a dull whine, accompanied by a falling cadence, which changed to a rising shrill as soon as the acme was reached, and the curve turned down. I was told that shells sounded different when going up than when coming down, but that this knowledge was not of value for practical purposes. I found that I could, with a trained musical ear, mark the spot where shells reached their acme, and so could give the almost exact range of guns.

Music and Animals

Music affects even the animal world. The flute pleases and thrills the horse. The drum and trumpet awaken the spirit in this noble animal so that he plunges headlong on to the battlefield. The Hindu snake charmer plays on his POONGI flute, and deadly cobras crawl out and weave their sinuous way toward their seductive charmers. Not long ago a musical experiment was tried out at the New York Zoological Park. The animals were tested on the "jazz music" that so many modern human beings seem to fancy. The animals did not like it. The monkeys, in particular, went wild in anguished revolt.

National Music

It is passing strange that some would like to nationalize music. Music belongs to no nation. The spell of music is the same whether it is sung and played in America or England, in France or Italy, in India or China, in Russia or South Africa. Music, like art and literature, is universal; it transcends all national boundaries. Rodin belongs just as much to Russia as to France; Shakespeare just as much to Europe and America as to England; Kalidasa just as much to England as to India; and Brahms just as much to Paris as to Vienna. As from the mountain top the world below is bereft of all national distinctions, so, viewed from the peak of higher understanding, nationality in art disappears.

It is cultural background, intellectual training, specialization, and execution that make the difference in the appreciation of music. If badly played, even Beethoven's symphonies would be a deadly drag. From my earliest days I have been interested in music, and music is my life; and yet, if I do not like the music of a Negro in Darkest Africa, that does not make that music less vital, less real to the African. It is my own fault that I do not appreciate such music. The first time I heard Chinese music I did not like it at all. But later on, when I heard a Chinese scholar sing, the deeper and inner message of Chinese music was revealed to me. To understand music of this sort we must study national background and tradition.

In examining the cubist and futurist arts of to-day, one may fail to understand the meaning of lines and surfaces. One may scorn a picture and call it grotesque, but to the artist it is real. Adherents to the traditional laws of pictorial art scoff at him, but he does not care. He looks at the picture he has produced from the angle of a highly accentuated imagination.

The same is true of music. The last movement of Beethoven's Fifth Symphony, played to an untutored listener, may be no more than a crude march, but to one trained in music it is sublime revelation—as though the soul of a mortal had burst through the shell of egotism to stand face to face with the Infinite. When I hear Beethoven's symphonies, I think

I know why he became deaf. It seems to me that he must have been so saturated with exalted music feeling that a little more would have devastated him physically. It seems almost as if he HAD TO BECOME deaf, to be shut in, in order to gain an intensified hearing of the musical inspiration within him. No sound from outside could help him any more. The sonatas that he wrote while deaf are the very essence of music.

Here it may be mentioned, by the way, that with the growing complexity of music, really great compositions are growing less in number. Haydn wrote one hundred and fifty symphonies, Mozart over forty, Beethoven nine, Tschaikovsky six, Schumann only four, and Brahms four.

The international animosities of the past few years have retarded the progress of music in the world. But in the task of reconstruction, of the regeneration of the human race, music will play a prominent part. I have, however, somewhat modified my views in this matter. Before the war I was enough of a dreamer to exaggerate the importance of music for the elevation of society. But I know Europe to-day, and I have seen things with my own eyes. Now I hold that when men, women, and children actually die of starvation, or eke out an existence of lingering death, music, even the very best of it, cannot help them! The artist himself cannot sing or play on an empty stomach. Give the hungry musician a slice of bread and a glass of water, if a cup of sugarless coffee is too much to expect—then his spirits will rise and he will produce good music. Give the hungry lover of music a bite of food—then he will enjoy music and smile. Music glorifies life but cannot preserve it. Music is the dome, a very beautiful dome, but not the foundation of the edifice of humanity.

As in music some notes mingle, so in life some vibrations are in accord. The underlying principle of this accord in life may be called love. Music and love are like twin sisters. Like flames of fire they both burn into the very core of our being. Music has often been defined as "the language of emotions," and the profoundest of all emotions is love. The dominant note of most of the beautiful songs is love. Most of the grand operas strive to unfold this glowing principle in life. Love invigorates art. One who cannot love greatly and unselfishly cannot accomplish great things in life. "Music," says von Weber, "is the purest, most ethereal language of passion." "I can grasp the spirit of music," says Wagner, "in no other manner than in love."

Most of the great musicians have been great lovers, for music creates love; it deepens and sanctifies love. Love has been the rudder to guide the ship of their lives.

In spite of all human thoughts and theories, life is still a mystery, love is a mystery, music is a mystery. No one can really define them. It is a supremely happy thing, nevertheless, that we can realize love and music in life. Both music and love blend with life as does color in a rainbow.

Began   *Finished*   No. words: 2500

$$\frac{\qquad}{\qquad} \times 60 = \underline{\qquad} \text{ W.P.M.}$$

_____   _____   No. seconds:

Checking Comprehension

1. The writer thinks that the potency of music (a) has always been recognized, (b) is something we have only recently realized, (c) is still not realized by most people, (d) has been greatly exaggerated.

2. The writer believes that (a) music in itself produces both good and bad effects, (b) that some music degrades, (c) that there is such a thing as bad music, (d) that music enhances and intensifies existing ideas and instincts, good or bad.

3. The writer explains the effect of music waves on the ill by saying that (a) they help patients to get their illness off their minds, (b) they remind the sick of days when they were well, (c) they adjust or maladjust the atoms and ions of our natures, (d) electrical waves are produced by music which definitely cure certain diseases.

4. The author found his musical ear was valuable during his war service for (a) giving the almost exact range of guns, (b) entertaining troops, (c) teaching proper voice control to officers, (d) improving military bands.

5. The author claims that music is the property of (a) the nation in which it was written, (b) no nation, (c) the nations that speak the same language as that of the composer, (d) the nations with the same cultural background as that of the composer.

6. The writer says that the differences in various peoples' appreciation of music are the result of (a) physical differences between peoples, (b) geographical and climatic factors, (c) early training in music, (d) cultural, intellectual, specialization, and execution factors.

7. The writer believes that Beethoven became deaf because (a) of a hearing defect that developed when he was very young, (b) he listened to loud music continuously for too many years, (c) the vibrations from his symphonies were of a type which affected the tympanum, (d) he had to be shut in, in order to gain an intensified hearing of the musical inspiration within him.

8. Really great compositions are (a) becoming greater in number, (b) less in number, (c) remaining about the same, (d) have promise of increasing greatly in the near future.

9. The writer states that international animosities of the past few years have (a) stimulated greater creative efforts on the part of a few individuals, (b) heightened musical progress within certain nations,

(c) retarded the progress of music in the world, (d) retarded the progress of music specifically in the United States.

10. The writer believes that (a) music and love are like twins, (b) music and art are twins, (c) love and art are twins, (d) appreciation of music and appreciation of art are synonymous.

Answers: 1)—, 2)—, 3)—, 4)—, 5)—, 6)—, 7)—, 8)—, 9)—, 10)—.

See Answer Key on page 376. Allow a score of 10 for each correct answer.

Rate: W.P.M. —————   Comprehension Score: —————

Vocabulary Study

Here is a list of words from the selections you have just read. Familiarize yourself with their meanings by looking them up in a dictionary if necessary. Then, write one of the words in the blank space in each of the following sentences to complete its meaning.

permeates	incendiary	accentuated
enhances	dynamic	animosities
consonance	therapeutic	ethereal
	regeneration	

1. Many people think that salt ————— the flavor of a melon.
2. The governor was forceful and energetic. He was said to be a ————— person.
3. The ————— cloud wafted lightly up into the heavens.
4. Officers were quite sure that the fire had been set by an

—————.
5. The mayor ————— the need for giving food to the flood victims.
6. When onions are cooking the odor ————— the entire house.
7. Many people harbor ————— against people who have harmed them.
8. Certain herbs have ————— values in treating sickness.
9. Vegetation undergoes ————— every spring.
10. As the two violinists played, their renditions were in perfect

—————.

See Answer Key, page 377. Allow 10 for each correct answer.

Vocabulary Score: —————

Follow-Up Suggestions

Applying the main-idea technique in your daily reading. You have been given some basic instruction and practice in the art of reading paragraphs. You have been launched on the technique of finding the main idea accurately and quickly. The extent to which you perfect this skill depends on you. You may sharpen this tool to a very fine point by continuing to use it every time you have occasion to read. Special practice periods are of course highly desirable as well.

From this time on, in all your reading, both informal and special practice, do three things:

a) force your speed;
b) take advantage of the signpost words;
c) apply paragraph-reading techniques.

Continue to keep a record of your speed and comprehension in each of your practice periods. You should begin to note substantial gains.

CHAPTER 7

Mining for Details

Can You Strike Pay Dirt?

Now you have learned the technique of gathering "bright and shining nuggets" which are more or less apparent on the surface. There will be many times when this technique of gathering the larger basic ideas will serve your purpose. There will be other times, however, when you will be obliged laboriously to "sift the sands for the gold dust," or mine for details.

As Bacon has so aptly said, "Some books are to be tasted, others to be swallowed, and some few to be chewed and digested." The concern of this chapter is with reading materials that have to be "chewed and digested." This is the kind in which you must carefully study every sentence, such as in the printed instructions which accompany income-tax forms. No speed reading for main ideas in this situation!

Most of us find it necessary to do reading of this type every day. Businessmen, especially, have to do a great deal of careful factual reading as a part of their daily routine. There are financial reports which grow out of the company's activities or which have a close bearing on them. There are letters, memos, ads which tell about new processes or machines. There are directions for conducting the business which must be followed exactly. There are explanations of policies and plans in which every word is important. And so it is that the businessman *must* give attention to details.

The same is true of those who are in professional work. The attorney and the physician must do exact and detailed reading; engineers have to read much technical material; the chemist, the physicist, and the biologist must read material in which every word is important. This is an age of technology and scientific advancement in every field. Each business or profession has its own flood of technical articles published weekly or monthly. Thousands of people find it necessary and desirable to read these periodicals in order to keep abreast of developments in their respective fields.

There is no question about the need for detailed reading, but there is a question in the minds of many people, it seems, as to the possibility of increasing speed and understanding in this kind of reading.

One man says, "I'm an engineer. My reading is *all* technical. I have to grasp every detail. Would it be possible for me to learn to read faster?"

Another says, "I'm a lawyer. Believe me, every word is important in a legal paper. Could I learn to do this kind of reading more rapidly?"

"My work is editing. I have to do meticulous reading of manuscripts all day long. I guess there is no chance for me to speed up this kind of reading, is there?"

"I work for stockbrokers. Three fourths of my time is devoted to research in which I have to read and digest financial reports. Would the modern techniques help me to cover this material more rapidly?"

The answer "Yes" was given to every one of these questions. Each of these persons took a course under the writer's supervision, and each one markedly improved his ability to do the particular kind of reading he had to do. Furthermore, each one reported at the end of the course that he could accomplish much more work in a day with greater ease and less fatigue.

One *can* improve the ability to do detailed, factual reading. Yes, you *can* strike "pay dirt" while mining for details, if you practice the suggestions given in this chapter.

Techniques for Grasping Details

Using old skills. The ability to do detailed reading rapidly and well is a very complex act requiring the combination and application of many different reading skills. That is why instruction in and practice on this type of reading was delayed in this book until you had already mastered several of the elementary skills.

In effective reading for details you need to know how to make use of preview so that you can decide whether the material is of sufficient interest to be read for details. You need to know how to pick out the main idea in paragraphs so that you will be in a position to see details as related to this idea. And of course you need the skill which you have already acquired in learning to read fast, in order to increase your tempo in reading for details.

Learning new skills. You need also to learn two very important new skills: first, learning to discriminate between main ideas and details; second, learning to organize details around the main ideas to which they are related. After considerable practice in analyzing paragraphs and organizing details, you will reach a point at which you will read factual material in groups of meanings rather than in isolated scraps.

As you read, think of the main idea as a magnet drawing the particles toward it—the "particles" being the smaller, detailed ideas. Then think of this main idea together with its cluster of sub-ideas as a unit. These are the basic processes which will enable you to grasp a series of minor details quickly and accurately.

The necessary written work may seem laborious and time-consuming, for you must thoughtfully read all the explanations and directions and write all the answers requested. As you practice, however, you will gradually abandon written work and detailed analyses and will mentally apply the new techniques as you read. Then you will be able to grasp details more speedily, as well as with greater effectiveness. So don't be discouraged with the length of time the ensuing exercises take. Once the foundation is thoroughly laid, a new house goes up rapidly. So it is with skill development in learning to read factual material. When you become adept at grasping clusters of details in their right relationships you will have become a skillful reader.

Diagraming major details. There are major details and minor details in most paragraphs. At first we shall concern ourselves only with major details. The simple paragraph below will be used in illustrating the procedures for noting the main idea together with its major details. Read this paragraph quickly and see if you can "spot" the main idea.

In a growing number of hotels and skyscrapers across the nation, façades of steel have replaced the foot-thick brick and mortar walls once used. Tests show that a steel wall four inches thick has better insulating qualities than a 12-inch thickness of masonry. In addition, steel-curtain wall panels save both time and labor. And the floor space conserved by use of the thin wall as against the thick wall in a big office building can mean a couple of hundred dollars a year in rentals.[1]

[1] "Steel Framing in Houses," *Science Digest*, February 1955, p. 95.

No doubt you discovered at once that the main idea is *A growing number of hotels and skyscrapers use steel instead of brick or mortar walls.*

Now find three details that are *related* to this main idea and sum them up in as few words as possible.

Your summary should be something like this: (1) a steel wall has better insulating qualities, (2) steel wall panels save time and labor, (3) a steel wall conserves floor space.

Now think of this whole mass of ideas as one related cluster of meanings, as in the diagram.

No doubt the three details are very easy for you to grasp. If so, they are easy to grasp because you sorted them from the main idea and related them to this main idea.

Now that you see what this beginning work is like you may be saying, "This will take a terribly long time." Please bear in mind, however, that through repeated use of these techniques you will eventually be able to apply them mentally without diagraming. Then you'll read details with speed!

No time limit is placed on the reading of the following practice paragraphs. In working with them you will be developing your skill to analyze paragraphs and to perceive relationships of their component parts. You should, however, work as fast as you can. Don't dawdle. Work at an energetic pace.

PARAGRAPH 1

Tropical fish are becoming increasingly popular. Varied in color, they are decorative for homes, offices, and even store windows. The raising of such fish is recommended as a relaxing hobby for people in jobs involving much tension. Many hobbyists have made money by breeding tropical fish varieties for which there is a special demand.[2]

[2] Max F. Baer, "Basement Farming Can Pay," *Journal of Living,* December 1953, p. 17.

Complete the diagram:

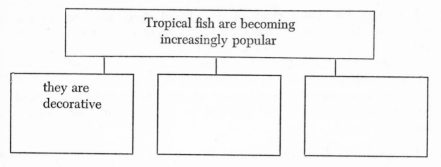

Check your work with the Answer Key on page 377. The wording doesn't have to be exactly the same as that in the Answer Key, so long as the ideas are comparable.

PARAGRAPH 2

There are a lot of things that should come before investing in securities —particularly if you're raising a family. First, an adequate insurance plan should give your dependents reasonable security. And if you are paying for a home, you will probably want to direct all your surplus dollars into paying off the real estate mortgage. Finally, you'll want to be sure of enough money for the children's education, and have a reserve fund of cash for emergencies like unexpected medical bills.[3]

Complete the diagram:

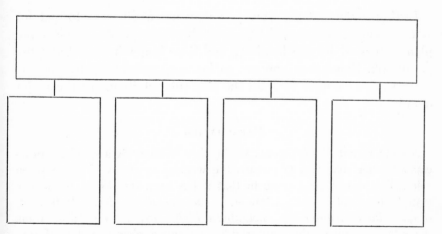

Check your work with the Answer Key on page 377.

[3] "You Don't Have to Be a Millionaire to Invest in Stocks and Bonds," *Putting Your Money to Work*, Merrill Lynch, Pierce, Fenner and Beane, New York, 1953.

PARAGRAPH 3

For some time Jones' chain of department stores has been recommended to stock buyers. It has 1,228,183 shares of common outstanding, selling on the New York Stock Exchange around 12-13 and paying a $1 annual dividend. No preferred is outstanding. The mortgages of $10,183,-000 are mostly on property in use by the Company, which would otherwise have to be rented. It is reasonably immune to bombing, and should benefit from the "tidal wave" of young people who will need clothing during the next few years.

Complete the diagram:

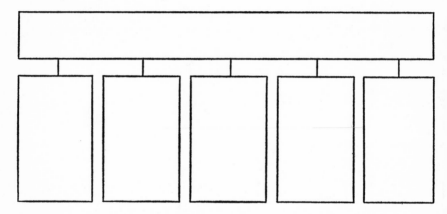

Check your work with the Answer Key on page 377.

Listing major details. Now you may use a different format for stating the main idea and grouping the major details. Follow the plan suggested by the headings and lines beneath each following paragraph. Remember you are to list only *major* details. For the moment don't bother with all the tiny sub-details under the major details.

PARAGRAPH 4

Among recent developments in the shoe industry is a specially processed leather sole said to possess the wearing qualities of composition soles. This outsole is unique in that it has been developed by a shoe manufacturer rather than a tanner. *It contains all the desirable features of an orthodox leather sole, including a high-porosity value.* In addition, it contains many of the comfortable, "cushiony" characteristics of synthetic or composition-type soles. Ordinary chrome-tanned leather is processed in a special manner in order to produce this new sole substance. The leather is leavened or plumped to loosen and spread its fibers so as to create numerous air cells in the material. It is claimed that the leather is strengthened, rather than weakened, by this process in which no grease or oil is used. Laboratory and field tests indicate that the new sole actually wears better than orthodox leather soles and is extremely light—*about half the weight of an ordinary sole*.[4]

MAIN IDEA   MAJOR DETAILS

_____   _____

_____   _____

_____

_____

_____

_____

_____

_____

Check your work with the Answer Key on page 378.

PARAGRAPH 5

The history of production is easily sketched. Early primitive man doubtless "manufactured" little, himself, but merely appropriated what nature provided—fish, game, and wild fruits. Slowly, through the centuries, however, he learned to work over the products of nature more and more, to make fishhooks from bones, to make spears, bows and arrows from trees, mallets from stones, clothing from hides. Such production was carried on by the labor of man alone, and on a very small scale. Later, animals were tamed and used in certain operations, especially in carrying burdens and in cultivating the soil, and this increase in the power of man's disposal caused a great expansion of production. Much later still, various natural forces were harnessed to production—wind, water, power, steam, and in very recent years the explosive power of gases, as in the automobile and tractor. At the present time it is estimated that the United States has available more than a billion horsepower of energy.[5]

MAIN IDEA   MAJOR DETAILS

_____   _____

_____   _____

_____

_____

_____

[4] "News of the New," *Babson's Reports*, December 1, 1954, p. 256.
[5] John Ise, "The Laws of Production," *Economics, Harper*, 1946, p. 16.

Check your work with the Answer Key on page 378.

PARAGRAPH 6

The essence of Cambridge is in its surroundings. It is in the crocuses beside the walks promising an end to the long winter, and then in the daffodils declaring it has ended. It is in the roses and lupines and the tumbled gravestones of St. Botolph's little churchyard. It is in the sound of the bells of Great St. Mary's Church, though academicians in rooms hard by curse bells and bell ringers vehemently. It is in the swifts flying into lovely Nevile's Court about May tenth to set about their expected building. It is on the meadows up the river to Grantchester, where all good lovers go for strolls.[6]

Complete the blanks below to show an outline of the paragraph.

MAIN IDEA   MAJOR DETAILS

_____   A. _____

_____   B. _____

_____   C. _____

                           D. _____

                           E. _____

Check your work with the Answer Key on page 378.

Identifying minor details. In some of your reading the grasping of major details which expand upon main ideas will serve your purpose. There may be other times, however, in which you will wish to concern yourself with the minor details which usually cluster about a major detail in much the same way as major details cluster about the main idea. If the content of what you are reading is so important to you that you want to get *all* details in a page of text, then try to grasp clusters of major details together with their minor details, keeping in mind the relationship of these clusters to the main idea.

PARAGRAPH 7

In the paragraph below there are: (1) a main idea, (2) one major detail, and (3) several minor details related to the major detail. Read the paragraph and see if you can detect these three types of ideas.

Increased production, reduced scrap, better quality control, easier scheduling, happier workers, and lower costs are benefits which appeal

[6] J. Frank Dobie, "Cambridge," *Holiday,* June 1950, p. 155. (Slightly revised.)

to management in any industry. This is doubly so in high-volume, close-margin candy making. Few industries are so dependent upon the rigid control of temperature and humidity as to avoid losses in production and maintain product quality. Often the difference between profit and loss may be a few temperature degrees or a slight change in the relative humidity. Thus, candy makers were among the first to realize the advantages to be derived from air conditioning. As a result many plants have complete integrated systems, serving all their manufacturing, packaging, and storage areas.[7]

The relationships between ideas in the paragraph above may be represented diagrammatically in this way:

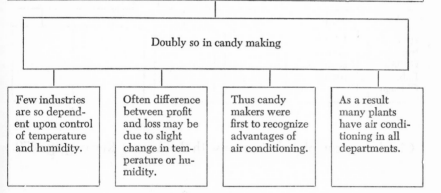

In this example it is evident that there are four minor details all closely related to the one major detail.

PARAGRAPH 8

In the paragraph below there is a main idea as usual. Then there are three major details, each of which has its own related minor ideas. See if you can find these clusters of major and minor ideas, then complete the diagram.

In the past few months a number of commercial meat tenderizers have hit the market, aimed particularly at cost-conscious Mrs. Housewife. Largely responsible for making this little dream come true is Lloyd A.

[7] Charles W. Vaughan, "How Welch's Profits from Humidity Control," *The Manufacturing Confectioner*, September 1954, p. 29.

Hall of the Griffith Laboratories, Chicago, who has come up with a new tenderizer containing papain. Papain is an enzyme, or organic substance, obtained from papaya, the edible fruit of a tropical American tree. Manufacturers of the domestic product are compounding Griffith's basic composition with flavoring materials, and obtaining a variety of distinctive individual products.[8]

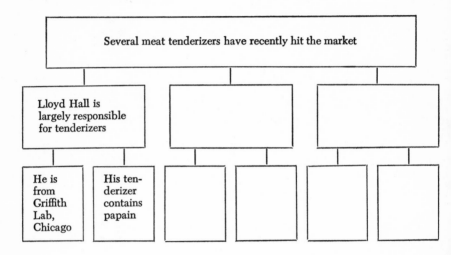

Check your completed diagram with the Answer Key on page 379.

PARAGRAPH 9

There is a boom in pharmaceuticals in Spain, and the newer drugs which have been found effective in the United States, Britain, France, and the other more advanced Western countries enjoy active sales. Sulfa drugs, antibiotics, and many of the "mycins" are produced under license by Spanish concerns. An entire building in Madrid is devoted to Pfizer products. The directors report that their business is rapidly expanding with the technical guidance of an American chemical engineer loaned by Pfizer to supervise plant construction and production controls, and to train the personnel in the high standards required by the food and drug laws in the United States.[9]

[8] "Tough Meat Made Tender," *Science Digest,* March 1952, p. 53. (Condensed from *Industrial and Engineering Chemistry,* December 1951.)
[9] "Spain," *The Atlantic Monthly,* April 1955, p. 21.

Complete the diagram:

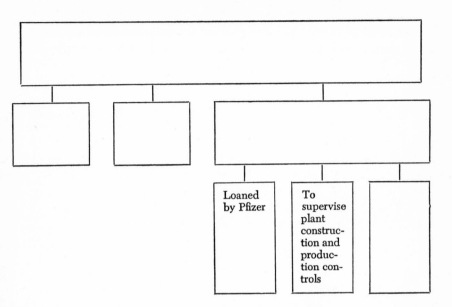

Check your work with the Answer Key on page 379.

PARAGRAPH 10

You should now be ready to progress from a diagram to an outline. In the somewhat more difficult paragraph below, find the main idea. Find two other ideas of next relative importance which are used in expanding upon the main idea. Each of these two sub-ideas has several detailed facts which cluster under it. Group these details in relationship to the larger sub-idea to which it is related, and also in relationship to the total topic.

If you read for the purpose of discerning the above pattern, you should have no difficulty in filling in the outline, although you may have to refer back to the paragraph for some of the details.

Public industries are much less important in the United States than in some other countries. In many countries the government runs industries. In several European countries, and in Australia, New Zealand, and Canada, the government, national or state, operates some or all of the railroads; in France and several other countries the government conducts the tobacco industry as a state monopoly; and various cities throughout the world operate some or all of the public utilities. Our federal government has no important industries except the post office, certain types of banks, and a few giant hydroelectric plants, including Tennessee Valley Authority and the Boulder and Grand Coulee Dams. None of these was established for the purpose of securing revenues; in fact, most of them were unattractive to private enterprise—a common reason for government operations.[10]

Write answers in as few words as possible.

I What is the main idea? _____
_____
_____

II What are the two major sub-topics or major details, and what are the minor details under each such sub-topic? (Refer back to the paragraph if necessary.)

A. (First large sub-topic) _____
_____

    (Related details)

      a. _____
      b. _____
      c. _____

B. (Second large sub-topic) _____
_____

    (Related details)

      a. _____
      b. _____
      c. _____
      d. _____

Check your answers with the Answer Key on page 379.

Paragraph 11

In working with this paragraph you will be more or less on your own, with only a few directions. Fill in the outline. Check your completed outline with the key on page 380. Correct your outline if necessary.

Gradually men have learned by experimenting that air is a real substance, that it has weight, that it exerts pressure, and that it is compressible. They have learned that it expands when heated and contracts

[10] John Ise, *Economics*, Harper, 1946, p. 482.

when cooled. They have also learned that air has inertia. It offers resistance to being moved. This knowledge of the air has made possible the invention of instruments to measure air pressure and pumps to compress it. It has made possible the invention of pneumatic tires, air engines, blast furnaces, vacuum tanks, balloons, dirigibles, airplanes, and a great many other appliances. While we know a great deal about the atmosphere, many possibilities remain, and there is much still to be learned about air.[11]

I (Main idea) ————————————————————————————

  A. Properties

    a. ————————————————————————————

    b. ————————————————————————————

    c. ————————————————————————————

    d. ————————————————————————————

    e. ————————————————————————————

    f. ————————————————————————————

    g. ————————————————————————————

  B. Inventions made possible

    a. ————————————————————————————

    b. ————————————————————————————

    c. ————————————————————————————

    d. ————————————————————————————

    e. ————————————————————————————

    f. ————————————————————————————

    g. (1) ——————— (2) ——————— (3) ———————

      Group three together

PARAGRAPH 12

Now outline a paragraph by yourself with no help at all.

1. Read and decide upon relationships of ideas.
2. Make your own outline.
3. Correct it by referring to the Answer Key on page 380.

A knowledge of the forces and resources of nature around you enables you to appreciate and understand your environment. It is science that has changed waste places into gardens; it has conquered many germ diseases; it enables man to control sources of power in nature; it enables him to travel under water and through air; it enables him to illuminate cities by the power of a distant waterfall; it has improved the quality of fruits, root crops, cattle, horses and sheep.[12]

[11] Ira C. Davis and Richard W. Sharpe, *Science*, Holt, 1943, p. 45.

Space For Your Outline

PARAGRAPH 13

You probably won't need further practice in actually writing the outline of a paragraph in order to perceive the relationships of its different parts. As an intermediary step between writing outlines and mentally grasping the "stripped-down structure" as you go along, write the numbers and figures which indicate different parts of an outline right into the text of the paragraph, thus:

I. The traditional procedure, so far as the investigation of the American financial institutions is concerned, has been to sit down and wait patiently until the symptoms have moved in orderly sequence from disturbing to alarming, to critical to fatal. (A) Then there would be an in-

12 *Ibid.*, p. 15.

vestigation. And (B) the principal object of the inquest, all too frequently, would be to find not the facts but a culprit.

Can you grasp all detailed facts in this paragraph as a whole by thinking in terms of relationships of ideas as expressed by the outline symbols?

PARAGRAPH 14

Try writing your own outline symbols into the text of the following paragraph. Use Roman numeral I for the main idea, capital letters such as A and B for important subordinate ideas, and Arabic numerals, such as 1, 2, 3, for details under subordinate ideas.

Characteristics which make automobiles the generally comfortable, smooth-running vehicles they are—as distinct from simple conveyances providing places to sit and engines to move them around—are built into every American passenger car today in varying degrees. They are the end-products of many things: a great amount of research, expert experience, technological know-how, management prejudices, consumer studies, dumb luck, and shrewd guesswork. As a result, the various brands of cars are notably unlike each other in their handling, economy, ease of repair, power and speed, riding qualities, noise level, driver vision, and safety.[13]

Check your work with the Answer Key on page 381.

PARAGRAPH 15

Another good technique to use when working directly with the text of detailed factual material is that of underlining. A single underline is used to denote the main idea; two underlines to denote the major details, and three underlines to denote the minor details.

Gardeners who have been waging losing fights against birds may find an electric snake just the thing to scare away the feathered seed-eaters. The imitation snake has a 12-foot cross-striped bamboo pole for a body and a heart-shaped aluminum head painted white with glaring black eyes. Balanced on the top of an upright, it rotates continuously driven by an electric motor.[14]

The main idea is that gardeners may find an electric snake just the thing to scare away feathered seed-eaters. The first major detail tells

---

[13] *Consumer's Reports,* May 1953, p. 182.
[14] "Inventions, Patents, Processes," *Science Digest,* March 1952, p. 95.

us that it is an imitation snake, and two minor details tell us how the imitation is accomplished: (1) it has a 12-foot, cross-striped bamboo pole for a body, and (2) a heart-shaped aluminum head. The second major detail is that it rotates continuously, and three minor details tell more about this rotation: (1) it is balanced, (2) on top of an upright, and (3) it is driven by an electric motor.

PARAGRAPH 16

Try underlining the paragraph below in the same way.

In the Hudson, opposite West Point, is a famous little island that recalls heroic days of the Revolutionary War. From one end of the island a great chain was stretched across the river to the cliffs below West Point, to keep back the British fleet. The links of the chain were forged in a blacksmith shop at New Windsor, New York, and were carried down the river on a log boom. A part of the chain is today on view at Washington's Headquarters, Newburgh, New York. Another section of the chain is to be seen at West Point.[15]

Check your work with the Answer Key on page 381.

PARAGRAPH 17

Now find out how well you can read and grasp details without the aid of "crutches" such as diagraming or outlining; just concentrate on a specific cluster of ideas in terms of a specific purpose.

Make a quick preview of the material in order to locate the cluster or clusters of details in which you have a special interest. It is unwise to attempt to grasp every little detail at once. Decide instead which group of details is of special interest to you, and then read carefully for a vivid impression of this particular cluster.

With your knowledge of paragraph structure and your practice in skimming, you should now be able to make this preview in from five to ten seconds.

After previewing, read the paragraph carefully, concentrating on special clusters of details.

The geckos lay their eggs in all manner of places, and most species seem to deposit two. When first laid they are soft-shelled and dent readily, hardening only after several hours of exposure. Within the eggs there are the usual albumin and yolk. The embryonic lizard takes on a recognizable form in about two weeks' time. The head is extremely large, and the eyes are well developed and prominent. The eggs hatch in about thirty days, although weather is a controlling factor. Most egg-

[15] Charles H. Dorr, "Constitution Island," *The Mentor*, September 1924, p. 53.

laying reptiles in the United States carefully place their eggs where they will get just the right amount of moisture and heat. The geckos of Hawaii, however, seem to drop theirs wherever they will not be readily seen. Auger holes in two-by-four ceiling rafters are usually jammed full. In such a position, rainfall and dew cannot reach them. Others are often found at the base of long-leaved plants. In this site the leaves act as funnels and the eggs are constantly drenched with water. But still they hatch! One of the favorite situations is within the iron framework of the common recessed lock. Climbing in the keyhole the females will first start filling the far corners, and each succeeding female is forced to lay closer to the opening until the chamber is eventually crammed to overflowing.[16]

Name three special places in which geckos lay eggs:

1. _____

2. _____

3. _____

Check your answers by referring to the paragraph.

PARAGRAPH 18

Preview the paragraph below, allowing yourself a maximum of five seconds.

Then read for the purpose of grasping details in regard to each of two processes: (1) mediation, and (2) arbitration.

Strikes and labor wars are expensive to workers, employers, and the general public; and the government has tried in various ways to help preserve industrial peace—through mediation, arbitration, and, in a few cases, through prohibition of strikes. In the process of *mediation,* an impartial third party, known as the mediator or impartial chairman, is called in; he confers with the employer and labor representatives in a friendly, informal way, and tries tactfully to get them together. If he is unable to do this, he is not expected to render any decision in the dispute. In the process of *arbitration,* an arbitrator or board of arbitrators is chosen, and after hearing the two sides it renders a decision which the disputants have agreed to accept; if either party is not satisfied with the decision, the dispute may come up for further action later. Both mediation and arbitration have achieved some success in promoting industrial peace.[17]

[16] Lewis Wayne Walker, "Mo'o, Spirit of Hawaii," *Nature Magazine,* November 1945, p. 469.
[17] John Ise, *Economics,* Harper, 1946, p. 417.

(a) How does the process of mediation work?
1. _____
2. _____
3. _____
4. _____

(b) How does the process of arbitration work?
1. _____
2. _____
3. _____

Correct your answers by referring to the paragraph.

PARAGRAPH 19

Now read for the purpose of concentrating on three different groups of details.

First: preview the paragraph for five seconds, and locate the main idea.

Second: Read carefully to grasp all details: (1) in the group that tells things that can be done with plastics, (2) in the group that tells what plastics are formed by nature, and, (3) in the group that tells what substances have been combined by different people to produce synthetic plastics.

Don't bother about dates, involved chemical terms, or other details. Just read for the details that you want to grasp for these three purposes.

Plastics are substances that can be molded, bent, or carved into various forms. Rubber and resins are plastics formed in nature, but synthetic plastics are of recent development. Carbolic acid entered the picture in 1872 when Professor Bayer discovered that carbolic acid and formaldehyde could be united to form a strong, hard, resinous material. This was merely a curiosity until 1909, when Dr. Leo H. Backeland developed a commercial process for producing this resin and fashioning it into various forms. His product is called Bakelite, after its inventor, or, chemically, "polymerized oxybenzyl-methylene-glycol-anhydride." Bakelite and closely-related plastics are products of the union of phenols and aldehydes.[18]

Checking Comprehension

Write one word in answer to each question or part of a question.

[18] Emmett James Cable, Robert Ward Getchell, and William Henry Kadesch, *The Physical Sciences*, Prentice-Hall, 1946, p. 429.

1. What is the main topic of this paragraph?
   _____

2. Mention three of the things which can be done with the substance discussed.
   (a) _____
   (b) _____
   (c) _____
3. What plastics have been formed by nature?
   (a) _____
   (b) _____
4. What substances have been combined by the different people mentioned below to produce synthetic plastics?
   (a) Professor Bayer
      1.
      2.
   (b) Dr. Backeland
      1.
      2.

Check your answers with the Answer Key on page 381. Allow a score of 10 for each correct response, regardless of whether it is designated with a capital letter, lower-case letter, or arabic numeral.

Speeded reading of details. Building groundwork techniques is the first consideration in improving one's ability to grasp details readily, but once you have perfected the basic techniques, it is safe to begin practice designed to increase your speed.

The excellent reader has not just one speed but many. He has an extremely rapid speed which he uses when he skims material for a definite purpose; he has a lesser but still *very* fast speed for reading narrative or nontechnical material; and he has a slower speed when reading factual material in which he wishes to grasp details. The skillful reader "shifts his gears" when reading for different purposes. Of his several rates of speed, all can be improved.

Your speed in reading factual material for details will never equal your speed in reading easy narrative material for general ideas. You can, however, increase your speed greatly even in reading content that is heavy with detailed facts. Once you acquire the basic skills of seeing relationships and fixing details in your mind, then you can practice the same speed-reading techniques with factual material as suggested in Chapter Three for the easier material.

Selection 1

Try a timed exercise in reading for details in a series of paragraphs. Preview first; find the main ideas; then read to grasp groups of details. Do not include the time it takes for your preview in the time recorded.

BEGINNING TIME:_____

HR._____ MIN._____

The Arts in America[19]

Obviously, there is a difference between the cultural background of the New Englanders of the late seventeenth and early eighteenth centuries, who wove, embroidered, made furniture, carved wood, and built houses which are still admired; and that of the nineteenth-century settlers in the Mississippi Valley and beyond, whose handicraft period was abbreviated by the swift spread of manufactured goods, with a resulting scantiness of creative tradition. Or if a creative tradition existed it was of a kind which could not survive the early primitive conditions. The modes of life changed too rapidly. And the Puritan tradition, the country over, though its influence has probably been exaggerated, operated for a long time to prevent any conscious and determined reaching out for aesthetic expression.

That the American people were, on the whole, unaesthetic rather than anti-aesthetic may be conjectured. When artistic stirrings began in the country they led inevitably, in the absence of national patterns, to importations from abroad; in most of our arts we have not yet ceased to import from abroad. The first really American paintings, for example, were American in subject matter rather than in method. First London, then Paris and Rome educated our artists. The growth away from this tutelage has naturally been slow. There is no reason to believe that it has been slower than might have been expected of any people under like circumstances. No permanent factors can be demonstrated in American life which deny us artistic parity with other nations. We are, and have been, going through a process of normal evolution.

At certain points this evolution has been more rapid than at others. This statement may certainly be made of architecture, though with special reference to the skyscraper; our homes, schools, churches, and public buildings are less individualistic; and a lay visitor to a modern architectural exhibition finds it hard to determine without lookng at the signatures which combination of cement, steel, and glass is American and which foreign. In painting we are by no means independent of

[19] Frederick P. Keppel, and R. L. Duffus, *The Arts in American Life*, McGraw-Hill, 1933, pp. 205-207.

Parisian influences. Our development has, however, gone far enough to indicate that a genuinely American expression is possible. In music we have contributed some new motifs, though not yet an internationally recognized composer of the first rank. In drama we have achieved a degree of individuality and independence. In motion pictures we have set world standards, though they cannot yet be said to be high standards. In motion-picture photography, as an art by itself, we have probably gone further than any other country except Germany. Indeed, it may be said that in the cinema we have displayed both our best and our worst.

In commercial and industrial design it cannot be denied that we have had an awakening, and that whatever may be the merits of our tastes as displayed in those fields we are at least aware of taste as a factor in them. Indeed, we may set this awareness down as the most significant feature of the present situation. Art education, direct and indirect; the appeal of advertising; higher incomes and shorter working days, as they had developed down to 1930; the need for leisure-time activities—all these have led to a turning toward the aesthetic satisfactions. We cannot escape the impact of such instrumentalities as the radio and advertising—we have to look and to listen, and we cannot avoid in the long run trying to improve the quality of these experiences.

Began   *Finished*   No. words: 466

$$\frac{}{} \times 60 = \underline{} \text{ W.P.M.}$$

_____   _____   No. seconds:

1. Name three (any three) artistic expressions of the early New Englanders which disappeared with the spread of manufactured goods:
   (a)
   (b)
   (c)
2. What three cities educated our early American artists?
   (a)
   (b)
   (c)
3. What progress have we made in regard to:
   (a) Architecture _____

   _____

   (b) Painting _____

   _____

   (c) Music _____

   _____

(d) Drama ————————————————————————————

(e) Motion pictures ————————————————————

4. What influences have led toward aesthetic satisfactions in America?
   (a)
   (b)
   (c)
   (d)
   (e)
5. Does the present development in painting indicate that
   (a) we shall develop an original art? (Underline *Yes* or *No*)
   (b) we shall develop an imitative art? (Underline *Yes* or *No*)
6. In what two types of design have we definitely had an awakening?
   (a)
   (b)

Check your answers with the Answer Key on page 382. Allow a score of 5 for each detail which is correct. Multiply the total number of correct answers by 20.

Rate: W.P.M. ————————   Comprehension Score: ————————

Diagnosing your needs. If you read the last selection unaided by pencil work, your score on the comprehension check will afford some indication of your need for further practice. In this chapter you are not expected to do so well as you will do in the following chapter. For the moment, the following relatively low scores are set up for your reference in checking your comprehension status in reading for details.

	TIME	COMPREHENSION SCORE
Excellent	4 to 5 min.	75-100
Good	5 to 6 "	60-80
Poor	6 to 7 "	50-70
Very poor	7 to 8 "	40-60

If your scores fell within the "Excellent" group, it isn't necessary for you to make further use of supplementary aids. You are ready to go ahead "on your own," reading and mentally grasping details in paragraphs as you follow the lines of print in entire articles.

If your scores fell within the "Good" group, you would profit by working more carefully with paragraphs, placing outline numbers in the text, or underlining parts to show relationships.

If your score was within the limits of the "Poor" or "Very poor" groups, it would be well for you to continue practice in making written outlines or diagrams. When you have gained additional facility in reading for details, then proceed to work through the remaining exercises in this chapter.

Selection 2

Read to find, first, the main idea in each paragraph, and, second, the cluster of details that expand that main idea. In the test main ideas or main topics will be stated and you will be asked to identify one of the details related to the main idea.

BEGINNING TIME:_____
HR._____ MIN._____

Mr. Seward's Bargain[20]

Always the Americans have been fond of looking ahead to a grandiose future. The history of their development as a people has incessantly fed their faith in progress; and progress they identified with their own continued growth. The unconditional surrender of the South in 1865 dispelled the threat of disunity, and the aspirations of the veterans lately returned from war looked ahead to the prospect of a constantly-expanding destiny. They differed only as to the form and direction they supposed that expansion would take.

Few, however, attached their hopes to the continent's northernmost extremity. Those little-known, desolate spaces, lost beneath the snow of almost-continuous winter, seemed doomed to perpetual emptiness. Little had come of the Russian attempts to plant settlements there. And, indeed, no sober statesman, reckoning the balance of possibilities, could foresee the future wealth of Alaska—the outpouring of gold and oil, of furs and fish, of gas, timber, pulp, and tin, with which it was ultimately to enrich the nation.

No more could such a man have guessed at the immense strategic significance of this corner of the North Pacific. True enough, the visionary Tocqueville had once predicted that the United States would someday face the Russian Empire in opposition. But to the Americans who noted it, that prophetic observation referred only to the rivalry between their system of government and the Czarist despotism. No one, of course,

[20] Oscar Handlin, *The Atlantic Monthly*, April 1955, pp. 63-68.

conceived that a shift of interests in the Pacific and a new geography of flight would give this region crucial value at a moment when the United States was locked in massive competition with Russia, with the outcome certain to determine the fate of the whole world. No one, therefore, was then concerned about what the disposition of power might be were Russia established in North America, only four hundred miles away from the borders of the United States. . . .

In the 1580's Yermak Timofeiev, a Cossack fleeing the consequences of his brigandage, pushed across the Ural Mountains and defeated the Tartars. Some fifty years later, the Russians had edged across the half-empty plains of Siberia to the Pacific at Okhotsk. Into the nomadic tribes, white traders and hunters and an occasional retinue of tax collectors insinuated themselves. In the 1720's Peter the Great occasionally turned his attention to the unexploited empire in the East, and it was he who formulated the plans to extend it to America.

At this time no one yet knew whether or not America was joined to Asia. Vitus Bering, a Dane in the service of Peter's new navy, was directed to find out. . . . His mission was to cover the six thousand miles from St. Petersburg to farthest Siberia, taking with him the necessary supplies to build his ships at the ocean's edge and then to map the uncharted seas beyond.

He left the Russian capital on his first journey in February, 1725; and three and a half years later, having built his own ships at the mouth of the Kamchatka River, he traced the northern outlines of the eastern Asiatic coast. At latitude 67° north, he satisfied himself that America and Asia were not connected, and turned back out of fear of the threatening ice floes. Returning to St. Petersburg, he persuaded the government to sponsor a second exploration. He set off again in February, 1734, at the head of a far more elaborate expedition. More than seven years of strenuous preparation and struggle with recalcitrant Czarist officials followed before his ships at last set sail from Avacha Bay in Siberia in June, 1741. This time his course was directly eastward and, before his death on an unknown island, he had chartered the Aleutians and the Gulf of Alaska and made the whole area Russian. . . .

For more than a century the Czars directed their energies in a drive toward the Balkans and the Black Sea. Now their advances toward Constantinople were a threat to the British. Were they to secure access to the Mediterranean, England's supremacy in this part of the world would be challenged. For almost forty years after Waterloo a series of parries and thrusts had occupied the statesmen of the two nations; and in 1854 the Crimean War had brought the issue into the open.

Russia's defeat in this war led to a time of reckoning. The massive incompetence of the Czarist administration called for a succession of internal reforms, and military failure called for a reassessment of the strategic situation. On the first score the government was attracted by the liberal economic policies that had succeeded so remarkably in Britain. To some Russians in the court such monopolistic companies as the Russian-American were relics of the past to be eliminated as quickly as possible, and strategically Alaska was in an exposed position, difficult to defend. During the war English sea power had dominated the Pacific. In any future conflict the British Navy could hardly be prevented from taking Alaska at will. Thus, in the 1850s, the question was increasingly debated in St. Petersburg whether the American territory was worth keeping at all. . . .

The events of the next five years made the Americans desirable purchasers from the Russian point of view. The Czar had no love for the western republic, nor any desire to strengthen or extend it. But Anglo-American tensions during the Civil War and the unsettled problems that continued to trouble the relations of Washington with London convinced him that the transfer of Alaska to the United States would weaken England or at least create an additional source of dissension. In 1865 the Russian government had signified its willingness to sell Alaska to the United States.

It was by no means certain, however, that the United States was willing to buy. Earlier suggestions looking toward the acquisition of this northernmost region of the continent had evoked no enthusiasm in Washington. Many Americans saw no necessity for further expansion while great areas of the country were still unsettled; and those who did thought that the proper direction of our growth was southeastward toward Cuba and the Caribbean. To almost everyone, Alaska seemed likely to be a useless encumbrance.

Only one statesman, nursing stale dreams as his career drew to a close, was convinced that Alaska was destined to be American.

William H. Seward also had been marked for assassination when Booth's bullet put an end to Lincoln's life; for the mad conspiracy had been directed at the Secretary of State as well as at the President. But Seward, wounded, had lived, while Lincoln died.

At the war's end, Seward was almost sixty-five and knew his active political career had not much further to go. He had largely put aside his personal ambitions. The presidency, for which he felt he was far better qualified than Lincoln, was now beyond his grasp; new and younger politicians were crowding onto the scene and would give but small regard to his earlier achievements. In the conflict between President Johnson and the Radical Republicans, principle led him to side with the Chief Executive—and that had cost him considerable public and party popularity. He would serve out his term as Secretary of State until 1869 and then retire. Yet Seward longed to leave behind him some enduring accomplishment that would fulfill the promise of his youthful career. . . .

Back in the 1840s Seward and most other Americans had believed it was their country's manifest destiny to occupy the whole continent. The advantages of their system of government and social order were so clear, they thought, that people everywhere would rush to adopt them once the opportunity was presented them. Indeed, it was only the obstruction of corrupt and undemocratic governments that prevented them from doing so. When the opportunity presented itself, the United States would brush aside those regimes, and the people would voluntarily adhere to the Union. In due course the whole continent would become the United States of America.

After 1846 the doctrine of "manifest destiny" seemed to Seward to have become entangled in the slaveholders' conspiracy to extend the area of servitude southward. Now that that danger had been averted, it was once more possible to extend the boundaries of the country outward in the interests of human liberty. The power of Spain was deteriorating and would not persist for long in the Western Hemisphere. The French had withdrawn from Mexico. Only the British and the Russians remained.

The English would be a problem, the Secretary of State knew. There was no likelihood that they would voluntarily relinquish their hold on Canada or on Central America, and powerful forces in the United States were interested in maintaining the peace that had prevailed since the establishment of the Oregon boundary in 1846.

Yet Seward was convinced that the day would come when we would move north. In 1861 he had been willing to provoke war with England and Spain in the rash hope that the shock treatment of trouble abroad would draw the seceded states back into the Union and, perhaps, add Canada to it as well. After 1865, when it was no longer necessary to keep England neutral, the day of reckoning seemed closer than ever.

For Seward, the acquisition of Alaska would eliminate one more alien power from the continent, it would extend American holdings, and it would threaten Canada from the north. Alaska was worth buying because it would open the way to expansion over the whole continent.

When the Russian ambassador returned from a visit to St. Petersburg in the early spring of 1867, the Secretary of State leaped at his suggestion that a sale might be made. The terms were quickly agreed upon, and the next year the ratification of the purchase was pushed through an apathetic Senate and a dubious House. The utmost political pressure and personal cajolery were necessary to get Congress to agree to the consummation of "Seward's folly."

Seward himself retired, and the new territory attracted little public attention thereafter. Even later, when discoveries of gold and iron more than repaid the cost of $7,200,000, Alaska excited only momentary interest among Americans, and then receded from their consciousness, taken for granted.

Yet, had this opportunity been passed up, the Russians might never have been dislodged. By the end of the century the whole situation had changed. The discovery of gold and other mineral resources suddenly gave the territory a new and unexpected value. Furthermore, the Czar was now acquiring the means to defend it. For the construction of the Trans-Siberian Railroad, which was completed at the turn of the century, narrowed the distance between St. Petersburg and the Pacific, and allowed the Russians to establish naval bases at Port Arthur and Vladivostok, which soon became important centers of power in the area. Not many years after 1867, the Russians might have been far from willing to give up Alaska.

In that event, the bases that today flank the northern ocean would not be American, pointing toward Asia, but Russian, pointing toward the United States. If our citizens, in the air age, still feel that distance from the potential enemy gives some security to their national borders, it is in no small measure due to Mr. Seward's bargain.

Began	*Finished*	No. words:	1860
			—— $\times$ 60 = ———— W.P.M.
_____	_____	No. seconds:	

Checking Comprehension

1. Americans have always had faith in the progress of our country. They have differed only in their decisions as to (a) how much progress should be made each decade, (b) how much money should be spent to promote progress, (c) form and direction of expansion, (d) who should be responsible for progress.

2. Men in the 1800's could not have guessed the strategic importance of Alaska because (a) they didn't realize how much gold there was in Alaska, (b) they didn't envision the advantage of extending American territory, (c) they were not concerned about what the disposition of power might be were Russia established in America, (c) they visualized Alaska as a land of perpetual winter.

3. Vitus Bering made two explorations of northern lands. On the second exploration he (a) sailed around Iceland and discovered a new island in the northern Atlantic Ocean, (b) charted the Aleutians and the Gulf of Alaska, and claimed the whole area for Russia, (c) traced the northern outlines of Russia and explored Kamchatka River, (d) discovered and claimed the New Siberian Islands for Russia.

4. Russia's defeat in the Crimean War led to a time of reckoning. As one result of this reckoning the Russians (a) decided to adopt the

liberal economic policies which had succeeded in Britain, (b) decided to continue their advance toward the Balkans and the Black Sea, (c) debated whether North American territory was worth keeping at all, (d) decided to conquer the British.

5. Americans became desirable purchasers of Alaska from the Russian point of view because (a) the Czar wanted to help America extend its boundaries, (b) the Czar thought the transfer of Alaska to America would weaken England, (c) the Russian Empire needed the money for reconstruction purposes, (d) the Czar held America in high esteem and wanted to cooperate with this nation.

6. One reason the prospect of purchasing Alaska evoked no enthusiasm in Washington was that (a) America couldn't afford to spend the amount of money needed, (b) Americans didn't want to deal with Russia, (c) busy Congress didn't want to be bothered with the Alaskan proposition, (d) Americans saw no necessity for further expansion while great areas of the country were still unsettled.

7. At the end of the Civil War Seward knew that his active political career was about ended. One of the reasons he realized this was that (a) he had lost considerable public and party popularity, (b) he had lost interest in politics, (c) his health was failing, (d) he had been told that he must soon retire.

8. After the Civil War was over, Seward again saw the possibilities of extending the boundaries of the United States over the entire continent. One of his reasons was that (a) Congress was developing more interest in expansion, (b) the power of Spain was deteriorating, (c) Mexico wanted to be taken into the United States, (d) England was not doing much to develop Canada.

9. Seward had several reasons for wanting to purchase Alaska. One of them was (a) to provide an outpost for defense of America, (b) to capitalize on Alaska's wealth in minerals and furs, (c) to threaten Canada from the North, (d) to have a United States territory named after himself.

10. Had the opportunity of buying Alaska been passed up, the Russians might never have been dislodged. One reason for this conclusion is that soon after its purchase (a) the Russians learned that the fur-bearing seals in Alaskan waters were valuable, (b) the Czar was acquiring means to defend Alaska, (c) the Czar realized the strategic importance of Alaska in America's defense, (d) Russia needed Alaska as a base from which to make Arctic explorations.

Answers: 1)——, 2)——, 3)——, 4)——, 5)——, 6)——, 7)——, 8)——, 9)——, 10)——.

See the Answer Key on page 382. Allow a score of 10 for each correct answer.

Rate: W.P.M. _____   Comprehension Score: _____

Selection 3

This is a maintenance selection provided for your practice in reading easy material. You have been doing the most difficult type of reading. Now "try your wings" again on light material.

Adjust your speed to a much more rapid rate than you were able to use in working with the detailed factual selections. Try to exceed the rate and comprehension scores which you made previously in Chapters Four, Five, and Six. Your comprehension check will not be based on details. It will be concerned with main ideas and large units of thought.

BEGINNING TIME:_____
HR._____ MIN._____

Some Queer Things Big Birds Do[21]

There are over 20,000 kinds of birds. They differ in their ways as much as in form and color—and some of their habits are very queer.

Penguins are the most devoted parents of all. The penguins inhabit the Southern Hemisphere, and the largest species, the "emperor," lives south of the antarctic circle. In July, during the depth of the long antarctic night, when the ice is firmest, the mother penguin lays her single egg. She makes a platform of her stumpy legs and feet, on which to cradle her treasure, and warms it with a soft flap of down-covered skin. When the mother finds it necessary to enter the water for a meal she passes the egg to one of an eager company that is always ready. For it seems that, while emperor penguins are inordinately fond of brooding, few females of a flock produce eggs.

The emperor penguin stands nearly four feet in height and weighs close to ninety pounds. Its relative, the king penguin, is slightly smaller and lives farther north, where there is a firm land, though its nesting habits are essentially the same.

A king penguin, the acquaintance of which I once made, in the Zoological Gardens of London, was a magnificent bird and brilliantly colored. He had also a most charming personality, and would turn his beak skyward with a musical whistle of ecstasy when one scratched his glossy black throat.

[21] *The Mentor*, June 1925, pp. 14-19.

Mammals frequently carry their young about from place to place, but this is rarely done by birds. Some ducks, such as the hooded merganser and the wood duck, nest in hollow trees, often at some distance above the ground. Just how the young get down has long been in dispute. Many observers have maintained that the mother carries them down in her bill or even on her back, but the truth seems to be that, in most cases at least, they scramble or leap to earth or water as best they can without assistance. . . .

However, birds do sometimes carry their young. The white mute swan of Europe often takes the cygnets on its back, either when they become tired or when danger is near. Some years ago I saw a splendid pair of South American black-necked swans on an estate in Holland. They had just brought off a brood of youngsters, and the family made a striking picture as they swam in a little slough covered with duckweed. When I approached the female gave some subtle signal which was readily understood, for the cygnets promptly scrambled upon her back and were rapidly borne away. Like most male swans with families to guard, the father was inclined to be pugnacious. He moved slowly toward me, wings raised and neck arched, throwing the brilliant blue and scarlet of his beak into sharp relief against the black—a picture of defiance.

There is a great diversity in the feeding habits of birds and some birds secure their food in strange ways. The flamingo, for instance, eats with his head upside down. The long, spindly legs, bare of feathers almost to the body, enable him to wade in fairly deep water; the gracefully-curved neck allows the head to reach the mud at the bottom, where he finds his food. When feeding, the bird inverts his head, so that the upper surface of the angular beak rests on the bottom. Then, paddling alternately with his webbed feet, he stirs up the mud, draws in a mouthful, and forces it out again by raising his tongue. The sides of the beak are furnished with a row of narrow plates, which act as strainers, and sift out the tiny animal life on which the bird lives. . . .

As far as I know, parrots are uniformly vegetarians by nature, but one kind, the "kea" of New Zealand, has developed carnivorous habits. The kea has an unusually long and pointed bill, as parrots go, well adapted to use in exhuming roots and tubers. When sheep were introduced into New Zealand the birds formed the unpleasant habit of alighting on the backs of these helpless creatures and excavating there for the fatty capsule of the kidneys. . . . So severe did the ravages of the keas become that the government offered a bounty for their heads.

Most birds work hard for a living and ply their trades with industry. But pirate birds have developed among them and live largely by robbing their more diligent fellows. The man-o'-war, or frigate, bird, a relative of the pelicans, is an expert fisherman in his own right, but when times are dull and food scarce he charges upon the smaller gulls and terns and forces them to disgorge the catch that they have stored for their own use.

Friendship among birds usually is the result of a mutual benefit. Species that have flocking instincts band together for protection, to make use of restricted nesting sites or often simply because food is available in a given locality. Unselfish attachment between individuals seldom exists among wild birds, but in captivity, where social barriers are more or less broken down, curious and thoroughly-platonic friendships are sometimes formed. . . .

Feathers are of as much importance to birds as clothes are to us. In most cases the plumage is fully renewed but once a year, and therefore the bird owner takes the greatest pains to keep his raiment in good condition until it is replaced. Special plumes and decorations, of course, are the most difficult to care for, but often these are required only during the breeding season, which is comparatively short. Particular as birds are about their plumage, I know of only one that goes so far as to provide its own decorations. The motmots are a brightly-colored South American group, with no close relatives and living in the depths of the tropical forests. The two central tail feathers are considerably longer than the others, and when they are renewed a portion of the web, just below the tip, is very lightly attached to the quill. As they grow, the bird constantly draws them through his bill, until finally the weakened web breaks away, leaving the shaft bare for a distance of an inch or more, with a little tab on the end. Thus the motmot secures the "racket" decoration, for which he is famed. . . .

The nesting customs of birds range from almost complete indifference to infinite solicitude on the part of the parents. In the East Indies there is a species related to the Australian brush turkey which merely deposits its eggs in the warm sand of the seashore and leaves them to be incubated by the sun's rays.

Originally the stork made its nest in trees, but now it almost invariably builds on the tops of buildings. In Denmark, Holland, and Germany, householders are delighted to have a stork guest nesting on the roof, as there is a well-grounded belief that the long-legged visitor is "a bringer of good." The wooing manners of the stork are extremely grotesque. With wings outspread it performs a kind of leaping dance, at the same time setting up a harsh chattering with the upper and lower parts of the beak. Storks commonly spend their summers in Europe and their winters farther east.

Began	*Finished*	No. words:	1500
			$\frac{}{} \times 60 = \underline{\hspace{1cm}}$ W.P.M
_____	_____	No. seconds:	

Checking Comprehension

1. There are over (a) 2,000 kinds of birds, (b) 1,000,000 kinds of birds, (c) 20,000 kinds of birds, (d) 60,000 kinds of birds.

2. Penguins (a) neglect their young, (b) lay more eggs than they can hatch, (c) are not interested in brooding, (d) are devoted parents.

3. Birds (a) carry their young in their bills, (b) carry their young on their backs, (c) carry them under their wings, (d) rarely carry them at all.

4. As an illustration of the strange feeding habits of birds the author discusses those of the (a) flamingo, (b) penguin, (c) wood duck, (d) swan.

5. All parrots are (a) vegetarians, (b) carnivorous, (c) both vegetarian and carnivorous, (d) vegetarian with one exception.

6. Most birds are (a) pirates, (b) work hard for their living, (c) are always expecting "handouts," (c) will "sing for their supper."

7. Friendship among birds usually results (a) when two flocks belonging to the same general family meet, (b) when birds get lost at migration time, (c) when they are nesting, (d) when it is to their mutual benefit to be friends.

8. As a general rule birds (a) depend upon wind and rain to take care of their feathers, (b) take good care of their feathers themselves, (c) pay no attention to their feathers, (d) try to pull out their feathers.

9. Birds are (a) always solicitous about building their nests, (b) range from indifference to solicitude, (c) are never indifferent, (d) are nearly always indifferent.

10. Originally storks made their nests (a) on the tops of buildings, (b) in trees, (c) in barns, (d) in low bushes.

Answers: 1)—, 2)—, 3)—, 4)—, 5)—, 6)—, 7)—, 8)—, 9)—, 10)—.

See Answer Key, page 382.

Rate: W.P.M. ————   Comprehension Score: ————

Vocabulary Study

The italicized words in the following phrases are taken from the selections you have just read. Underline the synonym or phrase beneath each italicized word which best defines that word. Check your answers with the Answer Key on page 382.

1. *Carnivorous* habits
   a) ferocious
   b) cannibalistic
   c) flesh-eating
2. White *cygnets*
   a) a constellation
   b) young swans
   c) flowers
3. *Inordinately* fond of fish
   a) occasionally
   b) excessively
   c) rarely
4. Bright *raiment*
   a) metal
   b) clothing
   c) sunshine
5. Fleeing from *brigandage*
   a) capture
   b) war
   c) robbers
6. *Nomadic* tribes
   a) dark-skinned
   b) roaming
   c) savage
7. *Recalcitrant* officials
   a) rebellious
   b) obliging
   c) reluctant
8. A *grandiose* future
   a) extensive
   b) famous
   c) impressive
9. A *manifest* destiny
   a) discouraging
   b) magnificent
   c) obvious
10. A *pugnacious* dog
    a) momentous
    b) animated
    c) inclined to fight

11. Followed by a *retinue*
    a) parade
    b) attendants
    c) well-wishers
12. A useless *encumbrance*
    a) bother
    b) task
    c) hindrance
13. Artful *cajolery*
    a) embroidery work
    b) delusive enticements
    c) pointillist painting
14. A familiar *motif*
    a) reason
    b) pattern
    c) fantasy
15. With expert *tutelage*
    a) instruction
    b) technicians
    c) adviser
16. An *apathetic* audience
    a) sympathetic
    b) impassive
    c) demilitaristic
17. A series of *parries*
    a) defensive movements
    b) obstinate activities
    c) refractive interference
18. *Consummation* of the plan
    a) initiation
    b) execution
    c) completion
19. A long *regime*
    a) system of government
    b) life
    c) scientific treatise
20. *Ravages* of wild beasts
    a) savageness
    b) destructiveness
    c) revelations

Vocabulary Score: —————

Follow-Up Suggestions

This is necessarily a longer chapter than the others. Learning to read details rapidly is the most difficult type of reading that a person has to do, and as such it requires more development and practice than some of the simpler skills.

Using Materials of Your Selection

If you did not do well in your test of Selection 2, page 133, then continue practice with individual paragraphs which you find in your trade or professional journals or books. Outline related ideas on a separate piece of paper or within the paragraph itself; or make notes on the margin of the page; or underline main ideas and major and minor details with one, two, and three lines, respectively. Continue to use these helps as long as necessary. As soon as you can, however, try to get away from the use of such "crutches," for they slow up speed.

When you have achieved a high degree of skill in working with separate paragraphs, proceed to carry out the following suggestions.

Set aside at least one fifteen-minute period each evening for practice on reading detailed, factual articles. In each of your practice periods, select an article of this type and apply the techniques which you have learned. Work with one paragraph and try to envision that as a whole. Then go on to the next paragraph and proceed as if it were a new unit. Stop frequently to sum up what you've gotten out of two or three paragraphs. You will soon be able to make an easy transition from one paragraph to another and to grasp details in increasing numbers of paragraphs.

As soon as you can read two or three paragraphs without stopping, make a new entry in your notebook: "Speed Record—Detailed Reading." Enter the date and the number of words per minute which you were able to cover in reading material packed with facts. Continue to keep this record each night until you read detailed material as fast as you want to. You should make regular rate increases in this kind of reading—but remember this rate will never be so high as your speed in reading easy, narrative material.

Check your grasp of facts after each reading by one of these methods: have someone ask you detailed questions; make an outline from your "mental picture"; write a summary of facts; or tell yourself the important thoughts, together with the cluster or clusters of details that belong with each one. You can of course check your responses by referring to the text. Continue to force your speed in reading this type of material, as you have been forcing it in reading selections of easier content.

You should also continue your speed and comprehension practice in reading easy nontechnical material, making regular records of your speed. Don't let your detailed reading slow down your very rapid rate of reading easy material.

CHAPTER ▶ **8**

Wake Up Your
Memory!

Are You the Hourglass Type?

COLERIDGE, the English poet, very succinctly classified adult readers as follows:

"There are four kinds of readers. The first is like the hourglass; and their reading being as the sand, it runs out and leaves not a vestige behind. A second is like the sponge, which imbibes everything and returns it in nearly the same state, only a little dirtier. The third is like a jelly bag, allowing all that is pure to pass away, and retaining only the refuse and the dregs. And the fourth is like the slaves of Golconda, who, casting aside all that is worthless, retain only pure gems."

This chapter is directed to those who are "like the hourglass; and their reading being as sand, it runs out, and leaves not a vestige behind." Truly these people must be the ones who in multitudes voice their problems in some such way as this: "I read and read and read, and when I have finished I don't know what I've read. A week later I may boldly state at an appropriate time in conversation that I read an article on atom bombing last week. Then I'm stopped cold—I can't tell a thing that I read in that article. Is it possible to improve my ability to remember what I read?"

Yes, although there is almost unanimous agreement that memory as a general ability in itself cannot be improved, in this specific field it is quite possible to develop competence in recalling what you have read.

Memory is one of the most complicated topics in the realm of psychology, and a great body of information has been accumulated in regard to it. A few simple psychological facts with direct bearing on reading retention are here presented on the assumption that you may be one of the many who haven't had the time or the inclination to study the findings of modern psychologists.

What About Memory Training Systems?

Most of the methods devised for training the memory are considered by modern psychologists to be artificial and unnatural. Certain criticisms leveled against them will help you understand why these quick, ready-made systems are not recommended.

The origin of systems for memory improvement dates back to the fifth century before Christ. One event is said to have first called to the attention of the early Greeks the possibilities of cultivating the ability to recall. Scopas, a wrestling champion at the Olympic Games, was honored at a feast, and the poet Simonides was called upon to speak. Between courses Simonides was told that a messenger was waiting outside to see him, so he left the banquet hall. He had scarcely gotten out when the ceiling and walls caved in, and all the guests were killed. Their faces and bodies were so mangled that not one of them could be identified. Relatives were distraught because they knew not which of the bodies belonged to which loved one. Simonides, accustomed to entertaining at feasts, had developed a scheme whereby he associated the name of each guest with his position at the table. With the use of this scheme, he now prepared a chart marking the position of each guest at the table, and, since the bodies were still in the same position, the dead were identified by means of Simonides' chart.

This feat naturally improved Simonides' reputation. Moreover, it proved that fixing a number of locations in mind in order and associating a person with each location was an aid to memory. Simonides consequently developed a system of artificial memory training which met with great success among the Greeks.

Basically this was his method: He instructed the student to form a mental picture of a house divided into many apartments, corridors, walls, and balconies. The student committed the plan of the house to memory, numbering each room, and in each room he mentally stored the memory of some special thing that he wanted to fix in his mind. When he wished to recall a particular thing he would mentally go from room to room, calling to mind the contents of each room in turn. Some of the present-day advocates of this system have a student mentally fill the rooms with furniture, then associate the things he wants to remember with different pieces of furniture. Others have a student associate the things he wants to remember with different pieces of furniture in his own home.

Frequently since Simonides invented his system of memory training, others have devised panaceas for those who wish to "train the memory." Instead of using rooms and furniture as mental depositories, some have a student associate what he wants to remember with letters of the alphabet. Others have the student exchange the consonants in the alphabet for numbers, then use the numbers in some special arrangement.

All such devices are called "Systems of Mnemonics." The word mnemonics is derived from a Greek word meaning "remembering."

For two thousand years these mnemonic systems have been exploited commercially, and no doubt you have seen them advertised in daily papers and have heard about them over television and radio. These methods are deplored by those who have made a scientific study of the process of recall and the conditions under which it operates. In the light of hundreds of investigations, psychologists consider the use of mnemonics very unsatisfactory and, indeed, undesirable. They claim that these systems are based upon imperfect or mistaken views of the nature of memory; that the spectacular results sometimes produced are mere tricks of unnatural associations which do nothing to strengthen the higher processes of the memory. They claim that such methods accustom the mind to associate ideas accidentally and arbitrarily and that, while this may serve to impress a few items on the memory, it does nothing toward making the mind retentive. Furthermore, the symbols used as "pegs" to aid in recall sometimes actually clog the memory.

A person using such a system soon finds it more difficult to remember all the "pegs" than the things they stand for.

On the other hand, if a person avoids artificiality and works in harmony with the natural conditions under which memory takes place, he will get permanent results. If he establishes the right conditions, the memory will do its own job.

What Factors Contribute to Memory?

We are told that memory is the show window of life. The inference is that we can gaze into the window of memory and again "look at" anything that has happened to us—not only events of firsthand experience, but also events we have heard of, seen in pictures, or read about. Of course this chapter is concerned with memory in connection with reading.

Psychologists have described three of the most important conditions which contribute to recall. These conditions are (1) the strength of the impression of the idea or ideas to be recalled, (2) the nature of the associations by which one idea is linked to another, (3) the frequency with which the impression is revived. These can be applied to your reading situation.

Intensity of First Impressions

In improving your ability to remember what you read, one of the most fundamental "laws" is to establish strong, sharp, vivid impressions of ideas or facts you mean to fix in your mind. Weak, feeble impressions do not cut deeply enough into your subconscious mentality to be pulled out again when you want them.

What are some aids that you can summon to assist you in making intensive first impressions?

Good physical condition contributes to vigorous impressions. In reading a selection in which there are details that you have reason to need later, be sure you are fresh and rested and feeling well. Under these conditions your energy will be most abundant and will serve you best. If you are fatigued or have a cold or a headache or are physically uncomfortable in some other way, do some light reading and save the "memory" reading for another time. Physical fitness provides you with a power-producing vehicle in which your mental activities may obtain strong, decisive first impressions.

Attention is an absolute prerequisite to intensive impressions. In fact, the intensity of the original impression is proportionate to the attention given the item to be remembered.

What is attention? It is the will directing the intellect into some particular channel and keeping it there.

What does this mean to you in terms of improving your ability to remember what you read? It means that you must give your whole undivided attention to that which you want to recall. You must *will* to fix vividly in your subconscious mind whatever you mean to recall. Your memory awaits your commands. If you say to it, "I want to recall this thing later. Take hold of it for me and keep it until I need it," it will obey.

Don't say, "But I have a poor memory." If you are healthy and have average intelligence you have as good a memory as anyone else. Memory is not an organ that is weak or strong. It is a function. Make use of it or let it lie dormant, as you prefer. But if you do the latter, don't blame your memory. Blame yourself for not using it properly.

The person who complains that he has a poor memory in recalling what he reads is the one who has not directed his attention strongly toward any particular items in the article. No doubt he has passed over the lines of print in an effortless manner, recognizing masses of words and myriads of meanings indiscriminately, conveying only weak and feeble impressions to his brain. Such impressions are not stamped into the "storage grooves" with sufficient impact to permit ready recall at a later time.

Knowing, then, that you are as capable as anyone else of recalling what you read, trust your memory. Don't condone it or view it with suspicion. Make such use of it that you won't have to excuse its failures.

In order to make the best use of your memory in retaining what you read, let us discuss aids for directing your attention to printed material for recall purposes.

Interest is a very important factor. We give voluntary attention to anything in which we are interested. A musician may give rapt attention to a musical rendition by a great master, but he may have the greatest difficulty in giving attention to a lecture on philosophy.

So it is with reading. If you are deeply interested in the content of a selection, you probably won't have to concern yourself about giving attention or about recalling these ideas later.

Purpose is important. Much of our reading is not of such a character that we do it as the result of a compelling interest. Very frequently, however, we have a purpose in reading material we wish to recall, whether or not we are very much interested in it. Purpose contributes to attention, also. If we just wander through an article with no purpose in mind, we do not bring strong attention to bear on the text. On the other hand, if we have a definite purpose, we focus attention on whatever will fulfill this purpose. Interest together with purpose constitutes a perfect team. Without interest, you must draw strongly upon your purpose and reserves of will power to make your attention strong enough to result in vivid impressions.

This book is equipping you with many techniques which will be useful to you in retaining what you read. These previously-learned techniques will now be integrated into your recall procedures.

Purpose, for example, is something which has been emphasized from the beginning. You have been urged always to set a purpose for yourself before reading. You have been told that having a definite purpose for reading a selection contributes both to your speed and comprehension. Now we tell you that whatever fills your purpose will probably be that which you will want to remember.

Concentration is a necessity. Purpose is one important phase of attention. A second significant aspect of attention is concentration, or the process of holding your attention in certain channels long enough to establish the vivid impressions which contribute so much to ready recall.

One of the common complaints of adult readers is, "I can't concentrate on what I'm reading." These individuals usually are able to direct their initial attention to some reading matter which they desire to retain, but they have difficulty in holding it to the task at hand. They should take the advice of the Bible: "Think it with all thy might. Do one thing at a time with all thy soul."

In discussing concentration, Atkinson[1] said: "Men of great intellectual power are noted for their developed power of attention and, on the other hand, imbeciles and idiots are almost destitute of concentrated attention. The great man's mind, consequently, is stored full of strong, intense impressions, which he brings into the field of consciousness in his every-day work, while the man of deficient attention has but a small stock upon which to draw, and he consequently fails to manifest force and resourcefulness."

[1] William Walker Atkinson, *Mercury Culture,* McClure, 1911, p. 15.

The power of concentrating attention on what you read again breaks down into two components: exclusion and "staying on the track." Exclusion means the ability to shut out *all* sights, sounds, and thoughts except the one on which you wish to concentrate, thus giving one hundred per cent of your attention to the reading content. Divided attention won't yield a vivid impression. If, when focusing your attention on a text that you wish to remember, you can become absolutely oblivious to everything else in the world, then you will get the strongest possible impression. As you have learned previously, strength of impression is in proportion to strength of attention.

According to one story, an Italian scientist was concentrating so intensively on his experiments that he was unaware of the fact that a battle was going on in the streets about him. When he came from his laboratory at nightfall he was annoyed to find that Napoleon's troops were occupying the town. Another story tells that Socrates once volunteered to serve in a campaign but, becoming involved in a philosophical speculation, stopped still until he reached the solution to the problem. At this point he discovered that he was standing alone on a plain and that the entire army was several hours' march away from him. When you arrive at a stage in which you can concentrate your attention on reading text to such an extent, you will have no difficulty in fixing vivid impressions for recall purposes.

If you haven't been in the habit of concentrating one hundred per cent on what you read, you will find that it will take will power and effort to form the new habit. But with practice you will eventually be able to concentrate your attention on those items you wish to remember almost automatically and with very little expenditure of effort. Be patient, for improvement in concentration is gradual; but once you have established a new mental pathway leading straight ahead without branching off at distractions, your mind will travel over this pathway without special effort. Clear away the brush and build a well-established mental road; then your mind will not explore the many bypaths into the forest of forgetfulness.

Have you noticed that you now are concentrating better than before you began to work with the techniques in this book? The answer should be in the affirmative because every technique learned so far has made its own contribution.

Take reading under time pressure, for instance. If you are forcing your speed to see how many words you can read and understand within a given time, you are apt to stick pretty closely to the job.

You won't have time to let your mind run off on side excursions. Striving to see if you can beat your own record in reading more words per minute is one of the best antidotes for an itinerant mind.

The skills that you have learned to use in tackling different types of reading materials for different purposes have also contributed to concentration of attention. People who are not equipped with specific reading skills often laboriously "plow through" everything in one manner. The application of just one general-reading procedure to all reading situations is in itself conducive to wandering attention. Knowing just how to undertake the job of reading a specific selection for a specific purpose, and how to use a certain combination of skills which best serve that purpose, enables you to get at the heart of things without lost time and effort. You already save time that you might otherwise spend in dispersing your attention here and there.

So, even though concentration has not been mentioned in preceding chapters, you have ever since the first page been developing skills which contribute to concentration. In addition to making use of skills previously learned, however, you now need to work *specifically* for a higher power of concentration.

Will power is of first importance. You must definitely make up your mind that you are going to direct your whole attention to the reading task at hand and that you are going to hold it there as long as necessary. Be the master of your own mind. Don't let your mind run around hither and thither diverting you from your purpose and wasting your time. Order your will power to take hold and direct the job. Every time you catch your attention wandering, command your will power to pull it back and put it to work at full force in getting the sense out of what you are reading.

Practice excluding all external stimuli such as airplanes passing overhead, people starting up a conversation in an adjoining room, children beginning to play a noisy game outside your window, your dog yipping for attention. Just ignore everything except the message which you are getting from your reading. This principle of *exclusion* is important. You can develop it to a high degree, by resolutely disregarding *everything* which is contesting for your attention. Wage a battle. See who wins. Will the winner be a combination of all things clamoring for your attention and diverting you from your reading, or will the winner be your will power which holds your attention one hundred per cent on your reading?

Of course if you now cannot concentrate, it would be a good idea to start your intensive practice at a time and in a place where your mind can be fairly free from outside impressions. As you habituate yourself to the use of undivided attention you can gradually emerge into situations where there are increasing numbers of potential distractions and still read with as much attention to the author's message as if you were marooned on Robinson Crusoe's island.

The time you can concentrate on one reading selection can be lengthened. If your power of concentration is weak, perhaps you won't be able to direct intense attention to reading material for longer than one minute at a time.

The instant your attention begins to wander and you think you can't compel it to stay with the text any longer, raise your eyes from the page and rest a moment. Then pick up where you left off and again direct your *whole* attention to the text. See if you can concentrate for a longer period this time. Even if it amounts only to two seconds longer, you have made progress.

Continue in this way. Every time concentration becomes a strain, rest a few seconds, then try again. Strive to lengthen the time you can concentrate, as you make successive trials.

Day after day resume your efforts to concentrate. If you engage in such practice only two or three times and then lapse into careless reading, your practice won't do you much good. But if you continue to give concentrated attention to your reading during a daily period for a month, you will notice considerable improvement. In addition to your regular practice periods, you should of course direct strong attention to the printed messages in all the reading you do throughout the day.

How Can Impressions Be Revived?

The first step in improving your ability to remember what you read is *establishing* vivid impressions of meanings conveyed through printed symbols. But this is only half the story. The process of receiving and storing vivid impressions is of great significance in memory improvement. Of equal significance, however, is the process of reviving these impressions when they are needed again. At the time you want to revive an idea a ray of consciousness passes over the stored-up impression and you re-read it not from the book but from your subconscious mind where it has been lying dormant.

Meaning contributes much to the revival of an impression. Psychologists in experiments have learned that meaningful text is recalled more readily and accurately than meaningless non-sense syllables. Applied to reading, this indicates that it is essential for you thoroughly to understand what you read if you wish to recall it.

Association is of even greater importance for recalling. Several different types of association have been used in memory training. Association by location was used by Simonides and many of his followers. There is also association by contiguity; recalling items because they occur in close succession to one another. This is used in memorizing the ABC's. We know that B comes next in order after A, and that C comes next in order after B, because we memorized the letters in that order. But if you were asked suddenly what letter comes after K you probably would have to go back and repeat the beginning of the alphabet in order to pull from your memory the name of the letter that comes after K.

Both of these types of association are mechanical and belong to what is generally considered the lower forms of memorization. They are usually based upon artificial associations which have little utility in real-life situations and as such do not tend to improve or strengthen the memory.

The third type of association, that of rational association of ideas, is the most natural and useful, and this is recommended for your use in improving your ability to recall what you read. According to this type, ideas are assembled because of their relationships, and any one idea in the chain of relationships helps to recall the others that belong with it. Thus the person who is trying to recall has several "handles" to take hold of in pulling back any one set of related facts or ideas which he has impressed upon his mind through previous reading.

Dr. Abercrombie says: "The habit of correct association—that is, connecting facts in the mind according to their true relations, and to the manner in which they tend to illustrate each other . . . is one of the principal means of improving the memory, particularly that kind of memory which is an essential of a cultivated mind; namely, that which is founded not upon incidental connections, but on true and important relations."[2]

Selectivity is very important in making use of the association-of-ideas technique. You need to select with care those ideas out of a

[2] D. Abercrombie, quoted by David Kay in *Memory, What It Is and How to Improve It*, Appleton, 1889, p. 280.

mass of related ideas which you wish to recall. The trouble with many people is that they read an article rather carelessly, not thinking particularly about relationships and cluttering their minds with numerous details, none of which "stand out." The habit of promiscuous reading without selection or reflection tends to weaken the memory. People who habitually do this kind of reading are usually the ones who complain that they can't remember a thing they have read. Casual reading without selection or reflection is all right if you are simply pursuing a story for a passing pleasure. But the procedures used in that type of reading won't work for you if you are reading an article in which there are facts or ideas that you want to remember.

Skills previously learned in this book have provided you with an excellent grounding for further developing your association ability for recall purposes. You have learned how to find the most important idea in a paragraph. Being able to select the important points in an article or chapter is a prerequisite for recalling what you read. If main points only are what you desire to retain, then you can direct your attention strongly to establishing vivid impressions of these few main ideas, and not impose upon your memory by expecting it to recall *everything* you read.

If the content of the article or book is so significant to you that you want to remember *details* to use in your work or conversation, then the techniques of "mining for details" furnishes you the foundation to stand upon while taking the next step of improving your ability to recall what you read in material packed with facts. With association techniques and the perception of relationships, you had practice in noting details as they were related to each other and as the entire cluster of details was related to an important idea.

After analyzing a selection for important ideas and clusters of details related to these important ideas, you probably found that you "knew it by heart." In other words, in directing your attention to the selection of the main idea and clusters of related details, you have succeeded in establishing strong impressions, and in organizing the details in related clusters you have built up associations which have helped you to pull back entire units of thought. So, in terms of conditions which contribute to recall, you have already had practice in putting the most important ones into effect.

Repetition is one new technique, however, which you may wish to apply. This is effective in promoting the conscious revival of ideas or facts read. Briefly stated, other things being equal the intensity of an impression can be increased by *repeatedly* reviving it. If you wish to remember something permanently, think about it off and on for several days and try to recall it frequently without referring to the book or periodical in which you read it. *Repeated* recall intensifies the impression.

Immediacy of recall after reading a selection is also very beneficial. It is helpful to stop at intervals while you are reading and sum up those points you will wish to recall. Each time you do this, recall your previous summary of points and add new ones. By the time you have reached the end of the selection you will have repeatedly revived impressions of all the points you want to remember.

Pencil work is used by some people as an aid to recall. There are some who find it helpful to underline the points they wish to remember. Others make a brief note of basic ideas here and there on the margin of the page. Others write a summary, an abstract, or an outline of an article or chapter. In all such cases, original impressions may be strengthened through the use of the additional activity of writing. Such techniques are often employed by students while studying for an examination.

If you habitually use written supplements to mental recall, there is the danger that you may lean too heavily on the written reminders instead of handing the whole job over to your memory. The ideal plan is to select, as you go along, those ideas which you would like to recall, concentrating attention on them and associating them in the proper relationship with successive ideas. If you practice this without the crutch of taking notes, you will soon be able to use the procedure automatically. When that time arrives you will have no further complaint about remembering what you read.

Practice in Recalling What you Read

You have just finished reading a background discussion on the nature of memory and the conditions under which recall best operates—all in relation to recalling what you read. Now you are in a position to take advantage of the instruction and practice which follow.

Recalling Main Ideas

Now you are about to have a guided experience in applying to a reading situation the points we have been discussing.

1. *Utilize your interest.* In the selection below five rules are given for staying on a diet. Perhaps you are on a diet. If so, you will have a strong interest in this topic. If you aren't on a diet yourself, no doubt someone who is close to you is going through the throes. In this case you may be interested in getting suggestions to pass on. Whichever the situation is, tap the interest that you have, and it will serve you as capital stock in your reading-to-remember process.

2. *Set your purpose.* Clearly set up a personal purpose for remembering these five rules.

   (a) You may want to remember them as frequent reminders to yourself to stay on your own diet.

   (b) You may want to remember them so that you can relate them to some other person who is on a diet.

   (c) You may wish to remember them for use in conversation whenever the topic of dieting comes up.

Whatever your purpose is, be sure you have it strongly in mind when you start to read.

3. *Establish strong impressions.* Establish a vigorous impression of each of the five rules. When you come to each rule concentrate on it with the idea of impressing it indelibly in your mind. Don't let any influence in your environment distract one iota of your attention. Give everything you have in the way of energy and attention to each rule.

4. *Build meaningful associations.* Read the information beneath each rule in order to build up meaningful associations. Perhaps at first you won't fully understand what the first rule means: "Find out the psychological basis for your overweight." When you read the explanation and the example that follows, you will understand exactly. At some future date you may be unable to recall the rule itself, but the story of the woman who ate too much because she was lonely may be just the right "handle" to help you pull back the rule. So, in addition to making an effort to impress the rules strongly on your mind, read the details about each of them for the purpose of building up associations which may furnish you useful "handles" in later recall.

5. *Make use of repetition.* After you have read the second rule, see if you can tell yourself both the first rule and the second rule. After you have read the third rule, see if you can state the first, second, and third rules, etc.

6. *Read and apply.* Now, as you read the article apply these various principles.

Additional suggestions numbered 7 and 8 will be given at the end of the selection.

Five Ways to Stay on a Diet[3]

Maybe it's because you can't get into last year's clothes. Or perhaps a candid snapshot or home movie showed you up in all your corpulence. Or maybe it was hearing your doctor say, "There's nothing at all the matter with you except that you're carrying too much lard around on your bones." Anyway, whatever it was that precipitated your decision, you've made up your mind to Do Something About It. If other people can take off weight, you tell yourself firmly, so can you!

And so you set your jaw as you march to the grocery to lay in a supply of string beans, lamb chops, and tomato juice. But even as you vow that *this* time you are going to stick with it until you get down to a decent weight, you hear your subconscious whispering to you from a corner of your mind, "No, you won't! You've tried it before, remember? You *know* you don't have enough will power to see you past the first few days."

Even before you begin your first day's dieting, the ghosts of all your past failures hover over your table. You feel impervious to temptation *now*, but a premonition of defeat is already nibbling away your determination. You're licked before you start, and you know it!

Take cheer! You *can* stay on a diet! Oh, you'll have a few pangs of hunger and occasional moments of discouragement, but if you'll follow five simple rules, you'll find that your will power has more starch in it than you ever dreamed possible. What's more, they will help you change your diet from an endurance test into a fascinating game.

Rule 1. *Find out the psychological basis for your overweight.* An eminent psychiatrist told me, not long ago, that he doubted if any universal truth had received so much publicity during the past few years as the fact that there is a psychological factor back of almost every case of overweight.

Books, magazines, motion pictures, and lecturers keep pounding home the tenet that people overeat to relieve bordom, to bolster inferiority complexes, soothe worries, and compensate for frustrations and disappointments.

A great many people, however, are like the middle-aged woman who recently complained to her physician, "I know that I eat too much simply because I'm lonely. I have too much time on my hands, and I eat because I have nothing else to do. But knowing the reason *why* I overeat doesn't help a bit. I still seem to get just as hungry!"

[3] Jean Z. Owen, *Your Health*, Spring Quarter, 1954.

"Madame," the doctor answered, "it isn't enough for people to discover and admit the cause of their 'nervous appetites'; the information is not a magic wand that can banish one's appetite instantly. You have acquired a bad habit. The knowledge of your motive in acquiring this habit can help you break it, but it can't do the whole job."

Examine your own life and your own personality carefully; see if you can discover why you started to overeat. Uncovering the emotional unrest that prompted you to adopt bad eating habits won't make fudge cake suddenly look repulsive to you, but it *will* help you say "no" a little more easily.

Rule 2. *Adopt a sensible reducing program.* Unfortunately, fad "starvation" diets have an emotional appeal to anyone beginning a reducing program. Whole-hog-or-none is the idea, and so you airily skip breakfast the first morning. Perhaps you decide to skip lunch, too. This isn't at all bad, you tell yourself joyfully, as you plan a dinner of a single lamb chop and a serving of spinach. At this rate you should be able to whittle off as much as a couple of pounds a day!

Your enthusiasm may carry you through two or three days of this type of dieting, but you will be forced to abandon it before there is any appreciable weight loss. Seeking to conserve every ounce of body strength, your metabolism will go into low gear. You will feel lethargic, headachy, and depressed. Your nerves will be at the snapping point. And so, finally, the law of self-preservation will take over, and your diet will be "temporarily" discarded.

No diet is safe and effective that does not provide three meals a day, balanced to include the food properties your body requires. Forgo the fad "quickie" diets; instead, adopt one that is sensible and well-balanced, medically approved. There is an execellent diet book that my own physician recommends: *The New Way to Eat and Get Slim,* by Donald G. Cooley, published in 1949 by Wilfred Funk. I've known any number of patients who have lost as much as a pound a day on this diet and felt fine. You can't lose weight faster than that, even on a starvation diet!

Follow a sensible diet, approved by your own doctor, and you will find that your body won't force you to go on a fattening "food binge" every few days.

Rule 3. *Keep a record of everything you eat.* One of my closest friends is a dietitian in a large hospital. For a number of years she was more than fifty pounds overweight, yet she was always counting calories, paring her meals to Spartan fare.

"It's my *business* to know food values," she was in the habit of saying unhappily. "I can help *other* people reduce, but my diets just don't seem to work on me."

Even her physician was almost convinced that she was a medical enigma—until she began to shed her excess poundage. Within four months she had reduced to her normal weight.

"How did you do it?" I asked her, admiring her svelte figure. "What made you start to lose all at once?"

She chuckled. "One day I was listing the caloric intake for one of the patients' charts, and I decided I was going to make a chart for myself," she told me. "You see, I thought I knew food values so well that I could keep a mental record of my own food. Not until I started tabulating every mouthful of food I ate, all through the day, did I realize how many 'nibbles' of food I was taking between meals."

Try her plan for just a few days, and you'll be amazed at the way it helps you put the brakes on your eating habits. If you know you are going to record it, you won't be nearly so inclined to reach for that solitary peanut, that tempting cookie, that spoonful of left-over pudding. And if you have dieted before, without satisfactory results, you may find, as did my dietitian friend, that it's the *little* things that often make the difference between success and failure.

Rule 4. *Don't talk about your diet.* To anyone who is trying to reduce, there is no subject in the world quite so fascinating as dieting. It takes almost superhuman control *not* to talk about it, yet nothing so endangers one's following a reducing program through to a successful finish.

There are several reasons why it is wise to refrain from wholesale discussion of your diet. In the first place, talking about it keeps your mind on the subject of food. Your mouth waters, your gastric juices bubble, and you experience sensations of hunger that would never be there if you were thinking about something else.

Secondly, it gives too many people a chance to butt in. For some inexplicable reason, a great many women can't abide the thought of some *other* woman going on a diet. As one acquaintance recently remarked, "A true friend is one who loves you even if you get thinner than she is."

Whatever is behind it, whether it be primitive jealousy or well-intentioned interference, people *will* try to undermine your self-control. Little phrases like "You're not a bit too heavy; you look just right the way you are," or "Oh, do break down and have another piece of pie; it won't hurt you" make it hard to stay firm-willed.

In the third place, talking about a diet makes anyone a bit of a bore. One of the most popular women I ever knew weighed well over two hundred pounds. She had a contagious sense of humor, plus a tolerance and understanding of people that made her beloved wherever she went.

Once on a diet, *however,* her whole personality narrowed. Her interests shrank until she could speak of little but calories, exercises, and measurements. By the time she had streamlined her body she had become so tiresome that people were actually avoiding her.

The motivating factor behind almost every attempt to diet is the desire to become more attractive. You will only defeat your purpose if, in becoming more physically attractive, you strip your personality of those qualities that make people like you.

Rule 5. *Prepare yourself ahead of time for "off" days.* Some days it's easy—even fun!—to diet. And then again there are days when you feel that it isn't worth the effort and you might as well chuck the whole thing.

You'll find it easier to get through those "off" days if you prepare yourself emotionally for them—*in advance.*

For example, there will be times when, no matter how much you really want to follow your diet, you can't do so without being rude. You're invited out to lunch or dinner and your hostess has baked a chocolate pie especially for you, and you can't refuse it without offending her.

On these days, a dieter is inclined to throw all caution to the four winds. "If I'm going to break my diet," he reasons, "I might as well *really* break it!"

This type of reasoning is as infantile as it would be to say, "Well, I've cut my finger. I might just as well rip my whole arm open and let it *really* bleed before I bandage it."

Don't forget that two high-calorie meals are twice as fattening as one! When courtesy forces you to abandon your diet—and such occasions are bound to arise—resolve, in advance, not to break it any more than you must, and *to get back on schedule the very next meal.*

Don't wait until "tomorrow" or "next Monday." Go back on your routine *immediately.* You'll find that the shorter the "lapsing" period, the easier it is to stick to your diet.

Most of us, I believe, are inclined to indulge ourselves with fattening food to compensate for disappointments and failures. For no logical reason, a pound of chocolates or a piece of rich cake seems to give us a temporary "lift."

For several years I was in the habit of salving my hurt feelings by eating a gooey sundae every time a manuscript was rejected. Oh, not consciously—I wasn't even aware that I was doing it until an outspoken friend brought it to my attention and suggested that I assuage my ego with something less fattening.

I learned that a "stolen" hour or two of reading, a ticket to a play, or a new phonograph recording gave me the same soothing sensation of pleasure without adding an ounce to my tonnage.

Lick the emotional factor in overweight by getting ready for bad days ahead of time. Don't fool yourself that you are above such childish nonsense. None of us ever gets past the point where we like to have our ruffled feelings soothed and our efforts rewarded.

A diet list isn't enough. Work out a plan to take care of the mental and emotional side of weight control. Prepare yourself for the common pitfalls that beset everyone who tries to reduce. Then get on your diet and see how quickly the ghost of your past failures evaporates. It's twice as easy to reduce if you keep your spirits up as your weight goes down.

You *can* stay on a diet.

Want to bet?

7. *Recall immediately.* As soon as you finish reading the article, repeat the five rules to yourself. No doubt you will find that you can do this perfectly. If you should have difficulty with one of the rules, however, find it again on the page, and establish another strong impression of this particular rule. Then say all the rules to yourself again, integrating this one into the list.

8. *Recall at delayed intervals.* Try telling the five rules to someone tomorrow, next week, a month from now. Delayed recall at intervals makes the impression more permanent.

Reading to Remember Answers to Questions

Try your speed on the following selection. You don't necessarily have to read slowly in order to memorize, particularly when you are not trying to retain details. You can now utilize two skills already developed in this book: (1) finding main ideas, and (2) rapid reading. In addition, utilize your new techniques of reading for recall.

1. Whip up your personal interest in sleep, perhaps by thinking about things that have happened to you in regard to sleep that were either satisfying or annoying.

2. Set for your purpose: to find and retain answers to some common questions about sleep.

3. Read rapidly, bestowing your attention intensively on

(a) the question, itself.

(b) the answer to the question.

4. After you have found a brief but complete answer to each question, reflect for a moment, associating the question and the answer firmly, and "depositing" both in your mind.

5. When you have finished reading the article, rapidly retrace your steps, reading the questions *only,* and trying to answer each question from memory. If you are not sure of your answer to a question, then renew your first impression by reading the answer

again, this time making sure that it is so deeply impressed that you will be able to recall it next time you try.

6. Compute your rate of reading.

7. Take the test following the selection.

8. Practice repetition and delayed recall at intervals by sharing the information with others.

Selection 2

BEGINNING TIME:_____

HR._____ MIN._____

Things to Know About Sleep[4]

Why do we sleep? We might better ask, "Why do we keep awake?" Sleep is a primitive state interrupted by wakefulness, according to physiologist Nathaniel Kleitman of the University of Chicago. We wake from necessity—of making a living and keeping alive—and from choice: to do the things we want to do. Sleep is fundamental to life itself: animals able to live 20 days without food have died after four or five when deprived of sleep; a man forced to stay awake would probably die after ten days, though he might live without eating as long as six weeks.

How much sleep is normal? Most people from 15 to 50 years of age average about eight hours out of the 24. But each person's normal needs differ. The person of limited interests takes more sleep than the mentally alert. The fellow looking forward eagerly to the day's activities is not a slugabed. This is testimony to our highly developed cerebration—the ideas and interests whirring about in our brains. Man probably sleeps fewer hours than any other animal.

If you don't have time to sleep eight hours, can you get by on five or six? More people ask this question than any other. The answer is: Try it and see. You are in the clear if you find that (a) you can wake at the right time without an alarm and (b) you are not sleepy during waking hours. A ten- or 15-minute snooze after lunch, in the late afternoon or after dinner, if you can work it in, may give you relief and leave you more alert for the ensuing hours. Just a stretch-out, with tight shoes off, even while you are awake, is beneficial.

Can you repay a sleep debt? Yes, unless you are too set in your habits of going to bed and getting up. Even though you have had an hour or two less sleep than usual each night all week, a late morning sleep can pay off the accumulated debt and leave you mentally and physically as alert as ever.

Do we need less sleep as we grow older? Yes. Newborn babies sleep

[4] Blade Clark and Norman Dine, *Reader's Digest*, September 1955, pp. 155-158 (Condensed from *Your Life*, September-October, 1955).

about two thirds of the time, adults only one third. Thus we double our period of wakefulness, and for every hour of sleep we can stay awake two hours instead of half an hour. Here is the average amount of sleep, by ages:

Age 6	about	11¼ hours
Age 10	"	10 "
Age 15	"	9 "
Age 20	"	8¼ "
Age 25	"	8 "
Age 60	"	7 "

But these are merely statistical averages. Some old people sleep exceptionally long hours. And those who appear to sleep few hours frequently take catnaps during the day.

Are some persons naturally inclined to sleep late? Yes. Experiments reveal that our ability to sleep varies with the time of day and night. This variation is reflected in our body temperature, which rises and falls about two degrees during each 24 hours, and is usually at its lowest from 2 to 6 a.m. As we get more active, the body turns the heat on; we are at our most alert mentally and physically when our temperature reaches its peak. . . .

We can adapt to different sleep schedules, but only after our body temperature has correspondingly shifted—and we eventually establish a new rhythm. The mother who is a night owl may force herself to rise early to get the children off to school for years, but when they grow up she is likely to revert to type and sleep until 10 or 11.

How harmful are sleeping pills? There are two types Powerful drugs, like the barbiturates, require a prescription. The milder sedative type does not. The barbiturate type is safe to use under a doctor's guidance. Getting the habit, however, is dangerous. You run the risk of using too many if the immediate results do not seem satisfactory, of sleeping in a drugged state when an emergency arises, and of letting a drug become a crutch. Moreover, the habitual user is likely to become irritable and difficult in personal relationships.

Non-prescription sleeping pills are safer because they are weak drugs and their effects are milder. (Some are related to the antihistamines, which have a well-known side effect of drowsiness.) Some people complain that they are too mild to be helpful. It is not yet known whether their constant use will have a bad effect on the brain or body.

Will coffee keep you awake? The stimulating element in coffee, tea, or cola drinks is caffein. Most habitual coffee-drinkers can ingest large quantities without marring their sleep. A minority, however, find caffein excessively stimulating. If these people drink coffee or eat a scoop of coffee ice cream for dessert at eight o'clock, they may not be able to sleep before 3 a.m.

Some *delude* themselves that coffee keeps them awake, and the delusion spoils their sleep. On the other hand, they can drink real coffee in the belief that it is decaffeinated and their sleep will be sound. This is merely one more evidence that the psychological factor in sleep is incalculable: any anxiety, whether about your sleep or coffee or unpaid bills, tends to keep you awake.

Are two hours' sleep before midnight worth four after? This seems to be an old wives' tale based on the obvious fact that since most of us have to rise early we get more rest if we go to bed early. Actually, it is not *when* you lie down that matters, *so long as you get your needed proportion of sleep to waking hours.* A few years ago a business-man inventor volunteered to try sleeping 30 minutes after every two and a half hours. After two years on this unsociable schedule he seemed to be in better health than before.

Can dreams mar your sleep? A vivid dream may result from great emotional agitation, which also produces bodily agitation. This agitation can produce pulse, respiration and visceral activity equal to the strain of running up a flight of stairs. Thus it can destroy rest.

Sleeping on your back increases the chance of lurid dreams. Their most frequent cause, however, is unresolved problems stirring emotions.

What is the best sleeping temperature? Fresh-air fiends who flood the room with cold breezes are inviting respiratory ailments and the hostility of chilled wives. The most favorable room temperature for restful sleep is about 55°, with a relative humidity of 45 percent. Individuals with a low metabolism, respiratory sensitivity, sinus problems, sluggish circulation or tendencies to arthritic or rheumatic twinges need a higher temperature.

It is true that lower temperatures favor deeper sleep than high temperatures. But whether the room is cold or warm, the climate under the blankets should remain constant—about a tropical 86°. A thermostatically controlled electric blanket can achieve this constant temperature.

Do we rest uniformly during the hours of sleep? No. Sleep comes in waves varying from deep to light, the first wave of about three hours' duration being the soundest. During the shallow phases we change position more often and dream more frequently.

Tests prove that rosy-fingered dawn has brass knuckles for most of us; light induces bodily activity and stimulates the kidneys. A bed either too Spartan or too sybaritic minimizes repose. Finally, any noise makes us move about in our beds.

You can increase the hours of rest in your sleep by making your bedroom as nearly light- and sound-proof as possible. A noise-muffling ventilator is good, as are sound-absorbing curtains or drapes.

How can you fall asleep again if you wake in the night? The ordinary person falls asleep again with the greatest of ease and doesn't even remember he waked. The insomniac is a special problem. Benjamin Franklin recommended two beds. Moving from a fatiguing, warm bed to a fresh, cool one was his method of invoking reluctant sleep. A neurologist recommends reliving the last dream situation lingering in one's mind, thus restoring the mental attitude conducive to the onset of sleep. Many persons recite soothing verses, repeat words or phrases, or count symbols. Others keep a carafe of a warm drink on the night table. These stratagems work best for those who think them up.

It is helpful to remember that the rest which comes from lying completely quiet is almost as good as sleep.

Is snoring curable? No. Its intensity, however, can be diminished.

Snoring is caused by nasal obstructions in the respiratory tract with a resulting vibration of the soft palate. Most snorers rhapsodize only when they sleep on their backs. A pad or rubber ball attached to the back of pajama or gown will discourage this position. Some surgeons have tried to shrink the offending soft palate to lessen its vibration; the operations have not yet proved widely successful.

The victims of snorers should try to recognize that snoring, after all, is only a sign of a contented sleeper. A victim might also equip himself with ear stops!

Is it bad to be roused suddenly from slumber? Yes. If you are having a nightmare, a shake, shout or strident alarm assaulting the senses may terrify you. Some doctors think the best way to be awakened is to have some obliging soul gently shake the corner of your blanket, bring you to your senses *gradually*. If there is no one to do this for you, be sure that your alarm clock has a soft, long call. Few persons sleep so deeply as to require a loud, shocking alarm.

Began   *Finished*   No. words: 1600

$$\frac{}{\text{No. seconds:}} \times 60 = \underline{\qquad} \text{ W.P.M.}$$

_____   _____   No. seconds:

Checking Comprehension

Answer Yes or No to each of these questions:

1. Is eight hours the normal amount of sleep for people fifteen to fifty years of age? _____
2. Can you repay a sleep debt? _____
3. Do we need less sleep as we grow older? _____
4. Are some persons naturally inclined to sleep late? _____
5. Are two hours of sleep before midnight worth four after? _____
6. Is the best room temperature for sleeping about 70°? _____
7. Do we rest uniformly during the hours of sleep? _____

8. Can the ordinary person fall asleep again if he wakes in the night? ————

9. Is snoring curable? ————

10. Is it bad to be roused suddenly from slumber? ————

See Answer Key on page 382.

Rate: W.P.M. ————   Comprehension Score: ————

Recalling Lists of Items

Sometimes we find a list of terms in a magazine or a book which we would like to remember. The list may consist of single sentences or phrases, each one constituting an isolated thought with some relationship to the general heading but none to the other separate phrases or sentences.

Such isolated items are usually difficult to recall because they are not embedded in related ideas which serve to build up associations as when a basic idea is supplemented by several related details. For help in recalling such a list, you need to rely to a large extent upon the strength of each separate impression.

There usually are some things, however, which you can do "on your own" to build up associations. You can sometimes organize and associate those items within the list that belong to a given classification; and you can associate these larger classifications with the major topic.

In working with the article that follows you will have an opportunity to apply these techniques.

1. Interest yourself in the topic of the selection. This will probably be easy to do, since all of us would like to know what our lives will be like twenty years from now.

2. Read the article for the purpose of finding out what it has to tell about our lives twenty years from now, and to see how many points you can remember to use in conversation later.

3. Read each item with the purpose of establishing a strong impression. Take time to reflect on each item if you like, comparing or contrasting it with your own personal experience. In doing this you will be building up associations of your own.

Do not time yourself in this exercise.

Additional directions will be given at the end of the article.

Selection 3

In Our Crystal Ball[5]

What will our lives be like 20 years from now?

All the experts associated with the COMPANION—our consultants and editor specialists—were asked that question recently by Article Editor Robert Moskin. They put their experience and their imaginations to work to foretell what they think our world may be like in 1975. Here are a few of the things they say we'll be enjoying by then:

• In the supermarket we'll only have to push buttons, not wire carts, and our purchases will assemble automatically at the check-out counter.

• We'll cook by radar in long, narrow ovens. Put the food in and it's perfectly done in seconds. There's no heat and you can cook right in your serving dishes.

• A trap door in the dining table will lead to a dishwasher into which you simply push the dishes. When they are washed, a gadget raises them again so you're ready to set the table.

• We'll preserve food by atomic-ray sterilization.

• Fabrics will repel dirt and no longer have to be cleaned.

• We'll have an electric memorizer that records a book you want to read in your unconscious brain. You'll just "tune in" and enjoy it later.

• You will take your baby to a psychological well-baby clinic as you take him to the pediatrician today.

• We'll be able to buy psychoanalysis insurance to protect us against mental illness.

• Teen-agers will plan longer careers and later marriages.

• We'll have a mood counter, like a Geiger counter, that tells you what your husband's mood is when you want to discuss a new hat.

• We may be taking hormones to change our moods, cheer us when we are exhausted and calm us when we are angry.

• Men will help with the housework even more than they do now.

These are a few of the things Bob Moskin described when he spoke to 1,100 teen-agers and their adult advisers and sponsors at the annual Junior Achievement awards banquet in Minneapolis. Chairman of the dinner was Philip Pillsbury, chairman of the board of Pillsbury Mills, who added to the prediction that we'll have some of the food wonders of our future even sooner than 1975.

4. Try to recall as many of the items as you can without referring to the article.

5. How many did you recall?_____

6. If you missed several, try some *logical* organization of your own. See how many of them can be organized around some common

[5] Woodrow Wirsig, *Woman's Home Companion,* August 1955, p. 14.

center to which they are related, and how many still stand out in isolation.

As an example, in studying the list you may find that (a) four of the items have to do with food from the time it is purchased until dinner is finished; (b) one of them has to do with clothes; (c) three of them have to do with members of the family (baby, teen-agers, husband); (d) four of them have to do with psychology—remembering, moods, psychoanalysis.

And all of these as they will be changed in twenty years!

7. Find the items that belong with each of these broader classifications.

8. Now, thinking in terms of changes which may take place in our lives in regard to food, clothing, members of the family, and psychology, again try to enumerate the twelve items, recalling the complete group associated with each classification.

9. How many did you recall this time? _____

This type of reading is not encountered frequently enough to warrant giving more space to it here. It is hoped, however, that in working through this exercise, you have "picked up" some clues to use should you, in the future, encounter in your reading isolated lists of items which you wish to remember.

Utilizing Preview Techniques

Preview techniques will assist you in retaining the gist of an article which contains subheads and which is accompanied by visual material.

Some people recall what they have seen in a picture, map, or chart more vividly than the more abstract concepts which they gather from printed words only. If such visual aids are provided in connection with an article containing information which you would like to recall, make the fullest use of them.

If the article has subheadings, then you may be sure that you are going to find in the text many ideas related to each heading. This being the case, you can use each heading as a nucleus around which to build your associations.

Converting the headings into questions is a very helpful procedure in reading to retain the gist of an article. You will be asked to use this technique in the exercise that follows.

1. As usual draw upon any inherent interest which you may have

in the subject of backaches. Perhaps you frequently have backache or have had backache in the past; or perhaps some member of your family has backache. Revive your remembrance of any personal experiences you have had with backache, as interest background for reading this selection.

2. Set this purpose for your reading: to find out and keep in mind information which will be helpful to you personally or to someone you know.

3. Preview the headings and change each one into a question. Write the question over each heading:

What Is the History of Low Backache?
What Are the Chief Causes of Backache?
What Is the Physical Structure of the Back?
What Are the Symptoms of Backache?
What Is the Diagnosis and Treatment?
What Are Preventive Measures?

4. Skim the first four introductory paragraphs for main ideas. Establish intense impressions of these main ideas with a view of retaining them. Associate them together as belonging to the history of backache.

5. Read the question which constitutes the first subheading, concentrating your attention strongly on this heading in order to establish a vivid impression.

6. Read rapidly to find the answer to this question and the details which build up meaningful associations with it.

7. Stop and reflect on the question and the answers, testing yourself to see whether you established deep enough impressions and sufficient associations to be able to recall them later. If not, reestablish your impressions and strengthen your associations until you think they will be effective in facilitating recall.

8. Continue to work with each subheading and the text beneath it in the same way.

9. Do this exercise under timed conditions. But don't let timing prevent you from concentrating and reflecting on the things that you are trying to remember. It takes time to concentrate and build associations if you are reading to recall rather than just reading for general and temporary impressions. Even so, you shouldn't dawdle over the selection. High tempo will sharpen your attention and concentration. So work as fast as you can while still accomplishing your purpose.

10. When you have finished reading, take the test.

Selection 4

BEGINNING TIME:_____
HR._____ MIN._____

Low Backache[6]

History of Low Backache

Low Backache is one of the most common medical problems today. It was probably known even to prehistoric and primitive man, but currently is one of the more serious by-products of civilization. Low backache may occur as a symptom of general diseases such as influenza or grippe, local disease such as inflammation of one of the pelvic organs, or as a consequence of disease or injury to the lower part of the back itself. The spine may be affected by such diseases as arthritis of various types, infection such as tuberculosis, and various types of tumors. In the majority of cases, however, low backache is due to a mechanical abnormality of the lower spine, with a superimposed strain or injury.

Some 50 years ago, the popular term for low backache was lumbago. This was a descriptive term, comparable to headache or stomach-ache, and had no specific meaning. It included a variety of diagnoses. Several decades ago the term "sacroiliac" became popular for all types of low backache. It was assumed that the sacroiliac joint slipped and that the slipping was the cause of the backache. In some cases, there was pain down the leg, called sciatica. The assumption was that the sciatic nerve was pressed upon as a consequence of the slipping where it crossed the sacroiliac joint. These theories were never proved. It is now known that the sacroiliac is one of the strongest joints in the body and that it probably does not slip except under very unusual circumstances. It is also recognized that such a minor slipping could not cause pressure on the sciatic nerve. The sacroiliac joint is occasionally affected by arthritis or infection, and it may be damaged with severe injuries such as fractures of the pelvis. It also relaxes toward the end of pregnancy. Otherwise it is rarely a problem.

It has been known for the past 30 years that the usual source of low backache is the lumbo-sacral joint. As this joint is very close to the sacroiliac, and not easy to distinguish, the cause for the confusion is obvious. The lumbo-sacral joint is the junction between the lumbar spine and the pelvis, specifically between the last lumbar vertebra and the sacrum. The average person has five lumbar vertebrae, but a small percentage of people have four or six. The number of lumbar vertebrae is not of great consequence. It is the construction of the lumbo-sacral joint

[6] M. Beckett Howorth, *Consumers' Research Bulletin*, August 1954, pp. 18-21.

that is of considerable importance, as well as the strains placed upon it.

Most vertebrate animals walk on all fours, with the spine in a more or less horizontal position. The higher apes walk in a semi-erect position, but frequently resort to the position on all fours. Man alone stands and walks erect. The infant's spine at birth is flexed or bent forward, and the hips and knees are drawn up. Gradually the spine and the legs straighten out in the first year of life so that the infant, when he stands, can assume the erect position. In this process the lumbar spine develops a hollow, or lordosis, whereas the process of becoming erect produces a mechanical strain between the movable lumbar spine and the fixed pelvis. The lumbo-sacral joint bears the whole weight of the trunk as well as the strains incident to the movements and use of the trunk. Nature has been unkind to man in fairly frequently producing deformities of various types at the lumbo-sacral joint. Man has been unkind to himself in using his back carelessly or recklessly, or in not keeping it in good physical condition.

Chief Causes of Backache

Posture is very often an important factor in low backache, not only the posture of the spine but also of the feet and legs. Good sitting posture is one of balance, with the head, shoulders, and trunk erect and centered over the pelvis. Good standing posture should also be erect and balanced, with the head, shoulders, hips, knees, and ankles in vertical alignment, without tension or strain. In this position there is little or no strain on the lower back. In the usual type of poor posture, the body makes an S curve as seen from the side, with the head and neck thrust forward, the upper back stooped, and the chest flat, the forward curve of the lower back increased, and the abdomen prominent or sagging, the pelvis well in front of the vertical line, the hips and knees hyper-extended or bent backwards. This posture is one of considerable strain on the low back, particularly for people who are long in the standing position. A person who is overweight or obese, with a large protruding abdomen, is thrown further out of balance, with increased strain on the low back. The same effect is seen in the latter part of pregnancy, but fortunately is of shorter duration.

The environment, as it relates to the back, is often of importance in producing back strain. A soft, sagging bed increases the strain on the back, whether the individual sleeps on his face, side, or back. On the face, the spine and hips are hyper-extended and stretched. On the side, the lower side is stretched, the upper side compressed, the spine curved to the side. Likewise a soft, low deep chair may be an important factor in backache. Many living room chairs are of this type, as well as many of the seats in airplanes, buses, and automobiles. Theater seats are often too small, crowded together, and sometimes have a back which is much too curved from side to side. Such shoes as sneakers, loafers, ballet slippers, and pumps, are light and comfortable on the feet, but they are not suitable for long standing and much walking, and are likely to increase the strain on the back. High heels are even worse in throwing the body off balance and increasing the tendency to poor posture as well as back strain. Knock-knees and poor foot posture also aggravate back strain.

Physical Structure of the Back

The support of the trunk is the spinal column, consisting usually of 24 vertebrae with their joints and ligaments. The ligaments of the spinal column bind the vertebrae together and support them strongly at the extremes of motion, but they are not subject to voluntary control. The spine receives additional support from the muscles which act upon it.

Several groups of muscles run lengthwise along the spine and are intimately connected with it. Other muscles, such as those of the chest and abdomen, while not directly connected with the spine, nevertheless act as spinal muscles. It is the muscles which give motion to the spine and control its position. The health and strength of these muscles is of utmost importance in protecting the spine from injury as well as in effective performance of the body. Inactivity of disuse results in weak flabby muscles which are of little service. Excessive activity may result in muscle injury due to strain or fatigue.

Symptoms

Low backache may occur at any age, but it is uncommon in children and most common in middle-age adults. It occurs in any race or in either sex but is more frequent in civilized urban communities.

The symptoms of low back trouble vary considerably in different individuals, and usually from time to time in the same person. The predominant complaint is an ache or pain in the lower back, sometimes on one side, sometimes in the middle. The pain may extend to the back of the hip, or even down the back or outer side of the thigh or leg as far as the foot. Leg pain of this type is commonly due to sciatic nerve root pressure or irritation. The back pain may begin suddenly or gradually. It may be associated with an injury or illness or may begin without apparent reason. The pain may be a dull ache or sharp; it may come and go or be present all the time. Ordinarily the pain varies in intensity somewhat with lying, standing, or sitting. It is apt to be worse after long sitting, especially in a poor chair, or lying on a poor bed. As time passes, the pain may improve, get worse, or remain the same, depending upon circumstances. An attack may begin with a definite injury such as a fall, a severe twist, a strain from doing heavy lifting, or by accumulated small injuries. Unaccustomed activities, such as heavy house cleaning, moving furniture, gardening, or other outdoor work, may provoke an attack. At times there is a "slip" or "crack" or feeling of "giving way" in the lower back at the onset of the trouble. . . .

Diagnosis and Treatment

Self-diagnosis and self-treatment are risky and should be avoided. There are, however, certain measures which are safe and often helpful that may be used for mild backaches of short duration.

The bed should be firm and flat. This requires a mattress with strong inner springs (not the type used in the usual commercial mattress), or a mattress of cotton felt or hair. A foam-rubber mattress is intermediate between the usual innerspring type and the felt or hair mattress. The box spring should be strong. With the usual type of box spring, it is better to put a board, such as a piece of plywood one-half to three-quarters inch thick, between the mattress and the springs. When the person lies upon it, the bed should remain flat.

The right kind of chair is one that is erect, firm, with arms, and adapted to the size and shape of the individual. The back of the chair should be curved to the shape of the normal trunk. The depth of the chair should be equal to the length of the thighs, and the height equal to the length of the legs below the knee.

Simple backache may be relieved by heat, supplied by a lamp, electric pad, hot towels, hot tub, or hot-water bag. The heat should be warm, not hot, and used for 20 or 30 minutes two or three times daily. For sleeping, a hot-water bag is safest. Heat which is too strong, or used too long, is apt to damage the skin. Diathermy or short wave produce heat deep in the tissues but should be used only under medical direction and supervision. Massage, if skillful and not too strenuous, may be helpful, but should not be given until the diagnosis is made.

Supports, such as adhesive strapping, a belt, or a corset, may be useful, although strapping tends to become loosened and is often harmful to the skin. Stronger supports should be reserved for prescription by an orthopedist.

The safest medicine for the relief of pain is aspirin, which may be taken in doses of five to ten grains and as often as three or four times a day. . . .

Manipulation is sometimes helpful for backache, although many persons have had repeated manipulations over a long period of time without any real improvement. Manipulation is most suitable for the type of back which snaps or cracks at the time of onset of pain, but should not be given without a preliminary careful medical examination, and X-rays. . . .

If a mild backache does not promptly improve or subside with the measures already indicated, it is imperative that a competent diagnosis be secured, followed by proper treatment under medical supervision.

Early attention to the problem is called for since it is more difficult to treat successfully backache of long duration. . . .

Sometimes there is a rupture of the disk between the vertebrae, with extrusion of the soft interior portion and with pressure against the nerve root, causing sciatica. Persistent or severe sciatica always calls for competent evaluation, usually by an orthopedist or neurologist or both. . . .

Preventive Measures

The most important aspect of low backache is prevention. Since low backache is so common, an understanding of its causes and prevention is of great value. Although the individual cannot alter the internal structure of his back, he can greatly reduce the stresses and strains which lead to pain. Preventive measures include a flat bed, proper chairs, and proper shoes. The avoidance or correction of obesity is of great importance. The avoidance or correction of poor posture is also of much value.

Proper use of the body is also essential. It is common, especially for housewives, to lift with the knees straight and the body bent forward at the waist. This puts the whole strain on the lower back, and is likely to result in backache or acute strain. It is far better to lift with the legs, starting with the legs flexed and then straightening them, with the trunk fairly erect, and the weight held in the arms close to the body. . . .

The basic principles of muscular activity should be observed. The muscles should be warmed up by graduated exercise at the beginning of each season's activity, and at the beginning of each day. Muscles which are soft and flabby from sedentary occupations or disuse during most of the year are not in condition for heavy work. Similarly, if heavy work is to be continued for several hours, it is better to take an intermission or to stop before real fatigue occurs.

In summary, low backache is not a simple disease, but a symptom due to a variety of causes. Simple low backache of short duration may be relieved by a group of simple measures. Persistent or severe low backache, particularly if accompanied by sciatica, requires a careful diagnostic examination by a competent physician or orthopedist and careful evaluation of treatment. Low backache can, to a large extent, be prevented by an understanding of its basic causes and the avoidance of abuse of the back.

Began   *Finished*   No. words: 2100

$$\frac{}{\text{No. seconds:}} \times 60 = \underline{} \text{ W.P.M.}$$

_____   _____   No. seconds:

Checking Comprehension

Write the correct words in the spaces to complete the sentences below.

1. Some fifty years back a popular name for low backache was

_____ .

2. It has been known for thirty years that the usual source of low backache is the _____ _____ joint.

3. The chief causes of low backache are (1) environmental factors and (2) _____ .

4. The structure of the spinal column is made up of 24 vertebrae and several groups of _____ .

5. Low backache is most prevalent in _____ adults.

6. The predominant symptom is an ache or pain in the _____

_____ .

7. Self-diagnosis and self-treatment should be _____ .

8. The safest medicine for relief of pain is _____ .

9. Preventive measures include the use of the right furniture and clothing, good posture, and avoidance of obesity. Another preventive measure is _____ _____ _____ _____ _____ .

10. Low backache is not a disease in itself but a _____ due to a variety of difficulties.

See Answer Key, page 382.

Rate: W.P.M. _____   Comprehension Score: _____

Recalling Details

Usually a person does not care to remember all the specific details in a long technical article. He is more apt to find a paragraph here and there which he considers to be so important that he would like to remember all the particulars in that certain paragraph. On the other hand, there may be occasions in which a person wishes to remember all details in a series of paragraphs.

In case you wish to remember the details either in a single paragraph or in a series of paragraphs, you have already learned the basic techniques. You know how to analyze a paragraph into its main idea, its major details, and its minor details in terms of their respective relationships. In using this procedure you have applied strong attention in order to make the analysis, and during the course of the analysis you built associations in terms of relationships. In other words, you have been using the techniques which contribute most to recall: establishing strong impressions and gathering vivid associations. Probably when you finished working with a paragraph in Chapter Seven you could have recalled it in all its details if you had tried. Missing in the process which you used in Chapter Seven were your *will* to remember, your *purpose* for remembering, and *practice in reviving* the details in your memory.

Since relationships or associations are so important in recalling details, it will help you to take an over-all view of relationships in a paragraph or in an entire selection, as you would take an over-all view of a park from a window in a hotel, or of a valley from the top of a mountain, or of a town from an airplane.

For the sake of illustration, let us suppose that you have viewed a city park for the first time from a high floor in a hotel. If so you probably took a bird's-eye-view mental snapshot of the entire park. In your first glance you noted that as a whole the park covered about two acres and that is was given over to recreational activities, which were located in different parts of the park. (This corresponds to "the main idea" in reading.) You might have concentrated next on a lake in one section of the park (corresponding to one of the important subordinate thoughts in reading) and noted that there were canoes and bathers (details belonging to the lake). You may have noticed also that another section of the park was given over to games (a second important subordinate), and that the game area made provisions for tennis, baseball, and quoits (details belonging to the game section). You may have noted next that another section provided for picnickers (a third important subordinate), and this section contained tables, benches, and outdoor fireplaces.

Turning from the window you no doubt could close your eyes and visualize this park with its sub-areas and the details that belonged in each. Your understanding of relationships would enable you to repicture mentally all details in the park, and you would see each detail in its right setting. You woudn't recall boats in the game section or an outdoor fireplace in the lake section. You would readily associate details with the area in which they were meaningful and appropriate.

If you apply this same technique in reading separate paragraphs and entire articles, you will find that it is very beneficial to you in recalling detailed facts. In reading, however, major "areas" and their details, clear-cut relationships and associations, are not so apparent. You must work out these relationships and organize them into a total structure bared to its *minimum essentials;* and then concentrate on this stripped-down structure. You will now be given some exercises designed to help you in recalling details in an article in the same way that you would remember details in a park after viewing it from a high window.

Exercise 1

Recalling exact details with the use of an outline. In working with the paragraph that follows, your first guidance will be directed toward establishing the "stripped-down" structure, and recalling the details through concentration on and association with this bare structure. The "structure" in this case will be an outline which you are to complete.

Read the paragraph below. Find the main idea. Find two other ideas of next relative importance which are used in expanding upon the main idea. Each of these two larger sub-ideas in turn has several detailed facts which cluster under it. So you need to grasp these details in each case in relationship to the larger sub-heading to which they are related and also in relationship to the total topic —just as you would view a park in terms of its separate areas and the details that belong to each.

If you read for the purpose of discerning the above pattern, you should have little difficulty in filling in the outline. Should there be details that you can't recall, refer to the paragraph for them. You are not asked to recall as a result of your first reading.

Technical division of labor developed with the growth of the factory system and is both the cause of the use of machinery and, in turn, the result of the use of machines. When tasks are reduced to simple repetitive motions, they can be done more cheaply by machines than by man. Machines are more regular and accurate in their motions than men, and they do not tire. But machines, once installed, call . . . for new types of labor—some to design, set up, and attend the machines; others to take charge of the general management of the factory; others to sell the product; and still others, largely unskilled, to feed the machines and take away finished materials.[7]

Write answers to the questions below in as few words as possible.

I. What is the main idea? _____

_____

II. What are the two major sub-topics, and what are the details belonging to each of those larger sub-topics? (Refer back to the paragraph if necessary)

   A. First large sub-topic: _____

_____

---

[7] John Ise, *Economics*, Harper, 1946, Chap. 6, p. 71.

Details under sub-topic:

(a) _____

(b) _____

B. Second large sub-topic: _____

Details under the sub-topic:

(a) _____

(b) _____

(c) _____

(d) _____

Check your answers with the Answer Key on page 383.

Now that you have extracted the essence of the paragraph, proceed to fix the major thoughts and minor details in your mind. Take a "snapshot" of the outline. Read with intensive attention directed to the purpose of recalling the entire structure.

Close your eyes and see if you can recall the larger ideas together with their details. Concentrate especially on the ones that you forgot. Then look at the entire group again, noting those particular facts in their relationship to the others with which they are associated. Now close your eyes and see if you can recall the entire outline with all its details, correctly and completely. You should be entirely successful this time.

Perhaps at this point you are saying, "I don't have time for all that." You don't need to take time for "all that" except on the rare occasions when you must remember exact details as a physician or a lawyer must do. Under such conditions you may find outlining helpful.

Exercise 2

Recalling minor details without the use of an outline. Try reading the paragraph below for the purpose of recalling major and minor details, without the use of any pencil assistance.

Analyze the paragraph for the main idea and the major and minor details. Concentrate on this structure with the intention of making a deep enough impression to be able to recall the entire paragraph. Build your associations in this case by thinking in terms of one idea logically leading to another.

After finishing your work on the paragraph take the test that follows.

Radiators for hotwater heating must have air valves for the escape of air when they are being filled and for the admission of air when they are being emptied. They could not be filled with water unless air was allowed to escape. Expansion tanks, sometimes placed in the attic, are used in hotwater heating systems to provide for the expansion of water when it is heated. But unless the level in the tank is regulated carefully, the water may overflow, and in extremely cold weather it may freeze. With the newer hotwater heating systems, the expansion tank is placed in the basement. Thus the water is allowed to expand into a tank which is partly filled with air. As the water expands, the air is compressed. When the water cools and contracts, the compressed air forces it back into the pipes and radiators. The flow of water in and out of the radiator may be controlled by valves which are constructed so as to operate automatically.[8]

Checking Recall

Write a word or a phrase to answer each question.

1) What is the subject of this paragraph? _____
2) What must they have for the escape of air? _____
3) They cannot be filled with water unless _____
   _____

4) Where are expansion tanks sometimes placed? _____
5)
& Unless the level in the tank is regulated what two things may
6) happen?
   (a) _____ (b) _____
7) Where is the expansion tank placed in the new systems?
   _____

8) As the water expands in the tank, what happens to the air?
   _____

9) When the water cools and contracts, what does the air do?
   _____

10) By what may the flow of water be controlled? _____

Check your answers with the Answer Key on page 383.

Recalling Numbers

It is of the utmost importance for a businessman to be able to recall accurately numbers which appear in the reading that he does in connection with his work or numbers which have a bearing on the interests of his firm. Perhaps nothing would be of greater

---

[8] Ira C. Davis and Richard W. Sharpe, *Science,* Holt, 1943, p. 83.

consequence to most businessmen than learning to recall numbers readily and accurately.

Some people seem to possess a photographic memory which enables them to revive the image of an entire series of numbers in exact reproduction. Perhaps this ability to receive and recall visual impressions could be cultivated to a greater degree in all of us. We don't know for sure that everyone could develop a high degree of visual imagery. If you think you might be able to develop a photographic memory for numbers, cultivate it and see.

Here we are relying upon sharp first impressions, plus logical thinking in terms of relationships, as the fundamental techniques for preparing to recall numbers met in a printed text.

Many people are of the opinion that factual material which includes numbers is more difficult to read and recall than text which contains words only. As a matter of fact, it is often easier to remember details containing number facts than word facts alone. Particularly is this true in cases where a pattern of number relationships can be worked out. This is the type of practice which you will be given in working with the exercises that follow.

Analyzing and Recalling Number Relationships

Exercise 3

1. Read the paragraph for the purpose of obtaining information about President Eisenhower's memoirs.

2. Analyze as you go along to ascertain the main idea and the minor ideas.

For anyone connected with the top management of the war, the writing of memoirs seems to be a profitable and a prevalent occupation. General Eisenhower is said to have sold his memoirs for a sum somewhere between $500,000 and $750,000. This information is reported with a comment which imputes to the General some extraordinary prescience in the matter of federal income taxes that saved him about $250,000.[9]

3. In answering these questions refer to the paragraph if necessary:

A. What is the main idea? Write it in the fewest possible words:

---

[9] *Taxes*, April 1948, p. 292.

B. What two facts are told which expand upon this idea? Write each one in the fewest possible words:

(1) ———————————————————————

(2) ———————————————————————

Your answer to the first question should be something like this: *Writing memoirs is profitable*. This idea is the "heart" of the whole paragraph.

4. Check your answers. After stating the main idea, the paragraph expands upon this basic thought by giving examples which reinforce it. Two detailed statements follow which are related to the main idea: (1) Eisenhower sold his memoirs for between $500,000 and $750,000, and (2) he saved $250,000 in income tax.

5. Try to recall your answers to the question. Lift your eyes from the page. Tell yourself the main idea and the two related lesser ideas.

6. Did you have some trouble in remembering the exact amounts of money? If so, use the technique of thinking in terms of relationships between the numbers. Fix one basic figure in mind and relate the other figures to it, proportionately. In this particular case, the basic number, a round one which is easy to recall, is $500,000. Concentrate on this figure and impress this one number on your mind as a "frame of reference" for recalling the others. How much more is $750,000 than $500,000? Then it would appear that the author didn't know within $250,000—that is, within ½ of the smaller sum or ⅓ of the larger sum—how much Eisenhower received. This is quite a margin of uncertainty. Thinking in terms of ½ of the smaller number and ⅓ of the larger, do you readily recall the two numbers in the first of the two minor statements?

Similarly, think in terms of number relationships in memorizing the third number mentioned. If Eisenhower saved $250,000 in income taxes, what part of the sum that he received was saved? If he received $500,000 he saved income tax totaling ½ of the full amount. If he received $750,000, what part of his total compensation did he save? The answer is ⅓, of course. Now, reply quickly: What were the two possible amounts Eisenhower received? How much income tax did he save?

Did the association of these numbers with their ideas, together with thinking about relationships between the numbers themselves, help you to grasp these exact figures clearly? Do you think that you would recall not only the detailed statements above but also the exact numbers if you wanted to use them in conversation next week?

The answer should be Yes to both questions if you followed through the procedures carefully and thoughtfully.

Exercise 4

1. Try working with this paragraph in the same way that you did with the one in the preceding exercise.

Mrs. Baker saved us money as a collector. She worked for 2 hours a day when we needed her over a period of 3 years. During this period her salary amounted to $1,514.25. Her collections of delinquent accounts over this same period amounted to $15,127.00. If these accounts had been collected by a commercial agency, they would have charged ⅓ of the total amount for their fee. So the saving was considerable.

2. Write your answers to these questions:
What is the main idea of this paragraph?

_____

What are the exact details which tell how Mrs. Baker saved her firm money?
(a) (The first set of details is concerned with two small numbers, one of which follows the other in consecutive order. Noting this relationship should help you to recall these numbers.)

_____

(b) (When writing the second detailed idea, use a round number. It will be easier to remember a round number than a sum involving a small amount in dollars and cents.)

_____

(c) (In writing the third detailed statement, again use a round number. Is there any similarity between the round number in (a) and the round number in (c)? What fractional part of the sum in (b) is the sum in (c)? Noting this similarity and relationship will help you to recall both numbers.)

_____

(d) (When writing your condensed statement of the fourth detail think about the fraction particularly. That's an easy number to remember.)

_____

(e) (Figure out in round numbers what the fractional part of the total amount would be in dollars. Write this sum on this blank. What is the relationship between this sum and the sum mentioned in (b), using round numbers in both cases?)

_____

Your statement for the main idea should be: "Mrs. Baker saved her firm money as a collector." This is the "hub" idea in the paragraph. The details related to this main idea are (a) she worked 2 hours a day for 3 years (the consecutive order of 2 and 3 makes it easy to remember these two numbers); (b) her salary was $1,500; (c) she collected $15,000 (the similarity of figures in the two numbers $1,500 and $15,000 and their relative proportion give you "handles" to take hold of in remembering them. At a glance you see that her salary was only 10% of her collections); (d) a commercial collector would have charged ⅓ of the total collections ($5,000). (The fraction ⅓ is a number that you will have no trouble at all in recalling. It adds to the meaning of the paragraph if you convert "⅓ of total collections" into dollars. And after following through the thread of thought to this point, you will probably want to subtract Mrs. Baker's salary from the sum a commercial collector would have charged and find how much money she saved her firm.)

As a result of your study and practice in building associations by noting relationships, you should recall the accurate answers to the detailed questions below with practically no effort at all. It is assumed that you are starting with this knowledge: the main thought of the paragraph is "Mrs. Baker saved her company money." Now test your recall of details:

1. How many hours per day for how many years did Mrs. Baker work for the firm? _____
2. What did she earn during that time? _____
3. How much did she collect for the company? _____
4. How much would a commercial concern have charged to make these collections? _____
5. How much did Mrs. Baker save her firm? _____

Check your answers with the Answer Key on page 383.

Exercise 5

Read the paragraph below for the purpose of remembering details, including all numbers. Associate the numbers both with the ideas and with each other. Use all the techniques you have used in preceding exercises.

Croesus was the first of all colossal millionaires. The extent of his wealth may be estimated by his gifts to foreign temples. His gift to the temple and people of Delphi, according to Herodotus, who copied from the records, was a pyramid of 117 bricks surmounted by a lion; the bricks each 18 inches long by 9 inches wide and 3 inches thick; the four top bricks of pure gold and weighing over 400 pounds apiece. The other 113 bricks had a certain alloy of silver added to the gold. The lion was of pure gold and weighed 800 pounds. The value of the pyramid in gold and silver alone was $3,500,000, and, with the addition of 15% for the work of the artists, amounted to over $4,000,000. Roughly, the purchasing power of money in the sixth century B.C. was twenty times what it is now. Therefore the modern equivalent of this gift would be $80,000,000.

Checking Recall

Write the answers to the questions below without referring to the paragraph.

1. In what order does Croesus come in enumerating the millionaires of the world? _____
2. To the people of what country did he make a gift? _____
3. How many bricks were in the pyramid? _____
4. What were the dimensions of each brick? _____
5. How much did the four pure gold bricks weigh? _____
6. How many bricks had silver alloy in them? _____
7. How much did the lion weigh? _____
8. What was the value of the pyramid in gold and silver alone?
   _____
9. What was the value when the work of the artist was included?
   _____
10. What would the modern equivalent of the gift amount to?
   _____

Check your answers by referring to the paragraph.

Selection 1

Read the selection below for the purpose of recalling the most important numbers. Use procedures previously suggested.

Time yourself on this one.

BEGINNING TIME:_____
HR._____ MIN._____

How Much Should You Spend for Entertaining Customers?[10]

If you spend $53 a month for entertaining customers, you're hitting the sum averaged by electrical distributors' outside salesmen across the

[10] *Electrical Wholesaling,* October 1954, pp. 50-51.

nation. That is assuming, of course, that you are among the 58 per cent who do entertain customers. This conclusion is drawn from a recent nation-wide survey conducted by ELECTRICAL WHOLESALING. A summary of the findings can be found at the top of the opposite page.

Actually, the monthly entertainment expenses reported by distributor salesmen ranged all over the lot. They started at $2 and climbed to $375. Only a fraction of the salesmen—10 per cent, to be exact—were within $10 of the $53 average. As a matter of fact, a much larger group—17 per cent—indicated customer wining and dining expenses of $100 and more a month.

This wide range probably reflects (1) a firm's liberality or lack of it when it comes to salesmen's expense accounts and (2) a salesman's inclinations and his evaluation of what it takes to get business in his territory. One thing is certain, however: there may be general agreement on the effectiveness of entertainment as a selling tool, but there's hardly any agreement on how much to spend.

One eyebrow-raising fact brought out by the survey is that the salesmen who spend the most for entertaining customers don't necessarily have the biggest incomes. Only one third of the salesmen who averaged $100 or more a month for entertainment expenses earn over $10,000 a year. The other two thirds earn between $4,000 and $9,999. The income of the salesman who reported an average business entertainment expense of $375 a month is in the $7,000-9,999 range.

Some regional differences showed up regarding entertainment. The most pronounced one involved the Northeast and the Midwest. Only 42 per cent of the salesmen in the Northeast entertain customers, while 73 per cent do in the Midwest. What's more, the midwesterners outspend their northeastern counterparts almost two-to-one—$62 a month as against $34.

The home is the site for some of the entertaining of customers done by electrical wholesale salesmen. A majority of 63 per cent said they occasionally make use of their homes for this purpose. Regionally, this practice finds most acceptance in the Far West, least in the Northeast.

A minority of salesmen—41 per cent—periodically send gifts to customers. Christmas provides the occasion for most of these goodwill gestures. The gifts most often given: food, liquor, candy, cigars, theater and sports tickets, appliances—in that order.

Began   *Finished*   No. words: 454

$$\frac{}{\text{No. seconds:}} \times 60 = \underline{} \text{ W.P.M.}$$

_____   _____

Checking Comprehension

From memory answer the questions in the spaces provided.

1. What is the average monthly bill for entertaining customers of electrical distributors' outside salesmen across the nation?

2. What per cent of electrical distributors' salesmen entertain customers?

3. What was the highest monthly entertainment expense reported?

4. What per cent reported expenses within $10 of the average?

5. What per cent reported monthly entertainment expenses of over $100 for customer entertainment?

6. What fractional part of the total number of salesmen who reported expenses of over $100 per month earn over $10,000 per year?

7. The author compared the entertainment expenses of salesmen in the Northeast and the Midwest. In which area do more salesmen entertain?

8. In which of the above areas are entertainment expenses higher?

9. What per cent of salesmen occasionally make use of their homes for entertainment?

10. What per cent of salesmen periodically send gifts to customers?

ANSWERS

1.   6.

2.   7.

3.   8.

4.   9.

5.   10.

Check your answers with the Answer Key, page 383.

Selection 2

Read the article below for the purpose of obtaining and recalling both numbers and detailed ideas. Use techniques suggested in the preceding exercises.

BEGINNING TIME:_____

HR._____ MIN._____

Time yourself and when finished take a test of your recall.

Watch That Turnpike![11]

As the sedan skimmed over the unbroken ribbon of the Merritt Parkway, Connecticut's super-highway, a feminine voice came in loud and clear from the back seat:

"Navigator to pilot! That blur you just passed was no cow. It was New Haven. Now throttle back, Jack, or the children and I will bail out at the next interchange."

Such aerial argot is peculiarly apt on America's new super-highways which offer motorists an exciting new "wild blue yonder." Drivers unfamiliar with their wonders have much in common with propeller pilots checking out on jets. Dead ahead for both lie new sensations in speed and travel.

Every foot of the road is designed for pushing past motoring's old 50-miles-an-hour barrier. It has no traffic lights, stop signs, cross streets, or pedestrians. It's flat and it's straight and, like a hopped-up rocket, it thunders across cities, lances through mountains, soars over rivers and zooms above plains. But like flying the "hot pipes," driving on this modern road requires a special combination of good eyes, good brakes, and good sense.

Millions of motorists will soon be acquiring that skill on the network of express highways being spun across the country. Fifteen states, including Ohio, West Virginia, Pennsylvania, New Jersey, New York, Colorado, Oklahoma, North Carolina, Kentucky, Florida, and California, are building or planning additional multi-million-dollar super-roads.

Most ambitious project is New York's 535 miles of Thruway, being laid at a cost of half a billion dollars. Virginia and North Carolina are planning 55 miles of ocean highway between Virginia Beach and Nags Head. Being blueprinted is a new road linking Dallas and Houston, supposedly more splendiferous, in the Texas tradition, than any other in the world.

All of these will be divided-lane, controlled-access expressways, 752 miles of which are already in use, with another 1,408 miles soon to come. Where they link, drivers will find themselves fitted with seven-league boots of wondrous power.

Take the New Jersey Turnpike, a 118-mile flying carpet that wings over the densest traffic in the world at a legal 60 miles an hour. From Manhattan's George Washington Bridge, it whips you breathlessly south to a point on the New Jersey shore opposite Wilmington, Delaware, in less than two hours. In pre-turnpike times that trip took from three to six hours.

En route you leap cleanly over 195 crossroads and railroads, vault 68

11 Jay J. Dugan, *Coronet*, April 1953, pp. 34-37.

waterways, and dart through a dozen heavily-populated areas. If westward bound, you will soon be able to bear right at Trenton and cross Pennsylvania in one swoop of 327 miles.

On that state's turnpike you lope across the farmlands of Lancaster County, soar over the Susquehanna River at Harrisburg, and plunge through seven tunnels in the Appalachian and Blue Mountains. Pittsburgh is a disappearing spot behind you, as you ease into the 241-mile Ohio Turnpike now being constructed.

Indiana and Illinois are now indicating that they plan to complete the circuit to Chicago. Thus you will be able to drive well over 800 miles from New York's 178th Street to the Windy City's Outer Drive without changing gears for a red light or an intersection.

These highways are super, all right, but are they safe?

Authorities say at moderately high speeds, *yes;* at excessive speeds, *no.* Their design virtually cancels the causes of most accidents—intersecting, approaching vehicles, pedestrians. Thus they carry more people more miles with fewer mishaps than average U. S. roads. Turnpike officials proudly point to Bureau of Public Roads' figures showing that for five years the fatality rate on controlled-access, express highways in 12 states was less than a third as high as rural road averages.

But here's the hook—they kill more people per accident! Or, as truckers put it, "When you get it on one of those race tracks, you're a gone goose!"

They show that fatalities per accident on expressways are many times greater than on roads with moderate speed limits. The average 35 mph stop-and-go city driver, they tell you, has not the conditioned reflexes, vision or distance judgment necessary for sustained travel over 60 mph. It takes practice to develop these faculties, and he simply doesn't get practice.

Above 60, they say, he's not driving his car, it's driving him. He's always behind it, trying to catch up. He doesn't project his line of sight far enough ahead to spot danger speeding toward him at 100 feet a second. Too soon, he is telescoped within a jungle of steel.

Turn a driver loose with 100-plus horsepower under his right foot, a wide, dart-straight roadbed stretching into the diminishing distance, with only an astronomical speed limit to inhibit him—and he does what comes naturally. Even geared-down drivers lose their speed sense after a while.

With no telephone poles, houses, or other reference points, they unconsciously accelerate, sometimes disbelieving their own speedometers. This speed-blindness occasionally persists after the expressway is left behind, causing collisions and other serious accidents on rural roads.

Speed limits are high on most super-highways. The Pennsylvania Turnpike allows you to watch the landscape rush backward at 70 mph. All the stops are out on the Detroit Industrial Expressway, where the only thing to prevent motorists from taking off is lack of a pilot's license.

"Brother, do you know it takes the length of a football field—nearly 300 feet—to stop a car doing 70?" asked a truck-and-trailer driver at a coffee stop just off the new Denver-Boulder Turnpike in Colorado. "And few people who've had to do it in a hurry are driving anything but harp-equipped clouds today." That driver's estimate is conservative; the stopping distance is actually a total of 444 feet.

The National Safety Council has analyzed the two most frequent accident types on expressways—rear-end crashes and single car collisions with stationary objects.

"The wide range of vehicle speeds on these roads causes most rear-end collisions," a Council spokesman said. "An overtaking car pulls out too late to pass the slower vehicle and shears off the other car's left rear end. Or he cuts back too soon and punches in his left front."

Modern highway designers are in the peculiar position of doctors who have cured many diseases, only to find that patients are dying of the medicine. In eliminating most motoring hazards, they have created one of their own. It is a sort of highway hypnosis, a fatal monotony encountered on long straight stretches.

With nothing to alert him—no approaching cars, intersections, billboards, curves, or hills—the motorist is imperceptibly lulled into a sense of security.

He maintains a constant speed, mile after mile. The engine—and on some roads the whump-whump of the wheels over paving joints—purrs him into drowsiness. He relaxes. His reflexes dissolve. He drowses. Then *wham*—he drives full tilt into a bridge abutment or the side of a mountain.

How can you get maximum safety and pleasure in driving these exciting new highways? With a car on whose brakes, lights, steering, tires, and horn you are willing to stake your life—and these few rules:

(1) Don't drive more than five or ten miles an hour above your normal maximum. The elimination of stops for cross-traffic, not break-neck speed, saves most of your time.

(2) Watch for slow-moving vehicles, especially trucks. A small change in grade, perhaps unnoticed by passenger-car drivers, will radically slow heavily-loaded commercial vehicles.

(3) Look farther ahead as you increase speed. Last-minute braking is not only dangerous but too often ineffective.

(4) Be alert. Change speeds occasionally, keep the car well ventilated, play the radio—and STOP when you feel drowsy.

(5) Maintain safe distance from other vehicles. Give them room. It doesn't cost anything.

(6) Watch for changing weather. Expressway driving takes motorists many miles in a short time. Slow down for rain, fog, sleet, and snow. Watch for wet and icy patches in the lee of hills and bridges.

(7) Don't stop in traffic lanes—pull well off the pavement. Other drivers don't expect parked cars.

(8) Take a "break" every 50 or 100 miles. If you're driving far, eat frequent small meals, but avoid big, heavy ones.

The simple fact of super-highway travel is that the roads were designed for speed but all drivers weren't. A healthy attitude was evidenced by a motorist who recently stopped at the George Washington Bridge Interchange of the New Jersey Turnpike.

"It's just 3 o'clock," he remarked. "At 60 miles an hour, I can make Wilmington by 4:58. At 70, I can save 17 minutes, at 80 I save 29 minutes —and if I did, I'd have to spend the time steadying my nerves.

"Guess I'll hold to a safe 60—then nobody will have to shovel me up from the wreckage."

Began   *Finished*   No. words: 1500

                              $\dfrac{}{} \times 60 =$ _____ W.P.M.

_____   _____   No. seconds:

Checking Comprehension

Below is a multiple-choice test, so choose the letter which represents the correct answer in each exercise and write it in the appropriate answer space.

1. Before the building of the new super-highways, the traditional speed limit was generally (a) 30 mph, (b) 40 mph, (c) 50 mph, (d) 60 mph.

2. The number of states building or planning additional super-roads is (a) ten, (b) fifteen, (c) twenty, (d) twenty-five.

3. One of the mountain ranges through which the Pennsylvania Turnpike passes is the (a) ̷ ̷e Mountains, (b) Green Mountains, (c) Catskill Mountains, (d) ̷ cono Mountains.

4. From New York it ̷ ̷ soon be possible, without changing gears at intersections, to re̷ ̷ (a) Pittsburgh, (b) Detroit, (c) Columbus, (d) Chicago.

5. The most s̷ ̷ ̷s disadvantage of the new super-highways is that (a) they h̷ ̷ ̷ higher accident rate than rural roads, (b) today's automobiles ̷ ̷oo powerful for them, (c) they require more maintenance th̷ ̷ ̷ral roads, (d) more people are killed per accident on them th̷ ̷ ̷ rural roads.

6. T̷ ̷ ̷istance required to stop a car moving at 70 mph is betwe̷ ̷ ̷ 200 and 300 ft., (b) 300 and 400 ft., (c) 400 and 500 ft., (d) 50ʊ and 600 ft.

7. The most serious element of danger of the super-highways is their (a) monotony, (b) slippery surface, (c) long grades, (d) tunnels.

8. A good speed for a super-highway is (a) your normal maximum speed, (b) five or ten mph above your normal maximum, (c) twenty mph above normal maximum, (d) any speed.

9. While driving on a super-highway, it is a good idea to (a) drive as long as you can without stopping, (b) take a "break" each 200 or 300 miles, (c) take a "break" each 300 or 400 miles, (d) take a "break" each 50 or 100 miles.

10. The motorist described in this article, who was driving the New Jersey Turnpike from New York to Wilmington, decided that his speed ought to be (a) 50 mph, (b) 60 mph, (c) 70 mph, (d) 80 mph.

Answers: 1)___, 2)___, 3)___, 4)___, 5)___, 6)___, 7)___, 8)___, 9)___, 10)___.

See page 383 for Answer Key.

Rate: W.P.M. ————————   Comprehension Score: ————————

Maintenance Practice

You have been reading to recall detailed information and numbers. Reading in order to establish strong impressions and to build associations for memory purposes is bound to slow you down—and that's all right. In order to maintain the speed which you have built up in reading material of medium difficulty for general impressions, you may now try reading an article of that type.

Selection 3

The selection below is of medium difficulty. See how rapidly you can cover it, reading for general impressions only, with no attempt to fix specific items for recall.

BEGINNING TIME:————————
HR.———————— MIN.————————

When to Change Jobs—and Why[12]

Many of us, of course, take new jobs because we are assigned them— or because the circumstances are so clear-cut that little choice is possible.

[12] Alan Gregg, *Harper's Magazine*, August 1955, pp. 71-76.

But in this country in the immediate future, the opportunities for new positions are going to increase dramatically, so that for many Americans the question of when to change jobs will become more acute than it has ever been in the past.

One might deduce this merely from the large and continuing growth in population, wealth, and number of organizations; but there are other favorable factors at work. Our job market is already large. We have in the United States one common language, a single currency, and a remarkable similarity of values, axioms, and cultural traditions. Furthermore, we ignore the obstacles of distance; we enjoy travel, and we believe in variety, change, and interchange. Mobility grows easier year by year.

I realize the absurdity of attempting to generalize about a career decision, so critical from the individual's point of view, where the circumstances that surround it are always variant and unique. I can speak with confidence chiefly in the field of medicine, and even there my experience of changing jobs has been mainly that of watching others engage in this anxious though stimulating process. But it seems to me to have features in common with other professions—features that are worth discussion if only because they are discussed so rarely when detached from specific cases. All will not go well automatically, merely because of the seemingly automatic growth of opportunity.

An early obstacle will be the very range of choice that confronts the employer. Who has the time to watch the quality, for example, of all the young physiologists in eighty-one medical schools and a dozen research institutions? Go to the meeting of the medical "Young Turks" at Atlantic City and reflect upon the problem of recognizing exceptional ability among these thousands of young men, many of whom certainly have exceptional ability.

The second obstacle is quite simply this: nowadays our list of acquaintances is long, but our intimates remain few—perhaps fewer than ever. Close, discriminating judgment of human character and intellectual potentiality has not kept pace in its growth, refinement, and dependability with the steadily-increasing job market.

I venture to mention a third reason for thinking that all may not go smoothly: It is my own conviction that suspicion breeds suspicion. Those institutions of whatever kind that blacklist and suspend individuals on the basis of unproven suspicion of subversion, in place of proven guilt, incur thereby a measure of aversion to working for them which is already hard to determine and may prove equally hard to control. Let us now pass to more agreeable subjects.

The offer of a position involves not only wisely appraising the candidate but also a wise—and under present circumstances an almost preternaturally wise—understanding by the candidate of what is involved in accepting the new position. Mistakes of judgment in such matters are already common enough. With the increasing number of opportunities they may become even more frequent. Perhaps we may best consider them by treating jobs in terms of the several stages that are possible in a given career.

As a device for exposition I shall follow a schematic division I saw years ago in a magazine. Modified to fit the careers of most professional people, it divides a man's working life into periods of fifteen years each, with the appropriate occupation or preoccupation of each period: (1) 20 to 35: *Learning;* (2) 35 to 50: *Doing;* (3) 50 to 65: *Directing;* and (4) 65 and onward: *Advising.* Such time periods are of course only approximate. I trust we all know that neither eternal youth nor occupational enthusiasm nor sclerosis of the spirit coincide very often or very closely with chronological age. But this arbitrary division can be useful as a framework to the extent that changes of occupation have very different implications according to your status, age, and major activities.

Learning

While you are in the Learning Period—that is, when you are not your own boss but working under instruction and direction—the *commonest* cause for wanting to leave is an inadequate salary; the *best* cause is the certainty that you are not learning much; the *least valid* cause is that you are living in Podunk; and the *least trustworthy* of causes is the feeling that you are being "neglected." On that last point, all young men who claim that they are being neglected, though they admit they are still learning a lot, would do well to realize that their chief may just be trying to find out whether they have enough drive to make good use of the spare time provided by apparent neglect. The Leiden pharmacologist Professor Storm von Leeuven once told me that he was no longer interested in bright young men with interesting ideas unless they were so possessed by those ideas that they spent all their free time trying to find out if the ideas were true. . . .

The positive reasons in the Learning Period—the attractions of the new place—usually relate to the widening of one's experience or new horizons or a higher salary or the chance to make new friends. These are excellent. Sometimes the advantage offered is the opportunity to prove to yourself that you can go it alone, that you can wean yourself from your past by accepting the challenge of a completely independent existence. Our educational system, especially on the Eastern seaboard, protects a good many young men from the rigors of freedom so much that the loneliness of complete independence rattles them. There is for such men a salutary clarity in the remark made by the Irish author George Moore to a young man inclined to pursue a literary career who asked his advice about doing so. Moore rather pointedly advised the young man against it. "But, Mr. Moore, you yourself decided in favor of a literary career!" Moore replied, "Yes, that's true—but I never had to ask!" . . .

Doing

Changes of a job between thirty-five and fifty involve some of the considerations already mentioned, but often with a different emphasis. The responsibilities of a family may very naturally increase the dissatisfaction of a low salary. The quality of education available to your children may be a cardinal factor in your decision to accept or decline an offer. President Dickey of Dartmouth tells me that a considerable concession is made by his college to faculty members who serve on the school board of Hanover and help make the local primary and secondary education satisfactory to faculty members with children. RCA, in its appeals to young engineers, takes account of the same concern.

One of the most familiar dissatisfactions in the Doing Period of thirty-five to fifty is work overload, especially for teachers. When the wave of children born in the past decade reaches the colleges in 1962 to 1972 the teachers' overload in the less foresighted institutions will be overwhelming. It will provide a reason for many a change in staff. It will make a buyers' market for industrial and research institutions that are looking for brains frustrated by overwork. . . .

One other cause of dissatisfaction in the Doing Period of thirty-five to fifty deserves mention, regrettable though it is. We cannot safely assume that all college presidents or deans or other sorts of managers will have an unerring flair for appreciating every kind of superior talent already in work in their own institution. Recognition may have to come from the outside. "A prophet is not without honor save in his own country." . . .

Directing

But it is in the next period, when directing becomes the major task, the period of fifty to sixty-five, that changing jobs presents the liveliest —or perhaps, more cautiously said, the deadliest—aspects. It is the time when most of us realize that it is now or never. But too few remember that bravado has been defined as frustration in action. And too few of us have heard, and harkened to, the gay wisdom of Christopher Morley's observation to the effect that any man who is worth his salt has by the age of forty-five acquired his crown of thorns, but the problem is to wear it over one ear. So it is in this period of life that the new director often shows a self-defeating sensitiveness about the way he is treated—and may, for instance, regard any budgetary cuts as examples of bad faith, whether or not they were due to conditions completely beyond the institution's control. . . .

The attractions of a proffered job to men of the age for directing usually center around the hope of having a free hand to get something done according to their own convictions, something of real significance. Customarily one expects salary, reputation, and social status all to be increased. It might also be noted that this glittering panoply will appeal the more to those whose character, talents, and good fortune have not already brought them a sense of substantial and unquestioned accomplishment.

But the hope of "having a free hand"—what of that? From what I have seen of men taking new jobs in this period, I would offer three or four observations tinged at times with a trace of warning. When you are offered a director's job, find out who is backing you and why or for what purpose. What does he expect you to do? Do you like him as a human being? Do you respect him? How long is he going to stay in a position to make good his promises, whether they are implicit or defined? Are you the candidate of a clique? Are you offered the job only because nobody knew anything against you? Does your appointment represent one phase of a quarrel you know nothing of? Are you following a man whose subordinates will think they prove their loyalty to him by opposing you? What fraction of his staff will you want to keep? What fraction will you *have* to keep, for other reasons?

Even when you have a completely new staff to assemble and the chance to do it, my vicarious experience in watching such opportunities unfold suggests that it is well to allow for the loss within five years of four or five out of every ten men you have picked to work with you. One may prove to be not what you expected. Another may find the position not what *he* expected. And between the losses due to accident, disease, and competition from the outside for some of your best men, you may very probably lose two or three more. In fact the obvious allure of an offer of "having a free hand" seems to me considerably discounted by what experience so often shows. . . .

All is not over even when the new job has been accepted. After about eighteen months in a new position the incumbent has acquired a clear idea of its limitations—and has still time to consider moving again. That is the most propitious time for another executive to interest a man he wanted but who seems to have escaped. His roots are not yet down. He may be secretly but profoundly disillusioned. I have seen such men and have seen them move again, in just such circumstances.

Advising

The last of my schematic groups—persons sixty-five and over, whom I would describe as Advisers—present phenomena that perhaps are new in human history. Scientific advances have been so spectacular, so numerous, and so radical that men over sixty-five cannot, as in times gone by, draw upon long experience on which to base all their advice. Concurrently, the proportion of men over sixty-five in the population increases. There have always, of course, been occasional vigorous and wise elderly men whose opinion was wisely sought. It was useful by so much as the culture of the society was traditional. But now we live in an adaptive culture; and there are many new technologies, new problems, new knowledge, and the certainty of still more discoveries whose long-term effects are not yet proven by young or old. . . .

In taking new jobs when you are over sixty-five, you may do well to be quite realistic about that age group. At no other time of his life is a man more likely to be tolerant of praise, so easily a dupe of flattery and a victim of "the V.I.P. treatment," and so pathetically ready to believe that he is indispensable. John Finley epitomized the sensible attitude for oldsters to take by his witty motto, "Nothing succeeds like successors." . . .

I favor making a relentless discount of the idea that many men over sixty-five or thereabouts are as good as they ever were in point of initiative, health, and adaptability to the unexpected. Furthermore, I find their reluctance to give younger men a chance is not much removed from cantankerous vanity indulged in the shelter of seniority. And the plain fact is that, however cogent be the arguments in individual cases, Nature seems not to be convinced by the theory that anyone is indispensable. I prefer to rely on the uniqueness of the special contribution by men over sixty-five rather than on their continuity, resilience, or indispensability. . . .

But the most interesting aspect of what the geriatrists prefer to call by the euphemistic name of "advanced maturity" seems to me to be an increase with age in the synthetic capacity of the mind—the capacity to generalize, rephrase, and put things in a quite new perspective, to regard interactions as well as actions, to detect the feed-back phenomena in human life. The repetitions made possible by long experience can discover uniformities of behavior, of cause and effect, of correlations, and of interacting factors that widen one's horizons in a most refreshing fashion.

And now, having outlined only a few of the phenomena of changing one's job in the four periods of learning, doing, directing, and advising, I shall end with some concrete bits of advice.

Too many of the final decisions about changing one's job are made when one is too busy with other things. Take a week off. Get plenty of sleep and rest. Nice decisions of major importance take an amount of nervous strength that you simply do not possess if you come tired to the task of deciding.

Visit the place of your proposed position and take your wife with you, for her life is involved as much as yours—often decisively, albeit differently.

Define to yourself, and if possible to some close personal friend, just what you are assuming as well as expecting more explicitly—but be chary of stipulating too much to your employer.

Distinguish between decisions that are irrevocable and those that can be postponed or reversed. Not all calls are last calls, nor all destinations final. And in a job that looks like a balloon ascension, look to the question of a parachute—an alternative if all does not go well.

Find out if possible who wanted you, and who else has been chosen by him, and whether he is in a position—as well as of a character—to make good his promises. . . .

I know full well that in this brief account I have not closed the subject: it would be quite enough to hope that a subject has been opened with detachment and possibly with profit. You can take advantage from these reflections only if you are disposed to add your own observations and corrections to this preliminary inventory. The time to read comes after you have thought, not as a substitute for thinking.

Began　　*Finished*　　　　No. words:　　2500

$$\frac{}{} \times 60 = \underline{} \text{ W.P.M.}$$

No. seconds:

_____　　_____

Checking Comprehension

1. The number of new positions is (a) increasing, (b) decreasing, (c) remaining constant, (d) fluctuating.

2. The commonest cause for a young man in the Learning Period to leave a position is (a) inadequate salary, (b) the certainty that he is not learning much, (c) the opportunity to take on increased responsibility, (d) the fact that he is in an out-of-the-way place.

3. If a young man changes jobs during the Learning Period the advantage offered is (a) an opportunity to live in the country, (b) a chance to start a business of his own, (c) a chance to choose the phase of the work he wants to do, (d) the opportunity to prove to himself that he can go it alone.

4. One of the most familiar dissatisfactions during the Doing Period is (a) not enough work, (b) work that is too routine, (c) work overload, (d) not enough opportunity for creative work.

5. The period of a man's working life in which he is most inclined to be oversensitive is the (a) Learning Period, (b) Doing Period, (c) Directing Period, (d) Advising Period.

6. When changing jobs during the Directing Period, the hope of "having a free hand" should be: (a) considered as an important inducement, (b) the supreme factor, (c) disregarded entirely, (d) considerably discounted.

7. The idea that men over sixty-five are as good as they ever were in initiative, health, and adaptability should be (a) respected, (b) accepted by employers, (c) relentlessly discounted, (d) used as an argument for employing men in this age bracket.

8. The man above sixty-five can make a contribution as an Advisor because (a) he is peculiarly well able to meet new problems, (b) he has proved indispensable to his company, (c) he has a synthetic capacity of the mind, (d) he has demonstrated his resiliency.

9. If you are offered a change in jobs you are advised to (a) accept immediately before the new employer changes his mind, (b) take time off your job to think about the matter, (c) discuss the matter at once with your present employer in the thought that he may give you a promotion, (d) keep turning the idea over in your mind whenever you can sandwich it in as you continue with duties in your present position.

10. One of the things you need to find out about the person who wants to give you the new job is (a) how he treats his help, (b) whether he is in a position to make good his promises, (c) whether he has the authority to offer you the job, (d) whether he, himself, has made good financially.

Answers: 1)—, 2)—, 3)—, 4)—, 5)—, 6)—, 7)—, 8)—, 9)—, 10)—.

See page 383 for Answer Key.

Rate: W.P.M. —————   Comprehension Score: —————

Speed Reading for Broad Ideas

Selection 4

In order to maintain your speed, see how fast you can read this easy article just for the purpose of finding broad ideas about the topic.

BEGINNING TIME:——————
HR.———— MIN.——————

Mental Indigestion[13]

Men engaged in a rather wide variety of business and professions are convinced that in their line of work ulcer is an occupational disease. Publishers, advertising men, taxi and bus drivers, lawyers, merchandising and industrial executives all claim it—some of them with a certain odd pride. This triumph of arrogance over pain stems from the legend that ulcer of the stomach or duodenum is above all others the affliction of

[13] Flanders Dunbar, *Mind and Body: Psychosomatic Medicine*, Random House 1947, pp. 155-173.

tycoons and so may be considered as a badge of success, or at least of superior quality.

Ulcer, they say, comes to a Go-getter. But in actual fact that is not true. All this particular kind of Go-getter really gets is his ulcer.

Nevertheless, the legend does reveal some popular understanding of the real nature of the disease—that it is a combination of physical and psychic factors which are all necessary to this particular kind of a sore interior.

There are four steps that go into the making of an ulcer—very few victims ever have more than one at a time although the pain is usually enough to make them refer to it in the plural—and the interplay of body and mind is decisive. The development is this:

First of all, an unduly large number of impulses, caused by emotional disturbances, are transmitted to the nerve fibers which run through the mid-brain to the intestinal tract. This part of the brain is believed to have, among its functions, that of emotional expression in the involuntary nervous system; that is, the nervous system over which man has no conscious control. It regulates the automatic functionings of the body, and these cannot be willed to behave thus and so. But they can be affected involuntarily through the involuntary nervous system.

Second, these impulses get passed along to the stomach and intestines where they affect the production of hydrochloric acid. This is their normal function; it does harm only when the acid is produced in larger quantities than are necessary for digestion. The immediate result is likely to be hunger pangs which in health are an indication that the body needs food. In this stage of ulcer development they prompt the consumption of more than is actually needed, so that the more the person eats the worse he gets.

Third, tension develops in the smooth muscles, whose work is especially beyond the power of the voluntary nervous system to control. The even contraction and relaxation of these muscles is disturbed. This may interfere with the normal rhythm of those muscles which govern the traffic between mouth and stomach. If their signals get mixed, the stomach will naturally be irritated by vomiting. Food which is kept in the stomach instead of being passed along in the normal course of digestion also irritates the lining.

Fourth, the victim then may eat something scratchy or irritating to the mucous membranes lining the stomach or intestines. The hydrochloric acid and the muscle tension combine to aggravate the slightest blemish caused on the wall of the digestive tract. The sore becomes noticeable, painful and infected, and can be seen by X-ray as an irregularity on the stomach wall. That is an ulcer.

Treatment in the past has generally worked backward from the symptom. The sore was the obvious seat of the trouble, so doctors tried to remove it by prescribing a soothing alkaline diet which would heal the ulcer, or they went to more drastic extremes and cut the ulcer out.

Recently there have been experiments in severing the vagus nerve, which carried the offending impulses. This last seems very much like cutting the telegraph wires from Washington to avoid hearing bad news. It does not halt the march of events, and the bad news will reach us one way or another. Probably it will come as all the more of a shock for the delay imposed by the roundabout route.

While the actual sore has to be healed, the permanent solution is to stop at their source the sequence of events which lead up to an ulcer. This has been recognized by medical practitioners for a long time; in fact, almost as long as medicine can be considered a science. The relation between the mind and the gastro-intestinal disorders has been accepted ever since Hippocrates, in the year 640 B.C., was reported to have cured King Perdicas of Macedonia by the analysis of a dream.

II

A Pattern for Ulcer

The existence of an ulcer is usually not a matter of any doubt to the physician. Yet there are times when the location of the sore and the reactions of the organs may conceal the irritated tissue from the fluoroscope. The facts may be revealed by a study of the victim's emotional problems, for the typical ulcer personality is not difficult to recognize if the physician has had adequate psychosomatic training.

I recall a young woman named Dorothy who was referred to a clinic as a purely psychiatric case. For more than a year and a half she had been complaining of pains which were definitely suggestive of gastric ulcer, but all the tests were negative. The doctors who had examined her became convinced that the symptoms were hysterical in origin, for they could recognize that she seemed to be laboring under a good deal of emotional strain.

They were right about the strain, but at the same time it was apparent that Dorothy followed the psychic pattern of the ulcer victim. It was not difficult to get at the bottom of her emotional problem. Unmarried and living alone wih her mother, who had decidedly puritanical reactions to her daughter's social activities, Dorothy was carrying on a love affair with the husband of one of her close friends.

Dorothy had a personality which inclined her to depend upon her mother for affection and support. At the same time she resented her emotional dependence on her mother and her mother's economic dependence on her. She could not shrug off her mother's views on virtue because she was accustomed to relying upon the older woman's judgment and needed to feel that she was approved. On the other hand, she could not accept the limitations on her own activities which this attitude implied.

She responded readily to treatment which revealed this situation to her, and the pain subsided. However, she could not be regarded as cured. She had a living to earn, and her job kept her from continued attendance at the clinic. When she was discharged, she was warned to have a medical check-up at least once a year and, if in between these check-ups the symptoms returned, to come back to the psychiatric clinic at once.

In due course the pains did return; Dorothy's emotional system had not been so thoroughly stabilized as would have been possible if she had been able to continue treatment. But when she arrived at the clinic, the psychiatrist happened to be on vacation, and she was referred to a neurologist.

For three years he treated her with sedatives, but at last the emotional and physical strain grew greater than drugs could cope with. Her lover decided to divorce his wife and marry Dorothy, a complex situation in which the young woman felt that she owed it to her friend to break off the affair with the man altogether. Immediately afterward she suffered hemorrhages, and for the first time became aware of the fact that she really had an ulcer.

"Last week," she wrote to the psychiatrist, "I was so sick I called in a doctor from the neighborhood and he said I was having hemorrhages from an ulcer in my stomach. If this is what you were treating me for six years ago, why didn't you tell me?"

She was promptly asked to come back to the clinic, and this time the existence of the ulcer could be confirmed without any trouble. In fact, it had progressed so far that she required blood transfusions. But for the accident of getting to a neurologist instead of a psychiatrist on her first return to the clinic she might have been helped to avoid this suffering. The possibility was more than hindsight for, at the time her job had prevented her from continuing psychiatric treatments, this note was added to her chart:

"This patient should be followed in Medicine (that is, by the general clinic). Although the immediate emotional problem has been relieved and with it her symptoms, she has the specific reaction pattern to any type of stress and strain which is characteristic of the ulcer patient."

The recognition of that particular pattern would do a good deal to prevent ulcer. However, the possessor of it does not usually consult a physician, particularly one trained in psychosomatic techniques, until the disease has developed to a point where a sore is actually present.

Therefore, the first step in treatment of the ulcer is to get rid of the sore. This can be done by diet, although often the obvious regime of milk and mush is psychologically harmful, or it may be necessary to operate if the ulcer has proceeded too far. Once the sore has been healed or removed, intensive treatment of the basic trouble can begin. In the meantime, psychotherapy can help prepare the patient either for an operation or for acceptance of his diet and pave the way for serious consideration of the underlying mental indigestion.

The rather clear pattern of emotional life is a good deal of help in treatment. Ulcer patients are generally a bit above average in intelligence, often very much above, and like to talk about themselves. They know very well that there is some sort of nervous or emotional basis for their pain, although they are inclined to blame other factors than the real ones.

"This happened to me because the government has made it so tough for us businessmen," they will say. Or, "My wife drives me nuts." Or, "I've had so much hard luck, Doctor, that it worries me sick."

Actually, these worries are more superficial than the majority of men like to think. Their trouble is deeper, but once they understand that fact, they cooperate quickly with the physician. That, too, is characteristic.

We find that most ulcer sufferers have always had feeding problems. If we can talk to their mothers, we learn that they usually had nursing difficulties in the very first few months of their lives. They were subject to colic later on. They may have inherited an organic weakness which predisposes them to ulcer when the necessary train of psychological explosive has been laid. One investigator has prepared statistics to show that among his ulcer patients, only 10.8 per cent were children of parents who had both been free of ulcers all their lives. In another 25.7 per cent, one parent had suffered from ulcer. That left the substantial majority as children of parents both of whom had been afflicted with the disease.

This indicates that the popular acceptance of ulcer as primarily a disease of men has little foundation in fact. For twenty-odd years, there was this much justification for the story: Most of the people who had ulcers were men. But that was only between 1914 and 1936. Since then, the proportion of women has been increasing, until now the sexes are about evenly susceptible. That this change in the sex distribution of ulcer is no phenomenon peculiar to the atomic age can be seen from the fact that, until about 1900, the chief victims of ulcer were women.

The truth is that the cultural conditions of the times, reacting upon the peculiar emotional system of the ulcer type, has a determining influence. The impulses passing through the mid-brain are altered by the conditions of life under which people find themselves, and ulcer results.

Began   *Finished*   No. words: 1875

$$\frac{\quad}{\text{No. seconds:}} \times 60 = \underline{\qquad} \text{W.P.M.}$$

_____   _____

Checking Comprehension

1. Men in a wide variety of businesses and professions take pride in their belief that (a) they know how to avoid ulcer, (b) they know a cure for ulcer, (c) ulcer may be considered a badge of success, (d) ulcer attacks only the "white-collar" class.

2. The first step in the development of an ulcer is (a) a continuous feeling of hunger, (b) tension in the smooth muscles, (c) an unduly large number of impulses transmitted to the intestinal tract, (d) something scratchy irritating the mucous membranes lining the stomach and intestines.

3. The cure for an ulcer is (a) a soothing alkaline diet, (b) cutting the ulcer out, (c) severing the vagus nerve, (d) to stop at its source the sequence of events which led up to an ulcer.

4. After Dorothy took treatment from a psychiatrist in the early stages of her trouble, (a) she grew worse, (b) was completely cured, (c) remained the same with much pain, (d) responded readily and the pain subsided.

5. The case of Dorothy was described to show that (a) unmarried women are more apt to have ulcers than married women, (b) girls who are too dependent on their mothers are apt to have ulcers, (c) recognition of her particular pattern would help prevent ulcer, (d) ulcer can sometimes be cured by psychiatrists.

6. The recognition of the pattern would help to prevent ulcer, but the trouble is that (a) patients are reluctant to give the information that the physician needs, (b) only a few physicians are acquainted with the pattern, (c) patients usually do not consult a physician trained in psychosomatic techniques until the sore is present, (d) treatment of the pattern is usually ineffective.

7. The first step in the treatment of an ulcer is to (a) treat the basic trouble which caused the ulcer, (b) get rid of the sore, (c) send the patient to a hospital for observation, (d) prescribe X-ray treatments.

8. Those who have ulcers are apt (a) to be too introspective, (b) to blame factors other than the real one, (c) to be uncooperative in accepting treatment, (d) to pay no attention to the doctor's diagnosis of emotional disturbances.

9. Most ulcer patients (a) have always had feeding problems, (b) have been free of feeding problems all their lives, (c) have had feeding problems in early life but not later, (d) have had feeding problems in adult life but not in childhood.

10. Ulcer at present is (a) primarily a disease of early children, (b) primarily a disease of men, (c) primarily a disease of women, (d) about equally distributed between the two sexes.

Answers: 1)—, 2)—, 3)—, 4)—, 5)—, 6)—, 7)—, 8)—, 9)—, 10)—.

See page 383 for the Answer Key.

Rate: W.P.M. _____   Comprehension Score: _____

Vocabulary Study

The italicized word in each of the phrases in the left-hand column was chosen from one of the selections you have read in this chapter. In the column to the right there is a word or phrase which has the same meaning as an italicized word in the left-hand column.

Find a word in the column to the right which is similar in meaning to an italicized word. Write the letter representing this word in the blank space on the line opposite the italicized word.

1. *Inexplicable* reason	(a) offered	_____
2. *Schematic* division	(b) unrecallable	_____
3. A *proffered* job	(c) summarized	_____
4. The *incumbent*	(d) slender	_____
5. A *propitious* time	(e) agreeable	_____
6. *Cogent* arguments	(f) sleepy	_____
7. *Geriatrics*	(g) a nerve specialist	_____
8. *Euphemistic* name	(h) according to a scheme	_____
9. Feeling *lethargic*	(i) a specialist in drugs	_____
10. A *svelte* figure	(j) favorable	_____
11. Finley *epitomized* attitudes	(k) soothe	_____
12. *Assuage* the pain	(l) not explainable	_____
13. *Corpulence* of figure	(m) gigantic	_____
14. Fatiguing *cerebration*	(n) medicine concerned with old age	_____
15. A *pharmacologist*	(o) even though	_____
16. No *phenomenon*	(p) bearing an obligation	_____
17. *Irrevocable* decisions	(q) forcible	_____
18. A *neurologist*	(r) obeseness	_____
19. *Albeit,* he spoke	(s) mental activity	_____
20. *Colossal* millionaire	(t) unusual occurrence	_____

Check your answers with the Answer Key on page 384.

Vocabulary Score: _____

Follow-Up Practice

Using materials of your own selection

In this chapter you have been given some information about conditions under which memory operates, and you have been provided with some experiences in working in harmony with these conditions. You have been introduced to techniques for reading to recall ideas and numbers. If you wish to develop yourself to a high level of efficiency in this respect, go on practicing these procedures whenever you read an article or chapter that you wish to remember. Make the best possible use of the techniques of establishing strong impressions, concentrating intensively, and building rich associations. These are the essentials in reading to remember, so work on them continuously until they become automatic.

CHAPTER 9

Riding Along

with an Author

Purposes and Patterns

In reading it is very important that you identify yourself closely with the author. Regardless of the chapter or article you choose to read you may be sure that it was written with a specific purpose, and the author proceeded toward his destination until his writing journey was completed. True, he may occasionally have taken detours, and here and there he may have driven rather deeply into a forest of details which he considered especially important or interesting, and at other points he may have speeded over open spaces which he considered unappealing or of little consequence. Regardless of the variations in route, the author always has a purpose for his writing journey; he always has a reason for taking the trip. If you will mount the saddle and travel right along with him toward the destination that he has in mind, your reading journey will be much more swift and sure than if you travel with a goal of your own which differs from his.

Authors' purposes for writing vary. The purpose determines the pattern into which the writing falls. If you learn to identify the pattern, you will be able quickly to recognize the author's purpose. With this information you will be able to adjust to the pattern, whatever it may be.

To use another analogy, when a tailor makes a suit coat he lays a certain pattern on the cloth and cuts a piece of material in the shape of that pattern with as little waste as possible. He lays a different pattern on the cloth if he is going to make a pair of slacks, and he uses still a different pattern if the goal of his efforts is to be a topcoat.

So does each author "lay a different pattern on the cloth" for each of his purposes. If you can decide on the garment he wishes to turn out, and will "lay the same pattern on the cloth" that he uses, you too will have less waste material left in the way of time and lack of comprehension.

Sharing-Experience Pattern

Perhaps the pattern most frequently met is the one in which the author wishes to tell about some personal experience. This experience is so interesting, unusual, or worthwhile in his opinion that he would like to share it with others, at the same time entertaining his readers.

To identify the sharing-experience pattern ask yourself, "Is he telling some actual, first-hand experience?" Additional clues are the use of the personal pronouns *I, we, our,* or *us.*

The sharing-experience pattern is easy to identify as well as easy to read. When you start to read such a selection, you may know that it is safe to proceed at the highest speed you can command. Usually comprehension difficulties are at their minimum in such an article. There are no detailed facts that you will have to recall. All you have to do is to enjoy the author's experience in the way you would if he were telling it to you orally.

Our largest catch, a 50-pound yellow, was caught near the close of the day. A group of grabblers flushed him in open water fifty yards above us. He lunged and butted his way through another group and appeared in our midst. Our first notice of his appearance among us was when he butted Charlie Cox squarely in the stomach. We closed in and undertook to corner him. He thundered, blustered, butted and chewed fingers until we finally managed to pen him against a log. With shouts of triumph we hoisted him ashore, and thus ended our day.[1]

[1] Ewart A. Autry, "Acres of Catfish," *Field and Stream,* May 1954, p. 121.

Question-Answer Pattern

The Question-Answer pattern, as its name implies, is one in which the author states a question, then proceeds to answer it. The question may be stated as the title of an article, as a subheading within the article, or at the beginning of a paragraph.

The question-answer style can be used in writing technical material, but usually it isn't. It more often appears as an "interest tickler."

The author may make one of two uses of the question-answer technique in his writing. He may use the question to excite curiosity so that you will be interested in reading what he has to say. On the other hand, he may use this technique in order to indicate his intentions in a concise and clear-cut form. This "sharpening" up of the subject by couching it in the form of a question may be his way of helping you understand his purpose at once.

The question-answer pattern has many advantages for the reader. For one thing, it states the reader's purpose for him. He doesn't have to formulate his own motive for reading the article. Second, it is easier to hold in mind a question than a topic sentence, for the question stands out sharply throughout the reading of the text that follows. Thus it furnishes a compelling and constant frame of reference with which details can be associated.

The question-answer pattern also has the advantage of easy identification. A glance reveals the question. When you encounter a question in a title, subdivision, or paragraph you know immediately that the author is going to answer the question.

The question-answer pattern also facilitates speed. If the content is of such a nature that you don't care about the details, simply read the question, glance through the text until you find the answer—and let it go at that.

Try this technique in reading the sample paragraph below.

What is time?—The shadow on the dial, the striking of the clock, the running of the sand, day and night, summer and winter, months, years, centuries—these are but the arbitrary and outward signs—the measure of time, not time itself. Time is the life of the soul.

—Henry Wadsworth Longfellow

Imparting-Information Pattern

This pattern also is easy to identify, but it is often difficult to read. Frequently this pattern contains many factual details. If you wish to remember these details you must use the very careful techniques already taught. Usually one quick glance at a selection will tell you if the author's purpose was to give information. If so, be prepared to adjust your speed to careful, detailed reading.

A sample of the "Imparting-Information" pattern is given below. Put yourself in a state of mind for reading a paragraph packed heavily with informative details.

The radioactivity of uranium minerals may be detected by use of Geiger and scintillation counters (Wright, 1953, 1954a; Brownell, 1950; Wilson and others, 1954). Their use gives the prospector an unusual advantage, for these instruments can detect the presence of radioactive minerals even if they are concealed from sight by a few inches or so of soil or rock. Geiger counters and scintillation counters have been developed in various shapes and sizes, suitable for use by the prospector on the ground, for carborne (Nelson, 1954) and airborne (Stead, 1950; Stead and Davis, 1952) reconnaissance, and for drill-hole logging (Faul and Tittle, 1951; DiGiovanni, and others, 1953). The scintillation counter is much more sensitive than the Geiger counter and therefore will detect much less intense radioactivity. For this reason, scintillation counters have now largely displaced Geiger counters in airborne reconnaissance. Light planes, such as those used by the Atomic Energy Commission, are used to search for specific deposits in broadly favorable areas (Tavelli, 1951; Foote, 1954). They fly at an altitude of about 50 feet and are equipped with scintillation counters that detect almost all abnormal radioactivity that field Geiger counters detect on the ground. Larger planes, like the Geological Survey's DC–3, are used for quick reconnaisance of large regions (Stead, 1950; Balsley, 1952). The Survey's plane is flown at an elevation of about 500 feet along traverse lines about a quarter of a mile apart, and records both radioactivity and magnetic measurements.[2]

Opinion-Reason Pattern

The writer uses this pattern in order to state an opinion and give his reason for it. You may have to read two or three paragraphs before you can determine whether the author is expressing his opinion and also whether he intends to give reasons supporting it. Some clues are such phrases as "I think," "I believe," "I prefer," "I judge," "I am sure," "in my opinion," "as I see it," "according to my viewpoint," "I regard," etc. If you find statements such as these and the reasons follow, then all you need to do is to get a concise understanding of the author's opinion, then find his reason or reasons

[2] U.S. Atomic Energy Commission, *Search for Uranium in the United States,* U.S. Gov. Printing Office, 1955, pp. 20-21.

for believing as he does. Synchronize your purpose and techniques to the author's style, and there will be no lost time or effort.

Try adjusting yourself to the opinion-reason pattern while reading the paragraph below.

From my earliest youth I have regarded slavery as a great moral and political evil.—I think it unjust, repugnant to the natural equality of mankind, founded only in superior power; a standing and permanent conquest by the stronger over the weaker.—All pretence of defending it on the ground of different races, I have ever condemned, and have even said that if the black race is weaker, that is a reason against and not for its subjection and oppression.—In a religious point of view, I have ever regarded and spoken of it, not as a subject of any express denunciation, either in the Old Testament or the New, but as opposed to the whole spirit of the gospel, and to the teachings of Jesus Christ.—The religion of Christ is a religion of kindness, justice, and brotherly love;—but slavery is not kindly affectionate; it seeks another's and not its own; it does not let the oppressed go free; it is but a continual act of oppression.

—Daniel Webster

Substantiated-Facts Pattern

This pattern usually begins with a conclusion and is followed by facts to prove this conclusion. The conclusion, however, sometimes comes at the end. This pattern is most frequently found in technical or scientific content, although occasionally in a popular article. This is the most convincing type of pattern an author can use in making his point.

In identifying this pattern, look for a definite statement in the form of a conclusion. Unlike the opinion-reason pattern, this statement will contain no personal pronouns, nor will it contain such verbs as "think" or "believe." It usually is a terse statement of fact. The series of statements which follows the conclusion offers substantiation in the form of data, scientific observations, experiments, or quotations.

This pattern usually must be read far more carefully and slowly than the experience pattern or question-and-answer type of material.

The meaning of every word must be grasped in order to understand the evidence presented. If you wish to remember the proofs, then you need to employ all your techniques for reading and recalling detailed facts. The conclusion stated by the author will of course be the topic sentence, and all the subsequent proving sentences will be related to this statement as reinforcing details.

Try out these suggestions in reading the substantiated-facts sample that is presented below.

1) Make certain that you comprehend the significance of the author's conclusion; 2) then mentally challenge him to prove it to you; 3) read on to see if his proof is convincing.

There are many visible evidences that the moon has little or no atmosphere. The illuminated portion of its surface is always visible. No haze, clouds, or dust storms have ever been observed. When the moon passes between the earth and the sun, no luminous atmospheric ring is visible. The moon's margin is sharp and black. When the moon passes between the earth and a star, the light of the star is cut off sharply and suddenly, not gradually. It is quite certain that if it ever possessed an atmosphere, it has lost it now.[3]

Applying What You've Learned

Following are selections which represent each of these patterns. Identify the author's pattern of writing, then try quickly to adjust to this pattern as you read. You will be rated on your accuracy in identifying the patterns, on your comprehension of each selection, and on your speed of reading.

The selections are assembled in three groups in order that you may obtain a check of your rate in reading different types of material: 1) easy short selections, 2) more difficult short selections, 3) long selections.

Practice Section I

Easy Short Selections

All five of these selections are easy to read and are of such a nature that you probably won't care to linger over details. Your test at the end will check your identification of the pattern and general comprehension in each selection. You will also be checked on the time it takes you to read all five paragraphs.

As you start to read each selection, quickly identify the pattern of writing and synchronize your reading pattern with the author's

[3] Emmett J. Cable, Robert Ward Getchell, and William Henry Kadesch, *The Physical Sciences*, Prentice-Hall, 1946, p. 585.

writing pattern. This will contribute much both to your speed and comprehension.

BEGINNING TIME:_____

HR._____ MIN._____

Selection 1

No Hollywood Star could be so temperamental, so hilarious, so touching, or so frightening as some of the actors that have performed their roles before my camera.

As a member of the Walt Disney wildlife camera crew, I spent two seasons filming the spectacular true-life adventure, *The Vanishing Prairie.* We followed and found our animal and bird actors in remote sections of the West—in the last retreats of the native wildlife of the Great Plains.

This was my greatest camera adventure.

My "actors" were unpredictable. They misbehaved continually. Small ones disappeared down burrows just when I was ready to start my camera. Of course they ran from me whenever I inadvertently revealed myself. They hid from me much more easily than I from them. Larger ones often charged me angrily when I got too close.

Yet all this was to be expected.

The story for this film was their story—the everyday adventures of the animals and birds of the vast American prairie. They wrote the script with nature as their director. My camera was merely the "invisible" intruder.[4]

Selection 2

Why, then, do doctors prescribe, and parents often demand the expensive formulations put out under the fancy labels? For the doctor, it is often the easy way out: the formula pad is handy, the infant is doing well under its hospital-prescribed mixture, and the parents will be satisfied to continue the "official" routine the hospital started. For the parents, the expensive product with the fancy label gives the satisfaction that they are not stinting, but giving their new child "the best."

But there are signs of change. Some hospitals have started to use sugar and milk—any brand—and to forego the free offers of the companies. Some pediatricians are following the same progressive technique. And some parents, even some whose babies started out on traditional and expensive formulas, are asking questions of their doctors, and beginning to realize that the most expensive course is not necessarily the best one.[5]

---

[4] Tom McHugh, "Animals Are Like People," *Field and Stream,* September 1954, p. 113.

[5] "Infant Formulas," *Consumer Reports,* October 1952, pp. 484.

Selection 3

The tropical rainstorm had stopped as suddenly as it had begun. Long shafts of yellow sunlight were lancing down through the dripping trees as I stepped from the porch of the trading station at Sietevaca, a tiny native village in eastern Honduras. At the end of the long boardwalk that stretched out into the murky, sullen water of the Patuca River a half dozen curious Hondurans were assembled to watch the rapid approach of a huge pitpan, or native dugout canoe.

Under normal conditions, the arrival of one cargo canoe would have been no cause for interest. But this pitpan was not filled with cargo. There were three men in the boat. One of them was lying motionless in the bottom, and the other two were excitedly calling to the onlookers to find the doctor. Stepping back up to the door, I called to Doc McGuartney, the only man within a radius of fifty miles who was qualified to call himself a physician, and waited while he heaved his ponderous bulk out of the wicker chair and lumbered toward the door.[6]

Selection 4

What can be done about emotionally-caused overeating?

To break the conditioned reflex of eating under stress, you must first recognize the wide prevalence of emotional conflict. Everyone has weaknesses, though we express them differently. Some people lose their appetite under stress; others overeat. Still others take to alcohol, or develop stomach pains, diarrhea, cardiac palpitation, or migraine headaches.

Breaking food reflexes must start with a conscious deliberate setting up of *different* reflexes. This takes time. A few days or weeks of dieting is not enough. Be prepared to allow months for the job, because only then can results become permanent.

Overeating is a habit. It can be broken, like all habits, by the substitution of other routines. Once you remove the need for overeating through self-understanding and tolerance, you can give yourself the motivation to carry through to a permanent goal.[7]

Selection 5

What is the reason for the existence of this great glacial system on this mountain? It is not simply the altitude of Mount Rainier, for there are other mountains which are slightly higher above the level of the sea. Both Mount Whitney in California and Mount Elbert in Colorado may boast

[6] William Thomas Helm III, "Spotted Killer," *Field and Stream*, September 1954, p. 43.
[7] Wilfred Dorfman, "How to Stop Overeating," *Journal of Living*, December 1953, p. 70.

of greater elevation, but neither possesses glacial systems. The reason is snow. Upon the broad flanks of this huge volcano, due to the great amount of moisture that is swept inland from the Pacific in the prevailing winds, occurs one of the heaviest snowfalls on record in our country. At Paradise Valley (5557 feet), which is widely known for its wild flowers during the summer season, it is not unusual for twenty-five feet of snow to be found upon the ground in midwinter, while unquestionably a great deal more snow falls at the higher levels where most of the glaciers are born. This snow, in packing down is transformed into glacial ice and keeps alive these remnants of the "ice age." Each winter it partly repairs the damage of the warm summer sun, but the glaciers are fighting a losing battle. Eventually, perhaps, at some time in the distant future these great glaciers, some of which are more than four or five miles long today, may be mere traces of their former magnificence.[8]

| *Began* | *Finished* | No. words: | 880 |

$$\frac{\quad}{\quad} \times 60 = \underline{\qquad} \text{ W.P.M.}$$

No. seconds:

Checking Comprehension

If necessary you may refer back to the selections in answering the first five questions about patterns, but do not refer back while answering the last five questions which check comprehension of content.

1. What pattern of writing was used in Selection 1? _____
2. What pattern was used in Selection 2? _____
3. What pattern was used in Selection 3? _____
4. What pattern was used in Selection 4? _____
5. What pattern was used in Selection 5? _____
6. The photographing of animals was discussed in one selection. Where was this photography done? _____
7. In one selection "formulas" are discussed. What kind of formulas are under consideration in this article? _____
8. What was the object of excitement in the selection with a setting in Honduras? _____
9. What is the cause of overeating as discussed in one selection? _____
10. The glacial system on Mount Rainer was discussed. What is the reason this glacial system exists? _____

The Answer Key is on page 384.

Rate: W.P.M. _____   Comprehension Score: _____

[8] C. Frank Brackman, "The Wonders of Mount Rainier," *Natural History*, March 1936, p. 257.

Practice Section II

More Difficult Short Selections

In this section you will again have practice in reading selections in different patterns. Unlike the selections in Practice Section I, however, these as a whole are of the detailed factual type. You will therefore need to read them at a slower rate.

You will be checked on the patterns of writing and also on some of the details in each selection. In addition, you will have an opportunity to check your speed.

When you are ready to start, jot down your beginning time, and when you have finished reading all five selections record your ending time.

Identify the pattern of writing in each selection and "read to the pattern." Force your speed as much as you can while still grasping the information. Don't feel frustrated, however, because you cannot read at such a high speed as in the preceding section. These selections are more difficult to read, and you will have to "shift your gears."

BEGINNING TIME:_____

HR._____ MIN._____

Selection 6

Improvement in machines has been the result of many factors, one of which has been the rapid advance in the science of metallurgy. There are now some 5000 different metal alloys, some of them much better than the metals formerly used. It has been claimed that the steel produced today wears nearly twice as long as most of the steel made fifty years ago. The advance has been phenomenal in some of the hard cutting metals. "A new material is now available which consists of a mixture of tungsten and titanium carbides cemented with cobalt. This is perfectly satisfactory for cutting steel, and it has been found to have 60 times the life in operation that the original cemented tungsten carbide had. Through chromium plating the life of various tools and parts has been extended from 3 to 20 times. By the use of tungsten carbide, Carboloy tools have been formed which operate in some cases 300 to 400 times as efficiently as the old steel tools. On a brass-plug job the number of finished pieces produced by old tools was 200; through the substitution of Carboloy tools this was increased to 15,000. Great improvements have been made in some articles through the use of the lighter metals and alloys, some of which are extremely strong as well as light. Scientists say that we are entering a new era in which steel will to some extent be displaced by these materials.[9]

Selection 7

Let me state at once my theme and my deep personal conviction: that, by not lifting the Language Curtain which she has lowered on her shores since the time of World War I, America persists in imperiling her international commitments and weakening her influence as a promoter of world peace and understanding. By indulging our linguistic and cultural isolationism long after we have abandoned political isolationism, we seem to others a nation of good intentions paving the road to an atomic hell. I am using the phrase "Language Curtain" deliberately to invite comparison with another more familiar and more metallic screen. Is it pure coincidence, one of the forgivable synchronisms, that the rise of the Soviet Union and the decline of foreign language study in this country began at precisely the same moment in history and have continued to do global damage together? This sounds like a charge of "guilt by association" against those responsible for the decline of foreign languages, but I reject the inference. It would be more accurate to call it guilt by dissociation, or going to another equally unfortunate extreme. There have been too many Americans whose smug answer to the problems of a shrinking, suspicion-ridden world has been "Let 'em learn English!"[10]

Selection 8

The rare 1913 nickel is not the Buffalo type but is the Liberty-head type. Shortly after their coining (only six were made), a then well-known coin dealer was detailed by the late Colonel Green to approach the mint regarding the sale. After negotiating for a short time, four of the six 1913 Liberty-head nickels were sold to him for $500 each, $2000 for the four. All were in brilliant uncirculated condition, and the fifth was kept for the United States Mint collection. No one knows what became of the sixth nickel, and this mysterious nickel is probably the reason so many non-collectors have been acquainted with the rarity of the 1913 Liberty nickel.

For years a well-known dealer advertised very extensively throughout the United States that he would pay $50 for a 1913 Liberty-head nickel, but this coin has never been found and probably never will be. The chances of anyone finding it are practically nil, for we must remember that the average life of a nickel in circulation is not over twenty years. There have been hundreds of millions of nickels coined since 1913, and

[9] John Ise, *Economics*, Harper, 1946, p. 509.
[10] William R. Parker, "The Language Curtain," *School and Society*, October 31, 1953, p. 129.

millions are in circulation all the time. Our population is in excess of 160,000,000 people, anyone of whom might have that poor nickel, so you can figure what odds there are against your ever finding it, or its still being in existence.[11]

Selection 9

Only an all-out war against the virus itself, if successful, would eradicate colds. Medical science now has a new weapon which could accomplish this.

"Ultraviolet 2537" has already been used in hospitals, clinics and other institutions, where it has proved itself an efficient germ killer. At the University of Toronto's Hospital for Sick Children, twice as many children suffered infections where the lamps were not installed as where the lamps were used. At the U. S. Naval Training Center, Sampson, N.Y., respiratory diseases, including colds, were reduced by one fourth by installing the lamps in the sleeping quarters, although mess halls and classrooms were unprotected. The Cradle Society, Evanston, Ill., reported a 90% reduction in the spread of upper respiratory infection among infants in cubicles equipped with "2537" as compared with those in untreated cubicles.[12]

Selection 10

When I speak of freedom, I believe that I approach a subject which is of interest to you not only in general but which must be definitely in your minds as you approach the matter of security, for I presume that we should all be ready to admit that the person who is truly free in this world is the most secure. He has the needed flexibility; he does not need to become a slave of any particular age and therefore unable to meet the revolutionary changes which inevitably come as we move from age to age.

Do you recall that in the passage on the grand inquisitor in Dostoevski's *Brothers Karamazov* he says, "I tell thee that man is tormented by no greater anxiety than to find someone quickly to whom he can hand over that gift of freedom with which he, ill-gaited creature, is born?"[13]

Began   *Finished*   No. words: 970

$$\frac{}{} \times 60 = \underline{\qquad} \text{W.P.M.}$$

No. seconds:

[11] Charles French, "Money of Yesteryear," *Hobbies*, October 1953, p. 120.
[12] John D. Murphy, "New Cure for Colds," *Strange Medical Facts*, November 1954, p. 6.
[13] Douglas Horton, "Slaves to Freedom," *Education for National Security*, American Assoc. of School Administrators, 1953, p. 5.

Compare your rate for reading easy, narrative material with that for reading detailed factual material. Is the latter rate lower than the former? If so, that is what you should expect. You should, however, show an increase in speed in reading both types of content.

Checking Comprehension

Write a brief answer to each question.

You may refer to the selections in answering the first five questions, but do not refer back in answering the last five questions.

1. What pattern was represented in Selection 6? _____
2. What pattern was represented in Selection 7? _____
3. What pattern was represented in Selection 8? _____
4. What pattern was represented in Selection 9? _____
5. What pattern was represented in Selection 10? _____
6. How many different metal alloys are there now? _____
7. According to one of the articles, the decline of foreign-language study in this country began at the same time in history as a certain foreign development. What was this foreign development? _____
8. What is the date and name of the nickel which is so rare? _____
9. The effectiveness of Ultraviolet 2537 was reported from three centers: University of Toronto's Hospital, U.S. Naval Training Center in Sampson, N.Y., and where else? Name the institution and its location. _____
10. Can you complete this sentence? ". . . the person who is truly free in this world is the most _____."

The Answer Key is on page 384. Allow yourself a score of 10 for each completely correct answer. In questions 8 and 9 you may allow yourself a score of 5 for each correct part.

Rate: W.P.M. _____   Comprehension Score: _____

Practice Section III

Long Selections

The short selections with which you have been working should have afforded you sufficient practice in identifying different patterns of writing and adjusting to them.

In each of the selections that follow, first of all identify the pattern of writing. If it is in the Question-Answer pattern, concentrate on the question or questions and then read for the purpose of finding the answer or answers. If the pattern is that of personal experience, probably all you will need to do is to live with the writer vicariously as he tells what happened. Should the giving-information pattern be used, then read carefully to find out what information the writer wishes to impart. If the pattern is of the opinion-reason type, focus sharply on the opinions expressed and then read to find out the author's reasons for holding them. Finally, if you encounter the substantiated-fact pattern, first look for the conclusions, and then find the facts which support each conclusion.

Read as fast as you can in terms of the pattern at hand.

Selection 1

BEGINNING TIME:_____

HR._____ MIN._____

Houses, Signs and Portraits Painted![14]

In the early part of the eighteenth century the *South Carolina Gazette* carried a notice "to gentlemen AND OTHERS" that portraits, engraving, heraldry, and house painting would be undertaken and performed by a native artist "at the lowest rate." This was the usual rather than the unusual thing in the days before and just after the Revolution. Only a fashionable painter could make a living by painting portraits, even though, in those pre-photographic days, that was the only means whereby a man might preserve his image for posterity. Nor could an artist hope to make a living in any one place, because commissions were too rare and competition too keen. He had to go from place to place, painting likenesses at a furious rate, working eight or ten hours a day, and resorting to every kind of time-saving device in order to keep the wolf from the door. If he were not a well-known artist his lot was even harder. He dared not even hope to make a living by his brush, but must eke out his livelihood in more practical fields of endeavor.

A painter whose services were in demand usually received about twenty-five dollars for a portrait; and it is recorded as an evidence of phenomenal success that one artist painted a hundred likenesses at this price in six months. A modern photographer would close up shop if business were as poor as that. The usual rate, however, was even lower, as the following advertisement from a Boston paper of 1790 shows:

[14] J. Pennington, *The Mentor,* October 1924, pp. 45-47.

"The public are respectfully informed that the artists who took the most correct likeness of the President of the United States and executed a medal of him are at the house of John Coburn in State Street and will continue for one month only to make the most correct likenesses in two minutes' sitting and finish them for one dollar to three."

Samuel B. Morse, inventor of the telegraph, made his living in his youth painting miniatures. His price was five dollars if the sitter provided his own ivory; the rate for profile drawings was one dollar. Morse afterward made several full-size likenesses, among them a well-known portrait of General Lafayette. John Wesley Jarvis, nephew of John Wesley, the founder of Methodism, devised two ingenious schemes for saving time in making likenesses. In his early days he invented a machine for drawing profiles on glass, the reverse then being blacked in very quickly. Later on, when he became more successful, he spent his winters in New Orleans executing commissions for portraits, and took with him a lesser light named Inman. Jarvis would paint the head and face and then turn the canvas over to have the background and drapery completed by Inman.

Sometimes the artist survived the struggle, and sometimes he did not. The scarcity of orders, the low prices paid, and the keenness of competition were not the only obstacles in the path of the artist. Puritan prejudice against him was strong. In the "Records of the Selectman of the Towne of Boston," this entry appears: "Lawrence Brown, a Limner, asks admittance to be an Inhabitant of this Towne, which is granted on Condition that he gives Security to Save the Towne Harmless."

There was also the difficulty of securing the materials of one's craft, which had to be imported and were therefore expensive. Benjamin West, called the father of American portrait painting, secured his colors and brushes in this way: The Indians taught him to make the reds and yellows they used for painting themselves, and his mother gave him some indigo. He had never seen a camel's-hair brush, but it had been described to him; so he took a goose quill and fastened to it some hairs from the cat's tail. Another ambitious youth who lived in the backwoods fashioned a palette from a piece of board in which was arranged a row of thimbles filled with various colors.

There was one unfailing expedient to which the Colonial artist could resort, and that was the painting of signs. In the days when shops and houses were not numbered, every business street presented a succession of golden balls, blue gloves, crowns and scepters, dogs, elephants, and horses. These signs very often had no relation to the nature of the business they represented. In Philadelphia, particularly famous for its signs, there was a representation of a cock in a barnyard "which for many years graced a beer garden in Spruce Street. The execution of this was so fine and the expression of nature so exactly copied that it was evident to the most casual observer that it was painted by the hand of a master."

The master whose hand had painted this sign, and many others in Philadelphia, was Matthew Pratt. From childhood Pratt had been interested in painting, and so he was apprenticed to his uncle to learn all branches of the business—that is, sign, house, and portrait painting. His first known portrait is one of Benjamin Franklin. After some months of study under Benjamin West in London, Pratt returned to Philadelphia. In spite of a reasonable number of commissions he was compelled to resort to sign painting as a means of supporting his family. Pratt's signs were a source of great pride to his fellow citizens. He painted the Federal Convention, showing "a group of personages engaged in public discussion," with the venerable head of Dr. Franklin conspicuously displayed in the foreground. Under it was the following rhyme:

These thirty-eight great men have signed a powerful deed
That better times to us shall very soon succeed.

Citizens crowded about busily engaged in identifying the figures in the group. Pratt's portraits were often excellently done. At his best he was the equal of Benjamin West, and a number of his paintings have been attributed to Copley. His picture "The London School" shows West's studio. In it the master is criticizing a picture held by Pratt, and in the foreground is a picture of Delanoy, the artist son of a Philadelphia oysterman.

There were other interesting figures among the early American painters. Charles Willson Peale was apprenticed to a saddler and subsequently worked as a coach builder, a clock- and watchmaker, and a silversmith. When a portrait painter came to town Peale decided to try his hand at the same craft; so he went to Philadelphia and purchased the materials he needed and a book of instructions.

While studying, unaided, Peale also learned to model in wax and to cast in plaster. He painted miniatures, engraved plates, and taught his brothers the art of painting—even as he was learning it himself. Peale was a soldier in the Revolution, founded a museum of natural history, and then went on a lecture tour. As he began to lose his teeth he found speaking difficult, so he gave up lecturing and began making dental plates—at first a set in ivory for himself, and then porcelain teeth for his friends. Among his clients was Washington, and in several of his portraits the Father of our Country wears a strained expression around the mouth due to an ill-fitting set of teeth made by Peale. Peale had many children, all named for famous painters. One of them, Rembrandt Peale became a good painter in his own right. The elder Peale founded the Pennsylvania Academy of Fine Arts in Philadelphia.

Another man to achieve unusual things was William Dunlap, one of the first to paint Washington and his wife. In addition to the vocation of portrait painter, Dunlap was a theatrical manager and playwright, an editor, author, poet, soldier, and farmer. He had only one eye, but his infirmity did not prevent his painting some large canvases of historical and Biblical scenes, in imitation of those of Benjamin West. The public paid twenty-five cents to see them when they were sent on exhibition.

Chester Harding was one of the most romantic figures of the period. A giant well over six feet tall, until he was twenty-one he lived the rough life of a pioneer. When the ambition to paint first struck him he left his father's farm, floated down the Allegheny on a flatboat, and set up shop as a sign painter in Pittsburgh. Finally, encouraged by Gilbert Stuart, Harding opened a studio in Boston. The backwoodsman-artist received so many commissions that even Stuart became envious.

There are countless others who deserve mention, who suffered for the sake of art and pursued it at all costs. Edward G. Malbone, the famous miniaturist, at one time painted theatrical scenery. Bass Otis, a scythe-maker's apprentice, painted many portraits and made the first lithograph ever printed in this country. Robert Fulton, inventor of the steamboat, painted portraits, landscapes, and miniatures in his early manhood.

The work of these early American portrait painters had "power and serenity." As a whole, their art may be summed up by a phrase used to describe the worthy Matthew Pratt's signs: "Here is no niggling in style or touch."

Began	*Finished*	No. words:	1400
			$\dfrac{}{\text{No. seconds:}} \times 60 = \underline{}$ W.P.M.
_____	_____		

Checking Comprehension

1. Before and just after the Revolution most artists (a) had enough portrait painting to do to earn a good living, (b) were very famous, (c) were very well paid, (d) often had to do other kinds of work to earn a living.

2. An artist of early times (a) set up a studio of his own in one town and stayed there, (b) usually worked with a group of artists in one studio, (c) traveled about from place to place, (d) settled in Boston to become a part of an art center.

3. In colonial times an artist usually received for painting a portrait: (a) about ten dollars, (b) about fifty dollars, (c) about one hundred dollars, (d) about twenty-five dollars.

4. The following inventor was an artist as a young man: (a) Eli Whitney, (b) Samuel B. Morse, (c) Cyrus McCormick, (d) Alexander Bell.

5. Benjamin West, one of the colonial painters, solved the problem of obtaining expensive red and yellow paints by (a) importing paints,

(b) using materials from his own fields, (c) having the Indians teach him how to make red and yellow, (d) using water colors.

6 The most common work by which artists supplemented their income was (a) farming, (b) selling landscape paintings, (c) teaching art, (d) painting signs.

7. The artist most famous for sign painting was (a) Matthew Pratt, (b) Benjamin West, (c) John Coburn, (d) John Wesley Jarvis.

8. One of the things which made William Dunlap famous was (a) modeling in wax, (b) being one of the first to paint Washington and his wife, (c) engraving plates, (d) painting signs.

9. Charles Willson Peale, in addition to painting, made: (a) ship models, (b) furniture, (c) houses, (d) dental plates.

10. Chester Harding set up his first shop as a sign painter in (a) Boston, (b) New York, (c) Philadelphia, (d) Pittsburgh.

Answers: 1)—, 2)—, 3)—, 4)—, 5)—, 6)—, 7)—, 8)—, 9)—, 10)—.

See the Answer Key on page 384.

Rate: W.P.M. —————   Comprehension Score: —————

Selection 2

BEGINNING TIME:—————
HR.————— MIN.—————

Statement of Donald B. Woodward[15]

Your letter of September 22 asks for a statement of what I believe to be "the specific implications and long-run effects on Government finances and on stability of the economy in following at this time a policy of allowing interest rates on short-term Treasury issues to rise."

1. *The question's setting.*—My response is necessarily conditioned by my concept of the environment and the Relationship the incidents you mention have to it. My reply may be clearer if those concepts are very briefly made explicit.

The American political economy of our age seems to me to be marked by two transcending imperatives: First, that freedom must be protected from tremendous exogenous threats; and second, that the economy must be protected from the disequilibration, indeed, the disintegration, of major depression and major inflation. (At the moment the greater danger seems to be major inflation, but emphasis on it alone could cause us to go to extremes; the major preoccupation of analysis with combatting depression between 1929 and 1941 so inhibited balanced thinking as to produce

[15] Donald B. Woodward, *General Credit Control, Debt Management, and Economic Mobilization*, U.S. Govt. Printing Office, 1951, pp. 77-79.

extensive antidepression policies when inflation was the problem.) And major depressions and inflations are occurrences involving credit and money in a great degree, if, indeed, they are not really essentially monetary phenomena.

These two imperatives are intimately interrelated at various levels. They can have and have had major consequences upon each other. Both major inflation and depression have weakened the country's power and consequently its ability to protect freedom, while the struggle to protect freedom has brought about conditions inducing at different times major inflation and depression. In view of these interrelationships, it is important to avoid partial views when these matters are considered.

During the course of national efforts according with the two great imperatives, two major developments have occurred during the past two decades which, in my opinion, bear with great force on your question. First, the public debt has grown enormously. Second, the value of the dollar as commonly measured by price indexes has fallen by only a little less than half.

The existence of the two imperatives, and the developments resulting from them, have greatly broadened the horizons and increased the depth of the question you ask.

I turn now to your question, which deals both with government finances and economic stability. Let me first consider the two parts separately.

2. *Government finances.*—The purpose of "following at this time a policy of allowing interest on short-term Treasury issues to rise" (to use your terminology and emphasis) is to curb the inflation manifested for some weeks in rising bank loans, commodity prices, and the like. "The specific implications and long-run effects on government finances" of such a policy depend preponderantly upon whether inflation is likely to be curbed by the policy followed.

It is traditional central bank and orthodox economic theory that rising interest rates penalize and dissuade those considering expansion of their businesses and also result in increasing saving and curtailed consumer demand; all this is supposed to operate in part directly from rising short-term rates, and in part from the effects of rising short rates on long-term rates (and the opposite effects are had from declining rates). This inhibiting effect supposedly is felt on the private sector of the economy and presumably, though this has been less clearly developed, on the public sector as well. This view of the functioning of rising (or falling) rates has long been and still is vigorously challenged as unrealistic and contrary to much available evidence; on the other hand, it has been supported by arguments of marginal economics and an array of evidence of the association of rising interest rates and the ending of booms. The evidence does not appear to validate either point of view conclusively.

But there is another consideration. The policy of raising interest rates to curtail inflation is now being followed in a new environment; the public debt has grown large. When Mary's little lamb grows to a size far surpassing an elephant, can it appropriately be treated any longer as a little lamb? If Mary does so, may she not be endangering the house she lives in, the school house, the lives of her schoolmates, the teacher and herself? Rising short-term interest rates produce rising medium-term and longer-term rates, and rising rates mean declining prices of Government securities. Many holders of government securities have been encouraged to believe that no one could take a loss on these issues; though, of course, no contract or commitment exists that prices will never go down. There is a risk that falling government security prices, with below-par quotations for a number of issues, may make for dissatisfaction among holders, with consequent sales (or presentation to the Treasury for redemption of demand issues) and declining willingness to invest in such issues in the future.

The present is a very unhappy time for such a question to be raised. The present is just on the eve of a period of years in which the vast amount of 10-year securities sold to finance World War II must be refinanced, when the volume of short-term debt is large, and when international conditions might require new and sizable deficit financing. During the next few years the Treasury must find buyers for literally many hundred billions of dollars of government issues. If prospective buyers question the attractiveness of the paper, then the banking system, including the Federal Reserve, will of necessity become the buyers, because it is inconceivable that the Treasury would be left without necessary funds. In that event, the money supply would be substantially increased, and this would be inflationary. The possibility, therefore, exists that very much of a rise in interest rates at this time might prove to be inflationary rather than anti-inflationary as intended, because of the change in the environment from the times when traditional central banking and orthodox economic theory were formulated.

But there is another aspect to the matter. Inflation, i.e., loss of purchasing power by the dollar, may also cause a diminution in willingness to hold promises to pay dollars in the future. Inflation already has raised questions about the desirability of holding government securities, and the further inflation proceeds, the greater may be the Treasury's difficulty in doing the refunding and financing it has to do in the next several years. And, in addition, inflation increases the cost of goods and labor.

Viewing these various aspects of the matter, I conclude that the most important consideration to government finance is that inflation be halted. If it is not, I judge that the Treasury is likely to experience considerable trouble during the next several years. This conclusion can be reached with confidence, however one may feel about the efficacy of changing interest rates as an anti-inflationary technique. I shall return to the question of technique later. But it should also be noted that serious deflation, which does not now seem likely for a long time to come, would also be quite harmful to the Treasury, and its prevention, as well as that of inflation, should be part of the continuing objective.

For purposes of completeness, I should add two points to these comments on government finances. First, higher interest rates mean that the Treasury will have to pay a higher interest cost than would otherwise be the case. Second, rising short-term rates mean that longer term issues are made less attractive to buyers relatively, so that any refunding of short paper into longer paper by the Treasury is made more difficult. But these are evidently of subordinate importance to the larger question just developed; and the higher interest cost argument has been tremendously over-exaggerated.

3. *Economic stability.*—The chief "specific implications and long-run effects . . . in the stability of the economy in following at this time a policy of allowing interest rates on short-term Treasury issues to rise" also relate to inflation control.

The time which has elapsed since the rise in rates was started has been very short, and the phenomena which have appeared can properly only be noted for consideration along with subsequent events which will provide greater perspective. Subject to this treatment are two items: (a) The Federal Reserve, in the weeks since the interest rate rise was started, has had to buy about $1.2 billion of government securities to maintain orderly market conditions; and during the period has turned from a seller of long-term issues to a buyer. (b) During this time the commercial loans of the commercial banks have continued to rise, which was under way prior to the action, and the total of such loans outstanding has reached a new high level for many years. These developments do not indicate immediate success in credit curtailment, and they raise the question whether limited increases in interest rates in the new environment of the vast public debt have any effect on the ability or willingness of the banks to accommodate their customers. Is the availability of credit significantly affected?

Yet such questions should not in any way obscure the fact that the interests of economic stability, just as the interests of government finance, require that inflation be halted, that if the decade of the 1950's is marked by any such robbery of the dollar as was the preceding decade, the United States will be harmed economically, and as well politically, internationally, socially, morally, and spiritually. And they should not mask the extremely intimate relationship between inflation (and depression) and monetary and credit developments.

4. *What conclusion?*—The territory over which we are now traveling is so new as to make evidence scanty and dogma dubious. Tentatively, and rather gingerly, I would advance the following hypotheses for consideration:

(a) Realization of this country's twin objectives of freedom and prosperity, in an environment including the large public debt and an already seriously depreciated dollar, require careful fiscal policy and operation and more extensive, skillful, and successful monetary management than ever before; and it is more true perhaps than at any previous time that "money will not manage itself."

(1) To the degree that monetary management and fiscal policy are inadequate or fail, the country probably will resort to direct price control, allocation and rationing. These deal only with the results of inflation, which they may suppress for a time; but they cannot prevent or cure inflation. While they may be necessary in a great national emergency, they cannot be used over any prolonged period of strain, and the attempt to do so would be catastrophic.

(b) The necessity for effective monetary management means that every possible technique and device should be utilized.

(1) A rigorous pay-as-you-go fiscal policy in inflationary periods, with strictest curtailment of public expenditures not absolutely essential, and a tax policy designed to stimulate production which is itself a major inflation control, is an essential procedure to prevent further aggravation of the already serious monetary problems.

(2) The central bank should be given and encouraged to seek the greatest possible latitude of operation consistent with the objective of economic stability. Developments, during the weeks since a policy of allowing interest rates on short-term and, to a degree, other Treasury securities to rise was adopted, have provided no conclusive evidence of the efficacy of that policy in halting inflation, which is its objective, and broader considerations also leave the question subject to controversy. This does not mean that the policy should be abandoned, or even that it should not be pursued further, but it does mean that the operation carries sizable risk to government finance and economic stability and should be very cautious.

(3) Because monetary management is so vital, and because the traditional techniques are so inhibited, the development of new techniques and devices is extremely urgent. Some selective credit controls have been utilized in recent years, e.g., consumer credit and stock-market credit, and now mortgage credit. And public-debt management has been utilized a little for monetary-management purposes. I believe that both these areas could be utilized much more effectively and extensively for and by monetary management, and so deserve more attention.

The Joint Committee on the Economic Report can most appropriately and usefully pursue this subject. The committee has a great opportunity to perform a significant public service.

Began   *Finished*   No. words: 1700

                                        —— × 60 = ———— W.P.M.

——————   ——————   No. seconds:

Checking Comprehension

1. This statement is Mr. Woodward's opinion on the advisability of (a) lowering the interest on long-term Treasury issues, (b) raising the interest on long-term Treasury issues, (c) lowering the interest on short-term Treasury issues, (d) raising the interest on short-term Treasury issues.

2. One of the "transcending imperatives" that Mr. Woodward mentions is that (a) freedom must be protected, (b) the present "boom" must be continued, (c) a more conservative government must come to power, (d) a less conservative government must come to power.

3. Two developments have occurred during the two past decades which have a bearing on the question being discussed. One is that the value of the dollar has fallen. The other is that (a) population has increased, (b) imports have decreased, (c) the public debt has grown enormously, (d) taxes are higher.

4. The question which the writer was asked to discuss consisted of two parts. One part had to do with government finances. The other part had to do with (a) interest on loans, (b) selling treasury bonds, (c) bank policies, (d) economic stability.

5. The possibility exists that a rise in interest rates at this time might be (a) anti-inflationary, (b) inflationary, (c) stabilizing, (d) not felt at all.

6. There are two viewpoints in regard to the functioning of rising or falling rates on our economy. Evidence (a) supports both of these points of view, (b) doesn't validate either point of view conclusively, (c) supports one point of view more directly than the other, (d) has nothing to do with either point of view.

7. The most important consideration in government finance is to (a) halt inflation, (b) maintain prosperity, (c) avoid too many controls, (d) bring business techniques into government.

8. Prior to Mr. Woodward's statement, increased interest rates on short-term loans had been in effect for several weeks. It is pointed out that during this time commercial loans had (a) declined, (b) continued to rise as before, (c) remained constant, (d) continued to rise, but at a lower rate than before.

9. The policy of allowing interest rates on short-term Treasury securities to rise (a) should be intensified, (b) should be discontinued immediately, (c) should be continued with caution, (d) is neither recommended or not recommended.

10. In the field of monetary management, the author says there is a need for (a) another expert opinion, (b) a survey, (c) new techniques and devices, (d) the hiring of more experts by the government.

Answers: 1)—, 2)—, 3)—, 4)—, 5)—, 6)—, 7)—, 8)—, 9)—, 10)—.

See Answer Key on page 384.

Rate: W.P.M. ————   Comprehension Score: ————

Selection 3

BEGINNING TIME:————
HR.———— MIN.————

General Introduction[16]

This report is prepared in response to a letter from the chairman of the Joint Committee on the Economic Report requesting a survey of foreign experience in the field of treasury-central bank relationships.

Almost all countries have central banks, and in all cases these institutions are separate and distinct from the treasury departments of their governments. The function performed by central banks in all countries is to regulate the supply of money in such a way as to serve national interests. Activities of central banks, designed to influence or control the availability of loan funds, necessarily affect interest rates paid by private and governmental borrowers. Conversely, actions designed to affect interest rates have repercussions upon the supply of credit. Because of the great importance of public debts in the financial structure of most countries, the need for coordination between monetary and credit policies, on the one hand, and public-debt management and fiscal policies on the other, has been recognized in almost all countries. Methods of working out a harmoniously-functioning relationship between treasury and central bank have varied widely. There is wide diversity also in the devices adopted in foreign countries to restrict the over-all supply of credit within the framework of policies which take account of large-scale financing needs of treasuries.

[16] *General Credit Control, Debt Management, and Economic Mobilization,* U.S. Govt. Printing Office, Appendix I, p. 80.

This survey of foreign experience is designed to provide background material for the study of problems of monetary policy in the United States. It will be immediately apparent, however, that devices which may have worked well in foreign countries may not be suitable here. Differences in political, economic, and financial structure between the United States and foreign countries, as well as among the foreign countries themselves, are so profound that a comparison of national monetary policies serves primarily to bring into sharper focus the peculiarities of national problems.

To illustrate this point, it may be well to review briefly some of the principal differences in underlying conditions among the countries whose experiences will be described below and between them and the United States.

Differences in economic structure and development are possibly most important in accounting for the lack of comparability of treasury-central bank relationships among various countries. Thus, in countries where there are highly developed money and capital markets, issues concerning monetary and debt management policies tend to revolve around questions of the interest-rate structure, since the rate structure affects, on the one hand, demand and supply factors in the money market and, on the other, the rates at which the treasury can place its obligations with investors other than the central bank. But in countries where the central bank is the principal source of funds for financing government deficits, market rates of interest are of less importance for debt management; in these countries agreement must be reached as to the amounts that can be advanced by the central bank to the treasury in view of the unstabilizing effect of these advances on the economy. Again, in a country where hyperinflation or currency reform has virtually wiped out the public debt, monetary problems are of a different nature from those characteristic of a country where the public debt is large in relation to national income and is widely dispersed among both bank and nonbank holders.

Wide differences among the various types of banking systems must also be recognized. Credit control techniques that are adequate in a country with a highly centralized multiple-branch banking system, in which bank policies can be influenced by direct contact and suasion, may be of little help in a country whose banks are numbered in the thousands. Also, differences in banking traditions and attitudes, such as the extent to which banks are willing or reluctant to hold long-term government securities or to borrow from the central bank, may mean that policies that are effective in some countries will not work elsewhere.

Began   *Finished*   No. words: 640

$$\frac{\quad\quad}{\text{No. seconds:}} \times 60 = \underline{\quad\quad} \text{ W.P.M.}$$

Checking Comprehension

1. This report covers the relationships in foreign countries between treasuries and (a) small banks, (b) central banks, (c) commercial banks, (d) savings banks.

2. The institution of the central bank exists (a) in all foreign countries, (b) in almost all foreign countries, (c) in a few foreign countries, (d) in no foreign countries.

3. The function of the central bank is to (a) regulate the supply of money, (b) keep smaller banks from financial difficulty, (c) handle the government's payrolls, (d) take care of the national budget.

4. The survey of foreign experience in banking was designed to (a) bring the United States into closer relationships with foreign countries, (b) find out how much these banks are aiding their government, (c) provide background for the study of monetary policy in the United States, (d) find out the average interest charged abroad.

5. Devices which have worked well in foreign countries (a) should be adopted here, (b) should be used in communist countries, (b) reveal how banks are aiding their government, (c) may not be suitable here, (d) reveal the average interest rate charged abroad.

6. The most important factor in accounting for incomparability of banks is (a) differences in the amount of money they handle, (b) differences in debts they owe, (c) differences in rate of interest charged, (d) differences in economic structure and development.

7. Another factor which must be recognized in considering differences in banks is (a) size of cities in which they are located, (b) the various types of banking systems used, (c) the climate of the country, (d) the products of the country.

8. In countries where there are highly-developed money and capital markets, policies tend to revolve around questions of the (a) interest-rate structure, (b) amounts of money advanced by the central bank, (c) administration of the national budget, (d) determination of wage and price standards.

9. In countries where the central bank is the principal source of funds for financing government deficits, agreements must be reached in regard to the (a) interest-rate structure, (b) amounts of money advanced by the central bank to the Treasury, (c) administration of the national budget, (d) determination of wage and price standards.

10. In some countries the national debt has been wiped out by (a) high taxation, (b) low government spending, (c) hyperinflation or currency reform, (d) deflation.

Answers: 1)—, 2)—, 3)—, 4)—, 5)—, 6)—, 7)—, 8)—, 9)—, 10)—.
See the Answer Key on page 384.
Rate: W.P.M. ————   Comprehension Score: ————

Selection 4

BEGINNING TIME:————
HR.———— MIN.————

Cigarettes[17]

Sixteen cigarettes of each brand, each cigarette from a different pack, were "smoked" in CU's laboratory tests for nicotine and tar in cigarette smoke. Twenty-seven brands, purchased in 19 cities throughout the United States, were included in the tests. All kinds of cigarettes were represented: regular-size and king-size; regular-price, low-price, and premium; the common American blend and Turkish and Virginia blends; low-nicotine, denicotinized, and untreated; flavored and mentholated; and untipped, cork-tipped, ivory-tipped, and filter-tipped. For so great a variety, most of the differences were, nevertheless, significant. Several positive conclusions can be drawn from the data.

The kind of tobacco

The test results indicate that the nicotine content of the smoke from a cigarette is influenced, first of all, by the type of tobacco used. The cigarette with the least nicotine in its smoke was one made with tobacco especially developed for its low nicotine content. This brand, JOHN ALDEN, had an average of only 0.4 milligrams of nicotine per cigarette in the smoke puffed in by the laboratory smoking apparatus. (A milligram is about 1/28,000th of an ounce.) Other cigarettes with less nicotine in their smoke than the big-selling brands were in general those made largely of Turkish tobacco. The low-priced YORKSHIRE cigarette was as low in nicotine as any of the Turkish types.

The "popular" brands

The most widely-advertised and widely-sold regular-length cigarettes— CAMELS, LUCKY STRIKES, CHESTERFIELDS, PHILIP MORRIS, and OLD GOLDS— were practically identical in the nicotine content of their smoke, which averaged about five times as high in nicotine per cigarette as the smoke from JOHN ALDEN.

The smoke of king-size cigarettes (about 3⅓ inches in length) generally contained about a fifth more nicotine than the smoke of regular-length

[17] *Consumers Reports*, February 1953, pp. 67-70.

American brands (about 2¾ inches in length), when both were smoked down to a butt of a little under an inch. When, however, the extra length of the king-size cigarette is left unsmoked—that is, when only as much of the longer cigarette is consumed as of a shorter one—the total nicotine from the king-size cigarette is lower. The single exception found—EMBASSY—gave only about as much nicotine as a regular cigarette, even when smoked down to a butt just under an inch.

Most filter-tip cigarettes tested—contrary to the statements in the ads for them—actually had about 20% more nicotine in their smoke than regular brands—as much as that of the typical king-size brands smoked down to about a one-inch butt. Among the filter-tip brands tested, there was the single exception already noted: KENTS were second only to JOHN ALDENS in freedom from nicotine in their smoke, averaging only about one milligram of nicotine per cigarette.

As the smoke passes through it, the tobacco in the cigarette itself acts as a fairly effective filter; CU's tests included a determination of the filtering effect of the length of tobacco which is replaced by other materials in filter-tip cigarettes. Two thirds of an inch of a regular-size cigarette were cut off, and the remainder smoked to the usual extent; 16% more nicotine was found in the smoke than in the smoke of uncut cigarettes.

Some special cases

Slightly above KENT in nicotine content—but appreciably below the big-selling regular brands—were SANO, a "denicotinized" cigarette, MURAD, a Turkish brand, and YORKSHIRE, the Sears brand, which appears similar to the more-widely-sold brands. Two other Turkish cigarettes, HELMAR and MELACHRINO, also ranked between KENT and the big sellers in nicotine content of their smoke, but they were only a little below the popular regular-size American blends.

Some brands—VIRGINIA ROUNDS and CRAVEN A—had a higher nicotine content than the popular brands, probably because of their particular blends of tobacco.

KOOLS, the largest selling mentholated cigarette, are, like so many other brands, promoted as being "mild," but in nicotine content of their smoke KOOLS were about the same as the popular regular brands.

Tars are not found in unsmoked cigarettes but are produced as a result of incomplete combustion. Because of the variability between different cigarettes of the same brand, and because of inherent shortcomings in available test methods, the differences in tar content between brands can be considered only approximate; differences of a few milligrams are of no significance. The tar content of the smoke from KENT cigarettes war found, however, to be consistently low.

Comparison with previous tests

The tests on which this report is based showed a somewhat higher nicotine content for many brands than was found in the limited tests of these brands reported on in June, 1952. CU pointed out at the time that the very small number of cigarettes of each brand tested made those results only approximate. The present results reflect the greater accuracy afforded by the greater number of cigarettes tested. The large difference found in the two tests with respect to KENT cigarettes appears to be mainly the result of a change in the filter during the interval. CU noted last summer that KENTS required "considerably more effort to draw on than do other cigarettes." This characteristic appears now to have been largely corrected with a looser and, therefore, a more permeable filter.

CU's current tests were for nicotine and tar content. Blindfold tests, which have been performed many times by many groups, including CU, and which have almost uniformly shown that smokers cannot with any regularity distinguish among the popular brands by taste, were not a part of this survey. In the course of its investigation, CU did have members of its staff who were habitual smokers try out various brands, but no attempt was made to conceal the names of the cigarettes being smoked. Some of the comments were interesting. With almost no exceptions the smokers showed the same reluctance to shift from their favorite brands that some advertising surveys have shown to exist widely. Many of the smokers said they would not shift from the brand they smoked to some of the brands even if these cost appreciably less.

Filter holders

The filter holders CU tested were the DENICOTEA, in which silica is used as the filtering agent; the MEDICA, in which a roll of paper is used; the PURA-SMOKE, in which alumina is used; the WEBER, in which charcoal is used; and the ZEUS, in which a cigarette in the tube acts as the filter. Two of each brand were tested.

Cigarettes held in the filter holders were "smoked" as for the cigarette tests, and the smoke was collected and analyzed by the same methods. A typical regular-size cigarette was used. Each holder was "smoked" on a run of five cigarettes. The two brands which proved most effective on the initial run—the ZEUS and the DENICOTEA—were further tested for their effectiveness when the same filters were used without change for longer runs. The filtering action of the DENICOTEA was determined for the last five of 15 cigarettes, and the effectiveness of the ZEUS for the last five of 20. Both were found effective even after such long use. (The DENICOTEA effectiveness had decreased and the ZEUS effectiveness had increased slightly.)

In length the holders ranged from 3½ to 4¾ inches; the long metal tube of the ZEUS holders was found to be more effective by itself in removing nicotine than some of the holders with the filters in them. When used without a cigarette inside as a filter, the ZEUS tube condensed nearly 20% of the nicotine in the smoke from the first five cigarettes smoked.

Most of the members of a panel of smokers who normally did not use cigarette filter holders found the odor of the filters after a few cigarettes extremely unpleasant. One may have to suffer through a period of building up a tolerance to the odor in order to be able to use one of these filters regularly. Some users found the extra effort of drawing through them objectionable; others disliked the weight of the holders. One found the smoke relatively tasteless, and noted that he smoked more cigarettes when using the filter. While cigarette holders have the advantage of keeping tobacco grains out of the smoker's mouth (an advantage shared by filter-tip cigarettes), they cause the smoke to impinge on a small area of the tongue, which can cause the same "bite" that pipes cause.

One unhappy tendency of smokers who use a filter holder is to smoke cigarettes down to the very end, thus negating at least a part of the nicotine-removing effectiveness of the filter. Another tendency, which has the same effect, is to smoke deeper puffs with a holder than without.

Began   *Finished*   No. words: 1360

$$\frac{}{\text{No. seconds:}} \times 60 = \underline{\hspace{2cm}} \text{ W.P.M.}$$

Checking Comprehension

1. According to the tests, one of the most important factors that influence the nicotine content of the smoke from a cigarette is (a) the type of tobacco, (b) the treatment of the tobacco, (c) the manner in which the tobacco is packed, (d) the type of paper used.

2. The nicotine content of the smoke of the five most widely-advertised and widely-sold regular-length cigarettes was found to be (a) variable, (b) highest in Camels, (c) lowest in Old Golds, (d) practically identical.

3. In general, the nicotine content of the smoke of king-size cigarettes was (a) about a fifth lower than that of regular-size cigarettes, (b) the same as that of regular-size cigarettes, (c) about a fifth higher than that of regular-length American brands, (d) higher than regular size in some, and lower in others.

4. The nicotine content of most filter-tip cigarettes was found to be (a) about 20% less than that of regular cigarettes, (b) the same as that of regular cigarettes, (c) about 20% more than that of regular brands, (d) 20% higher than that of king-size cigarettes.

5. Test results for tars in cigarette smoke (a) proved the superiority of king-size cigarettes, (b) proved the superiority of filter-tip cigarettes, (c) proved the superiority of mentholated cigarettes, (d) showed Kent cigarettes to be low.

6. The report refers to a previous test made for nicotine content in 1952. It points out that the results of this test were only approximate because of (a) poor testing methods, (b) insufficient experience in testing, (c) poor equipment, (d) small number of samples used.

7. The study revealed that when a suggestion is made that a smoker change his brand of cigarette, the reaction is (a) willingness to change, (b) willingness to change if the price of the suggested brand is lower, (c) willingness to change if laboratory tests show the suggested brand to have a lower nicotine content, (d) reluctance to change.

8. Two brands of filter holders were tested initially and then were tested again for their effectiveness after long use. After the second test it was found that (a) they were both effective, (b) neither one kept its effectiveness, (c) one brand kept its effectiveness while the other did not, (d) no conclusions could be reached.

9. Smokers who did not use filter holders found that a filter (a) made the smoke taste better, (b) caused the odor to be unpleasant, (c) enhanced the aroma, (d) caused them to smoke fewer cigarettes.

10. According to the article, one unhappy tendency of smokers who use a filter holder is (a) to run out of filters, (b) to hurt their teeth by gripping the filter holder, (c) to smoke cigarettes down to the very end, (d) to smoke more than other smokers.

Answers: 1)—, 2)—, 3)—, 4)—, 5)—, 6)—, 7)—, 8)—, 9)—, 10)—.

See the Answer Key on page 384.

Rate: W.P.M. ————   Comprehension Score: ————

Selection 5

BEGINNING TIME:————
HR.———— MIN.————

The Curse of Tondo[18]

What happens when a place is cursed? Does the curse linger on through the ages, bringing evil to all who fall under its spell? Is this true of Lake Elsinore in Southern California?

[18] Belle C. Ewing, *The American Mercury*, July 1954, pp. 125-126.

This blue, mystic lake lies in an inland California valley which is teeming and steaming with hot springs. Rimmed by shaggy mountains whose forested crests are reflected in its clear waters, Lake Elsinore is the very personification of peace—but on it rests the curse of Tondo.

Lake Elsinore has had a colorful history. Much of it lies buried in legend, and it is difficult to separate fact from fiction. There have been stories of underground volcanoes on the lake bottom, erupting, killing fish and discoloring the water. There have been tales that, although portions of the lake were shallow even in wet years, other parts are bottomless abysses. There have been stories of a playful sea serpent that lived in its depths.

Long noted for its scenic beauty and health-giving waters, the lake was a famous resort in the Nineties.

But long before the first white man had set foot along the shore of the lake, this part of California had been the home of the Soboba Indians. Their chief was Tondo, a stern and unforgiving man.

He had a daughter, Morning Star, who was in love with Palo, son of the chief of the Palas, a neighboring tribe. The Sobobas and Palas were sworn enemies. For a time the lovers met secretly. Then one day they were discovered by Tondo. His rage was terrible to behold. He forbade the lovers ever to meet again.

Morning Star tried in every way to appease her father's anger, to soften his heart toward Palo. But in time she saw that it was useless; that he would never give his consent to their marriage. Vowing that they would never be separated, the Indian maid and her lover walked hand in hand into the lake, as the dreary November sun cast long shadows on the land. They were followed by a group of orphan children whom Morning Star had befriended. All walked into the lake, singing the mournful death song of their people, while Tondo stood on the shore and cursed the lovers, cursed the blue water into which they all walked to their death.

Ever since that day it would seem that a jinx has been laid over Lake Elsinore. Old-timers tell of a great upheaval in the lake which caused water to spout into the air like a geyser and turn blood-red. Later, it became known that three hundred springs of boiling mud and water were born in the valley during that upheaval. The springs reeked with sulphur.

Shortly after this, mysterious lights were seen dancing over the water. The Indians declared that the spirits were having a powwow.

For many years after this phenomenon the lake remained peaceful. Then boats were overturned for no apparent reason, and few of their occupants ever returned to tell the story. This continued for several years. At the same time, strong swimmers dived into the lake never to reappear.

In 1833 and again in 1846, fish in the lake suddenly died.

In the spring of 1850 came the Battle of the Gnats. They bred in the water of the lake and swarmed over the land. They invaded the country-side until the harassed inhabitants called for help.

And in this century, in July 1951, the sky-blue waters of the lake vanished like mist before a noonday sun. When the bottom was laid bare there was no trace of a volcano, the bottomless pits, or the other disturbances of legend or fact.

The copious winter rains of 1951-1952 have replenished the lake. But what menace does its haunting beauty hold today? For tomorrow?

The once mighty Sobobas are few now. But the old men swear that their ancestors still haunt the lake; they claim to hear their voices in the rustle of the tules—see them walk across the water, bearing in their hands a spirit light. They nod grizzled heads and murmur that the great Tondo's curse will forever remain upon the lake. Only Time, the wise and silent one, can tell.

Began   *Finished*   No. words: 700

$$\frac{}{} \times 60 = \underline{} \text{ W.P.M.}$$

———   ———   No. seconds:

Checking Comprehension

1. Lake Elsinore is considered by legend to be (a) beautiful, (b) temporary, (c) full of gold, (d) cursed.

2. This lake is located (a) in a volcanic crater, (b) in the desert, (c) in a valley, (d) near the ocean.

3. During the Nineties the lake was famous (a) as a resort, (b) as the center of a mining area, (c) as a stopping place for people going West, (d) as a Pony Express station.

4. Chief Tondo was (a) a kind man, (b) a stern man, (c) a great leader who united two Indian tribes, (d) a bitter enemy of the white men.

5. Probably Chief Tondo's rage was due to the fact that (a) Palo was not wealthy enough, (b) Morning Star was too young to marry, (c) Tondo's tribe and Palo's tribe were enemies, (d) Palo had murdered Tondo's brother.

6. Morning Star and Palo finally (a) married, (b) killed Tondo, (c) killed themselves, (d) walked to their death in the lake.

7. Old-timers tell of a great upheaval in the lake. They say that at that time, the water turned (a) red, (b) blue, (c) green, (d) yellow.

8. When boats were mysteriously overturned in the lake, their occupants (a) swam ashore, (b) righted the boats, (c) had to avoid vicious fish, (d) usually never returned.

9. On two occasions, fish in the lake (a) suddenly died, (b) became plentiful, (c) developed weird shapes, (d) became very large.

10. When the lake dried up in 1951, it was found that (a) there was an old volcanic crater at the bottom, (b) there were deep trenches at the bottom, (c) there were relics of Indians on the bottom, (d) there were no traces of disturbance on the bottom.

Answers: 1)—, 2)—, 3)—, 4)—, 5)—, 6)—, 7)—, 8)—, 9)—, 10)—.

See the Answer Key on page 385.

Rate: W.P.M. ————   Comprehension Score: ————

Vocabulary Study

Each line extending across the page below contains one word which appears in a selection in this chapter. Two other words appear which are miscellaneous in meaning. There is a fourth word in each list related in meaning to the first word. Underline the related word in each horizontal list.

1. *extempore*	unpremeditated	inadvertently	peremptorily
2. *agitation*	palpitation	instigation	commotion
3. *phenomenon*	eventuality	incontrovertible	marvel
4. *anachronism*	synchronism	simultaneousness	incongruity
5. *scrutinizer*	examiner	inquisitor	intruder
6. *nomenclature*	escutcheon	terminology	heraldry
7. *inventive*	endowment	adulatory	ingenious
8. *perceived*	received	manifested	discerned
9. *preponderantly*	precipitate	dominantly	prevalence
10. *interpolation*	insertion	diminution	abatement
11. *languish*	attenuate	curtailment	pine
12. *tentative*	indubitable	provisional	enigmatic
13. *efficacy*	puissance	omnipotence	opalescence
14. *infringe*	implicit	encroach	include
15. *transcending*	surpassing	culminate	pre-eminently

Check your answers with the Answer Key on page 385.

Follow-Up Practice

Using materials of your own selection. Continue with your regular practice periods each evening. Devote some of your practice time to improving your speed and comprehension in reading non-technical material and some to improving your ability to read and recall detailed facts. Keep a record of your speed and comprehension in reading both types of material.

In all the reading you do in connection with your duties, continue to apply the techniques that you have learned up to this point, including the new technique of identifying patterns of writing. As soon as you pick up something to read, decide upon the pattern, then read in accordance with the author's design. The continuous application of this technique to every situation should contribute much to your skill in reading all types of material.

CHAPTER 10

The Knack

of Skimming

Swallows Skim—So Can You!

THE swallow skims swiftly through the air, catching and devouring insects while simultaneously flapping his wings to propel his body. He even drinks as he skims along over brooks, ponds, and rivers, gathering drops of water in his beak with no cessation in flight. This versatile creature doesn't pause or labor over any one insect or any one pool.

The swallow's mode of skimming for food and water may be likened to the method used by skilled readers who skim over the pages of print, gathering what they want as they "fly" along. With instruction and practice a reader can become extremely adept in "catching" what he desires from reading while "on the wing." This is the type of reading in which some people cover 1,000 words per minute and are able to repeat the gist of what they have read.

What Can Skimming Do for You?

There is no reading asset of greater value to the present-day adult than this highly-developed skill. Skimming enables a person quickly to select material which he wants to read and to discard that in which he is not interested or which is inconsequential to his purpose. The ability to skim expertly makes it possible for the businessman to clear his desk rapidly. If he is skilled in skimming, just a few swift glances will enable him to segregate and organize a miscellaneous pile of papers. Quickly he can toss into the basket those materials which hold no interest for him, stack in a pile those things which he needs to read carefully, and place in another pile those pieces which he may later skim once more for main ideas. Probably two thirds of the stack on his desk (and this includes correspondence) can be disposed of through the skimming technique.

Clearing a desk quickly is not the only function of skimming. All of us find the skimming technique useful in newspaper and magazine reading. We skim to find the articles we wish to read and those which we prefer to skip. Probably almost everyone has developed some initial skill in skimming, through contacts with newspapers and magazines.

Skimming is useful also in choosing a book to read, whether it is fiction or nonfiction. It is advisable to skim through several different books for general impressions. Such a procedure yields guidance in the choice of the book which seems to hold the best promise of personal satisfaction and pleasure. In selecting a factual chapter or article, either in a book or magazine, it is helpful to be able to locate a topic of special interest by skimming.

Rarely does the person who is skillful in skimming complain that he doesn't have time to cope with the mass of reading material which confronts him.

Techniques of Skimming

While skimming is the most useful of the reading skills, it is also the most complex. Skimming is a hierarchy built upon and utilizing all other reading skills which have been discussed in this book. That is why this chapter on skimming was delayed until the other skills had been presented. There is no easy trick which will enable you immediately to become an expert in skimming. All you have done so far has built the foundation, and new techniques will be suggested in the pages that follow. A high degree of proficiency can come only as a result of stepped-up practice in applying both the old and the new techniques in the right proportions at the right times.

Some specialists use the term *scanning* to designate the process of quickly locating a particular fact or figure within a selection, while the term skimming is used for the process of quickly passing over an entire selection or passage to get a general impression of it. The difference is in the purpose rather than in the process. For this reason both are treated in this chapter under the general heading of skimming.

Applying Skills Previously Learned

A strong, leading-on purpose is absolutely essential in successful skimming. Your intent in reading must be clearly formulated and kept uppermost in your consciousness, for how can you skim unless you know what you are skimming for? Is it to find something which you may enjoy as recreational reading? Is it to find an informative article which will contribute to your business, professional, or general knowledge? Is it to find main ideas or just one specific fact? Is it to grasp the meaning of something to which you must give attention in your office communication? Whatever your reason, cleave to it throughout your skimming process.

The procedures suggested in regard to speed reading have special significance for you now. In skimming you need to force your speed, to accelerate your reading tempo far beyond that used in your fastest reading of even easy material. In skimming you really "fly" over the pages, but you should learn effective procedures for getting what you want while "flying," or the flight will be wasted effort.

Recognizing the signposts, finding main ideas, previewing, detecting patterns of writing, searching for and remembering clusters of related details are all techniques which you call into action as you skim for different purposes. You have no doubt mastered these techniques by now, and you can now integrate them into your new stepped-up super-speed skimming.

Knowing how to preview, for example, will often serve you as the first step in your skimming process. If it is a book that you wish to skim, flash your eyes over the table of contents to get an over-all view of the material which the book contains and to decide whether you would be interested in the book as a whole or just in certain chapters.

If the book doesn't have a table of contents, flick the pages through hastily for fleeting glimpses at the chapter titles. Should any of the titles intrigue you, note subheadings and visual aids, if any are provided.

If this book is factual in nature, it will probably contain an index. Suppose you are interested in finding information about just one topic. It is possible that this information can be found only in one paragraph, so consult the index for the one word that names the topic, then turn quickly to the designated page, and read.

The preview procedure not only provides you with a skimming technique for rapidly grasping information about a book, chapter, or article as a whole, but it also enables you to discard or select sections if you decide to dip into the text. So, in all of your skimming, preview first.

If, after the preview, you decide to skim a chapter, then two other techniques that you have learned will be your useful allies: 1) finding the main idea, and 2) identifying patterns of writing.

If the author has used the relating-experience or the imparting-information pattern and you wish only to get his most important ideas, quickly locate the main idea in each paragraph. Sweep your eyes straight down the middle of the page or column until you find in each paragraph the phrase that names the topic of the paragraph and tells what this subject does, what happened to it or what property it possesses which makes it worth a paragraph. Once the main idea is found, flash your eyes to the next paragraph, locate the important idea there, and so on. With practice you can become highly skilled in skimming for main ideas. Watch out for the signposts, though, as you race along. If you note the go-ahead and turn-about words, you will not have to retrace your steps.

Should the author's pattern be the question-answer, the opinion-reasons, or the conclusion-facts type, then the pattern can facilitate your skimming process in locating the important idea. Should the pattern be that of question-answer, perhaps you will wish to skim only to find the answer or answers and won't bother about the details. If the pattern is that of opinion-reasons, maybe you will wish to skim only for the opinion or opinions and will not care to read the reasons. Should the pattern be of the conclusion-facts type, possibly you will care only to grasp the conclusion as quickly as you can and will be satisfied to omit the facts that substantiate the conclusion.

Referring again to the question-answer pattern, in skimming a very good use can be made of this pattern by changing each subheading into a question and then skimming for the answer to the question.

These techniques can be used in situations in which you are interested in finding main ideas, opinions, conclusions, or answers to questions. There may be situations, however, in which you want to skim for a certain detail or cluster of details. In such cases skim until you find the section of content that deals with the detail or details in which you are interested, and then use your techniques for grasping related clusters of details. Should you find it important to remember the details, apply your techniques for recalling them.

New Skills to Learn

Developing a new attitude toward reading is a prime requisite in learning to skim at a high speed. This new attitude is a combination of resigned willingness to pass hastily over a page without reading all that it has to say and of release from a feeling of guilt because you haven't done thorough reading. For many people whose daily work requires meticulous reading, such as editors, lawyers, physicians, and scientists, considerable effort and will power is necessary to "break loose" and cover quantities of material without reading every word.

There is much reading that must be done meticulously, of course, but most people could skim through, without loss, a great deal of the material they now read carefully. To do this, one must cut all moorings with past reading habits and recklessly take a chance at merely catching snatches of printed symbols here and there. It is necessary to cultivate an attitude of abandon while engaging in the high-powered skill of skimming.

In so far as new techniques are concerned, the first is that of skimming for main ideas *only*. Ignore all content in a selection except the main idea in each paragraph. This will be your first experience in this book at skipping over large sections of content. Do this with no feeling of restraint. Be satisfied to find the main ideas only and rush on.

Another new technique is that of making use of *key words* only. Certain words are important in conveying the general meaning of a selection, and others aren't. Developing skill to read only the key words and omitting all words of lesser importance greatly facilitates skimming.

And you should use a new pattern of eye movements—the pattern in which you sweep your eyes from the top to the bottom of pages. No doubt you have developed excellent speed by this time in reading horizontally from left to right. The next step is to develop skill in making fleeting eye sweeps vertically. The old habit of reading from left to right has been ingrained in your nervous system since childhood, and it may be difficult to develop vertical eye movements to a point at which they are as facile and fleeting as your horizontal eye movements.

Normally, our eyes move from left to right across the page, and for this reason all of us are accustomed to using our *lateral* field of vision. We fixate at a point on a line and read all the words we can see at the left and right of this fixation, then move on to another fixation and repeat the perception process. But it happens that we also possess a vertical field of vision which usually lies dormant in so far as reading is concerned. It is possible to cultivate this to take in words above and below the point of fixation, as well as at the left and right of it. Undoubtedly the phenomenal skimmers who claim they can grasp 3,000 or 4,000 words per minute make use of their vertical field of vision.

The formerly-learned skills to be integrated into the new procedures are forcing your speed, heeding signposts, finding main ideas, detecting patterns of writing, grasping clusters of details, and impressing them upon your mind. The new attitude and skills which you are to develop are (a) cultivating a willingness to skip large portions of content, (b) making use of key words, (c) developing facility in using a vertical pattern of eye movements, and (d) developing ability to use your vertical field of vision.

Cultivating the habit of skipping large sections of content. In working through the two selections below, resign yourself to passing over large portions of text with no attempt to find out what is said in the parts you are skipping.

Also make a conscious effort to speed up your vertical eye movements. Try sweeping your eyes down through the print on any one page and up to the top of the next page just as fast as it is physically possible for you to do so.

Skimming for Main Ideas

In this selection skim for main ideas only and omit everything else.

1. Preview the title and subheadings.
2. Decide upon the pattern of writing.

3. Formulate your purpose for reading the article. For practice purposes let's agree that you want to read to find the answer to the question, "What was the hoax?"
4. Grasp the main idea in each paragraph as quickly as you can, then sweep your eyes with high speed straight to the next paragraph, grasp the main idea in that paragraph, and so on. Pay no attention to anything but main ideas.
5. Time yourself allowing a total of one minute. Stop at the end of one minute whether or not you have finished.
6. Take the comprehension test which is based upon main ideas only.

Selection 1

BEGINNING TIME:————————
HR.———— MIN.————————

The Famous Fossil Hoax[1]

The hoax of the Wurzburg fossils, a far-reaching piece of foolery perpetrated two hundred years ago by German university students, ranks in ingenuity with the "Balloon Hoax," the *New York Sun* "Moon Hoax," and other celebrated practical jokes of history.

The butt of the fossil joke was a serious-minded old professor, Johann Beringer, who held an honorable position as a Doctor of Philosophy and Medicine in Wurzburg University. The doctor, highly respected for his learning and studious habits, was appointed private physician to the reigning Prince Bishop of the old university town. He was distinguished as a scholar and writer in the fields of zoology, botany, and medicine.

Of all the problems then engaging scientific minds, none had caused more contention than the origin and meaning of fossils. It was claimed by some that the creation of fossils was due to an unknown influence of the stars. Another theory explained fossils as the remains of oceanic animals and plants stranded on the land by the Flood. It was not until about 1800 that it was determined that fossils were relics of animal and vegetable life that existed in prehistoric times and had become entombed in rock, in frozen mud, in the beds of rivers, even in the soft gum of cone-bearing trees.

The science of paleontology, or the knowledge of fossils, attracted Professor Beringer. He advanced an original theory that fossils were merely a capricious fabrication of the Creator, placed in the earth to test human faith. He was so keen about this pet notion that some of his

[1] Leon Augustus Hausman, *The Mentor*, February 1922, pp. 40-42.

pupils at the university could not forbear playing a trick on the old professor.

With the connivance of some of his own colleagues, the students prankishly fashioned "fossils" out of clay and hid them among the rocks of a hillside where they knew Beringer used to roam around on geological exploration. It was not long before the venerable professor chanced upon the fictitious deposits during one of his walks. Completely deceived, over-joyed at his discovery, Beringer hurried back to the university and ex-hibited the organisms he had found.

The jokers, perceiving with glee the success of their jest, now went further and buried the most fantastic figures their imaginations could suggest. Not content with these they even buried inscriptions, worked out on "fossil" shells, one of them being the name of God himself, in Hebrew!

Professor Beringer's elation upon the discovery of these latter forms knew no bounds. He was now completely convinced of the soundness of his doctrine, and made ready to publish the results.

The semireligious fervor of the honest old scholar swept all before it. Despite the advice of level-headed friends, he hurried his ponderous work to completion.

And now for the strangest part of the story. The jesters came forward and confessed. They exposed all they had done. To their confusion, Beringer refused to listen. The hoaxers reiterated their statements that the whole thing was a colossal joke. Beringer could not be convinced. He conceived this as a base trick of his adversaries. He suspected them of trying to rob him of the glory of proclaiming his discoveries and establishing the truth of his theory. He hurried into print. His *magnum opus* appeared!

The entry of the volume into the world of learned literature was heralded by a shout of laughter! The author's name became a byword in the universities of Europe. Some declared his book was only an attempt to fool the scientific world, others set it down as the product of a mind diseased.

Copies of the weighty volume, printed in Latin, bore the title *The Figured Stones of Wurzburg*, and was illustrated with "marvelous like-nesses of two hundred figures, or rather, insectiform stones." It was pub-lished in Wurzburg in 1726. The pompous dedication, full nine pages long, is to Christopher Francis, Prince Bishop of Wurzburg. After the dedication and the preface, comes the body of the work, descriptive of Beringer's discovery of the fossils, the manner of their exhumation and examination, the account of the attempt of his colleagues to dissuade him from the work, and the description and significance of the "fossils" themselves. At the end of the volume are plates. . . .

For a time there was question in some parts of the scholastic world as to whether or not Beringer's book was of value, a condition which spurred the deceived scientist to greater efforts in his own defense.

But, as the truth became generally established, Beringer himself was finally undeceived. The blow staggered him; he was overwhelmed.

From the pinnacle of learned dictatorship, which he had formerly occupied so securely, he beheld himself tumbled headlong, almost in a night.

In a frenzy he attempted to buy up all copies of his book that had been issued. His most assiduous efforts were futile, however. Finally he desisted and surrendered to despair. His life's work was treasured and exhibited by many as an object of ridicule.

The broken-hearted scientist fell ill under the strain and died shortly afterward, with the laughter of the scientific world ringing in his ears.

Even after Beringer's death there was no end to the tragic joke. A bookseller, one Hobhard of Hamburg, seeing an opportunity to make capital out of Beringer's misfortunes, bought up all available copies and not only reissued them, but compiled a second edition which achieved a large circulation!

Checking Comprehension

1. The hoax of Wurzburg (a) boomeranged on the perpetrators instead of hitting its mark, (b) ranks with the greatest practical jokes of history, (c) brought eventual fortune to the man at whom the joke was aimed, (d) was really not a hoax in the true sense of the word.

2. The butt of the joke was (a) a university student, (b) a professor, (c) a physician, (d) a minister.

3. The science of paleontology is concerned with (a) bacteria, (b) the planets, (c) medicine, (d) fossils.

4. The jokers fashioned their fossils out of (a) soap, (b) wax, (c) clay, (d) wood.

5. The hoax was perpetrated by (a) Beringer's colleagues, (b) students with the connivance of his colleagues, (c) students without the knowledge of his colleagues, (d) none of the foregoing.

6. The jokers (a) placed their most fantastic figures on the professor's desk, (b) placed them on a stairway leading to his classroom, (c) buried their second batch in a place where Beringer would discover them, (d) placed them in a glass case containing fossils.

7. When Beringer discovered the fossils he (a) was delighted, (b) ignored them, (c) returned them to whom he considered to be the rightful owner, (d) recognized them as fakes.

8. When Beringer was informed about the hoax, he (a) refused

to believe it at first, (b) withdrew from the university staff, (c) wrote a public confession and apology, (d) went into seclusion.

9. After finding the fake fossils, Beringer (a) punished the jokers, (b) gave lectures on the discovery, (c) published a book, (d) sent articles to a newspaper.

10. In the end Beringer (a) convinced others that he was right, (b) received recognition from other scientists, (c) died because of the strain which accompanied his discovery of the truth about the fossils, (d) tried to capitalize financially on the sale of his books.

Answers: 1)—, 2)—, 3)—, 4)—, 5)—, 6)—, 7)—, 8)—, 9)—, 10)—.

See the Answer Key on page 385.

Comprehension Score:————————

Skimming for a Cluster of Details

In this next selection you will use a technique for grasping detailed facts about some *one* item under a title, ignoring everything else in the article. Use your vertical eye movements in skimming the pages from top to bottom until you find the paragraph or paragraphs concerning the phase of the topic in which you are interested. Then use the techniques which you learned for grasping details. If you wish to remember the details, use the techniques to impress them upon your mind.

Suppose that while you are looking through a magazine you come upon this informative article, "Stalking a Hurricane." You don't care about reading details concerning hurricanes in general, but you are interested in that phenomenon called "the eye of the hurricane," and you want to obtain specific details about it.

With this purpose in mind:

1. Skim through the article, using vertical eye movements at your highest speed, until you come upon mention of "the eye of the hurricane." Don't try to read any of the text until you find this particular section. And don't worry because you skip paragraph after paragraph without knowing what they say.

2. When you find "the eye" slow down, reading and absorbing each detail about the eye of the hurricane and fitting each detail into a pattern of relationships to the main idea and to one another. Of course you should do this detailed reading as fast as you can and still be sure you are grasping all details.

3. When you reach the point in which nothing more is said about "the eye," stop reading.
4. Allow yourself no more than one minute for this exercise. If you can do it in less time, so much the better.
5. After you have read for the specified length of time, take the comprehension test which in this case is concerned *only* with details concerning the eye of a hurricane.

Selection 2

Stalking a Hurricane[2]

Why are there fewer deaths and less property damage from hurricanes? Are the "big winds" getting weaker? Or fewer in number?

Not at all. The hurricane remains one of the most powerful forces on earth. During the 1952 hurricane season, six of these colossal whirlwinds roared through the American tropics with momentum enough to carry several of them on into northern areas as the worst storms of the year. But property damage set no records, and no deaths could be attributed directly to any of them.

Yet in 1935 a hurricane whiplashed across Florida and the dead totaled 400. In 1928 another Florida hurricane took 1,800 lives. At Galveston, Tex., in 1900, a hurricane killed more than 6,000, and as late as 1942 casualties from the big winds were still numbered in scores.

The explanation of reduced casualties and smaller property damage in recent years is, in three words, *better advance warning.* . . .

During the progress of a major hurricane the Miami Hurricane Warning Center, for example, issues four "advisories"—weather versions of a wartime communiqué—daily, based on reports received during the previous six hours. Each Weather Bureau office in the network then distributes the forecast as widely and as rapidly as possible. Precautions against hurricane damage—such as boarding up houses and shops, flying planes to safer regions, moving small craft, etc.—are expensive, so everyone wants to know: "Is it the real thing?"

In the meantime a search plane has made contact with the enemy. Far ahead through the rain squalls the pilot sees a dark, ominous-looking mass of whirling clouds, mist, and water that seems to reach up into the heavens and stretches fully 30 miles from side to side.

When the plane radios confirmation of the hurricane's existence, the first act of the Hurricane Warning Center is to give it a name. If this is the second hurricane of the season, it might be called "baker," from the

[2] E. John Long, *Science Digest,* September 1953. (Reprinted from *Nature,* August 1953.)

International Phonetic Alphabet used in radio voice communications. The first might have been called "Able," the third might be "Charlie," etc.

Because a hurricane's safest point of entry is usually its westward side, the plane approaches from the west. And from now on, every 15 minutes information obtained from meteorological instruments and by radar will be radioed to Miami.

The pilot brings the plane down to an altitude of 800 feet—or even to 400 feet if visibility is poor. The plane shudders and shakes as it bucks the outer rings of light thunderstorms and 35-mph winds which try their hardest to drive it southward.

After nearly an hour of sampling the air on the fringes of the hurricane, the pilot heads directly into it. The heavy, four-engined ship pitches and yaws, dives and soars again, until its creaking frame seems to be tearing apart. Sea and sky dissolve in pelting rain and spray, and the shrieking wind drowns out even the roar of the engines, straining at full throttle.

An interminable quarter hour of this—and suddenly the plane breaks through the storm into the clear. All pitching and tossing ceases, the howling gale quiets as if a valve had shut it off, and bright sunshine pours through the drenched windshield. Down below, the sea shows a few whitecaps, but the whole aspect is one of peace and calm. The transition is so sudden and unexpected that it comes as a shock, even to crews who have experienced it many times.

This strange world, called "the eye of the hurricane," is one of the weirdest, most awesome sights on earth. The eye is roughly circular. Its boundary is a vertical curtain of black, reaching from the ocean far up to the open sky above. It is difficult to believe that beyond this ebony cylinder, now 10 to 15 miles in diameter, is a watery chaos, revolving furiously in a counterclockwise direction as it is driven by gales of from 180 to 200 mph.

Strange things have been observed by planes cruising "the eye." Flocks of birds sometimes take refuge there, moving along within the comparative safety of the storm's vortex, which may have a forward motion of only 10 to 15 mph. Ships sometimes seek "the eye" to ride out the worst of the storm's violence before resuming their course. One plane observed a fishing boat, with the crew on deck sunbathing, within a hurricane's eye.

As the hurricane-stalking plane cruises around the eye, the "dropsonde" operator goes into action. As the dropsonde, an instrument dropped from the plane by parachute, slowly descends it automatically records atmospheric pressure, temperature, and humidity of the air, and relays these to the plane by a self-contained radio transmitter.

But now the fuel is getting low, so the pilot plunges back into the black wall of the hurricane, choosing the western or "weak" side, where, experience has taught him, a hearty tailwind can be picked up. Fifteen minutes more of furious buffeting, and the tired crew heads for the barn, clipping through squalls that would be bypassed by ordinary pilots.

Although many hurricanes simply veer back out to sea and finally subside in the colder climate of the North Atlantic, each of them is constantly pursued by watcher planes, which radio back the vital information needed to chart its course and to warn shipping and other planes in its path.

. . . . . .

What actually causes a hurricane?

Scientists have two theories. One, the convection theory, holds that it starts when a large mass of warm air rises in the doldrums of the open Atlantic, east and south of the West Indies. Sea-level air rushes in to replace the vacuum left by the rising warm air. The rotation of the earth deflects the slowly-moving air mass into a counterclockwise swirl. Soon a vigorous wind system is set up, and a full-blown hurricane is roaring on its way. Although it appears to take generally a westward course, the earth is really moving eastward under it.

The second theory is the counter-current theory. It explains that opposing tradewinds, warm and cold, cause the initial air lift; thereafter it is like the other theory.

Checking Comprehension

Follow the usual procedure in working with the statements below.

1. The adjectives used to describe "the eye" in the article are (a) black, very dangerous, (b) windy, strange, treacherous, (c) weirdest, most awesome, (d) powerful, terrifying.

2. The shape of "the eye" is (a) circular, (b) cylindrical, (c) eliptical, (d) conical.

3. "The eye" is bounded by (a) a black circular band, (b) horizontal black bands, (c) heavy orange lines, (d) a vertical curtain of black.

4. The diameter of "the eye" is (a) approximately 1 mile, (b) approximately 5 miles, (c) approximately 6 miles, (d) 10 to 15 miles.

5. The hurricane is driven by gales (a) 180 to 200 mph, (b) 40 to 60 mph, (c) 400 to 500 mph, (d) 10 to 20 mph.

6. "The eye" is (a) furiously active, (b) drenched with rains, (c) sometimes calm enough so that birds or ships can take refuge in it, (d) cold and snowy.

7. "The eye" (a) has no motion, (b) moves around in circles, (c) moves forward at about 100 mph, (d) may move forward with a motion of only 10 to 15 mph.

8. As the search plane cruises around "the eye" it (a) flies through it and reports its location, (b) flies into it and stays there, (c) avoids it, (d) puts the dropsonde into action.

9. The functions of the dropsonde are to (a) record the direction and velocity of the wind, (b) record the diameter and height of "the eye," (c) record the atmospheric pressure, temperature, and humidity, (d) record the size of the area which the hurricane is covering.

10. When fuel gets low the search plane leaves "the eye" on the western side because (a) the plane is facing the sun, (b) the hurricane is strongest in the west, (c) the "eye" is in the western part of the hurricane, (d) experience has taught him a hearty tailwind can be picked up there.

Answers: 1)—, 2)—, 3)—, 4)—, 5)—, 6)—, 7)—, 8)—, 9)—, 10)—.

The Answer Key is on page 385.

Comprehension Score:————————

Using Key Words in Skimming

Grasping key words is another short cut to the super-speed of skimming for general comprehension. Usually the import of a selection is carried largely through nouns, verbs, adverbs, and adjectives. Familiarity with the English language enables a person who practices the skill mentally to supply words of lesser importance, without stopping to read each one of them.

Examples of words of "lesser importance" are the articles *the, an,* and *a*; pronouns such as *you, your, it, they, them, we, my, their, our, his, her*; prepositions such as *in, of, with, to, by, at, for, from, on, over,* and *under*; and many other words which are not absolutely essential in "putting across" the stripped-down import of a sentence.

In the selection that follows, the less important words have been omitted.

1. Skim through the key words as rapidly as you can, trying to follow the trend of the author's message.
2. Allow yourself 30 seconds only to skim the article with the use of the key words.
3. Take the comprehension test after you have skimmed the article.

Selection 3

My Neighbor the Hippo[3]

_____ mud hut _____ _____ I lived _____ five years _____ British East Africa _____ situated _____ two miles _____ Lake Elmenteita. _____ remote stretch _____ water remains _____ _____ _____ undisturbed _____ white men. Except _____ _____ _____ naked savage _____ spear _____ club, no human being troubles _____ lives _____ _____ _____ waterfowl _____ scarlet flamingos.

I used _____ wander _____ _____ _____ shores because _____ knew _____ _____ depths _____ inhabited _____ hippopotami. _____ certain seasons _____ sunrise _____ sunset _____ air would resound _____ _____ _____ _____ bellows.

_____ "zee-koes," _____ "cows of the lake," _____ _____ Dutch pioneers call them, seldom leave _____ water _____ _____ daytime, _____ _____ _____ _____ return _____ _____ first indication _____ danger. Throughout _____ _____ _____ noons _____ lounge _____ _____ _____ _____, sometimes floating _____ _____ surface, sometimes walking _____ _____ _____ _____ bottom _____ _____ lake, _____ sometimes lying _____ _____ muddy reach _____ _____ great _____ heads resting _____ each other.

But toward sundown _____ preposterous _____ animals, growing impatient for _____ land pastures, draw _____ toward _____ shore. _____ can catch sight _____ _____ heads appearing _____ _____ _____ _____ _____, _____ close _____ _____ _____ seem possible _____ cast _____ stone down _____ _____ _____ mouths _____ yawn _____ _____ _____ _____ _____ _____. _____ span _____ _____ hippopotamus's open mouth _____ _____ _____, _____ jawbone _____ _____ _____ _____ _____ four feet.

I used _____ believe _____ _____ never wandered far _____ _____ _____ _____ _____ midnight excursions, but _____ _____ _____ _____ _____ _____ _____ found grass _____ _____ _____ chewed _____ hippos _____ _____ three miles away. _____ _____ moonlight night _____ _____ stood _____ _____ _____ hill _____ observed _____ country _____ acres around dotted _____ _____ _____ _____ forms moving _____ forward _____ _____ lowered heads _____ enormous mouths drew in _____ _____, _____ _____ grass.

_____ every direction _____ _____ _____ _____ _____ "hippo paths"— _____, _____ _____ tracks _____ led through _____ rushes _____ brushwood. _____ tracks _____ distinguished from _____ of _____ rhinoceros; _____ walking, _____ hippopotamus moves _____ front _____ hind foot _____ two parallel lines _____ _____ _____ center ground under _____ body _____ not trodden _____ _____ _____. _____ so short _____ _____ legs

[3] Llewellyn Powys, *The Mentor*, June 1922, pp. 30-31.

_____ _____ _____ rainy season, _____ _____ soil gives, _____ _____ bodies
drag _____ earth.

_____ _____, for all _____ grotesque appearance _____ hippopotamus
_____ _____ exquisitely designed _____ _____ unusual conditions _____
_____ existence: nature _____ contrived _____ anatomy _____ _____ _____
_____ _____ _____ eyes, nostrils, _____ ears can remain above water _____
_____ rest _____ _____ body _____ submerged. _____ _____ ears _____
nostrils _____ _____ fitted _____ _____ valves capable _____ shutting _____
_____ water when _____ sinks below _____ surface. _____ specific gravity
_____ hippopotami _____ such _____ _____ sink _____ _____ greatest depth
without _____ _____ trouble; _____ do not dive, _____ _____ allow themselves _____ disappear like submarines. _____ _____ also good swimmers.

One calf _____ born _____ _____ time. _____ sees light first _____ _____
hidden lair _____ _____ rushes near _____ water, _____ _____ mother
conducts it shortly after birth.

During _____ infancy _____ mother never remains under _____ water
_____ _____ long period, _____ may be seen rising _____ _____ surface
_____ _____ _____ _____ little hippo standing _____ _____ wrinkled neck.
Hippopotami _____ devoted mothers.

_____ fight between full-grown hippopotami _____ _____ something
_____ witness! _____ watched one _____ _____ _____ quarter _____ _____
hour. _____ took place _____ _____ rushes under _____ _____ bank. I had
been attracted _____ _____ place _____ _____ succession _____ _____ _____
roars, _____ peered over _____ rocks. _____ _____ early morning. The lake
_____ radiant _____ _____ _____ _____ _____ _____ _____ sun, _____ poured
down _____ _____ _____ grass, _____ rushes, _____ baboon-haunted ledges
_____ _____ _____ _____. _____ amphibia below appeared _____ _____ like
two prehistoric monsters, tusking _____ gnawing _____ _____ _____,
struggling _____ _____ _____ _____, _____ giving vent _____ _____ _____
_____ snorts _____ must have been heard _____ _____ _____ vultures far
up _____ _____ _____ sky.

_____ one time, during _____ _____ dry spell, _____ _____ lake water
_____ _____ stagnant _____ ill-tasting, _____ hippo made _____ habit _____
drinking _____ _____ _____ _____ farm troughs. If _____ had been content _____ drink decently _____ would not have had _____ _____ objec-
tion, but nothing _____ do him but _____ _____ place _____ _____ feet
_____ _____ iron sheeting, bending _____ twisting _____ like tinfoil. _____
actually caught _____ at it one night, _____ rewarded _____ _____ _____
bullet _____ my rifle; but _____ got back _____ _____ lake, _____ _____ _____
_____ _____ three weeks later _____ _____ _____ _____ _____ body came
drifting _____ _____ _____ shore. _____ _____ _____ _____ well _____ steer
clear _____ dead floating hippopotami, because _____ _____ accumulation
_____ gas puts _____ _____ _____ strain _____ _____ wrinkled hide _____
_____ _____ explosion takes place. _____, _____ _____ shot one but _____

regret, _____ the misgiving that _____ _____ _____ accelerating _____
coming _____ _____ day when _____ _____ _____ _____ animals _____
_____ extinct.

Checking Comprehension

1. The area in which the story takes place is inhabited only by (a) civilized white men, (b) savages, (c) civilized Indians, (d) wild animals.

2. The writer, in his wanderings (a) stayed close to shore because the depths were inhabited by hippopotami, (b) stayed close to shore to make certain that he would not lose his way, (c) went out into the center of the lake in order to observe better the shore movements of the hippopotami, (d) went to the center of the lake occasionally to observe the hippopotami at close range.

3. The hippopotami come to shore (a) toward sundown, (b) at sunrise, (c) rarely, (d) at noon.

4. During their midnight excursions the hippopotami (a) stay on the shore of the river, (b) never go more than a few rods away, (c) travel 10 or 15 miles inland, (d) have been known to chew grass three miles away.

5. Hippopotami tracks are distinctive in that they (a) form double parallel lines in the center of the ground under their body, (b) are heavier than those of other animals, (c) form an irregular pattern, (d) distribute their footprints at regular intervals.

6. The writer remarks about the anatomy of the hippopotamus by saying that (a) it is most massive, (b) it is amazingly well equipped for combat, (c) it is exquisitely designed for its mode of living, (d) it varies from hippopotamus to hippopotamus within the species.

7. A mother hippopotamus (a) frequently abandons her calf, (b) is sometimes cruel to her young, (c) leaves the care of the calf to the father, (d) is a devoted mother.

8. The writer shot a hippopotamus one night because he was (a) tearing up the writer's farm trough, (b) drinking water at the trough, (c) scaring the farm animals, (d) frightening the writer himself.

9. Three weeks after the shooting (a) the writer discovered the animal alive, (b) the writer found the body in a thicket, (c) the body drifted up on the shore, (d) the incident was repeated with another hippopotamus.

10. After shooting the hippopotamus (a) the writer regretted having accelerated the extinction of hippopotami, (b) claimed that the

hippopotamus managed to get back to the water, (c) encountered several other hippopotami to his dismay, (d) tried to help the animal.

Answers: 1)___, 2)___, 3)___, 4)___, 5)___, 6)___, 7)___, 8)___, 9)___, 10)___.

The Answer Key is on page 385.

Comprehension Score:_____

Grasping Key Words Only

The unimportant words have been retained in the selection below. You are now ready to take the more advanced step of reading text with the less important words in it but ignoring these words as you skim through, grasping key words only.

1. Skim at your highest speed, reading key words only as nec-essary in following the trend of thought.
2. Allow yourself exactly two minutes to skim, noting key words exclusively. If you can cover the article in less than two minutes, so much the better.
3. Take the comprehension test at the end of the article.

Selection 4

The Birds' Beauty Parlor[4]

Nature provides no beauty specialists for birds. It is a case of every bird his own manicurist, tailor, and bath attendant.

Frequent baths are an important feature in the daily round of bird life. Anyone that has watched the family canary at his morning plunge knows how thoroughly the work is done. When the bather emerges, he spreads his feathers by means of the delicate muscles provided for the purpose, and, shaking his body with violence, invites the application of air to as much of the surface as possible. The intricate process of rearranging his disordered plumage is accomplished with his beak. When the toilet has been completed, each feather is in perfect alignment, every particle of dirt has been removed; the plumage has the sheen of lustrous silk.

If the dexterity of the canary arouses our admiration, what shall we say of a bird like the pelican? His beak, nearly eighteen inches long, is armed at the tip with a heavy pointed hook. Each feather is drawn through that mighty beak with the utmost delicacy; each crevice is searched as with the finest comb.

[4] Lee S. Crandall, *The Mentor*, May 1929, pp. 49-51.

Every kind of bird bathes in its own particular way. Where the canary and the sparrow plunge bodily in, the barn swallow dips lightly, cutting graceful arcs over the water.

A few birds never wash in water. Turkeys, pheasants, and the common hen have a deep-seated prejudice against water. Yet they do bathe, in their own fashion, in dust or sand. Everyone has seen the humble hen engaged in the pleasant duty of dusting herself in the warm silt of a country road. Her motions are those of the canary in his tub. Clouds of powdered loam rise gently into the summer air; quantities are sifted through the plumage, suffocating tiny parasites.

Pigeons confine themselves exclusively to water. On the other hand, the "English" or house sparrow, and many of our native species, use both water and dust for cleansing purposes. Often, in crossing a dry back-country pasture, one comes upon an open space dotted with tiny hollows in the dry earth, like diminutive buffalo wallows—the dusting places of field or vesper sparrows.

Greasing the bodies of long-distance swimmers is not a new idea. Ducks have used it for generations. The phrase "like water off a duck's back" refers to the damp-proof quality of the plumage of waterfowl. All ducks seek their living in or about water.

For success in such a life it is necessary for the duck to shed water not only from its back, but from every portion of its body. A duck rises from the water as freely as a land bird from the ground; wet wings would be a serious handicap. As might be expected, the duck accomplishes this desirable result by the use of grease, and he carries his own grease pot. At the base of his tail lies an organ known as the oil gland, which secretes the necessary unguent in sufficient quantity for the purpose. Though ducks spend most of their time in the water, they nevertheless find frequent washing and dressing of the plumage a necessity. After each bath the feathers are arranged with care, and oil is spread throughout.

Birds use powder too. In many groups, notably the herons, the parrots, and some birds of prey, there occur tufts of matted feathers known as powder-down patches. These feathers grow continuously but never fully mature, because their tips constantly break off. The resulting detritus is a fine, greasy powder of much the same consistency as fuller's earth. This powder works its way through every portion of the plumage, adhering closely to the surface of the feathers.

In the herons, the powder-down patches are found in large masses on the breast or thighs, partially hidden by the surface feathers. The African gray parrot, famous for its ability as a mimic, has another point of distinction—it powders its face! This portion of the bird's anatomy is free from feathers, but is always thickly coated with the fine, white product of the powder-down patches.

Just what the full function of this powder may be is not known; in some cases it serves as waterproofing. The pigeons have no definite patches, but certain small feathers of the flanks serve the same purpose, as they slowly disintegrate. The plumage of pigeons is thoroughly saturated with powder, so much so that it remains on the hands if the bird is handled, or will soil a black cloth if it is used to wipe the feathers.

Care of the nails is another refinement practiced in the birds' beauty parlor. Daily contact with earth, sand, and rock keeps pace with the growth of nails or claws, so that they are always of the correct length. Canaries and other cage birds, as well as poultry or pigeons kept on board floors, soon demonstrate the lack of natural trimming. The nails not only become extremely long but also acquire a curious spiral formation, like an exaggerated ram's horn. They must then be manicured (or, rather, pedicured) in the human fashion, or they are likely to become entangled in cage wires with tragic result.

"Scarce as a hen's tooth" is scarce indeed, for hen's teeth are rare. Birds have no need for dentists. Yet the horny sheaths of beaks grow as persistently as do the nails and must be kept trimmed in much the same manner. Constant use in finding and eating food does much of the work, but many birds add the finishing touches by whetting their beaks on wood or stone. A piece of cuttlefish bone is a necessary item in a canary's cage, not only for the lime it supplies but also for use as a grindstone.

In the matter of clothing, birds are rather stingily treated. No bird has more than two full suits a year; some acquire an extra new coat and waistcoat in the spring, but many must make the old ones do. This is why birds are so particular in the care of their plumage. No needle mends their rents; no tailor provides new raiment. Worn or broken feathers are not replaced until the next molt. But, curiously, if a feather is lost completely, the follicle from which it grew is immediately stimulated to action and a new plume is produced, from four to six weeks being required for it to mature.

When hatched most young birds are provided with swaddling clothes of softest down, in varying amount, though some, like the great caciques or oropendulas of tropical America, come into the world quite frankly stark. With song birds, in particular, it is essential that they should be able to leave the nest and fend for themselves as quickly as possible, so the wings must make rapid growth. In from ten to fourteen days most fledgings of this group leave the nest, with the body completely clothed in the first suit of real feathers, the wings well grown, but the tail still stumpy and apologetic, since uncertain wings have little need for a balancing device.

In late summer and early autumn, the time of the great annual molt, all northern birds receive new clothes for old. Youngsters hardly more than two or three months out of the nest doff their juvenile raiment and acquire plumage that usually, though not always, resembles that of adults. Some, like the cowbird, have a complete change, including the wings and tail; others, such as the towhee, waxwing, and catbird renew the small body feathers only, the others remaining the same.

Once this annual change of clothing has been made, many birds must be content with it for a full year. Our two rather shady European immigrants, the house sparrow and the starling, are among those provided with sparse wardrobes. But both of these birds take the canny precaution of adding a suit of overalls, each feather being margined with a broad, dull edge, which hides the brighter colors underneath. During the rigors of a hard winter, these protectors gradually become weathered and worn, and by April have disappeared completely. Then the proud owner stands forth resplendent, his well-burnished spring ensemble glistening brilliantly in the warm sunshine.

Among the birds that enjoy a partial renewal of plumage in spring is the scarlet tanager. At the autumnal molt the adult male exchanges his brilliant red body plumage for a winter overcoat of somber olive, like that of his mate. In early spring the dull body feathers are replaced by the scarlet jacket that makes him the most brightly colored of North American birds.

Few indeed are the varieties of birds that are granted two complete costumes each year. Most conspicuous among these varieties is the bobolink, which leaves us in autumn clothing almost exactly like that his wife and children are wearing, but returns in spring from far Brazil, arrayed in formal bridegroom's regalia of dazzling black and white.

For the most part, birds are satisfied with Nature's allotments and accept such attire as she distributes, be it plain or gaudy. Only one group is known to attempt improvements. This comprises the motmots, tropical birds of jay-like appearance, though not related to those noisy, sagacious creatures. The two central feathers of the motmot's tail project considerably beyond their fellows. When they first appear they seem to be quite normal, except that close examination shows a portion of the web, at each side, to be lightly attached to the shaft. When these feathers have reached nearly their full length, the motmot sets to work, drawing the tips slowly through his beak and constantly picking at them. The effect of these attentions soon becomes evident, for presently the weakened web yields, leaving an inch or more of the shaft quite bare. The tip remains intact, forming a distinct spatula at the end of the feather. This ornament is obviously a source of great delight to its owner, for he sits for hours proudly swinging to and fro his newly decorated tail.

Checking Comprehension

1. Nature has created each bird (a) to be a beauty specialist for himself, (b) naturally beautiful without need of beauty treatments,

(c) dependent upon man-made aids to achieve its fullest beauty, (d) dependent upon beauty specialists provided by nature.

2. Regarding bird bathing the author says that (a) some birds don't require bathing, (b) birds have a variety of ways of bathing, (c) bathing is an important daily feature in bird life, (d) some birds require more bathing than others.

3. Birds who never wash in water clean themselves by (a) pulling out soiled feathers, (b) shaking themselves, (c) fluttering in dust or sand, (d) scraping their feathers with their beaks.

4. Greasing their backs is a practice used for generations by (a) pelicans, (b) pigeons, (c) ducks, (d) all birds.

5. The powder that many birds use comes from (a) flowers, (b) certain kinds of fruit, (c) tufts of matted feathers, (d) dried leaves.

6. Manicuring of wild birds' nails is accomplished by (a) shedding the nails, (b) daily contact with earth, sand, and rock, (c) breaking off the nails, (d) doing nothing, since the nails never grow.

7. In the matter of clothing, nature treats birds (a) generously, (b) stingily, (c) a little better than most animals, (d) badly.

8. All northern birds have their great annual molt (a) in the spring, (b) in midsummer, (c) in late summer and early autumn, (d) while they are south in the winter.

9. Birds who are allowed two complete costumes a year (a) are many, (b) are few, (c) do not exist, (d) are extremely rare.

10. The motmot is distinctive in that it (a) receives three complete sets of feathers per year, (b) has the most beautiful feathers of any bird, (c) has a huge topknot on its head, (d) decorates its own tail feathers.

Answers: 1)—, 2)—, 3)—, 4)—, 5)—, 6)—, 7)—, 8)—, 9)—, 10)—.

See the Answer Key on page 385.

Comprehension Score:————

Skimming with the Use of Vertical Field of Vision

Now you will be introduced to the highest skill in the hierarchy of skills in skimming—that of using your vertical field of vision. The development of this skill enables you to see two or three words or figures or phrases *above* and *below* the point at which your eyes are fixed, without moving the eyes up or down. In making use of this skill you simply hold your eyes in one place and take in everything within your range of vision, *vertically*.

Exercise 1

Grasping three sets of figures in a vertical column. First try to see three sets of figures in a vertical column at one glance.

1. In this vertical column look squarely at the middle figure, and read all three figures *without moving your eyes:*

    12:15
    12:30
    12:45

2. Try doing the same thing in reading the three groups of figures in the lists below that begin respectively with a) 4:00, b) 9:15, c)11:10, d) 7:15, e) 5:05.

1:15	7:15
1:30	7:30
1:45	7:45
2:15	8:00
2:30	8:25
2:45	8:40
3:00	9:15
3:25	9:30
3:45	9:45
4:00	10:05
4:15	10:35
4:35	10:55
5:05	11:10
5:25	11:35
5:50	11:55
6:00	12:05
6:15	12:15
6:30	12:30

Exercise 2

In this exercise you are requested to use your vertical eye movements and vertical field of vision. But you will also need quickly to switch to the use of your horizontal eye movements and your horizontal field of vision as you work through the exercise. In other words, you will alternate, using your vertical eye movements and

DAYTIME

7:00—WRCA: News;. Bill Cullen
WOR: News .Reports
WABC: Ernie Kovacs Show
WCBS: News; Jack Sterling
WNYC: Sunrise Symphony
WQXR: N. Y. Times News
7:05—WQXR—Bright and Early
7:15—WOR: John Gambling
7:25—WABC: News; Ernie Kovacs
7:30—WRCA: News Reports
WCBS: News; Jack Sterling
WQXR: Business Picture
7:35—WQXR: Breakfast Music
7:45—WRCA: Bill Cullen
WCBS: News Reports
WNYC: Weather; News
7:55—WABC: News; Ernie Kovacs
8:00—WRCA: News Reports
WOR, WCBS: News
WNYC: Around New York
WQXR: N. Y. Times News
8:05—WQXR: Breakfast Music
8:10—WRCA: Bill Cullen
8:15—WOR: Dorothy and Dick
WCBS: Bob Haymes Show
8:25—WABC: News; Ernie Kovacs
8:30—WRCA: News; Bill Cullen
8:40—WNYC: Social Security
8:45—WNYC: Food Talks
8:55—WABC: News Reports
9:00—WRCA: News; Bill Cullen
WOR: News Reports
WABC: Breakfast Club
WCBS: News; Lanny Ross
WNYC: Masterwork Hour
WQXR: N. Y. Times News
9:05—WQXR: Just Music
9:15—WOR: Second Breakfast
9:30—WRCA: Pegeen Fitzgerald
WOR: McCanns at Home
WCBS: Martha Wright
WQXR: Piano Personalities
9:45—WQXR: Composer Varieties
9:55—WRCA: Visit With Josie
10:00—WRCA: Mary M. McBride
WOR: News Reports
WABC: My True Story
WCBS: Arthur Godfrey Time
WQXR: N. Y. Times News
10:05—WRCA: Dr. Norman Peale
WQXR: Morning Melodies
10:15—WRCA: Weekday: Margaret
Truman, Mike Wallace;
Harold Arlen, Guest
WOR: Martha Deane: Anna
Kross, guest
10:25—WABC: Whispering Streets
10:30—WNYC: You and Health.
10:45—WABC: When a Girl
Marries
★WNYC: Dedication of
Library
11:00—WOR: News; Story Time
WABC: Companion

★WNYC: U. N. General
Assembly
WQXR: N. Y. Times News
11:05—WQXR: Mid-Morning Music
11:15—WABC: Paging the New
11:30—WOR: Queen for a Day
WABC: News Reports
WCBS: Make Up Your
Mind: Denise Lor, Guest
11:35—WABC: Walt Disney's
Magic Kingdom
11:45—WCBS: Howard Miller
WQXR: Luncheon Concert
11:55—WNYC: News
12:00—WRCA: News; Al Collins
WOR: News; Your Baby
WABC: News Reports
WCBS: Wendy Warren,
News
WNYC: Midday Symphony
WQXR: N. Y. Times News
12:05—WOR: Luncheon Concert
12:10—WOR: Answer Man
12:15—WOR: McCanns at Home
WABC: Frank Farrell Show
WCBS: Backstage Wife
12:30—WOR: News Reports
WCBS: Helen Trent
12:45—WOR: Luncheon at Sardi's
WCBS: Our Gal Sunday
12:55—WABC, WNYC: News
1:00—WABC: Paul Harvey, News
WCBS: Road of Life
WNYC: Famous Artist
WQXR: N. Y. Times News
1:05—WQXR: Midday Symphony
1:15—WABC: Arthur Van Horn
WCBS: Ma Perkins
1:30—WRCA: Sydney Smith
WOR: America's Front Door
WCBS: Young Dr. Malone
WNYC: Chemical Society
1:45—WCBS: The Guiding Light
WNYC: Weather; News
1:55—WABC: News Reports
2:00—WRCA: News; Weekday
WOR: News; Letter to
Lee Graham
WABC: Tedd Lawrence
WCBS: Second Mrs. Burton
WNYC: Board of Education
Series
WQXR: N. Y. Times News
2:05—WQXR: Footlight Favorites
2:15—WCBS: Perry Mason
2:25—WABC: News
2:30—WOR: Martin Starr
WABC: Martin Block:
Make-Believe Ballroom
WCBS: This Is Nora Drake
WNYC: For the Ladies
WQXR: Alma Dettinger;
Other People's Business
2:35—WOR: Radio Playhouse
2:45—WCBS: The Brighter Day
3:00—WOR: News Reports
WCBS: House Party
★WNYC: U. N. General
Assembly
WQXR: N. Y. Times News
3:05—WOR: Radio Playhouse
WQXR: Symphonic Matinee
3:30—WRCA: Hotel for Pets
WCBS: Galen Drake
3:45—WRCA: The Doctor's Wife
3:55—WNYC: News
4:00—WRCA: Right to Happiness
WOR: Drive East
WCBS: News; Lanny Ross

WNYC: Critics' Choice
WQXR: N. Y. Times News
4:05—WQXR: Concert Hall
4:15—WRCA: Stella Dallas
4:30—WRCA: Widder Brown
WQXR: Jacques Fray
4:45—WRCA: Pepper Young
4:55—WNYC: News
5:00—WRCA: Woman In .My
House
WOR: Bob and Ray
WCBS: News, John Faulk
WNYC: Adventures in Jazz
WQXR: N. Y. Times News
5:05—WQXR: Cocktail Time
5:15—WRCA: Claude Rains
5:30—WRCA: Lone Ranger
★WNYC: A. F. L.-C. I. O.
Unity Convention
5:45—WOR: Les Paul-Mary Ford
5:50—WOR: Sports; News
5:55—WRCA: Weather Reports
WCBS: News

EVENING

6:00—WRCA, WCBS: News
WOR: Lyle Van, News
WNYC: Window on the
World: Kenneth Bird
WQXR: N. Y. Times News
6:05—WQXR: Dinner Concert
6:15—WRCA: Jimmy Powers .
WOR: Dorothy and Dick
WCBS: Herman Hickman
WNYC: Veterans' News
6:25—WCBS: Weather Report
6:30—WRCA: Tex and Jinx
WOR: News Reports
WCBS: Martha Wright
WNYC: Canadian News
6:45—WRCA: Three Star Extra
WOR: Stan Lomax, Sports
WABC: Sports, Bill Stern
WCBS: Lowell Thomas
WNYC: Weather Report;
U. N. News
7:00—WRCA: Symphonette
WOR: Fulton Lewis Jr.
WABC: John Vandercook
WCBS: Larry LeSueur
WNYC: Masterwork Hour
WQXR: N. Y. Times News
7:05—WCBS: Tennessee Ernie
Show, With Doris Drew
WQXR: To France With
Music; Jacques Fray
7:15—WOR: Today's Business
WABC: Quincy Howe, News
7:20—WOR: The Answer Man
7:25—WABC: Wall Street Final
7:30—WRCA: Morgan Beatty
WOR: Gabriel Heatter
WABC: Events of the Day
WCBS: Bing Crosby
★WQXR: Hambro and Zayde
7:45—WRCA: One Man's Family
WOR: Basil Heatter
WCBS: Edward R. Murrow
7:55—WABC: News Reports
8:00—WRCA: News Reports
WOR: Official Detective
WABC: The World and You
WCBS: My Son, Jeep
WQXR: N. Y. Times News
8:05—WRCA: Great Gildersleeve
★WQXR: Symphony Hall
8:15—WCBS: Yours Truly,
Johnny Dollar
8:25—WABC: News Reports
8:30—WRCA: This Is My Story
WOR: Crime Fighters

WABC: Your Better
Tomorrow
★WCBS: Arthur Godfrey
Digest
★WNYC: Man's Right to
Knowledge
8:55—WABC: News Reports
9:00—WRCA: News Reports
WOR: News Reports
WABC: Sound Mirror
WCBS: News Reports
★WNYC: Cooper Union Forum
WQXR: N. Y. Times News
9:05—WRCA: American Adventure
WOR: Special Edition
WCBS: Jack Carson Show
★WQXR: The Spoken Word
9:15—WOR: The Book Hunter
9:25—WABC: News Reports
9:30★WRCA: Conversation
WOR: Martha Deane
WABC: Offbeat
WCBS: Amos 'n' Andy
WQXR: Listening Booth
9:55—WCBS: News
WABC: News Personality
WNYC: News (FM to 3)
10:00—WRCA: Fibber and Molly
WOR: News; Weather
WABC: Edward P. Morgan
WCBS: United Jewish Ap-
peal Drama: The Stow-
away
WQXR: N. Y. Times News
10:05★WQXR: Panorama
10:15—WRCA: News Reports
WOR: John Gambling
WABC: How to Fix It
10:30—WRCA: News Reports
WABC: George H. Combs
10:35★WRCA: Tex and Jinx Show
10:45—WABC: Platterbrains
11:00—WRCA, WOR, WCBS: News
WQXR: N. Y. Times News
11:07—WQXR: Recorded Previews
WABC: Les Griffith, News
WQXR: Record Previews
11:10—WCBS: Eric Sevareid
11:15—WRCA: Dan Peterson
WOR: Ruby Mercer
WCBS: Christmas Chimes.
11:20★WRCA: Tex and Jinx Show
11:30—WOR: Music
WABC: Music
★WCBS: This Is New York
12:00—WRCA: News; Tex and Jinx
WOR: News; Music
WABC: Mostly Music
WCBS: Music Till Dawn
WQXR: N. Y. Times News
12:05★WQXR: Midnight Symphony
12:15—WOR: Dance Time
12:30—WRCA: Music Through the
Night, With Fleetwood
1:00—WOR: Mitch Reed Show

vertical field of vision, then your horizontal eye movements and horizontal field of vision. Your speed will depend upon the rapidity with which you can make these changes in your mental and visual processes.

Suppose the radio schedule above appears in the morning newspaper. You decide you would like to hear the news while you are eating lunch between 12:15 and 12:45. What is the quickest way of finding the station which will present a news program at that time?

1. Preview to locate the heading which tells you which section is devoted to *daytime* programs.

2. Using your vertical eye movements glance down the first column, back to the top of the second column, and down again until you find 12. This should require only two or three sweeps of your eyes.

3. Look at the middle figure in a group of three twelve o'clock figures, and read not only this middle figure but also the one above and below it *without moving your eyes*.

4. Once you find the 12:15, 12:30, 12:45 group, glance quickly at the words to the right of these numbers in search of the one word *news*.

5. Then with one quick backward fixation, grasp the call letters of the station. All of this should take about one second.

6. Try it.

Use the same techniques in locating each of the following as fleetingly as possible:

(a) Galen Drake's program in the middle of the afternoon.

(b) A Bing Crosby program early in the evening.

(c) Edward P. Morgan's commentaries during the ten o'clock evening programs.

(d) A program called "This is New York" which appears during eleven o'clock hour at night.

Exercise 3

In the table[5] on page 264 statistics are given in regard to the number of failures in different fields of industry during 9 months in 1954 and 1955, respectively. The table also presents the amount of liabilities for each industry during these periods. The liability figure in each case represents millions of dollars; for example: 7.8 means 7 and .8 millions of dollars.

In working with this table make use of your vertical field of vision in scanning to locate the names of certain industries for a further investigation in regard to the failures and liabilites.

Fixate in the middle of the first group of names, then in the middle of the second group, and so on, until you find the industry you are

5 From *Dun's Review and Modern Industry,* November 1955, p. 25.

FAILURES BY DIVISIONS OF INDUSTRY

(*Current liabilities in millions of dollars*)	Number 9 Months 1955	Number 9 Months 1954	Liabilities 9 Months 1955	Liabilities 9 Months 1954
MINING, MANUFACTURING..	1635	1710	120.9	138.1
Mining—Coal, Oil, Misc....	41	36	3.5	7.8
Food and Kindred Products.	120	131	11.8	13.9
Textile Products, Apparel...	376	408	18.2	21.9
Lumber, Lumber Products..	239	247	10.0	12.0
Paper, Printing, Publishing..	80	98	3.0	8.1
Chemicals, Allied Products..	39	61	3.0	4.8
Leather, Leather Products..	69	78	4.1	5.5
Stone, Clay, Glass Products.	38	42	1.6	1.2
Iron, Steel and Products....	89	87	10.3	9.0
Machinery...............	216	225	31.9	34.7
Transportation Equipment..	38	40	3.8	4.7
Miscellaneous.............	290	257	19.8	14.7
WHOLESALE TRADE........	891	857	39.3	41.6
Food and Farm Products...	220	219	9.9	10.5
Apparel..................	49	37	1.8	1.0
Dry Goods...............	39	49	1.3	2.2
Lumber, Bldg. Mats, Hdwre.	101	84	5.2	3.9
Chemicals and Drugs.......	28	32	0.9	0.6
Motor Vehicles, Equipment.	54	44	1.3	1.6
Miscellaneous.............	400	392	18.9	21.7
RETAIL TRADE............	4036	4174	88.6	114.7
Food and Liquor..........	785	740	13.1	10.6
General Merchandise.......	146	141	4.3	6.1
Apparel and Accessories....	658	629	13.0	12.2
Furniture, Furnishings.....	561	731	16.4	37.1
Lumber, Bldg. Mats, Hdwre.	230	231	6.6	6.7
Automotive Group.........	392	459	8.9	17.6
Eating, Drinking Places....	733	737	15.3	14.2
Drug Stores..............	96	119	2.1	2.6
Miscellaneous.............	435	387	8.8	7.5
CONSTRUCTION............	999	956	57.4	39.3
General Bldg. Contractors..	320	337	28.3	20.6
Building Subcontractors....	624	579	22.3	16.6
Other Contractors.........	55	40	6.8	2.1
COMMERCIAL SERVICE......	636	668	24.0	24.8
TOTAL UNITED STATES......	8197	8365	330.2	358.5

Liabilities are rounded to the nearest million; they do not necessarily add to totals.

THE FAILURE RECORD

	Sept. 1955	Aug. 1955	Sept. 1954	P.C. Chg.†
DUN'S FAILURE INDEX*				
Unadjusted.......	37.5	37.4	37.5	0
Adjusted, seasonally	43.6	41.6	44.1	—1
NUMBER OF FAILURES	822	888	819	+0.4
NUMBER BY SIZE OF DEBT				
Under $5,000.....	129	157	121	+7
$5,000–$25,000....	388	431	400	—3
$25,000–$100,000..	227	223	231	—2
$100,000 and over..	78	77	67	+16
NUMBER BY INDUSTRY GROUPS				
Manufacturing....	168	158	153	+10
Wholesale Trade...	99	107	113	—12
Retail Trade......	366	430	406	—10
Construction......	114	134	88	+30
Commercial Service	75	59	59	+27

(*LIABILITIES in thousands*)

CURRENT..:.........$33,120	$36,028	$36,381	—9
TOTAL............. 33,348	36,425	37,757	—12

*Apparent annual failures per 10,000 listed enterprises, formerly called DUN'S INSOLVENCY INDEX.
†Per cent change, September 1955 from September 1954.

BUSINESS FAILURES *include those businesses that ceased operations following assignment or bankruptcy; ceased with loss to creditors after such actions as execution, foreclosure, or attachment; voluntarily withdrew leaving unpaid obligations; were involved in court actions such as receivership, reorganization, or arrangement; or voluntarily compromised with creditors out of court.*

CURRENT LIABILITIES, *as used in* The Failure Record, *have a special meaning; they include all accounts and notes payable and all obligations, whether in secured form or not, known to be held by banks, officers, affiliated companies, supplying companies, or the Government. They do not include long-term, publicly held obligations. Offsetting assets are not taken into account.*

looking for. You don't have to read all the names in any one group. Look at a point in the middle of the group and, holding your eyes right there, gather a reading impression of the phrases above and below the point at which your eyes are fixated. In doing this you will be making full use of your vertical field of vision and will thus save a great deal of time which otherwise might be wasted in reading each separate line individually and horizontally.

Now, to apply the techniques you have just read about, see how quickly you can find the name of each of the following industries by making just one fixation in the middle of a group of names and using your *vertical* field of vision:

Paper, Printing, Publishing
Chemicals and Drugs
Automative Group
Building Subcontractors

Did you discover that you could find these names readily with the use of your "above" and "below" field of vision, without moving your eyes from the middle point at which they were fixated? Most people could improve their scanning ability tremendously by making greater use of their vertical field of vision.

In scanning this table for information you will also have to make some use of your horizontal field of vision. After you find the name of the industry in which you are interested, you will want to read the two numbers at the right which give comparative figures in regard to the number of failures the industry had and the two comparative figures which appear still further at your right in regard to the number of million dollars the industry lost. In finding these two bits of information make just one fixation for each of the pairs of figures. This fixation should be in the column of vacant space midway between the two groups of figures, so that you can take in both groups with the use of your horizontal field of vision and without moving your eyes. As an example, suppose you wish quickly to grasp the comparative figures showing the number of failures for Paper, Printing, and Publishing: look directly at the middle of the space between 80 and 98. As you fixate precisely in the middle of this space you should be able to see the 80 clearly at the left, and the 98 clearly at the right.

Similarly, if you wish to grasp quickly the comparative numbers which represent the number of million dollars of liabilities in this industry during the two periods look straight at a spot halfway between the 3.0 and 8.1, at which point you can see both numbers without moving your eyes.

If you proceed in this way, you will make only three fleeting fixations in locating the name of an industry in any one group and in grasping the two sets of figures concerning it. In the first of these fixations in which you are locating a name within a group of names, you use your vertical field of vision, and in the other two in which you are grasping two figures at a time you use your horizontal field of vision. You must make the switch from the vertical to the horizontal with great speed.

See how fleetingly and accurately you can complete your scanning for the different items needed in filling in the blanks below. After each hasty scanning in connection with an item, write the correct numbers in the blank spaces.

Name of industry	Number of Failures		Liabilities in million of dollars	
	1955	1954	1955	1954
Textile Products, Apparel	___	___	___	___
Stone, Clay, Glass Products	___	___	___	___
Dry Goods	___	___	___	___
Lumber, Bldg. Mats., Hardware	___	___	___	___
General Building Contractors	___	___	___	___

Check your answers with the table.

Exercise 4

Now that you have had some experience in using your vertical field of vision in scanning groups of numbers and groups of words, try using it in skimming a selection consisting of sentences and paragraphs.

Increasing numbers of magazines are using double columns these days. This practice facilitates skimming with the use of vertical eye movements and the vertical field of vision. Often it is possible to sweep the eyes straight down through the middle of one of these narrow columns, taking in the central area of two lines at a time with the use of the vertical field of vision. In the great majority of cases, this central section of the lines contains enough words to convey the information given in the selection even though the words at either side of the central section are not seen. If you find that you aren't following the thought at a certain point while using this procedure, you can always glance quickly to the left or right to catch a key word needed in completing the meaning. Even if you do have to take a side excursion now and then to catch a key word, you can still cover the selection very much more rapidly by reading the central part of two lines at a time than by moving your eyes back and forth across all the lines of print.

1. Sweep your eyes straight down through the middle of the short selection on page 267.

2. Gather all the important details you can by reading the central portion of two lines at one fixation and without changing the position of your eyes.

3. If you lose the thought at any point, catch a necessary key word with a fleeting left or right glance.

4. Allow yourself exactly five seconds to skim the article in this way.

5. Take the comprehension test after you have finished skimming the article.

Facts About Hamsters

Hamsters have been increasing in favor as laboratory animals. They're also kept as pets.

Hamsters can be bought from the same source as white mice. Price is $2.50 to $3.00 a pair. Keep your hamsters in a room with a temperature between 55° and 70° F. Keep them in metal cages, or in wooden cages protected on the inside with hardware cloth to keep them from gnawing their way out. A cage 12 x 15 x 12 inches will house a pair, while a cage 35 x 25 x 15 inches will take care of eight to ten animals. An adult hamster needs about 10 to 15 grams of food per day (1/3 to 1/2 ounce).

You can breed your animals throughout the year, but most litters are produced between November and May. A female will produce only five or six litters in her lifetime. The gestation period is about sixteen days. The number of young per litter averages about seven.

Hospitals, laboratories, biological supply houses, schools and certain other institutions offer the best market for the sale of hamsters. You should assure yourself of such a market before you raise many hamsters for sale.

Checking Comprehension

(Write "True" or "False" to the left of each statement.)

_____ 1. Hamsters are decreasing in favor.

_____ 2. They are bought from the same source as white mice.

_____ 3. The price of a pair of hamsters is from $5.00 to $10.00 per pair.

_____ 4. They may be kept in a metal cage protected with hardware cloth.

_____ 5. One pair should have a cage 40 x 20 x 40.

_____ 6. A hamster needs 10 to 15 grams of food per day.

_____ 7. They produce litters in June and July.

_____ 8. The female produces ten to fifteen litters in a lifetime.

_____ 9. The gestation period is ten days.

_____ 10. You might be able to sell some hamsters to laboratories.

Check your answers with the article itself to find how well your vertical field of vision worked for you.

Selection 5

Try skimming a longer selection with the use of the same techniques. Allow yourself no more than 10 seconds.

Sweet But Nonfattening[6]

ABSOLUTELY NONFATTENING . . . . Thrills your taste, trims your waist . . . . All the flavor is in, all the sugar is out . . . . Insist on frosty, taste-tingling refreshment with this revolutionary new sweetening discovery!

With just such high-pitched promotional fanfare, soft-drink manufacturers this year have been vigorously pushing the sales of dietetic beverages—products in which the sugar normally present has been replaced by a synthetic, nonfattening sweetener. These products go under various trade names, and many of them are booming. One company which only recently began selling low-calorie soft drinks expects its gross sales of these products during the year to total about $5 million in the metropolitan New York area alone.

Today, dozens of beverage manufacturers are hopping aboard the bandwagon, not merely to keep the diabetics of the nation happy but primarily to appeal to the millions of calorie-conscious folk trying resolutely to lose weight—or at least to hold their own. Incidentally, it's no trade secret that the leading users of dietetic soft drinks are women.

Most of the new dietetic beverages contain between 0.1 and 0.3 percent of a calcium salt usually designated as calcium cyclamate or Sucaryl. (There is also a Sucaryl based on sodium and more closely related to common salt, but it is not used so much.) Because a noncaloric sweetener is used in place of sugar, the average 12-ounce bottle of dietetic beverage supplies only about 3 calories, as compared to the 200 or more found in the conventional soft drink.

As manufacturers hasten to explain, synthetic sweeteners are definitely not sugar substitutes. The key distinction is that the synthetics, unlike sugar, provide flavor only, not food value. Thus far, only two synthetic sweeteners have been approved by the Food and Drug Administration for use in foods. These are saccharin and Sucaryl.

Saccharin, produced by Monsanto Chemical Co. and intermittently by Lapaco Chemicals, has been manufactured commercially in the United States ever since the turn of the century. In fact, John F. Queeny's first production of saccharin in St. Louis in 1901 not only broke Germany's monopoly on saccharin but also marked the birth of Monsanto Chemical itself. Sucaryl, on the other hand, is a relative newcomer.

[6] *Science Digest*, December 1953, pp. 77-79.

Abbott's commercial production of sodium Sucaryl began in the spring of 1950. A year later, Abbott began producing calcium Sucaryl, which has a special appeal to people on sodium-free diets. Both salts have approximately 30 times the sweetness of sucrose.

The relative advantages and disadvantages of saccharin and Sucaryl have been the subject of continuing debate. The principal point of contention is the relative aftertaste of both products. There are people who rave about saccharin, will use nothing else. Others would go without any sweetening whatever rather than subject themselves to what they regard as saccharin's objectionably bitter or metallic aftertaste.

Of course, in anything as subjective as taste, there are bound to be clashes of opinion. Although it is frequently stated that Sucaryl in normal use is less apt to impart an aftertaste than saccharin, it is still true that, at concentrations greater than 0.5 to 0.8 percent, most people think Sucaryl also tastes bitter.

Moreover, because saccharin has 14 times the sweetening power of Sucaryl, it is vulnerable to overuse. The problem of aftertaste, therefore, is often accentuated. On the other hand, Monsanto claims that its saccharin does not contain the trace of impurity responsible for saccharin's bitter aftertaste.

Today, producers of synthetic sweeteners not only must face the competition of rival manufacturers but also a welter of national and state regulations. For example, the use of saccharin in foods is prohibited in 27 states in the United States. In 17 of these states, all synthetic sweeteners are banned. Despite these handicaps, the market for synthetic sweeteners is expanding.

With horizons broadening, what about possible new synthetic sweeteners? Oddly, there is very little research being done today that is directed specifically toward the synthesis of new sweeteners. One reason is that not much is really known of why certain select compounds actually taste sweet.

In all likelihood, new synthetic sweeteners will continue to be discovered by accident in totally unrelated fields of research. Thus, new sweeteners await the fortunes of laboratory workers who have the foresight—and courage—to taste their own compounds.

Checking Comprehension

Write "True" or "False" before each statement.

———— 1. The sales of nonfattening beverages are booming.

———— 2. The manufacture of dietetic beverages is being conducted by two manufacturers only.

———— 3. Calcium salt and Sucaryl are one and the same thing.

———— 4. The synthetic sweeteners provide real food value.

———— 5. Saccharin has been produced for over two centuries.

————— 6. Sodium Sucaryl has been produced only recently.

————— 7. The principal point of contention over the relative advantages of saccharin and Sucaryl hinges on the aftertaste of the two products.

————— 8. Saccharin has much more sweetening power than Sucaryl.

————— 9. There are no state regulations in regard to these sweeteners.

————— 10. Very little research is being conducted in regard to these sweeteners.

See the Answer Key on page 385.

Comprehension Score:—————

Skimming Page-Wide Material with Vertical Eye Movements

In the selection below the content appears in full-page width. See if you can use your vertical eye movements and vertical field of vision in skimming this article which contains wider lines than the ones with which you have been working.

This selection will also offer you a good opportunity to try the technique of converting subheads into questions and then skimming to find the answers to these questions.

Follow this procedure:

1. Preview to determine the pattern of writing.
2. Set up as your general purpose reading to find the answer to the question in the title.
3. Preview the subheads and convert each one into a question as you glance at it. Perhaps your converted sub-heads will take forms similar to those below.

Subheading	*Converted*
It Was Clearly Petunia	Who considered it to be "Clearly a Petunia?"
Entrée to Kitchen Gained	How was the entrée gained?
Unsettling Discovery Was Made	What was the "unsettling discovery"?
Gardener Forced to Confess	What did the gardener confess?
If Not a Petunia, Then What?	What Was It?

4. Skim the selection, trying to move your eyes straight down through the middle of the page, "catching" all you can as you swiftly pass over the central portion.
5. With watch in hand allow yourself exactly 10 seconds for skimming. Ready. Start!

Selection 6

What Was It[7]

It Was Clearly a Petunia

It all began sometime ago when the days were still warm. The lady of the house started it by saying she would like to have a potted geranium in the kitchen window during the winter, since there would be no garden to look out upon until late next spring. Later, the gardener, inspecting a small bed where perennials for next season were taking root, found growing between two rows of carnations what clearly was a misplaced petunia—very small, very young, and very determined. With a true gardener's sense of thrift, instead of pulling up and throwing away what clearly was a petunia, the gardener obtained a large flower pot, carefully lifted the plant into it, and brought pot and plant into the house well before the first frost.

Entrée to Kitchen Gained

As tactfully as possible the gardener suggested to the lady of the house that a potted petunia might be a more welcome addition to the kitchen window during the winter than a potted geranium. The lady of the house demurred, commenting that she never had heard of anyone having a potted petunia in the kitchen. It was, however, such a small petunia that, resting in the center of the big flower pot, it had somewhat the appeal of a lost small child. The gardener thoughtfully observed that he had to put the petunia somewhere, and inquired if he might leave it in the kitchen until a better place could be found. As the days passed he observed with interest that what plainly was a petunia was being watered regularly and growing, and that he heard no more requests for geraniums—which, privately, he did not care for, anyway.

Unsettling Discovery Is Made

Some days later the gardener noted, casually, that what plainly was a petunia was growing rapidly, the picture of health. He mentioned the encouraging growth to the lady of the house, who, as if waiting for just

[7] "Topics of the Times," *New York Times*, November 20, 1954.

this opening, asked if he would mind very much moving the plant, in its pot, to some more desirable location, as its spreading leaves were beginning to get in the way at mealtimes. Obligingly the gardener picked up the flower pot and moved it into the dining-room window, as he did so getting a good view of the plant's leaves for the first time in weeks. What plainly had looked like a petunia when it was transplanted was beginning not to look like a petunia at all.

Gardener Forced to Confess

Having advertised his importation as a petunia the gardener was, understandably, reluctant to mention his discovery, and decided to let matters rest. Unfortunately, they did not rest long; the next day, looking out of the dining-room window over her second cup of breakfast coffee, the lady of the house asked the gardener if he was sure that what he had planted in the pot was in fact a petunia. The gardener had to confess that, whatever it was, indeed it did not now seem to be a petunia. It surely was not a geranium. It plainly was not a number of other things. But what it really was, he said, he did not know.

If Not a Petunia, Then What?

The gardener now wishes he had confessed nothing and had stuck to his story that this was a petunia. For the plant—now a foot tall with spoon-shaped leaves perhaps ten inches long—occupying a conspicuous place in the dining room, has become a conversation piece; all who come to dine ask about it, or if they fail to do so the lady of the house tells them the story of her "geranium," much to the gardener's discomfiture. The gardener, after consulting a number of books, has tentatively concluded that he is wintering a fine specimen of Nicotiana, but he is not positive. If it is indeed Nicotiana and grows no more rapidly than the Nicotiana in last summer's garden, it will be a long time before he can be sure. The gardener's only hope is that if he is nursing carefully an unidentified weed it will eventually bear large blossoms—resembling, preferably, geranium or petunia.

Checking Comprehension

1. Who considered it to be "clearly a petunia"? _____

2. How was the entrée to the kitchen gained? _____

3. What was the "unsettling discovery"? _____

4. What did the gardener confess? _____

5. What was it? _____

Check your answers with the Answer Key on page 385. Allow 20 for each correct answer.

Comprehension Score:_____

Skimming with the Technique of Your Choice

You have now tried skimming for main ideas, skimming with the use of key words, skimming with the use of vertical eye movements and vertical field of vision. Perhaps you have found that some one of these techniques has more promise for your own personal skimming use than the others; or it may be you have found that the combination of all three of these procedures serves you personally to the best advantage; or maybe you like to use one technique for one purpose and a different one for another purpose.

Choose the technique or combination of techniques which you think you personally can use to the best advantage in skimming the following article.

Selection 7

1. Skim this article to find out whom the author is writing about and why this person was a "Master at His Trade." In doing this you will of course gather general information on the topic.
2. Allow yourself 5 seconds for skimming.
3. Take the comprehension test which follows the article. This test will be based on general information—not details.

A Master at His Trade[8]

The ballplayers always said that Bill McGowan was the best umpire in the American League. No higher praise ever could be given an umpire, and perhaps that can serve as McGowan's epitaph. He'd have liked it that way because he was as devoted to his profession as Bill Klem had been. The American League had retired the ailing McGowan earlier in the week on a handsome pension. But he died yesterday before he had an opportunity to enjoy it.

The proudest moment of his life was in 1948 when the American

8 Arthur Daley, *New York Times*, December 10, 1954.

League virtually admitted that he was its best arbiter. Once upon a time world series assignments were the supreme accolade, but they are on a rotating basis now and therefore meaningless. However, the junior circuit had the first and only play-off in its history in 1948 when the Indians and Red Sox tied for the championship. It was imperative that only the best of the Men in Blue handle that game. Significant indeed was the fact that Bill McGowan was named umpire-in-chief.

Bill was always an eager beaver, a hustler. And his enthusiasm never waned during his thirty seasons in the big leagues. But that's why he was so good, though his overenthusiasm twice drew him suspensions, a rarity in itself. Even then, the ballplayers never said grumpily, "Served him right." Instead they said softly, "Too bad about Willie, isn't it?"

In the Mirror

When McGowan entered the American League in 1924, he even brought his job into his hotel room with him, so unceasing were his efforts to improve himself. Soon he had his roomie, Roy Van Graflan, doing the same thing.

"Y're out!" Bill would bellow, jerking his thumb peremptorily in front of the mirror. Then he'd try it again with a different inflection and a different gesture, experimenting with his techniques. And pretty soon Van Graflan was doing the same thing.

"Y're out!" Van would scream, as the two of them practiced for hours on end. Finally a booming voice came echoing up from the hotel courtyard.

"Shut up!" howled a complaining nonsleeper. "Hey, don't you guys ever call anyone safe?"

It also was in a hotel that McGowan had one of the most soul-shattering experiences of his career. It happened when he was a young and green umpire. He'd noticed how well dressed his fellow arbiters were and asked for an explanation. After all, umpirical salaries were stringently modest in those days.

Wholesale Price

"It's easy," one of them said. "We lead lonely lives, apart from the ballplayers. But we're constantly coming in contact with traveling salesmen. So just butter up to a few of them, entertain them a bit, and you'll be able to get shirts, suits, shoes, and everything you need at wholesale prices. Sometimes they'll even give you samples for free."

McGowan cased the lobby and picked on a likely prospect. He struck up a conversation with him, learned that he was a salesman, and buttered him up. The stranger couldn't pick up a tab. McGowan wined and dined him, carefully avoiding even a hint of the nefarious purpose behind his hospitality.

"It's been a wonderful evening, Bill," said the stranger as they parted.

"By the way," said Bill, "you never did mention what firm you're traveling for. Which one is it?" "The Baldwin Locomotive Company," said the stranger.

McGowan's two suspensions deserve mention. The first was the outcome of an incident at home plate in a game between the Senators and Indians in Washington. Joe Papparella ruled that Eddie Stewart was out at home with the winning run, and the Washington players came storming out of the dugout in violent protest.

New Man on Job

Technically speaking, the call was none of McGowan's business. But Papparella was a new man on the job, and Bill rushed to his rescue. But in taking the heat off his fellow worker, he set himself ablaze. Words were spoken that should never have been spoken. So McGowan was suspended to cool off. But that was why he got even more than the normal satisfaction out of being named umpire-in-chief a few months later in the play-off game. It was a vindication of sorts.

The other suspension resulted primarily from a run-in with players and then erupted in the wrong direction, toward the press box. It was a Tiger-Brown game in St. Louis, and McGowan thought the Tigers were unnecessarily rough in their riding of Satchell Paige. He furiously ordered them to stop and cleared off part of the Detroit bench. The baseball writers asked for details of the still-seething McGowan.

"Tell 'em I'll write a letter," snapped His Nibs.

"We didn't know you could write," was the unnecessarily rude message he received in return.

"If you guys could write, you'd be in New York," was McGowan's final insult. The press-box tenants took umbrage and filed formal protest with President Will Harridge of the American League. McGowan was suspended.

For all of that, though, he was a mighty fine umpire. The fellows who'll miss him most will be the ballplayers who always affectionately called him "Willie."

Checking Comprehension

1. Bill McGowan was famous in (a) tennis, (b) basketball, (c) baseball, (d) football.

2. At the time the article was written, McGowan was (a) retired, (b) working in connection with a World Series game, (c) just elected an official, (d) deceased.

3. The proudest moment in his life was the American League named him (a) captain, (b) coach, (c) director, (d) umpire-in-chief.

4. Bill was (a) a pessimist, (b) optimist, (c) enthusiast, (d) chronic complainer.

5. Bill even practised (a) in his kitchen, (b) while traveling on the train, (c) before the mirror in his hotel room, (d) in his locker room.

6. It was indicated that McGowan's salary was (a) high, (b) exorbitant, (c) modest, (d) increased three fold during his last ten years of work.

7. Bill picked a man from the lobby to entertain, thinking that this man was a good prospect for (a) helping Bill get a salary raise, (b) helping him get a promotion, (c) letting him have clothes at wholesale prices or for free, (d) teaching him a new trick in baseball.

8. The article mentioned that McGowan was suspended (a) once, (b) twice, (c) many times, (d) never.

9. One of Bill's suspensions resulted from (a) unfair play, (b) ill health, (c) a hot exchange of words with the press, (d) a quarrel with the President of the American League.

10. Ballplayers regarded Bill with (a) jealousy, (b) animosity, (c) pity, (d) affection.

Answers: 1)___, 2)___, 3)___, 4)___, 5)___, 6)___, 7)___, 8)___, 9)___, 10)___.

See the Answer Key on page 386.

Comprehension Score:_____

Selection 8

1. Skim the following article on tipping for the purpose of finding the answer to the author's question in the subtitle, "A National Racket?"

2. In realizing this purpose you will on the whole skim only for general ideas, but you will also have to grasp some of the details in the way of figures. So you will use a combination of techniques in skimming this article: general skimming, and grasping and remembering details.

3. Allow yourself ten seconds to skim this article, then take the comprehension test.

Tipping[9]

A National Racket?

We Americans hand out approximately $750,000,000 annually in tips, or three quarters of a billion dollars, according to the United States Department of Commerce. Of this amount about $450,000 goes to restaurant employees. The rest greases the open palms of hotel "gimme" boys, taxi drivers, beauticians, barbers, parking-lot attendants, bartenders,

[9] Oneta Aldrich Wakeford, *American Mercury*, June 1954, pp. 127-129.

and a host of others who expect gratuities from the public for their services.

In spite of these magnanimous figures, however, tipping is generally an unpopular and disliked custom in the United States, and it always has been. As far back as 1896, the secretary of the Journeyman Barbers International Union of America condemned tipping as "humiliating and degrading." In 1905 the Anti-Tipping Society of America had 100,000 members, the majority of them salesmen. Within the next few years anti-tipping laws were passed in Arkansas, Iowa, Mississippi, South Carolina, Tennessee, and Washington. This legislation was short-lived, however, for in 1919 the Iowa law was repealed as unconstitutional and the other states soon followed suit.

Today, of course, we're all aware of how widespread the practice of tipping is, and how many categories of workers it covers. It has become mainly a "pressure" custom. And while we go along with it outwardly, the majority of us actually feel that it is wrong in principle. According to a recent survey on the subject, 65.1% of the persons queried definitely disapprove of tipping, only 22.2% approve, 12% are undecided.

A laborer should be worthy of his hire, no matter what his field. He shouldn't have to depend on the gratuities of the public. Yet, the United States Chamber of Commerce reports that there are 1,800,000 persons who depend on tips for the major part of their income.

Tipping itself has a servile aspect. One does not tip an equal. Even the way tipping is usually handled is undignified payment. Either the coin is slipped under the edge of the plate, out of sight, or into the servitor's hand quickly, almost stealthily, as if the transaction weren't quite above board. In the words of Edward Corsi, Industrial Commissioner of New York, who conducted hearings several months ago on proposed minimum wage laws that would affect his state's 250,000 restaurant workers: "Tipping is unworthy of labor in the twentieth century. It makes a servant out of the worker. It is a disgraceful thing that the worker has to depend on tips for a living."

This dependency on tips puts the worker in an unfair position. He has grown to expect them as his earnings, and not as a token of appreciation for extra service he has given. He is often filled with resentment when he isn't tipped, or not tipped highly enough because, to him, those gratuities are important as bread-and-butter money. Of course, there are a few servitors who, after the essentials are paid for, can well afford a shiny new Cadillac! Some headwaiters, for instance, who work in expensive nightclubs which dot the country from east to west, have reported yearly incomes of $35,000. At least six in New York earn $50,000. These naturally, are the exception.

The customer, on the other hand, is placed in an uncomfortable position, as well as what he thinks is an unfair one. The uncomfortable feeling comes usually from not knowing exactly how much he should tip. Practically everyone above the age of fifteen has read the "etiquette rules" of how much to tip and when. But if these rules were printed in books or magazines four or five years ago, he can be sure that they're substandard for today's tipping. Prices have gone up, and if the customer doesn't know it, or acts as if he doesn't, he'll receive bullet glances which denounce him as subhuman. For instance, ten or fifteen cents to a train porter for carrying one bag used to be acceptable. The present price is twenty-five. Ten per cent of the restaurant check was a standard rule a few years back. Today, it is fifteen, and in the so-called better places, more. As one waiter put it: "When I work in a swanky hotel I count on at least twenty per cent."

Because there are so many variations to the rules, a customer is often in a quandary as to whether the "rule" holds good in his particular situation. Take the case of a woman going into a beauty shop. She is armed with the "social knowledge" that she'll be expected to tip the operator fifteen per cent of her total bill. However, by the time she's had a haircut, shampoo, set, and manicure, not one operator but four have waited on her. If, for instance, her bill is $6.00 won't the required 90 cents tip, divided four ways, look stingy, and not be what each expected?

The term "tip" originated in a London coffee house in Fleet Street where Samuel Johnson and his cronies frequently visited during the eighteenth century. On the table was a bowl with the words, "To Insure Promptitude," printed around it. The phrase was later shortened to "Tip," taking the first letter of each of the three words.

Today, a person is expected to leave a tip even though the service has been slow and indifferent. The unfairness of the tipping racket, as far as the customer is concerned, hinges on the feeling that he is being pressured into carrying part of the employer's burden. If he pays a good price for his haircut, why should he tip the barber? Isn't it up to the employer to provide a decent wage for him? Or, when he stays in a hotel and pays that bill, why should he give the maid extra money for coming in to clean his room? Isn't her salary a definite duty of hotel management?

It seems to him that tipping is the employers' way out of responsibility. They pass the buck of their workers' salaries on to the customer.

Most of us continue to tip, even though we dislike the practice, for one or all three of the following reasons: (1) Conscience. We recognize the injustice of the worker's meager wage and feel that we must add to his take-home pay. (2) Social pressure. We don't wish to look like cheapskates to our associates or to the workers themselves. (3) Moral weakness. We lack the courage of our convictions that the principle of tipping, as it is being used today, is inherently wrong for our democratic way of life.

It is with a kind of mental relief that passengers ride the airlines, where no tipping is allowed. Many supermarkets which hire boys to carry bags or boxes of purchased groceries out to the car for the customer have signs requesting no tipping. A few (too few!) restaurants in various parts of the country have similar signs. To the customer, such signs are like a beautiful oasis in a "gimme" desert.

In some foreign countries such as Finland, a service charge is added to restaurant and hotel bills. I believe most of us would prefer this system to our present one.

The tipping racket can be stopped only when the three groups—employers, workers and customers—decide that it is an archaic and unfair practice and proceed to do something about it.

Checking Comprehension

1. The United States hands out in tips each year (a) millions of dollars, (b) hundreds of dollars, (c) thousands of dollars, (d) a very small amount.

2. In the United States tipping (a) is generally approved, (b) is generally disliked, (c) attracts indifference, (d) is regarded as unconstitutional.

3. Anti-tipping laws in the United States have (a) been short-lived, (b) been suggested but never passed, (c) been a success where they have been tried out, (d) been successful in only a few cases.

4. Tipping places the worker in the class of (a) a laborer, (b) a servant, (c) one's equal, (d) one who deserves recognition.

5. In following the rules for tipping, a customer may (a) acquaint the person who serves him with the rules, (b) always tip exactly the right amount, (c) disregard the rules entirely, (d) be in a quandary because of variations in rules.

6. As the years go by the amount given for tips (a) has become standardized, (b) is generally less than previously, (c) is generally higher than previously, (d) is higher for some services and less for others.

7. The word "tip" originated in (a) a French restaurant, (b) a Norwegian Smörgasbord, (c) a London coffee house, (d) an American hotel.

8. Nowadays you are supposed to leave a tip (a) only when the service is as good as usual, (b) only when you ask for something special, (c) only when the person serving you is unusually attentive, (d) even though the service has been slow and indifferent.

9. It seems that tipping is a good way for an employer to (a)

recognize his help, (b) avoid his responsibility, (c) aid his help in avoiding income tax, (d) find out which one of his employees have special abilities.

10. In Finland tipping is (a) regulated, (b) not emphasized, (c) added to the bill, (d) paid by the employer.

Answers: 1)—, 2)—, 3)—, 4)—, 5)—, 6)—, 7)—, 8)—, 9)—, 10)—.

See the Answer Key on page 386.

Comprehension Score:————————

Vocabulary Development

The italicized words appeared in the selections which you have just read. One of the phrases, *a*, or *b*, or *c*, completes each sentence. Check the phrase which correctly completes each of the sentences.

1. A *capricious* person would
   a. do surprising things
   b. usually be angry
   c. make a good soldier
2. He *reiterated* the
   a. machine
   b. building
   c. statement
3. An *assiduous* worker would
   a. work with chemicals
   b. be indefatigable
   c. try to please the boss
4. The president *demurred* because
   a. he disliked the plan
   b. he favored the plan
   c. he was using the plan
5. The *detritus* consisted of
   a. fleecy clouds
   b. tree-trunks
   c. tiny particles of rock
6. To take *umbrage* is to
   a. accept a bribe
   b. be resentful
   c. take the total weight of a cargo

7. A man in a *quandary* is
   a. successfully resisting temptation
   b. engaged in mining
   c. perplexed
8. Munificent *gratuities* were dispensed by
   a. a kindly old beggar
   b. the deacon of a small parish
   c. an industrial tycoon
9. *Nefarious* deeds were performed by
   a. iniquitous men
   b. chivalrous knights
   c. indigent but righteous men
10. The *peremptory* statement was made to
   a. encourage discussion
   b. ensure fairness
   c. silence all objections
11. The *exhumation* was done by
   a. a physician
   b. an undertaker
   c. a gravedigger

12. The *paleontologist* was examining
    a. blood cells
    b. fossils
    c. minerals
13. The boat slowly approached the *vortex*
    a. to dock
    b. to take it on board

    c. because it was drawn to it
14. *Doldrums* occur when
    a. stimulants are imbibed
    b. life becomes meaningless
    c. the wind is from the south
15. An *arbiter*
    a. will work diligently
    b. will settle the dispute
    c. will record the proceedings

Check your answers with an Answer Key on page 386.

Vocabulary Score: —————.

Follow-Up Practice

Using materials of your own selection. Continue with your daily practice periods and, beginning with your next period, devote a part of your time to practice in skimming. Skim to find an article that you want to read. Skim to locate a certain fact or figure. In a factual article skim to get main ideas. In easy narrative material skim to follow the trend of thought. Set a time limit of one minute and see how much you can get out of an article in that time.

Also try skimming quantities of the material which you meet in your daily work or recreational activities. Use various combinations of the techniques suggested in this chapter, for these changing combinations aid in accomplishing your different purposes. As you become more and more expert, try the flashing-from-top-to-bottom-of-the-page technique more frequently. With practice you can really become very skillful in gathering meanings through the use of one vertical sweep of your eyes right down through the middle of the column or page. When you can do this effectively, you will know that you are an expert skimmer.

CHAPTER 11

How to Get the Most

out of Reading

a Newspaper

Where to Find Things in a Newspaper

Newspaper Make-up. A knowledge of newspaper make-up can save the busy reader a great deal of time. Most newspapers have a definite pattern for the arrangement and location of different types of articles, and full awareness of this pattern contributes considerably to effective newspaper reading.

The front page of a newspaper is used as a sort of showcase. In this showcase the newspaper exhibits its most important, most interesting, most attractive wares. In the better newspapers an attempt is made to group the various items so that those belonging to the same general category are close together. A nice balance of topics is usually discussed on the first page and the typographical arrangement is attractive.

The most important piece of news ordinarily appears in the upper right-hand column of the first page. If you have time to read only one news item, this article is the one you probably should choose, for you may be sure that the editor considers it the most outstanding news of the day. The position for this lead article probably developed from the fact that newsstands in the past usually folded and arranged newspapers in such a way that only the upper right-hand corner of the paper showed.

The second most important article is usually placed in the upper left-hand corner of the first page. Other significant items are variously placed on the front page according to their relative importance. The distribution of news items then continues throughout the first section of the paper, on the front and back pages of the second sections, and with items of lesser importance interleaved throughout the pages.

Usually the sections devoted to editorials, sports, finances, radio and television programs, weather, and want ads appear in the second section or still further back if there are more than two sections.

The Index. For your convenience in quickly locating the kind of material in which you have a special interest, newspapers carry an index on page 1 or on page 2. Busy readers could save much time if they would make greater use of the newspaper index.

The format of the index varies from paper to paper, but its function is always the same—to tell readers where they can find what they want without thumbing through pages.

Sample indexes from several papers appear on page 284.

Regardless of the form, the purpose of an index is to help you locate things quickly. If you are not already making use of the index in the paper you read, locate it, try using it, and prove to yourself what a timesaver an index can be.

What Skills to Use in Newspaper Reading

There is nothing so specialized in newspaper reading that it requires the use of any technical reading skill not employed in reading other types of material. On the other hand, newspaper reading

Features

News summaries on page 4

You'll Find Inside:

FEATURES INDEX

French Troops Kill 31 Rebel Algerians

French troops fight bloody desert battle with a rebel band in Algeria, killing 31. Story on Page 15, Part 1.

Where To Find It

makes use of *all* the skills you have developed while working with this book.

Skimming you will use more widely in newspaper reading than in any other kind of reading. You skim the entire paper each day to find articles which interest you sufficiently so that you want to read them. After selecting an article you may skim it to find the answer to a certain question, to get the main idea, to find a specific fact, to follow the plot of a story, etc.

Your *preview* techniques help you quickly get the gist of many articles. Editors frequently divide articles by means of subtitles. Often articles are accompanied by a photograph, map, chart, or graph. Knowing how to preview will enable you to get all the information you want out of an article without reading it.

Finding the main idea in a paragraph will serve you well in reading a newspaper for the general trend and the most important points.

Reading for details will come in handy, of course. You will find technical articles and financial reports in the newspaper, as well as in books and periodicals. When you come across an article which is significant to you personally, then call into play the specialized technique for mining for details.

If you find some rules, lists, or information that you would like to be *able to recall exactly,* you will of course use the techniques for waking up your memory.

In a newspaper you will find all the different *patterns of writing*: narrative, question-and-answer, information, opinon-reason, substantiated-fact. Decide which pattern applies to the particular article you are about to peruse, and "ride in the saddle with the author."

In summary, it may be said that there is no other single source of reading material which demands the use of so many different reading skills. The great variety of interests to which the newspaper caters necessarily brings to its pages all types of material for all kinds of purposes. To be an effective newspaper reader one must run *the entire gamut of reading skills* and become proficient in all of them.

If there is one unique achievement to be developed in newspaper reading, it is that of flexibility; that of being extremely facile in changing from the use of one skill or set of skills to another, from one speed to another. Developing a higher degree of adjustability in accordance with changes in material or changes in your purposes for reading is the next skill that you must cultivate.

Preliminary Planning for Newspaper Reading

The first step is to plan a pattern of reading for yourself.

Establish a definite time for reading the newspaper every day. If you ride to and from work on a bus or train, plan to use that time for reading the paper—perhaps a morning paper on your way to work, and an evening paper on your way home. If you drive to work, set aside fifteen minutes each morning after breakfast and from fifteen to forty-five minutes again each evening after dinner. Of course any time arrangement convenient for you will do. The important thing is to devote the same definite period to newspaper reading regularly every day.

After deciding upon your newspaper-reading period or periods, budget your time. Allow about the right amount of time for reading different types of content in terms of their relative importance. Unless you plan for the best use of your reading time you may find yourself spending practically all the period on sports and columnists' articles, never getting around to the really important news.

Each person's time budget will differ in terms of his interests. Presented here is a sample of one person's program for newspaper reading. This man is a very fast reader, as you should be at this point, and he is able to get practically everything he needs out of the newspaper in one half hour.

Skimming	2	minutes
News	15	"
Financial pages	3	"
Sports	2	"
Drama, Music, Books	2	"
Radio, TV Programs	1	"
Editorials	1	"
Columnists	1	"
Advertisements	1	"
Comics	1	"
Crossword puzzle	1	"

This man places the least important things last on his list. If he runs out of time before covering all the items, then those of lesser consequence are the ones neglected.

Tackling the Job

First skim all the headlines on the front page. These headlines name the news items which the editor considers the most important. This should take about half a minute. If you did no more than this you would have a fairly good idea of the news events of the day.

Now spend a minute or so skimming through the entire paper in order to make mental notes of items to be read later. Use the index and the news summary.

After this swift bird's-eye view, return to the front page and read most of that. There may be some articles, however, in which the first paragraph or two suffice to give all the information you desire.

After covering the first page, proceed to read widely throughout the paper. Don't confine your reading to the one subject of sports or finances or any other special interest. Make yourself read on a variety of subjects and, first thing you know, you'll be interested in all of them.

In reading broadly, however, take care to read selectively. Don't try to read everything printed on any page (unless it is the first page). Select the most informative, interesting, or entertaining articles on each of the different subjects.

It is helpful to use the trick of turning headings into questions. If you read with a question uppermost in your mind you will find this technique to be a whipper-up of interest and a sharp-pointed tool. The question guides you in getting directly to the heart of the news. Having a question in mind contributes both to your speed and comprehension.

Here are some examples of titles which have been converted into questions:

Title	*Questions*
School Pay Rises Listed by Board; Teachers Object	Why do they object?
Report Bids U.S. Alter Aid Policy	Whose report? How did they want the policy altered?
Navy Jet Project Held Total Loss	Who held it a total loss?
Federal Reserve Under Heavy Fire	Why? For what? By whom?

It is helpful to think of news as a continued story. Make a practice of following the same news stories as they develop day by day. Try to anticipate what will happen next. Look forward to reading the next "installment" to find out.

Make use of the visual aids. Much enlightenment can be gained not only from looking at the photographs in the newspaper but also from studying the maps, diagrams, graphs, and charts—all of which are intended to help you to grasp information quickly.

Try to improve your vocabulary. The diversity of topics in a newspaper necessarily calls into use an extensive vocabulary. For this reason your newspaper reading offers a rich opportunity to extend your own vocabulary. It would be impractical to run to a dictionary every time you meet an unfamiliar word in the paper. Neither is it advisable just to skip over such a word saying, "I don't know the meaning of that, so let it go." Usually, if you stop to think about the word in terms of the context, you can figure out its meaning. The more you use context clues, the more adept you become in determining meanings through the use of this technique. Of course the dictionary should not be disregarded. It is a good idea to look up in the dictionary the few words that really "stump" you and concerning which you are curious.

Read several different newspapers to get different points of view. There is no doubt one paper which you buy regularly. Don't exclude other papers because of this favorite. Buy various papers and check their news stories and viewpoints with those of your own favorite paper.

Supplement what you read in newspapers with news presented through other communication agencies. Radio, television, moving pictures, lectures are all news-gathering and news-distributing media that provide you with a rich fund of information, to serve you in arriving at your own conclusions.

Finally, read *critically*. *Think* while you read. Read with an open, inquiring mind for the purpose of obtaining all of the information you can. But don't be too hasty in arriving at conclusions. Accept, reject, or change your mind only when you have facts and unbiased evidence. The chapter on how to analyze propaganda will be valuable to you in reading the newspaper critically.

In evaluating the slants and biases of others, don't forget to examine yourself for your own predispositions. Possibly some of your own biases color a news story or an editorial in a way which the writer never intended. In newspaper reading self-analysis is as important as propaganda analysis.

Vocabulary Development

The press, like many other fields of specialization, has its own vocabulary. Each of the following sentences contains an italicized word or phrase which has a specialized meaning in newspaper work. Use context clues to get the meaning, then take the test.

1. The sensational story was printed on the first page with a *banner line* heading it.

2. The paper had gone to press when only the *dogwatch* was on duty.

3. The reporter checked the police *blotter* to see if a lead for an interesting story might be found.

4. The banner line was printed in *bold face* type.

5. "Take the *dummy* in to the editor, so he can check it before you take it to the typesetters," said the assistant editor.

6. During the war important pictures were transmitted from London to the United States by *facsimile.*

7. "The *lead* on that article should give a better idea of the content of the story," complained the editor.

8. The *Linotype* operators can't change a word in the type without destroying the whole line of print.

9. Consult the *masthead* for information about the administration of the newspaper.

10. The cost of *newsprint* has been rising steadily, partly because of a developing lumber shortage.

11. "Print the banner line in *upper case!*" shouted the copy editor.

12. The *break-over* for that front-page story should be carried to page ten.

13. "Figure out a more suitable *caption* for that picture," the editor instructed the writer.

14. A reporter will be assigned to write a *feature* story on the president's inauguration.

15. "Use that humorous little article about licensing cats as *filler* on page one," said the editor.

16. Papers never use *lower case* letters for banner lines. They are too inconspicuous.

17. In the *morgue,* the editor found pictures dating back to the early 1900's.

18. "*Kill* that story before it goes any further," said the editor.

19. Through his *scoop*, Joe Black earned the envy of the other reporters and the plaudits of his editor.

20. All *copy* must be on the editor's desk by 1:15 P.M. if it is to make the first edition.

Definitions

Below are the definitions of the italicized words or phrases in the sentences above. Write the correct italicized word on the space at the left of each definition.

a) _____ loose-leaf book used by the police for registering arrests

b) _____ a process by means of which a picture or text is transmitted by radio and upon reception is automatically reproduced on paper

c) _____ paper on which newspapers are printed

d) _____ capital letters

e) _____ headline in large letters running across top of first page

f) _____ heavy type

g) _____ title or explanation accompanying a picture

h) _____ a layout of printed matter used as a guide for making up a page

i) _____ skeleton staff which stays on duty after the last edition of the paper has gone to press

j) _____ part of story continued from another page

k) _____ a distinctive or prominant article, story, or picture

l) _____ a story with little news value used to fill space

m) _____ first few sentences or first paragraph or two of a news story containing summary or introduction to story

n) _____ shows title, ownership, management, subscription and advertising rates of the paper

o) _____ typesetting machine that casts solid lines of type called slugs from molten metal

p) _____ small letters

q) _____ file of stories, biographies, cuts, and other clippings for reference—place where the material is kept

r) _____ to strike out copy

s) ———————— all manuscripts or typewritten matter prepared
for printing

t) ———————— an important story printed before other newspaper reporters get it

Check with the Answer Key on page 386.

Maintaining Your Skills

This chapter is an easy one to read and you should have covered
it very rapidly. You need continuous practice, however, on several
of the specific skills which you have been developing. This follow-
up practice is necessary in order to maintain a high level of competence in reading different types of material for different purposes.
The exercises on the next few pages should provide this maintenance
practice for you.

Maintaining Ability to Remember What You Read

Turn back to the list of suggestions under the heading "Tackling
the Job," pages 287-288. Try to fix in your memory the list of things
to do in reading a newspaper. Have in mind some person to whom
you would like to give this information. Use any of the techniques
described in Chapter Eight which you think would be useful to you
in recalling this list.

Check your recall by referring to the list itself.

Maintaining Ability to Read for Details

This is a selection for use in maintaining your ability to read for
details. Read it as rapidly as you can while still grasping the details
and their relationships. Your test will check major details.

Selection 1

News for the Million[1]

I

The original idea for the *News of the World* came from a 64-year-old
ex-bankrupt who had been jostling about in the British newspaper busi-

[1] Claud Cockburn, *The Atlantic Monthly*, August 1955, pp. 73-75.

ness right through the rise and fall of Napoleon Bonaparte, the War of 1812, the adult life of Jane Austen, and the construction of the first railroads. His name was John Browne Bell, and in October, 1843, he announced by placard and handbill a new weekly newspaper.

"News for the Million. The Novelty of Nations and the wonder of the World. 48 Large Folio Columns. Price only 3d. The Size of The Times." (The *Times* at that period sold at 5d. and had a circulation of 23,000.) "Our object," proclaimed the first issue of the *News of the World*, "is to establish a First Class Journal at a Price which shall place it within the reach of All Classes of Readers. . . . Our practice is the FEARLESS ADVOCACY OF TRUTH."

Blazing a trail from which the paper has never, in one hundred eleven years, deviated far, the three items most prominently displayed in the first issue concerned THE CHEAPEST AND BEST MODE OF ADVERTISING—which naturally turned out to be a First Class Journal within the reach of All Classes of Readers; THE POLITICIAN AND THE STATE OF THE NATION; and EXTRAORDINARY CHARGE OF DRUGGING AND VIOLATION. With this menu, Mr. Bell became the progenitor of the largest circulation newspaper in the world. Today the *News of the World* forms the whole, or a part, of the Sunday newspaper reading of almost half the entire population of Britain between the age of sixteen and the grave. More than 20 million is the number of its weekly readers, according to a semiofficial survey by the Institute of Incorporated Practitioners in Advertising. Of these, over 8 million are the paying customers, the officially attested paid circulation. Two other British Sunday papers—*Sunday Pictorial* and *People*—are runners-up, with paid circulations of a little better than 5 million each. The distinguished *Sunday Times* and the *Observer* stand respectively 50,000 above and 50,000 below the half-million mark. And this has been the rough shape of things as regards the *News of the World* since before World War I. It is as characteristic and pervasive an expression of the British way of life as the warm-beered British pub and the shuffling queues outside Lord's cricket ground; as accurate a partial reflection of the mind and face of Britain as are the parliamentary debates or a statement by the Executive of the Trades Union Congress.

This is so little of a paradox that it could be described as an undeniable fact—were it not sure to be ferociously or titteringly denied by millions of British newspaper readers, including several million weekly addicts of the *News of the World*.

"Sordid," "inexpressibly vulgar," "squalid recorder of squalid crime," "panderer to the lowest human instincts"—a person does not need to be a hypocrite to apply any or all of these epithets to this most popular of all British newspapers. The only hypocrites concerned are those who pretend that the epithets are mysteriously inappropriate or else that, equally mysteriously, this newspaper is not "truly representative of British taste." As a people, the British do not much care to be judged by the *News of the World*. They just buy those 8 million copies of it every Sunday and provide it with the highest advertising rate of any Sunday newspaper.

At the end of an English Sunday, the earnest inquirer could—on the basis of firsthand information received from sincere Britons at all social levels—report that nobody above the lowest income-tax groups reads it at all, except by accident or under some unexplained duress; that respectable members of the working class buy it only to take home to their wives, who have it in the home only because their husbands like to read it; and that its main circulation must be in some other part of the country, among people of lower taste. Persons who admit to reading it are apt to do so apologetically or with an air intended to suggest that the bit of them that reads the *News of the World* is hardly the real Them.

On the other hand, if the earnest inquirer persists long enough to uncover unabashed addicts, he will eventually find several million citizens who would consider it a frivolous waste of time and money to get any other paper. To them, "the paper"—as something to read, rather than a betting sheet with other stuff printed on the back of the lists of today's runners—means the *News of the World* and nothing else. For them, events only assume full reality on being reported in the *News of the World*.

A fairly large volume of the stream of sincere denunciation regularly directed against the paper from pulpits and the platforms of women's clubs has it obvious historical springs back in the days when the upper class found it difficult to forgive the lower class for learning to read at all, and predicted disaster and abuses. With a circulation of which over 56 per cent is rated by the Hulton Survey of the Press as "working class," the *News of the World* is the natural target for the descendants of those Viewers with Alarm. At least since World War I, "the sort of man who lies in bed on Sundays reading the *News of the World*" has become a conventionalized image of what any given critic means by national decadence.

Lying in bed with the *News of the World* is the thing people are alleged to be doing when they are failing to do whatever this or that enthusiast—for churchgoing, walking vigorously through the countryside, or cultivating the garden to make us independent of foreign food and close the dollar gap—thinks they ought to be doing.

As an ingredient of the kind of music-hall joke which the British love because it is just like the ones Father used to make, the *News of the World* is as well established in the public esteem as cheese. Man lying in bed reading it is still the central figure of the jest, but is here regarded in a more sympathetic light, a symbol of amiable and universal human weakness, like using the housekeeping money to buy beer or bet the horses.

II

The front page of the *News of the World*—in style, layout, and estimate of news values—is normally as serious as that of almost any newspaper in the English-speaking world, and a great deal more so than that of most. Its younger competitors—and this applies to others besides the tabloids—have increasingly adopted a vile technique (based partly on a discouraged conviction that everyone will have heard the general news on the radio, anyway) by which an editorial conference decides, some time on Saturday (even, occasionally, on Friday), what will be "our" front-page splash this Sunday, and goes remorselessly to town with this "exclusive" offering, regardless of almost anything that may have come up in the meantime.

The "exclusive" may be anything from a "hard-hitting exposure" of something or other—a spy ring or the impending collapse of the automobile industry—to inside news of a rift in the Cabinet or the Court, but it is so puffed up and noisy that almost every other item of interest has to creep away and curl up somewhere on the inside pages.

The *News of the World* has maintained a fairly sturdy and consistent resistance to this malpractice; and although it will devote at least as much care and money as anyone else to the comprehensive front-page presentation of, say, yet one more "extraordinary case of drugging and violation," there will almost certainly be room for a report, at intelligible length, of a minor war, a new scheme for old-age pensioners, a major scientific development, a reshuffle of the Cabinet, and even, if circumstances warrant, a further "extraordinary case of drugging and violation."

One gains the impression that people at the *News of the World* still believe that what 48 per cent of the population of Great Britain want to get first from their Sunday newspaper is a reasonably clear, not excessively peptonized or childishly overdecorated, account of the main things of general interest and importance that are going on. And this is encouraging, for surely the people at the *News of the World* should know.

The editorial page strengthens the general impression. The editorial itself—politically almost dead center, and thus unexacerbating rather than exciting—at least eschews that rib-poking, back-slapping mateyness with which several of the competitors find it desirable to approach the mysterious millions. The largest space on the page is likely to be occupied by an article—which could probably have appeared in the *Times,* certainly in the *Daily Telegraph,* and improbably anywhere else except the *News of the World*—by a Member of Parliament such as Sir Robert Boothby, or some other figure chosen because he has something to say rather than because he came into journalism with a big future behind him.

At this point, the visiting stranger begins to think he has been hoaxed, or that the English are crazier than he had been led to suppose. And then his eye takes note of those long, steady columns which form the bulk of the *News of the World* and are the basis for the jokes, the legend, the denunciations, and, of course, the supreme circulation. One hundred and eleven years later, these, without so much as a tremor of sensationalism in presentation or style, carry on the tradition of the first issue—testify to the old faith that although people are interested in advertisements and in the state of the nation, they like them a lot better if they are absolutely sure that in a minute or two there will be some fairly clotted cases of drugging and violation to sit quietly down with.

With their meager, almost colorless headlines and lack of all other decoration, these serried columns—recording in language which is something between a ritual and a code the most popularly appealing of the crimes, misdemeanors, and sexual mishaps of the citizenry brought to light during the previous seven days—constitute the heart and driving power of the *News of the World*.

Their raw material is the volume of straightforward, dead-pan reports from *News of the World* "stringers" covering police courts and magistrates' courts all over the country, supplemented in major divorce cases and other cases of importance at the assize courts by staff reporters. Selection of what is *News of the World*-worthy starts, of course, at this level.

So far as major cases are concerned—a multiple murder, for example— the *News of the World* cannot claim to offer the customers any service strikingly superior to that of its rivals (although it will probably give the matter a little more space and sometimes, through its exceptionally close and mutually profitable relations with the police, a detail not vouchsafed to others). It is in its technique of selection among the more homely, everyday rapes, breaches of promise, assaults, and indecent suggestions that the *News of the World* is unique. Broadly speaking, one might say that its tendency is to prefer the "It might have been me" type of crime or misdemeanor to the merely exotic or lurid. A great part of the appeal of the *News of the World* lies in the fact that in its compendious pages crimes, and particularly sexual misbehavior and impropriety of every kind, are seen as going on pretty well all the time, everywhere; they are woven into the texture of familiar life. The spotlighted stage upon which the criminal classes perform has been taken away, audience and players are at one; the curate at Woldmere who made that "certain suggestion" to the boy scout might have been our curate, here; the lewd schoolmaster who "disordered the clothing" of Mary Ann "with a view to committing an offence" is of the same clay as Mr. Jones. All of them might have been us.

Other papers often give the impression that it is only a special sort of people that are up to no good. *News of the World* readers know that almost anybody may be up to no good, with special reference to those sly ones who mask themselves in respectability as bank managers, clergymen, elderly solicitors—"He locked the door, saying the consultation must be confidential, and subsequently made a certain suggestion"—and men with eight-room homes in a good part of town. It is in every way a comforting thought. We always suspected things were that way, and they are; and nobody is really any better than anyone else.

The homely, family relationship established between the *News of the World* and its readers is more than one of mere "atmosphere" or sentiment. It maintains an Advice Bureau which replies to an average of between 6500 and 7000 readers' letters a week. By well over a quarter of a million people it is regarded as the most reliable and discreet of family lawyers and doctors, and it expends a great deal of effort and money to justify this faith. To deal with legal queries alone, it maintains a full-time staff of highly qualified lawyers; medical inquiries receive as expert medical advice as is available to anyone on the basis of consultation by mail; and the thousands of queries from soldiers and their parents, arising from the introduction of compulsory national service, are as likely as not to be studied and answered by high-ranking officers "retained" for the purpose by the paper.

Although the American-type comics have recently held the spotlight as potential menaces to the moral state of Britain, the debate over the significance and Moral Consequences of the *News of the World* goes on year in, year out.

Reginald Cudlipp, fortyish, gravely urbane editor of the *News of the World* since November, 1953, is not much moved by the familiar and unceasing attacks; he considers that most of them are based either on ignorance of the *News of the World* or on an absurd lack of touch with human nature. His explanation of the 20-million readership is simple and impressive.

"The person," he remarked to this writer, "who has no interest in the *News of the World* has no interest in Life."

Began   *Finished*   No. words: 2386

────── × 60 = ────── W.P.M.

─────   ──────   No. seconds:

Checking Comprehension

1. The name of the man who originated *News of the World* was (a) Napoleon Bonaparte, (b) Winston Churchill, (c) John Browne Bell, (d) Alexander Hamilton.

2. The object of *News for the Million* was (a) to be the largest newspaper in the world, (b) to be the best newspaper in the world, (c) to contain easier reading material than other papers, (d) to have a first-class journal that would sell at a price within the reach of all classes of readers.

3. Its weekly readers number (a) about a million, (b) more than twenty million, (c) half a million, (d) fifty thousand.

4. British people who admit to reading the paper do so (a) with pride, (b) with open praise of the paper, (c) with the approval of their entire family, (d) apologetically.

5. The circulation to the "working class" is rated as (a) over 56 per cent, (b) 100 per cent, (c) 25 per cent, (d) 10 per cent.

6. The central figure of a current jest about the *News of the World* is (a) a man drinking beer, (b) a man eating cheese, (c) a man cultivating a garden, (d) a man lying in bed reading.

7. The *News of the World* (a) leaves its Sunday front-page exclusive until the last minute so that it can capitalize on the latest news, (b) prepares its Sunday exclusive one week in advance, (c) prepares its Sunday exclusive on Friday or Saturday regardless of what may happen in the meantime, (d) has resisted using this malpractice.

8. The heart and the driving power of the *News of the World* lies in (a) its interesting coverage of world news, (b) its comic strips, (c) its sports news, (d) its columns having to do with the most appealing crimes, misdemeanors, and sexual mishaps.

9. The Advice Bureau of this newspaper is staffed with (a) editors who give answers to all questions sent in, (b) women who give general advice on love and marriage, (c) highly-qualified lawyers, doctors, and high-ranking officers of the army, (d) clerical workers who send out form letters in answer to inquiries.

10. The editor's explanation of the success of the paper is that (a) it gives accurate news, (b) the person who has no interest in the *News of the World* has no interest in life, (c) it plays up crime, (d) it has a long historical background.

Answers: 1)___, 2)___, 3)___, 4)___, 5)___, 6)___, 7)___, 8)___, 9)___, 10)___.

The Answer Key is on page 386.

Rate: W.P.M. ————   Comprehension Score: ————

Maintaining Speed in Reading Easy Material for Main Ideas

Read this selection as rapidly as you can to get the main idea of the paragraphs. The test which follows will check your comprehension of main ideas only.

Selection 2

BEGINNING TIME:_____
HR._____ MIN._____

Country Editors Play Many Roles[2]

The country editor of today is far removed from his prototype of two or three decades ago. It would be strange if an age that gives to the farmer his improved self-binder, to the physician his X-ray machine, and to the merchant his loose-leaf ledger, had done nothing for the town's best medium of publicity. The perfection of stereotype plate manufacture, by which a page of telegraph news may be delivered ready for printing at a cost of approximately twenty cents a column, and the elaboration of the "ready print" or "patent inside," by which half the paper is printed before delivery, yet at practically no expense over the unprinted sheets, have been the two great laborsavers for the country editor. Thereby he is relieved, if he desires, of the tedious and expensive task of setting type in order to give the world's general news, and the miscellaneous matter that "fills up" the paper. His energies then may be devoted to reporting the happenings of his locality and to giving his opinions on public affairs. By his doing of these, and by his relations toward the public interests, is he to be judged.

After all, no one man in the community has so large an opportunity to assist the town in advancement as the editor. It is not because he *is smarter* than others, not because he is wealthy—but because he is the spokesman to the outside world.

He is eager to print all the news in his own paper. Does he do it? Hardly. "This would be a very newsy paper," explained a frank country editor to his subscribers, "were it not for the fact that each of the four men who work on it has many friends. By the time all the items that might injure some of their friends are omitted, very little is left."

"I wish you would print a piece about our schoolteacher," said a farmer's wife to me one afternoon. "Say that she is the best teacher in the county."

"But I can't do that—two hundred other teachers would be angry. You write the piece, sign it, and I'll print it."

"What are you running a newspaper for if you can't please your subscribers?" she demanded—and canceled her subscription.

So the country editor leaves out certain good things and certain bad things for the very simple reason that the persons most interested are close at hand and can find the individual responsible for the statements.

[2] Charles Moreau Harger, "The Country Editor of Today," *The Atlantic Monthly,* January 1907, pp. 89-91, 95.

He becomes wise in his generation and avoids chastisements and libel suits. He finds that there is no lasting regard in a sneer, no satisfaction in gratifying the impulse to say things that bring tears to women's eyes, nothing to gloat over in opening a wound in a man's heart. If he does not learn this as he grows older in the service, he is a poor country editor.

His relations to his subscribers are intimate. There is little mystery possible about the making of the paper; it is as if he stood in the marketplace and told his story. Of course, the demands upon him are many and some of them preposterous. Men with grafts seek to use the paper, people with schemes ask free publicity. The country editor is criticized for charging for certain items that no city paper prints free. The churches and lodges want free notices of entertainments by which they hope to make money; semi-public entertainments prepared under the management of a traveling promoter ask free advertising "for the good of the cause." Usually they get it, and when the promoter passes on, the editor is found to be the only one in town who received nothing for his labor.

It is characteristic of the country town to engage in community quarrels. These absorb the attention of the citizens and feeling becomes bitter. The cause may be trifling: the location of a schoolhouse, the building of a bridge, the selection of a justice of the peace, or some similar matter, is enough. To the newspaper office hurry the partisans, asking for ex parte reports of the conditions. One leader is, perhaps, a liberal advertiser; to offend him means loss of business. Another is a personal friend; to anger him means the loss of friendship. The editor of the only paper in town must be a diplomat if he is to guide safely through the channel. In former times he tried to please both sides and succeeded in making enemies of everyone interested. Now the well-equipped editor takes the position that he is a businessman like the others, that he has rights as do they, and he states the facts as he sees them, regardless of partisanship, letting the public do the rest. If there be another paper in town, the problem is easy, for the other faction also has an "organ."

Out of the public's disagreement may come a newspaper quarrel—though this is a much rarer thing than formerly. The old-time country newspaper abuse of "our loathed but esteemed contemporary" is passing away, it being understood that such a quarrel, with personalities entangled in the recriminations, is both undignified and ungentlemanly. "But people will read it," says the man who by gossip encourages these attacks. So will people listen to a coarse street controversy carried on in a loud and angry tone—but little is their respect for the principals engaged. Country editors of the better class now treat other editors as gentlemen, and the paper that stoops to personal attacks is seldom found. Many a town has gone for years without other than kindly mention in any paper of the editors of the other papers, and in such towns you will generally find peace and courtesy among the citizens.

Of course, there are politics and political arguments, but few are the editors so lacking in the instincts of a gentleman as to bring into these the opposing editor's personal and family affairs. It has come to be understood that such action is a reflection on the one man who does it, not on the object of his attack. This is another way of saying that more real gentlemen are running the country newspapers today than ever before. This broadening of character has broadened influence. The country paper is effecting greater things in legislation than the county conventions are.

"The power of the country press in Washington surprises me," said a Middle West congressman last winter. "During my two terms I have been impressed with it constantly. I doubt if there is a single calm utterance in any paper in the United States that does not carry some weight in Washington among the members of Congress. You might think that what some little country editor says does not amount to anything, but it means a great deal more than most people realize. When the country editor, who is looking after nothing but the county printing, gives expression to some rational idea about a national question, the man off here in Congress knows that it comes from the grassroots. The lobby, the big railroad lawyers, and that class of people, realize the power of the press, but they hate it. I have heard them talk about it and shake their heads and say, 'Too much power there!' The press is more powerful than money."

This was not said in flattery, but because he had seen on Congressmen's desks the heaps of country weeklies, and he knew how closely they were read. The smallest editorial paragraph tells the politician of the condition in that paper's community, for he knows that it is put there because the editor has gathered the idea from someone whom he trusts as a leader—and the politician knows approximately who that leader is. So the country editor often exerts a power of which he knows little. . . .

The evolution of the country weekly into the country daily is becoming easier as telephone and telegraph become cheaper, and transportation enables publishers to secure at remote points a daily "plate" service that includes telegraph news up to a few hours of the time of publication. The publishing of an Associated Press daily, which twenty years ago always attended a town's boom and generally resulted in the suspension of a bank or two and the financial ruin of several families, has become simplified until it is within reach of modest means.

Instead of the big city journals extending their sway to crush out the country paper, it is more probable that the country papers will take on some of the city's airs, and that, with the added touch of personal familiarity with the people and their affairs, the country editor will become a greater power than in the past. For it is recognized today that the publication of a paper is a business affair and not a matter of faith or revenge. If the publication be not a financial success, it is not much of a success of any kind.

The old-time editor who prided himself on his powers of vituperation, who thundered through double-leaded columns his views on matters of world importance and traded space for groceries and dry goods, has few representatives today. The wide-awake, clean-cut, well-dressed young men, paying cash for their purchases and demanding cash for advertising, alert to the business and political movements that make for progress, and taking active part in the interests of the town, precisely as though they were merchants or mechanics, asking no favors because of their occupation, are taking their places. This sort of country editor is transforming the country paper and is making of it a business enterprise in the best sense of the term—something it seldom was under the old regime.

This eulogy is one often quoted by the country press: "Every year every local paper gives from five hundred to five thousand lines for the benefit of the community in which it is located. No other agency can or will do this. The editor, in proportion to his means, does more for his town than any other man. Today editors do more work for less pay than any men on earth."

Like other eulogies it has in it something of exaggeration. It assumes the country editor to be a philanthropist above his neighbors. The new type of country editor makes no such claim. To be sure, he prints many good things for the community's benefit—but he does it because he is a part of the community. What helps the town helps him. His neighbor, the miller, would do as much; his other neighbor, the hardware man, is as loyal and in his way works as hard for the town's upbuilding.

In other words, the country editor of today assumes no particular virtue because his capital is invested in printing presses, paper, and a few thousand pieces of metal called type. He does realize that because of his avocation he is enabled to do much for good government, for progress, and for the betterment of his community. Unselfishly and freely he does this. He starts movements that bring scoundrels to terms, that place flowers where weeds grew before, that banish sorrow and add to the world's store of joy; but he does not presume that because of this he deserves more credit than his fellow businessmen. He is indeed fallen from grace who makes a merit of doing what is decent and honest and fair.

Began	*Finished*	No. words:	1890
			$\frac{}{\text{No. seconds:}} \times 60 = \underline{}$ W.P.M.
____	____	No. seconds:	

Checking Comprehension

1. The country editor of today (a) has changed little through the years, (b) is a prototype of what he was at the beginning, (c) is far removed from his prototype of two or three decades ago, (d) is practically the same as his prototype of two or three decades ago.

2. The country editor leaves certain good things and certain bad things out of his paper because (a) he personally is interested in some items and not in others, (b) because he thinks some are good newspaper material and others are not, (c) he doesn't have room for them in his paper, (d) the persons most interested are close at hand and can find the individual responsible for the statements.

3. The country editor's relations to his subscribers are (a) strained, (b) intimate, (c) aloof, (d) democratic.

4. A country town (a) seldom has quarrels, (b) never has quarrels, (c) has quarrels as a natural characteristic, (d) mends its quarrels quickly.

5. Country papers (a) have no weight in Congress, (b) mean a great deal more in Congress than people realize, (c) are never read by Congressmen, (d) are considered by Congressmen to represent politicians.

6. The evolution of the country weekly to the country daily is becoming easier because (a) editors are becoming more competent, (b) townspeople are insisting on a home-town daily, (c) quicker typesetting methods make a daily paper possible, (d) communication and transportation facilities are cheaper and better.

7. The big city journals will probably (a) take over the small country papers, (b) crush out the country papers, (c) have some of their city airs taken over by the country editor, (d) have to go out of business.

8. The present-day country editor (a) trades space for groceries, (b) thunders his own views on matters of world importance, (c) prides himself on his powers of vituperation, (d) is making a business enterprise of the country paper in the best sense of the term.

9. The eulogy that editors do more work for less pay than any men on earth is (a) exaggerated, (b) absolutely true, (c) has no truth in it at all, (d) is recognized by everyone.

10. The new type of country editor (a) believes that he does little good in his town, (b) claims to be the leading benefactor of his town, (c) assumes no particular virtue because he is an editor, (d) thinks that he should have all the credit for town improvements.

1)—, 2)—, 3)—, 4)—, 5)—, 6)—, 7)—, 8)—, 9)—, 10)—.

The Answer Key is on page 386.

Rate: W.P.M. ————   Comprehension Score: ————

Maintaining Speed in Skimming

To maintain your skill in skimming, use this very famous editorial which has been printed thousands of times. Allow yourself thirty seconds for skimming it, then take the test.

Selection 3

Editorial on Santa Claus[3]

We take pleasure in answering at once and thus prominently the communication below, expressing at the same time our great gratification that its faithful author is numbered among the friends of *The Sun.*

Dear Editor: I am eight years old. Some of my little friends say there is no Santa Claus. Papa says, "If you see it in *The Sun,* it's so." Please tell me the truth, is there a Santa Claus?

Virginia O'Hanlon

115 West 95th Street.

Virginia, your little friends are wrong. They have been affected by the skepticism of a skeptical age. They do not believe except they see. They think that nothing can be which is not comprehended by their little minds. All minds, Virginia, whether they be men's or children's, are little. In this great universe of ours man is a mere insect, an ant, in his intellect, as compared with the boundless world about him, as measured by the intelligence capable of grasping the whole truth and knowledge.

Yes, Virginia, there is a Santa Claus. He exists as certainly as love and generosity and devotion exist, and you know that they abound and give to our life its highest beauty and joy. Alas! how dreary would be the world if there were no Santa Claus. It would be as dreary as if there were no Virginias. There would be no childish faith then, no poetry, no romance, to make tolerable this existence. We should have no enjoyment, except in sense and sight. The eternal light with which childhood fills the world would be extinguished.

[3] *New York Sun,* New York, September 21, 1897.

Not believe in Santa Claus! You might as well not believe in fairies! You might get your papa to hire men to watch in all the chimneys on Christmas Eve to catch Santa Claus, but even if they did not see Santa Claus coming down, what would that prove? Nobody sees Santa Claus, but that is no sign that there is no Santa Claus. The most real things in the world are those that neither children nor men can see. Did you ever see fairies dancing on the lawn? Of course not, but that's no proof that they are not there. Nobody can conceive or imagine all the wonders there are unseen and unseeable in the world.

You may tear apart the baby's rattle and see what makes the noise inside, but there is a veil covering the unseen world which not the strongest men, nor even the united strength of all the strongest men that ever lived, could tear apart. Only fancy, poetry, love, romance can push aside that curtain and view and picture the supernal beauty and glory behind. Is it all real? Ah, Virginia, in all this world there is nothing else real and abiding. No Santa Claus! Thank God! he lives and he lives forever. A thousand years from now, Virginia, nay, ten times ten thousand years from now, he will continue to make glad the heart of childhood.

Checking Comprehension

1. This editorial first appeared in (a) *New York Times,* (b) *New York Herald Tribune,* (c) *New York Sun,* (d) *Chicago Tribune.*

2. The letter quoted was written by (a) a young woman, (b) an eight-year-old girl, (c) a ten-year-old boy, (d) a four-year-old girl.

3. The name of the writer was (a) Mary, (b) Eva, (c) Christine, (d) Virginia.

4. The editor who wrote the editorial told the girl that she had been affected by (a) the Christmas spirit, (b) untruths, (c) older children, (d) skepticism.

5. He said that in our great universe man is a mere (a) insect, (b) babe, (c) calf, (d) atom.

6. He said that Santa Claus exists as certainly as (a) children exist, (b) as Christmas comes once a year, (c) as the snow falls in winter, (d) as love and generosity and devotion exist.

7. He said if you don't believe in Santa Claus you may as well not believe in (a) fairies, (b) ghosts, (c) witches, (d) God.

8. He said if you have never seen fairies dancing on the lawn (a) it is proof that your vision is poor, (b) it is proof that you've never looked for fairies, (c) it is no proof that fairies aren't there, (d) it is proof that they aren't there.

9. He said not even the strongest man can tear apart (a) a baby's rattle, (b) a spider's web, (c) a mountain of stone, (d) a veil covering the unseen world.

10. He said that Santa Claus would continue to make glad the heart of childhood (a) one hundred years from now, (b) ten times ten thousand years from now, (c) ten million years from now, (d) one hundred thousand years from now.

Answers: 1)__, 2)__, 3)__, 4)__, 5)__, 6)__, 7)__, 8)__, 9)__, 10)__.

The Answer Key is on page 386.

The Answer Key is on page 386.

Comprehension Score:_____

Follow-Up Practice

Continue to do all the things you have learned in this chapter as you read your newspaper each day. Just reading about the procedures suggested won't do you much good. You must actually put them into practice every time you pick up a paper. If you do this you will be rewarded with marked improvement in your newspaper reading.

CHAPTER 12

How to Detect and

Analyze Propaganda

You and Propaganda

"SHE is beautiful. She is engaged. She uses Thingum's Cream." She may not be particularly beautiful. She may have tried Thingum's cream once upon a time and found that it caused a rash on her face. Still she may have accepted $100 to permit her picture to be published in the home-town newspaper. And as an aftermath she may have ceased to be engaged when her boy friend's family found out about it.

At least that is what happened behind the scenes when one such glamorous ad appeared. Perhaps many girls who read the ad, however, bought the cream believing that it would cause them to become beautiful, and engaged.

Possibly you read the story about the Texas candidate for constable who tried a drastic propaganda technique. Highly desirous of being elected, and fearing that his strong and popular adversary would win the majority of votes from the kindly, warmhearted folk in the county, the night before the election he set fire to his own car. "Poor man. Such dreadful luck!" so went the talk of the town. And he was elected. His opponent, who was acquainted with propaganda techniques, insisted that the "unfortunate" man be brought into Court and questioned about the conditions surrounding the destruction of his car—and the truth was revealed.

One man was running for an office which the people in his town believed was no longer necessary, so he promised to abolish the office if he were elected!

Have you heard of the annual "barber campaign" conducted by a progressive manufacturer of farm machinery, before making public announcement of an innovation? The company sponsors a series of dinners to which they invite barbers throughout the Midwest's rich farming area. At these dinners, the barbers are told about the new improvements not yet revealed to anyone else. Barbers, of course, are known to cultivate the art of pleasant conversation while customers are in the chair, and those invited to such a dinner glibly talk of this dinner to which barbers as a special prestige group are invited, and, of course, they convey to their customers information about the new products.

You and I too are in the midst of communication networks which are teeming with propaganda. Dozens of times every day we are confronted with printed or spoken messages in which someone is trying to influence our buying or thinking. In this highly competitive age we are apt increasingly to become targets of this control of our thoughts and actions by others. As we float along in the stream of literature intended to mold public opinion, we may either sink or swim. We can succumb to the propagandists and let them make our decisions for us, or we can become so well acquainted with propaganda techniques that we are able to evaluate what we read and pass judgment upon it. Aldous Huxley has aptly said "In a land where there is no water, he [the propagandist] digs in vain."[1]

Think back to the source of your decision as you answer the questions that follow.

Who or what influenced you to buy the clothes you are wearing? The particular brand of coffee you had for dinner? The house you live in? The cigarettes you smoke? The toothpaste you use? The television set you view? The automobile you drive?

Who influenced you to join the club to which you belong? To

[1] Lincoln Steffens, *Autobiography*, Harcourt, Brace and Company, 1931, p. 238.

select the particular place where you spent your last vacation? To decide whether to travel by bus, train, boat, or airplane? To belong to the Republican, Democratic, or some other party? To vote for the last candidate for whom you cast a ballot?

If you reply "No one, positively no one!" to all these questions, then either you have learned to detect and analyze propaganda and have thus escaped its effect on you; or, not being aware of the techniques of propaganda, you have let it work upon you in such a subtle way that you don't know you are being influenced.

What is Propaganda?

Propaganda has been defined as "any attempt to persuade persons to accept a point of view or to take a certain line of action. The genesis of propaganda is intent. Though persuasion often takes place accidentally or incidentally, we are primarily concerned with deliberate efforts to convince." [2]

There is, however, a type of propaganda which is unintentional. "Intentional propaganda is a systematic attempt by an interested individual (or individuals) to control the attitudes of groups of individuals through the use of suggestion and, consequently, to control their actions; unintentional propaganda is the control of the attitudes and, consequently, the actions of groups of individuals through the use of suggestion." [3]

The opposite of propaganda is the scientific method by which we gather relevant data and apply it to our specific problems, leading to rational discussion and action in the light of all available evidence. In many situations, however, we are forced to make judgments in terms of spoken or written statements for which there is no scientific evidence.

In itself propaganda isn't necessarily something to scorn. It is an essential feature of a democratic society where there is freedom of speech and the press. As Hummel and Huntress say, " . . . [It is] no more evil because of its frequent misuse than drugs or dynamite, the characteristics of which it shares. We live our lives surrounded by propaganda, we create enormous amounts of it ourselves; and we form most or all of our cherished beliefs with its aids." [4]

[2] D. Lincoln Harter and John Sullivan, *Propaganda Handbook*, 20th Century Publ. Co., Philadelphia, 1953, p. 6.

[3] Leonard W. Doob, *Propaganda; Its Psychology and Technique*, Holt, p. 89.

[4] William Hummel and Keith Huntress, *The Analysis of Propaganda*, The Maple Press Co., York, Pa., 1949, p. 3.

This chapter is concerned only with intentional propapanda. It is limited further to propapanda as it appears in printed communication.

What Instruments of Printed Communication Are Used by Propagandists?

Every medium containing printed sentences or even phrases is a medium which is used to disperse propaganda: newspapers, magazines, books, billboards, leaflets, pamphlets, and handbills.

The *newspaper* finds its way into nearly every American home and brings to many people the first account of events of the world. The better newspapers increasingly pride themselves on accuracy of reporting, and as a whole the newspaper is not nearly so instrumental in the role of propaganda agent as it was twenty-five years ago, particularly in so far as political issues and candidates are concerned. Even so, reporters are human beings who have biases which are consciously or unconsciously reflected in their stories; an editor decides whether the story should have a position of prominence or be placed on a back page; and headlines are phrased to inspire the public to buy the paper. The person who thinks something is true just because he saw it in print is being unrealistic.

Advertisements scream out propaganda and, since a large share of a newspaper's income is derived from advertisements, it is not likely that this type of propaganda will soon be reduced. Editorial writers and columnists try to persuade and convince. Cartoons are powerful molders of opinion, and even the comics may be used as a means to influence.

The *magazine* also is a very effective medium of propaganda. It has the advantage that its bulk, artistic make-up, and higher price give it more prestige. Besides, it usually represents a more specialized interest than a newspaper does. Some magazines cater to current events, some to the interests of housewives, some to affairs of businessmen, some to sports enthusiasts, some to those engaged in hobbies, some to those enamored of love and sex, some to those seeking health, some to those inclined toward mechanics, etc. Intentional propaganda in such periodicals is directed toward the special interests of the group most likely to read that type of magazine.

Articles on controversial issues in magazines may or may not be propaganda. This depends upon whether or not the writer is offering all available evidence from which he draws his conclusion, or whether he simply asks others to believe what he wants to put across. All types of content in magazines can be used as carriers of propaganda, even fiction. Even reviews of plays, motion pictures, and concerts can fall into the category of propaganda if the reviewer wants to promote a certain entertainment.

It is in the magazine, of course, that the advertiser has a chance to make an "all-out" appeal to a special group. No expense is spared to utilize art, words, space, and the services of psychologists to exert effective appeals to the reader. Most magazines foster the reader's contact with these ads by starting a story or article in the first section of the magazine and continuing it on later pages between columns of attention-compelling ads. Like newspapers, magazines depend upon advertisers for a larger part of their income, and for this reason propaganda-bearing ads are apt to continue.

Books have a profound effect in molding public opinion. They are written by people who have followed one line of thought through in considerable detail, they are free from advertising, they are dignified in appearance, they cost more than newspapers and magazines, and they are generally recognized as important cultural contributions. Usually those who read books are the ones who control government, industry, and education. For this reason the influence of books is significant.

A book is written by a thinker of his day and age, and published when a publisher believes the time is ripe for releasing the author's message to the public. *Uncle Tom's Cabin* influenced public opinion greatly in regard to the slavery question and Ibsen's *Doll's House* contributed mightily to the emancipation of women. Among the better class of books which influence thinking in regard to national and international problems are political novels such as *The Clansman* by Thomas Dixon; nonfiction books such as *Our Times* by Mark Sullivan; and memoirs of political leaders such as Winston Churchill. Of course there are hundreds of books geared to the interests of the masses: on love, sex, popularity, beauty, health, luxury, appetite, success, travel, curiosity, and how to get rich. These books may contain the most flagrant and undesirable propaganda and may exert considerable influence in shaping the attitudes of those who read them.

Billboards are powerful conveyors of propaganda, and their messages reach hundreds of people who don't even read a daily newspaper. Highly-paid psychologists and ad writers are employed to create short messages so charged with appeal that they accomplish their purpose as the result of one quick reading-glance. Some of the cleverest and most compelling propaganda is to be found on billboards.

Leaflets, pamphlets, and handbills are valuable tools of the propagandist. Such printed materials are paid for by those with ideas which they want to put into effect. Printed mediums of these types do not have the benefit of a reputable publisher who might question the content or of a careful editor who might request substantiating data. The promoters often keep themselves and their motives concealed, concentrating limelight on the benefits which *you* will realize by buying the commodity, patronizing the place, joining the group, or voting for the candidate.

The important thing for a reader to know is how to detect propaganda so that he will be aware of reading situations in which someone is trying to influence his thinking or behavior. If he has some skill in propaganda analysis he will be less likely to succumb unless, after due consideration of all factors concerned, he decides of his own accord that it is beneficial for him to do so.

How to Detect Propaganda

Effective propaganda makes a strong appeal to human needs, interests, curiosities, loves, hates, prejudices, fears, lusts, cupidities, or amusements. Your first step in detecting propaganda is to identify the technique used.

To make a list of human interests and desires and ways in which the propagandist appeals to them would be an involved task. Different schools of psychology have compiled such lists, and they vary. In any event, no such list would be sufficiently inclusive. The propagandist doesn't care whether motives are innate or the result of environment. All he cares about is that they exist in the people to whom he wishes to appeal.

There are some propagandist techniques which are so inclusive that they appeal to whole clusters of interests. Seven of these techniques are generally recognized as basic.

Bad names. One of the propagandist's most usual techniques is that of using disagreeable words to arouse our fear, hate, or disapproval, without giving any evidence to support the point he is making. The "bad word" technique is the one used in some political campaigns: mud-slinging, name-calling, innuendos.

Shortly before presidential candidates had been nominated, the statements below were published about a governor whom many people thought would run on the Democratic ticket. The "bad names" are italicized.

GOP Chiefs Lash H———— Regime

————————, Dec. 30 (AP).—Republican legislative leaders slapped a *"do-nothing"* label on Gov. H———— today as a man whose main interest is the White House.

Senate Majority Leader J. M———— and Assembly Speaker D. B———— charged H's ———— administration with a "pattern of *broken* promises, fiscal *misrepresentation* and general *retreat* from the high standards of good government in the state."

They declared that H———— has *failed* on the state's highway-rebuilding program and on farm problems, and *accused* him of *courting union bosses* while *neglecting* rank and file union members. They said the quality of government has *deteriorated* and the *morale* of state workers has *broken* down.

This is the "bad name" technique at work in politics!

This technique is also used with high frequency in advertisements in which the propagandist tries to cause you to apply several unpleasant words to yourself and thus to be so moved that, in order to overcome the disgusting state of affairs, you will purchase the product he is trying to sell. One ad for tablets to increase weight was headed, "Why Be *Skinny?*" There was a picture of a very thin girl in a bathing suit while a man looking at her was saying, "No *Skinny Scarecrow* for me!"

Some of the text in the ad read as follows:

Why should you *dread* going to parties and socials, simply because you look *scrawny* and *spindly?* Why ever feel *self-conscious* about your body again. If you're *underweight* or just a little on the *thin* side, due to *faulty* appetite or *bad* dietary habits, you can put on up to a pound a day of attractive weight without exercise, *dangerous* drugs or *special* diet. Don't be a *wallflower* because you have a figure like a *broomstick.* Gain more weight!

Glad names. Quite the opposite is the "glad name" or "glittering generalities" technique. With the use of pleasant words, a halo of desirable associations is built around a person or thing to such an extent that the reader is moved to adore, respect, and vote for the person, or to buy a product in order to have all the desirable qualities mentioned.

A magazine article concerning Richard Nixon is a very good example of the "glad name" technique:

While politicos debate pro and con the Nixon qualifications, there stands out from the historic picture one paramount intriguing question: How did Dick Nixon get where he is today, at the age of only 42? How did he *achieve* in nine short years since he entered politics a spot for which many *able* men of *dedicated careers* have labored a lifetime in vain?

The answer seems to be a combination of Nixon's qualities of *integrity, sincerity, hard work, drive, decision, intelligence,* and *administrative ability,* plus the breaks. *Action* and *decision,* for better or worse, have keynoted his life.

Perhaps one great factor is that Dick Nixon represents the American ideal of the *self-made* young man, as well as today's typical businessman *hero.* In a business-geared state he has *succeeded* in politics not through any great *dedication* to a *lofty* cause or any *tremendous personal magnetism,* but by *hard-headed savvy* and *flexible application* of *streamlined modern big* business, public relations and even advertising methods. He stands in the *vanguard* of the *new* postwar generation of political *leaders, unfettered* by cumbersome tradition, and even his detractors must admit that he has brought a *brisk* and *energetic new* atmosphere to Capitol Hill." [5]

In advertising, the "glad name" technique is used more frequently than the "bad name" technique.

This cream truly works *miracles* on your skin. Pat a small amount on at night. In the morning you'll be *amazed* to see how *lovely* you are. Skin *smooth* and *fresh! Soft* as *velvet! Glowing* and *radiant!* A *new, beautiful* you!

The use of these glad words appeals to a woman's desire to be beautiful and is supposed to cause her to buy the cream in order to become lovely.

Transfer. Another commonly-used technique is that of transfer, by which the propagandist tries to get us to transfer our respect,

[5] Edward S. Sullivan, "The Man Who Lives One Heartbeat Away from the White House," *Conflict,* February 1956, pp. 10-12.

admiration, or reverence from something to which we have already attached one of these attitudes to something else. A candidate for office may be played up as a "typical American." Or the leaders of a cause may make a strong point of having God's sanction, in the hope that the public will transfer reverence for God to the cause. The flag, Uncle Sam, or a cross is frequently pictured in conjunction with a printed message in which the propagandist wants us to transfer our respect for the government or the church to his idea.

In advertisements famous people in the show business, sports, or society are frequently used for transfer purposes. For example, a well-known woman is shown examining crocheted articles in a full-page ad of manufacturers of crochet thread. The two-line heading reads, "Delighted with the pretty things you can crochet with top quality thread for only 98¢."

The ad doesn't state that the woman pictured crochets or that she uses the thread or that the crocheted articles shown are in her home. There is no connection between her and the crochet cotton advertised. She is pictured in the ad purely for transfer purposes.

Testimonial. This method of appeal is very much like transfer, except in this case some noted person goes so far in the printed material as to say that he uses the object of the propaganda. A famous tennis champion says that he is going to vote for Mr. So-and-So. The readers should inquire, "What difference does that make to me?" What motive or reward prompted the tennis player to let himself be quoted? What qualifications has he for judging candidates?

The picture of a famous movie actress appears in an ad for a low-caloried drink.

Movie actresses must have slim, attractive figures. I keep my figure trim by drinking No-Weight beverages.

(Signed) Shirlene Glamour

Probably the actress rarely or never drinks No-Weight beverages and keeps her figure trim through exercise and diet. Yet without a doubt untold numbers of girls rushed to their grocer for a case of "No-Weight" as soon as they finished reading the ad.

Plain folks. Admiration of the humble, unpretending, common man is an American tradition. The Pilgrim Fathers despised anything that was "hi-falutin" or smacked in any way of artificiality or affectation. One reason Lincoln has been idolized is that he came from a lowly family. Propagandists often go to great lengths in painting a word-picture of the person they wish to promote, to convince the public that he is just an ordinary man. The candidate for office may be shown driving a tractor, shoveling snow off the walk in front of his home, playing with his dog, coming from Sunday School, and so on. Sketches may be printed about his boyhood similar to this:

For Dick Nixon, the California small-town boy who carried groceries, played the piano in church, worked his way through college, sweated it out under Jap bombardment in the Pacific, and came up the hard, slugging way in politics through the House and Senate, stood in a phenomenal position in the center of the world stage.[6]

So what? Several million other boys in America might have had similar experience, yet we wouldn't consider them all competent leaders in government. In such cases the propagandist expects that our identification with our own early hardships, together with our admiration for the common man, will move us to vote as he wishes.

A recent article about a young baseball player told that he mowed the lawn and walked the dog, helped his wife by drying the dishes and caring for the baby. It was hoped that readers would develop a deep admiration for this man as a common person.

The band-wagon technique. The band-wagon technique is used to get us to accept something because everybody else is enthusiastic about it. It is based on the theory that you will want to think, vote, or buy what the great majority favors. If everybody else is doing it, then you should do it too. You wouldn't want to be different from other people.

The hat salesman is using this technique when he says, "They're all wearing the narrow brim this year." If you have already built up your resistance to band-wagon propaganda, you will probably reply, "Well, show me something less common."

Using the band-wagon technique the propagandist frequently directs his appeals to groups of similar religious belief, groups of similar racial descent, groups engaged in the same type of work: "All of us farmers want prices raised, and we know that Davis is the man that will do this for us."

Or he appeals to the desire of the masses to be on the winning side. "Don't throw your vote away. Vote for Gregory. He's sure to win anyhow."

[6] *Ibid.*

In advertising, this technique is used very frequently. "Nine out of ten use Gribber's Shaving Cream." "Cigs outsell all other cigarettes in America." "10,000 Americans switched to Sunny South Whiskey last month, why not you?" "Everybody's doing the Mambo. Let us teach you how."

Card stacking. This is the most subtle and probably the most dangerous of the propagandist's techniques. Even though you are acquainted with propaganda procedures you will be tricked with this every once in a while—unless you are very careful.

A cardsharp can cheat his victim by arranging the cards in the deck in such a manner that he will receive the winning combinations when the cards are dealt. Similarly the politician or ad writer may show only what is favorable to his purpose. He glorifies points which contribute to his ends but omits or misrepresents those which might influence you in the opposite direction. By card stacking an ordinary candidate for office can be built up as an intellectual giant, a wise administrator and a benevolent leader. His detrimental qualities are concealed.

Nowhere is this technique more frequently used than in advertisements. In reading about one cigarette you are told that it "lasts longer, tastes better, contains finer tobacco." Lasts longer—than what? Tastes better—than what? Contains finer tobacco—than what?

How to Analyze Propaganda

Questions to Ask.

Having an initial awareness of propaganda is not sufficient. You also should be able to analyze it.

As a frame of reference for analysis of propaganda found in printed material, five leading questions are offered:

1. Who is the propagandist?
2. Whom is he serving?
3. What is his aim in writing on this subject?
4. To what human interests, desires, emotions does he appeal?
5. What technique does he use?
6. Are you or are you not going to permit yourself to be influenced through the tactics of this propagandist?

Let's apply these questions in evaluating the selection below.[7]

MEN! Send for this Money-Making Outfit FREE!

See How Easy It Is to Make
up to $15.00 in a DAY!

Do you want to make more money in full or spare time . . . as much as $15.00 in a day? Then mail the coupon below for this BIG OUTFIT, sent you FREE, containing more than 150 fine quality fabrics, sensational values in made-to-measure suits, topcoats, and overcoats. Take orders from friends, neighbors, fellow-workers. Every man prefers better-fitting, better-looking made-to-measure clothes, and when you show the many beautiful, high quality fabrics —mention the low prices for made-to-measure fit and style—and show our guarantee of satisfaction, you take orders right and left. You collect a big cash profit in advance on every order, and build up fine permanent income for yourself in spare or full time.

No Experience Needed

It's amazingly easy to take measures, and you don't need any experience to take orders. Everything is simply explained for you to cash in on this wonderful opportunity. Just mail this coupon now and we'll send you this big, valuable outfit filled with more than 150 fine fabrics and everything else you need to start. You'll say this is the greatest way to make money you ever saw. Rush the coupon today!

Sample Suits to Wear

Our plan makes it easy for you to get your own personal suits, top-coats, and overcoats without paying 1¢—*in addition* to your big cash earnings. Think of it! Not only do we start you on the road to making big money, but we also make it easy for you to get your own clothes without paying one penny! No wonder thousands of men write enthusiastic letters of thanks.

Just Mail Coupon

You don't invest a penny of your money now or any time. You don't pay money for samples, for outfits, or for your own suit under

[7] Advertisement in *True Detective Magazine,* October 1952, p. 106.

our remarkable plan. So do as other men have done—mail the coupon now. Don't send a penny. Just send us the coupon.

1. Who is the propagandist? The man who wrote the article.
2. Whom is he serving? The company who is advertising.
3. What was his aim in writing this article? To persuade men to engage in the work of soliciting orders for the company.
4. To what human interests, desires, emotions does it appeal? To interest in making more money; to desire to look well.
5. What technique is used? *Glad words.*
6. Are you influenced? We hope not.

If you should be inclined to undertake the job of selling mail-order clothes, you should make careful inquiry into the entire proposition. Your decision would then come as the result of thorough investigation and not as the result of a persuasive advertisement.

Making Your Own Evaluations

Read each of the following examples and analyze it, using the set of questions given on page 316. Write your answers to the questions as applied to each example. Check your answers with the Answer Key on pages 386-387.

Exercise 1

Wonder Tooth-Whitener

A toothpaste that is different. Used by most of your favorite actors and actresses for years. Gives you a glamorous smile. Makes people admire you. Have beautiful, white teeth! Buy Tooth-Whitener today.

Exercise 2

The Communist leader described as "crude interference" President Eisenhower's Christmas message to the peoples of Eastern Europe expressing hope for changes in their regimes. However, Mr. Khrushchev tempered his remarks by saying he did not wish to attack the President, "for whom I have special respect."

The criticism voiced by Mr. Khrushchev and Marshall Nikolai A. Bulganin, the Premier, at the final session of the Supreme Soviet embraced "Western colonialism," military blocs, and attempts to deal with the Soviet Union from "positions of strength."

Missile Development Hinted

Premier Bulganin in his speech indicated that the Soviet Union had devoted particular attention to development of missiles in recent years.

(According to Reuters, the Soviet Premier said: "Rocket missiles have been developed particularly over the past few years and, we can say, are becoming intercontinental weapons.")

Mr. Khrushchev and Marshal Bulganin left no doubt they would present an unyielding front to the Western powers on all major issues. They also made clear that Moscow was now relying heavily on the support of India, Burma, Afghanistan and other Asian nations to swing the power balance against the capitalist countries.[8]

Exercise 3

Khrushchev said that although "we do not want to boast about our military and technical strength," he wished to remind the West about the recent Soviet hydrogen bomb explosion.

"The power of this weapon was equivalent to many million tons of ordinary explosives," he said, "and it can be considerably increased."

"People who are trying to increase tension should remember the results of this test," Khrushchev said.[9]

Exercise 4

Do You Desire Power?

Power to make you successful in all you undertake? Power to command a higher salary? Power to lead others? Power to be popular? Power to make a person love you? I will send you information which is the result of scientific research. This information will aid you to become more influential. Pay on delivery $5.00 plus postage.[10]

Maintenance Exercise

Do not let this temporary analytic practice interfere with the rapid tempo you have been developing in preceding chapters. Below is a selection for your use in maintaining and increasing your speed and comprehension. Read as rapidly as you can while perceiving main ideas and their clusters of details.

[8] Welles Hangen, "West Denounced," *New York Times,* December 30, 1955, p. 1.
[9] *New York Journal American,* December 29, 1955, p. 1.
[10] Adapted from an ad in *Conflict,* February 1956, p. 69.

Selection 1

BEGINNING TIME:_____
HR._____ MIN._____

The Role of Propaganda in a Democracy[11]

The advance of technology brought about the development of large-scale industry, which, in its turn, made conflicts within modern society greater, and propaganda sharper. Today we see numerous conflicts within our society—conflicts between groups of workers and groups of owners, between groups of workers and other groups of workers, between groups of owners and other groups of owners, between farmers and consumers, between workers and farmers, between farmers and manufacturers, as well as conflicts within these groups themselves.

Moreover, as we have already noted, the growth of technology also made modern society more complicated, more subject to dislocation and to periods of depression, unemployment and starvation—effects which are responsible for the growing conflicts within society.

But technology is largely responsible also for the development of democracy within the United States. First, technological expansion fed upon literacy—literacy among millions of workers. The development of the public school system of this country answered a growing technology's demand for literate men and women. Secondly, the rapid advance of technology broke down class differences to a very great extent; it created conditions for a fluid and moving population. During expansion of the last one hundred years and more, American workers found it comparatively easy to rise from one class to another. A shoemaker or a shoe salesman could become in the space of half a lifetime the owner of a great chain of stores; a bricklayer the leading banker of the midwest.

In previous periods the demands of so-called lower classes could be disregarded; they had no power, and, moreover, they "knew their place." The literacy of the American people brought them power as workers, as consumers, and as voters. Their growing power and their literacy, both attributable in part to the advance of technology, contributed to the growth of propaganda efforts and techniques. Today, powerful propaganda appeals are made for their support—as workers, as consumers, as voters.

In a democracy such as the United States there is a battle of propagandas—a "free for all" with many groups fighting for supremacy in commercial, political, religious, and social areas. Every four years in presidential election campaigns we see the political battle dramatized—a

[11] Violet Edwards, *Group Leader's Guide to Propaganda Analysis*, Institute for Propaganda Analysis, Inc., New York, 1938, pp. 58-65.

battle for control of great blocs of votes. One of the chief weapons used to gain the support of these millions of votes is propaganda. In the recent primary elections throughout the country, propaganda has taken many forms—investigations, personal appearances of high national officials in cities thousands of miles away from the capital, demonstrations, and even the singing of "hillbilly" songs.

Just as propaganda is the chief weapon in an election campaign, so is propaganda the chief weapon in labor-capital conflicts. For example, victory for an employer in a strike often depends upon his success in rallying other groups in society to his support by propaganda. He often uses propaganda to discredit the strikers. Likewise, victory for employees in a strike usually depends upon their success in rallying other groups to their support by propaganda against employers and by creating public opinion and action sympathetic to their own demands and program.

However, conflicts between capital and labor are not always, even in a democracy, settled by the free flow of propaganda. Lack of money to support a propaganda campaign may intervene; the government may sometimes act as "referee"; force, at other times, may be resorted to.

But generally the success of either side depends upon two things: (1) the success of their propagandas, defined here to mean the effectiveness of their threats; and (2) material conditions in and through which their propagandas operate. The interaction of material conditions and the propaganda of organized groups may be illustrated in the following instance.

The city project council in New York City, a part of the great national unemployment relief measures, in 1936 prepared slips for their members to give to merchants and shopkeepers when they paid for purchases. Upon these slips was printed the information that the money paid for articles was "relief" money. Thus, the Council attempted to show the shopkeeper the direct relationship between his sales, their buying, and government spending, and to rally him to its side—to the continuance of government aid. Their purpose was to show the merchant the unity of interest which existed between them, the unemployed workers, and himself, a representative of the middle class.

A period of depression such as that which led up to President Roosevelt's national unemployment program brought the working people and the middle classes—merchants and farmers—into closer agreement concerning their economic welfare. On the whole they agreed upon the necessity of a large government unemployment spending program. And, on the whole, men of wealth were opposed to this program.

In contrast with a democracy is the authoritarian state where propaganda is a weapon reserved solely by the state. The state has exclusive use of that weapon; it is a government monopoly. Nazi Germany, for example, used that weapon to gain adherence to its program. Groups in

German society whose interests were hurt by the Nazi program could not appeal to other groups. The government did not permit any propaganda in opposition to its own propaganda. It even banned radio reception of propaganda from other countries.

In Soviet Russia, too, only one propaganda is permitted—the propaganda of the Communist Party. Propaganda methods of the two countries are much the same—youth movements, demonstrations, parades, pageantry.

The *Chicago Daily News,* reporting on the Nüremburg Party Congress, once said: "Reichführer Hitler today mobilized his deadliest weapon—propaganda." In the authoritarian countries of the world propaganda is backed by force. Jail and even death by the execution squad face those who attack the government or any of its principles. Political opposition ranks with the most serious crimes.

We sometimes find the combination of propaganda and force even in a democracy. Occasionally, during the last few years in the United States, the mayor of a city or the governor of a state in which a strike was going on reinforced the propaganda of either the strikers or the employers by exerting his executive powers, backed by the power of the police or of the National Guard. Whenever this occurs, propaganda in a democracy takes on a resemblance to the propaganda of authoritarianism.

Propaganda is undemocratic in two other respects in the United States: first, in the sense that those individuals or groups in American society who have the most money can obtain the best facilities through which to carry on their propaganda—full-page advertisements in the newspapers and magazines are costly, and "time on the air" is beyond the financial resources of many individuals and groups; and, secondly, censorship and force—and censorship and propaganda—are closely allied in practice and in anti-democratic action. In the United States we saw this combination in Huey Long's domain of Louisiana. The application of any kind of force, such as censorship, in determining an election or the course of events, is a movement away from democracy.

In a democracy it is not the propaganda that is bad, but a monopoly of the propaganda. In this connection, the *Springfield Republican,* commenting on a conference devoted to the discussion of propaganda, declared: "Freedom of speech, and of the press, to the extent that Americans enjoy them, necessarily afford full scope for propaganda from everybody, everywhere, at any time.

"Free propaganda is nothing but free publicity for the views, interpretations, arguments, pleadings, truths and untruths, half lies and lies of all creation. Propaganda is good as well as bad. 'We are surrounded by clouds of propaganda,' complained the speaker at Williamstown; and so we are. It is up to each of us to precipitate from those clouds the true and the false, the near-true and the near-false, identifying and giving to each classification its correct label. If this task is far beyond the facilities or ability of most of us, the fact has to be accepted as the price we pay for liberty."

It has been argued by some that the multitude of conflicting propagandas in a democracy makes for confusion and, consequently, inaction—especially when immediate action is needed. And it certainly is true that democracies are slower to act than are the authoritarian states. This, however, is the price we must pay for democracy. We don't act quickly—but, theoretically at least, when we do act, it is in accordance with the decisions of the great majority of the people, decisions reached after the people have had the opportunity freely to consider all sides of the question, all propagandas. The quality of that consideration depends, of course, on many factors, such as access to many opinions, many points of view, and the ability to evaluate these. As has been pointed out, for one reason or another this does not always work out in practice; but it is the major job of the schools to see that it does.

ENDING TIME:_____
HR._____ MIN._____

Began   *Finished*   No. words: 1523

$$\frac{}{\text{No. seconds:}} \times 60 = \underline{} \text{ W.P.M.}$$

_____   _____   No. seconds:

Checking Comprehension

1. At the present time there are conflicts between a) workers and owners only, b) workers and workers only, c) farmers and consumers, farm workers and manufacturers only, d) practically all groups as well as cliques within the groups.

2. Technology is largely responsible for democracy because a) it produced more goods for the public and reduced prices, b) it demanded literacy and broke down class differences, c) the manufacturers of technology products were democratic people and promoted democracy among their employees, d) none of the above answers is correct.

3. The following forms of propaganda were used in a recent primary election: a) news items and pamphlets, b) testimonials and appealing pictures, c) stacking the cards and using band-wagon techniques, d) investigations, personal appearances, demonstrations, hillbilly songs.

4. In conflicts between capital and labor success depends upon a) success of their propagandas plus material conditions in and through which their propagandas operate, b) willingness to listen

to reason and make concessions, c) the length of time that the parties involved can go without work, d) the strength and endurance of picket lines.

5. Roosevelt's national unemployment program brought the following classes of people closer together: a) men of wealth and farmers, b) men of wealth and merchants, c) merchants and farmers, d) men of wealth and factory workers.

6. In the authoritarian state of Nazi Germany a) propaganda was used by all groups to further their personal interests, b) it was used by groups opposed to the government, c) it was used freely by different groups in expressing points of view over the radio, d) it was used solely by the government in support of its own policies.

7. Propaganda methods in former Nazi Germany and in Russia are the same in the use of a) television and radio broadcasts, b) testimonials and recommendations, c) youth movements, demonstrations, parades, pageantry, d) soap-box orators and cranks.

8. In our democracy propaganda takes on a resemblance to the propaganda of authoritarianism a) occasionally in a city or state, b) repeatedly in all of the state governments, c) often in most cities of the country, d) never.

9. Propaganda in the United States is undemocratic because a) the news is suppressed in newspapers and periodicals so that people don't know what's going on, b) individuals or groups with the most money can obtain the best facilities for propaganda, and censorship is sometimes used in determining an election or the course of events, c) the president controls the decisions of the public by thinking of himself and his close advisors, d) elections do not represent the will of the people.

10. The quality of decision made by the great majority of people depends upon a) how often they listen to radio and television, b) how much they read in newspapers, periodicals, and books, c) their ability to investigate a candidate's background, d) their access to many points of view, and the ability to evaluate these.

Answers: 1)___, 2)___, 3)___, 4)___, 5)___, 6)___, 7)___, 8)___, 9)___, 10)___.

Rate: _____   Comprehension Score: _____

Check your answers with the Answer Key, page 387.

CHAPTER 13

Untangling the Snarls

of Legal Language

Words! Words! Words!

"I AM thinking of sunshine, flowers and birds;
While these lawyers are giving me words, words, words." [1]

William Kent, a famous judge who often served as referee on the trial of causes, penned these lines one fine summer's day while listening to jury testimonials. Not only you and I, but even judges themselves sometimes feel this way about lawyers' words.

The early Scribes had to write all legal documents by hand, and they were paid by the word. According to tradition, it was for this reason they made their legal forms as wordy as possible. Perhaps we of today are still hampered because of the early Scribes' desire to earn a good wage.

Certainly lawyers are students of language. Success in court is

[1] Adapted from Charles Edwards, *Pleasantries About Courts and Lawyers*, Richardson, 1867, p. 362.

often dependent upon the wise use of language, and clients are protected in negotiations by the use of exact terms which will withstand contest. Through experience lawyers have found out how many different questions may arise to cause trouble after a document is signed, and so they have learned to insert clause after clause as protection for their clients against contingencies.

As a result certain forms have evolved through the centuries. As one loophole after another has come to light a new phrase has been added or an old one reworded. In other words, the legal forms used today have been thoroughly tested.

What to Do About It

Many of us may never have to go to court, but all of us at one time or another must deal with such legal papers as leases, deeds, wills, insurance policies, and contracts. When we first take a printed legal form into our hands and realize that we are supposed to sign it, we may either panic and not read it at all, or try to wade through it with distress and frustration.

There is a third alternative. Instead of becoming benumbed and befuddled when confronted with a legal form, we should learn how to attack it intelligently and to read it understandingly. The complaint that we didn't understand a phrase in one of these documents will never relieve us of having to meet a legal obligation.

The interpretation of legal forms is a very appropriate topic for a book on reading improvement, since the interpretation of such forms is really a specialized type of reading comprehension.

Reading an Order for a New Car

Perhaps the simplest and at the same time the most common legal form which readers of this book may have to sign is an order for a new car. Such an order looks unpretentious and easy to understand. It is usually written in terms of modern language instead of in formal legal phraseology. The reading trouble in such a case is usually one of omission. The majority of people who order a car sign a paper after having glanced at the *face* of the form only and probably not reading *all* of that.

At the bottom of the page there is in fine print:

I have read the matter on the back hereof and agree to it as a part of this order the same as if it were printed above my signature. The front and back hereof comprise the entire agreement affecting this order and no other agreement or understanding of any nature concerning same has been made or entered into. I hereby acknowledge receipt of a copy of this order.

This means of course that when you sign the face of the order form you have bound yourself to all conditions stated on the back. So you ought to read carefully and understand the printed matter on the back of the agreement *before* you sign on the dotted line.

This appears on the back of the agreement:

It is further understood and agreed:
The order on the reverse side hereof is subject to the following terms and conditions which have been mutually agreed upon:
1. John Doever, Inc., has reserved the right to change the list price of new motor vehicles without notice. In the event that the list price of the new car ordered hereunder is so changed, the cash delivered price, which is based on list price effective on the day of delivery, will be changed accordingly. If such cash delivered price is increased the Purchaser may, if dissatisfied with such increased price, cancel this order, in which event if a used car has been traded in as a part of the consideration herein, such used car shall be returned to the Purchaser upon the payment of a reasonable charge for storage and repairs (if any) or, if the used car has been previously sold by the Dealer, the amount received therefor, less a selling commission of 15% and any expense incurred in storing, insuring, conditioning, or advertising said car for sale, shall be returned to the Purchaser.

When you sign on the face of the order you acknowledge that all the terms on this side of the page "have been mutually agreed upon."

If you had decided to turn your old car in immediately but hadn't really taken the step as yet, no doubt you would change your mind after reading the first paragraph.

Read the second paragraph on the back of the order:

2. If the used car is not to be delivered to the Dealer until the delivery of the new car, the used car shall be reappraised at that time and such reappraisal value shall determine the allowance made for such used car, but if such reappraisal value is lower than the original allowance shown on the reverse side hereof Purchaser may if dissatisfied with such reappraisal value, cancel this order, such right to cancel, however, must be exercised prior to the delivery of the new car to the Purchaser and the surrender of the used car to the Dealer. The Purchaser agrees to deliver the original Bill of Sale and the Title to any used car traded herein along with the delivery of such used car, and the Purchaser warrants such used car to be his property free and clear of all Liens and Encumbrances except as otherwise noted herein.

So if your used car has not been turned in before arrival of the new car it will be reappraised at the time of the delivery of the new car, but you can refuse acceptance of the price only if you made this clear *before* you let the dealer deliver the new car and turned your old car over to him. This information alone might prove to be worth a good many dollars to you.

Paragraph 3 also has stipulations which are important to you:

3. Upon the failure or refusal of the Purchaser to complete said purchase for any reason other than cancellation, on account of increase in price or decrease of used-car allowance on reappraisal as specified in paragraph 2 above, the cash deposit may be retained as liquidated damages, and, in the event a used car has been taken in trade, the purchaser hereby authorizes Dealer to sell said used car, and the Dealer shall be entitled to reimburse himself out of the

proceeds of such sale, for the expenses specified in Paragraph 1 above and also for his expense and losses incurred or suffered as the result of Purchaser's failure to complete said purchase.

Such penalties are worth noting in advance.

Paragraphs 4 and 5 deal with model changes and delays arising from natural causes; they are easily understood and probably what you would expect anyhow, but in Paragraph 6 you may be surprised to learn what taxes you have to pay on a new car.

6. The price of the car quoted herein includes reimbursement for Federal Excise taxes, but does not include sales taxes, use taxes, or occupational taxes based on sales volume (federal, state or local), unless expressly so stated; the Purchaser assumes and agrees to pay, unless prohibited by law, any sales, use, or occupational taxes as aforesaid, imposed on or applicable to the transaction herein set forth, regardless of the person having the primary tax liability.

Had you only read the face of this order you probably would have insisted that the dealer or manufacturer was responsible for such taxes, not the buyer.

Section 7 states what the manufacturer warrants in regard to your new car.

7. It is expressly agreed that where there are no warranties, expressed or implied, made by either the Dealer or the Manufacturer on the vehicle, chassis, or parts furnished hereunder, except the Manufacturer's warranty against defective materials or workmanship, as follows:

"The Manufacturer warrants each new motor vehicle, including all equipment or accessories (except tires) supplied by the Manufacturer, chassis, or part manufactured by it, to be free from defects in material and workmanship under normal use and service, its obligation under this warranty being limited to making good at its factory any part or parts thereof which shall, within ninety (90) days after delivery of such vehicle to the original purchaser or before such vehicle has been driven 4,000 miles, whichever event shall first occur, be returned to it with transportation charges prepaid and which its examination shall disclose to its satisfaction to have been thus defective; this warranty being expressly in lieu of all other warranties, expressed or implied, and all other obligations or liabilities on its part, and it neither assumes nor authorizes any other person to assume for it any other liability in connection with the sale of its vehicles.

"This warranty shall not apply to any vehicle which shall have been repaired or altered outside of an authorized service station in any way so as in the judgment of the Manufacturer to affect its stability and reliability, nor which has been subject to misuse, negligence, or accident.

"The Dealer agrees to install any part or parts furnished under the Manufacturer's warranty above on the motor vehicle covered in this order without charge to the owner of such motor vehicles.

"This warranty does not apply to second-hand cars or cars not mentioned in the above order.

"The Dealer also agrees to promptly perform and fulfill all terms and conditions of the Owner Service Policy."

Did you know that you had to prepay transportation charges in sending a defective part back to the factory? Did you know that the factory reserves the right of deciding whether or not the part is defective? Did you know that this guarantee would not be effective if you had let the car be repaired at any service station other than one authorized by the manufacturer?

8. In the event that the transaction referred to in this order is not a cash transaction, the Purchaser herein, before or at the time of delivery of the car ordered, and in accordance with the terms and conditions of payment indicated on the front of this order, will execute such other form of agreement as may be indicated on the front of this order.

9. In case the car covered by this order is a used car, no warranty or representation is made as to the extent such car has been used, regardless of the mileage shown on the speedometer of said used car.

So there is a lot of *careful* reading to be done in connection with the simple act of ordering a car!

Reading an Automobile Insurance Policy

When you are ready to insure your car, you tell your insurance agent what you want. He prepares a policy and mails it to you with a statement of how much you owe him.

As in the case of all legal papers that you sign, it is a mistake to treat an insurance policy lightly. You should carefully read, study, and interpret every word in it, for many points are involved.

One of the legal words appearing in insurance policies is "insurer." The insurer is the party or company who insures against the loss. The one who is to receive the protection is called "the insured." The sum which the insured pays for insurance protection is called the "premium." The amount which can be collected in case of loss is often called "the face of the policy." "Contingency" is a word frequently used in insurance policies; in this context it means "dependent upon an uncertain event." "Coverage" means the specific casualty or casualties covered by any one of the classifications for which insurance may be taken out. The phrase "limits of liability" refers to the maximum amount for which the company will be liable in case of casualty in any one type of coverage.

The amount specified under "Limits of Liability" for E Collision and Upset is sometimes confusing because of the "deductible" specification. This provision simply means that the insurance company will pay the "Actual Cash Value" of the damage after deducting the amount specified as deductible. In the sample policy, $50 is deductible. If you were the holder of this policy the company would not pay for any damage amounting to $50.00 or under. You would have to pay that yourself. If the amount were $150, then you would pay $50 of it and the company would pay $100.

Reading with Guidance

Your chief reading responsibility lies within the content printed on the inside pages and the back of the policy. Let's look at some of the sections of a sample policy,[1] to find out if there is anything there which you should know about.

The companies severally agree with the insured, named in the declarations made a part hereof, in consideration of the payment of the premium and in reliance upon the statements in the declarations and subject to the limits of liability, exclusions, conditions and other terms of this policy.

In the first sentence, reproduced above, you find a general statement to the effect that the companies will pay the insurance subject to all of the agreements specified. Then follow the "Insuring Agreements."

INSURING AGREEMENTS

I **Coverage A—Bodily Injury Liability:** To pay on behalf of the insured all sums which the insured shall become legally obligated to pay as damages because of bodily injury, sickness or disease, including death at any time resulting therefrom, sustained by any person, caused by accident and arising out of the ownership, maintenance or use of the automobile.

"Coverage A—Bodily Injury Liability" tells you for what the companies are liable in regard to the injury of a person by your automobile. They promise to pay whatever they are *legally obligated* to pay—not whatever is asked but the amount that is legally decided upon as that which they are obligated to pay. Notice also that "maintenance" of your car is mentioned in this paragraph as one of the conditions under which insurance can be collected. Since "maintenance" is included, you could then collect insurance if, for example, a mechanic were working on your car and a wrench slipped from his hand, flew into space, and hit and injured a passerby. It is important for you to know that insurance can be collected for injury resulting from maintenance of your car as well as for injury resulting from its use.

Coverage B—Property Damage Liability: To pay on behalf of the insured all sums which the insured shall become legally obligated to pay as damages because of injury to or destruction of property, including the loss of use thereof, caused by accident and arising out of the ownership, maintenance or use of the automobile.

Coverage C—Medical Payments: To pay all reasonable expenses incurred within one year from the date of accident for necessary medical, surgical, ambulance, hospital, professional nursing and funeral services, to or for each person who sustains bodily injury, sickness or disease, caused by accident, while in or upon, entering or alighting from the automobile if the automobile is being used by the named insured or with his permission.

Coverage D—Comprehensive Loss of or Damage to the Automobile, Except by Collision or Upset: To pay for any direct and accidental loss of or damage to the automobile, hereinafter called loss, except loss caused by collision of the automobile with another object or by upset of the automobile or by collision of the automobile with a vehicle to which it is attached. Breakage of glass and loss caused by missiles, falling objects, fire, theft, explosion, earthquake, windstorm, hail, water, flood, vandalism, riot or civil commotion shall not be deemed loss caused by collision or upset.

Coverage E—Collision or Upset: To pay for direct and accidental loss of or damage to the automobile, hereinafter called loss, caused by collision of the automobile with another ob-

[1] Merchants Indemnity Corporation of New York; Merchants Fire Assurance Corporation of New York.

ject or by upset of the automobile, but only for the amount of each such loss in excess of the deductible amount, if any, stated in the declarations as applicable hereto.

Coverage F—Fire, Lightning and Transportation: To pay for direct and accidental loss of or damage to the automobile, hereinafter called loss, caused (a) by fire or lightning, (b) by smoke or smudge due to a sudden, unusual and faulty operation of any fixed heating equipment serving the premises in which the automobile is located, or (c) by the stranding, sinking, burning, collision or derailment of any conveyance in or upon which the automobile is being transported on land or on water.

Coverages B, C, D, E, and F are all very clearly stated. They should be read and interpreted carefully, however, so that you will understand all of your rights in case you have one or more of these types of insurance.

Coverage G—Theft (Broad Form): To pay for loss of or damage to the automobile, hereinafter called loss, caused by theft, larceny, robbery or pilferage.

In the paragraph concerned with Coverage G, you might puzzle over the differences between "theft, larceny, robbery and pilferage." A *thief* is one who steals furtively. *Larceny* is defined as "the unlawful abstraction, without claim or right, of the personal goods of another with intent to defraud the owner." *Robbery* is "taking away of property of another unlawfully, by force or fear." *Pilferage* means petty stealing, such as taking a radiator cap or a rear-vision mirror from a car. At a casual glance these four words mean the same thing, but legally there are differences in their meaning, as explained above.

The remaining articles having to do with Coverages H, I, and J are quite clear, but of course should be read and interpreted if you have these particular types of insurance.

Coverage H—Windstorm, Earthquake, Explosion, Hail or Water: To pay for direct and accidental loss of or damage to the automobile, hereinafter called loss, caused by windstorm, hail, earthquake, explosion, external discharge or leakage of water except loss resulting from rain, snow or sleet.

Coverage I—Combined Additional Coverage: To pay for direct and accidental loss of or damage to the automobile, hereinafter called loss, caused by windstorm, hail, earthquake, explosion, riot or civil commotion, or the forced landing or falling of any aircraft or of its parts or equipment, flood or rising waters, external discharge or leakage of water except loss resulting from rain, snow or sleet.

Coverage J—Towing and Labor Costs: To pay for towing and labor costs necessitated by the disablement of the automobile, provided the labor is performed at the place of disablement.

II Defense, Settlement, Supplementary Payments: As respects the insurance afforded by the other terms of this policy under coverages A and B the company shall:

(a) defend any suit against the insured alleging such injury, sickness, disease or destruction and seeking damages on account thereof, even if such suit is groundless, false or fraudulent; but the company may make such investigation, negotiation and settlement of any claim or suit as it deems expedient;

Section II has to do with "Defense, Settlement, Supplementary Payments." In (a) you find out that the companies will defend you in any event, but that they may make additional investigations and that it is entirely within their jurisdiction to make any settlement that they wish.

(b) pay all premiums on bonds to release attachments for an amount not in excess of the applicable limit of liability of this policy, all premiums on appeal bonds required in any such defended suit, the cost of bail bonds required of the insured in the event of accident or traffic law violation during the policy period, not to exceed the usual charges of surety companies nor $100 per bail bond, but without any obligation to apply for or furnish any such bonds;

In (b) you discover that the companies are under no obligation to apply for or furnish bail bonds. You do find, however, that they will pay all premiums on bonds to release attachments for an amount which doesn't exceed the total amount of insurance for which you have applied in the current policy. You also find that they will pay premiums on appeal bonds and the cost of bail bonds in an amount not to exceed that charged by surety companies and not to exceed $100 per bail bond.

(c) pay all expenses incurred by the company, all costs taxed against the insured in any such suit and all interest accruing after entry of judgment until the company has paid, tendered or deposited in court such part of such judgment as does not exceed the limit of the company's liability thereon;

(d) pay expenses incurred by the insured for such immediate medical and surgical relief to others as shall be imperative at the time of the accident;

(e) reimburse the insured for all reasonable expenses, other than loss of earnings, incurred at the company's request.

The amounts incurred under this insuring agreement, except settlements of claims and suits, are payable by the company in addition to the applicable limit of liability of this policy.

In studying (c), (d), and (e) you gather that the company will pay: costs of a suit together with interest up to the amount for which the companies are liable; immediate medical and surgical relief necessary at the time of accident; reasonable expenses incurred at the companies' request, except for loss of earnings.

On Your Own

Now you read and analyze the remaining parts of this insurance policy which are presented without the aid of discussion. When you have finished you will be given a test on important points made from the standpoint of the part which you yourself might have to play in this agreement, and the benefits or penalties which might accrue to you personally if you insured your automobile under the sample policy.

III Definition of Insured: With respect to the insurance for bodily injury liability and for property damage liability the unqualified word "insured" includes the named insured and also includes any person while using the automobile and any person or organization legally responsible for the use thereof, provided the actual use of the automobile is by the named insured or with his permission. The insurance with respect to any person or organization other than the named insured does not apply:

(a) to any person or organization, or to any agent or employee thereof, operating an automobile repair shop, public garage, sales agency, service station or public parking place, with respect to any accident arising out of the operation thereof;

(b) to any employee with respect to injury to or sickness, disease or death of another employee of the same employer injured in the course of such employment in an accident arising out of the maintenance or use of the automobile in the business of such employer.

IV Automobile Defined, Trailers, Two or More Automobiles:

(a) **Automobile.** Except where stated to the contrary, the word "automobile" means:

(1) **Described Automobile**—the motor vehicle or trailer described in this policy;

(2) **Utility Trailer**—under coverages A, B and C, a trailer not so described, if designed for use with a private passenger automobile, if not being used with another type automobile and if not a home, office, store, display or passenger trailer;

(3) **Temporary Substitute Automobile**—under coverages A, B and C an automobile not owned by the named insured while temporarily used as the substitute for the described automobile while withdrawn from normal use because of its breakdown, repair, servicing, loss or destruction;

(4) **Newly Acquired Automobile**—an automobile, ownership of which is acquired by the named insured who is the owner of the described automobile, if the named insured notifies the company within thirty days following the date of its delivery to him, and if either it replaces an automobile described in this policy or the company insures all automobiles owned by the named insured at such delivery date; but the insurance with respect to the newly acquired automobile does not apply to any loss against which the named insured has other valid and collectible insurance. The named insured shall pay any additional premium required because of the application of the insurance to such newly acquired automobile.

The word "automobile" also includes under coverages D, E, F, G, H and I its equipment and other equipment permanently attached thereto.

(b) **Semitrailer.** The word "trailer" includes semitrailer.

(c) **Two or More Automobiles.** When two or more automobiles are insured hereunder, the terms of this policy shall apply separately to each, but a motor vehicle and a trailer or trailers attached thereto shall be held to be one automobile as respects limits of liability under coverages A and B and separate automobiles as respects limits of liability, including any deductible provisions, under coverages D, E, F, G, H, I and J.

V Use of Other Automobiles: If the named insured is an individual who owns the automobile classified as "pleasure and business" or husband and wife either or both of whom own said automobile, such insurance as is afforded by this policy for bodily injury liability, for property damage liability and for medical payments with respect to said automobile applies with respect to any other automobile, subject to the following provisions:

(a) With respect to the insurance for bodily injury liability and for property damage liability the unqualified word "insured" includes (1) such named insured, (2) the spouse of such individual if a resident of the same household and (3) any other person or organization legally responsible for the use by such named insured or spouse of an automobile not owned or hired by such other person or organization. Insuring Agreement III, Definition of Insured, does not apply to this insurance.

(b) This insuring agreement does not apply:

(1) to any automobile owned by, hired as part of a frequent use of hired automobiles by, or furnished for regular use to the named insured or a member of his household other than a private chauffeur or domestic servant of the named insured or spouse;

(2) to any automobile while used in the business or occupation of the named insured or spouse except a private passenger automobile operated or occupied by such named insured, spouse, chauffeur or servant;

(3) to any accident arising out of the operation of an automobile repair shop, public garage, sales agency, service station or public parking place;

(4) under coverage C, unless the injury results from the operation of such other automobile by such named insured or spouse or on behalf of either by such chauffeur or servant, or from the occupancy of said automobile by such named insured or spouse.

VI Loss of Use by Theft—Rental Reimbursement: The company, following a theft covered under this policy, shall reimburse the named insured for expense not exceeding $5 for any one day nor totaling more than $150 or the actual cash value of the automobile at time of theft, whichever is less, incurred for the rental of a substitute automobile, including taxi-cabs.

Reimbursement is limited to such expense incurred during the period commencing seventy-two hours after such theft has been reported to the company and the police and terminating, regardless of expiration of the policy period, on the date the whereabouts of the automobile becomes known to the named insured or the company or on such earlier date as the company makes or tenders settlement for such theft.

Such reimbursement shall be made only if the stolen automobile was a private passenger automobile not used as a public or livery conveyance and not owned and held for sale by an automobile dealer.

VII General Average and Salvage Charges: The company, with respect to such transportation insurance as is afforded by this policy, shall pay any general average and salvage charges for which the named insured becomes legally liable.

VIII Policy Period, Territory, Purposes of Use: This policy applies only to accidents which occur and to direct and accidental losses to the automobile which are sustained during the policy period, while the automobile is within the United States of America, its territories or possessions, Canada or Newfoundland, or is being transported between ports thereof, and is owned, maintained and used for the purposes stated as applicable thereto in the declarations.

It would be a good idea for you to pause at this point in your reading and do some self-checking. Glance back over the headings of the sections you have read "on your own." See if you can tell yourself, in your own words, the important points.

Now go ahead with your interpretations of the remaining paragraphs.

EXCLUSIONS

This policy does not apply:

(a) while the automobile is used as a public or livery conveyance, unless such use is specifically declared and described in this policy and premium charged therefor;

(b) under coverages A, B, and C, to liability assumed by the insured under any contract or agreement;

(c) under coverages A and B, while the automobile is used for the towing of any trailer owned or hired by the insured and not covered by like insurance in the company; or while any trailer covered by this policy is used with any automobile owned or hired by the insured and not covered by like insurance in the company;

(d) under coverages A and C, to bodily injury to or sickness, disease or death of any employee of the insured while engaged in the employment, other than domestic, of the insured or in domestic employment if benefits therefor are either payable or required to be provided under any workmen's compensation law;

(e) under coverage A, to any obligation for which the insured or any company as his insurer may be held liable under any workmen's compensation law;

(f) under coverage B, to injury to or destruction of property owned by, rented to, in charge of or transported by the insured;

(g) under coverage C, to bodily injury to or sickness, disease or death of any person if benefits therefor are payable under any workmen's compensation law;

(h) under coverages D, E, F, G, H, I and J, while the automobile is subject to any bailment lease, conditional sale, mortgage or other encumbrance not specifically declared and described in this policy;

(i) under coverages D, E, F, G, H, I and J, to loss due to war, whether or not declared, invasion, civil war, insurrection, rebellion or revolution or to confiscation by duly constituted governmental or civil authority;

(j) under coverages D, E, F, G, H, I and J, to any damage to the automobile which is due and confined to wear and tear, freezing, mechanical or electrical breakdown or failure, unless such damage is the result of other loss covered by this policy;

(k) under coverages D, E, F, G, H, I and J, to robes, wearing apparel or personal effects;

(l) under coverages D, E, F, G, H, I and J, to tires unless damaged by fire or stolen or unless such loss be coincident with other loss covered by this policy;

(m) under coverages D and G, to loss due to conversion, embezzlement or secretion by any person in lawful possession of the automobile under a bailment lease, conditional sale, mortgage or other encumbrance;

(n) under coverage E to breakage of glass if insurance with respect to such breakage is otherwise afforded.

CONDITIONS

1. Notice of Accident—Coverages A, B and C: When an accident occurs written notice shall be given by or on behalf of the insured to the company or any of its authorized agents as soon as practicable. Such notice shall contain particulars sufficient to identify the insured and also reasonably obtainable information respecting the time, place and circumstances of the accident, the names and addresses of the injured and of available witnesses.

2. Notice of Claim or Suit—Coverages A and B: If claim is made or suit is brought against the insured, the insured shall immediately forward to the company every demand, notice, summons or other process received by him or his representative.

3. Limits of Liability—Coverage A: The limit of bodily injury liability stated in the declarations as applicable to "each person" is the limit of the company's liability for all damages, including damages for care and loss of services, arising out of bodily injury, sickness or disease, including death at any time resulting therefrom, sustained by one person in any one accident; the limit of such liability stated in the declarations as applicable to "each accident" is, subject to the above provision respecting each person, the total limit of the company's liability for all damages, including damages for care and loss of services, arising out of bodily injury, sickness or disease, including death at any time resulting therefrom, sustained by two or more persons in any one accident.

4. Limit of Liability—Coverage C: The limit of liability for medical payments stated in the declarations as applicable to "each person" is the limit of the company's liability for all expenses incurred by or on behalf of each person who sustains bodily injury, sickness or disease, including death resulting therefrom, in any one accident.

5. Limits of Liability—Coverages A, B and C: The inclusion herein of more than one insured shall not operate to increase the limits of the company's liability.

(c) file proof of loss with the company within sixty days after the occurrence of loss, unless such time is extended in writing by the company, in the form of a sworn statement of the named insured setting forth the interest of the named insured and of all others in the property affected, any encumbrances thereon, the actual cash value thereof at time of loss, the amount, place, time and cause of such loss, the amount of rental or other expense for which reimbursement is provided under this policy, together with original receipts therefor, and the description and amounts of all other insurance covering such property.

Upon the company's request, the named insured shall exhibit the damaged property to the company and submit to examinations under oath by anyone designated by the company, subscribe the same and produce for the company's examination all pertinent records and sales invoices, or certified copies if originals be lost, permitting copies thereof to be made, all at such reasonable times and places as the company shall designate.

Checking Your Interpretation

Read the statements below. Choose the statement which you think is correct in each exercise and write the corresponding number in the answer space below.

1. Definition of "insured" includes a) the manager of a parking lot where damage occurs, b) any employee of the owner of the car who injures another employee with his employer's car, c) a mechanic who is working on the car in a garage, d) any person or organization who is legally responsible for the use of the car and to whom the owner has given permission for such use.

2. The word "automobile" may include a) a utility trailer which is being used as your home, b) the use of a substitute automobile while your automobile is being used by a visiting relative, c) a new automobile to replace the old one without additional charge for premiums under any conditions, d) each automobile and trailer attached to it if the two are insured in the same policy in so far as bodily injury and property damage liabilities are concerned.

3. Bodily-injury liability, property-damage liability and medical payments provided for in a policy apply to a car other than the one described in the policy providing the other car a) is being driven by your wife even though she may be residing at an address different from your own, b) is being repaired by a garage mechanic, c) is a truck used in your business, d) is driven by your domestic servant.

4. Rental reimbursement a) will be made in case of theft at the rate of $10 per day up to the amount of $200, b) will begin immediately upon report of theft, c) will be made only in case of a private passenger car not used for public conveyance or owned and held for sale by a dealer, d) will continue until the car is returned to you.

5. In the above policy, rental reimbursement for a stolen car will be made if the car is: a) a truck, b) a delivery wagon, c) a trailer, d) a private passenger automobile.

6. This policy would apply to accidents which take place in a) Canada, b) Panama, c) The Bahamas, d) Mexico.

7. The policy would apply to accidents occurring on board a ship while a car is being transported from the United States to: a) Spain, b) England, c) Brazil, d) Hawaii.

8. This policy does not apply a) under coverages D, E, F, G, H, I, and J to tires except in case that the insured has a blowout while driving at a moderate speed, b) under coverage E for breakage of glass regardless of whether or not insurance has been provided elsewhere for such breakage, c) under coverage B if the property damaged is owned by, rented to, in charge of, or transported by the insured, d) under coverages A and B while the automobile is used in towing a trailer owned or hired by the insured which is not covered by like insurance in the same company.

9. When an accident occurs the insured or someone on behalf of the insured should as soon as practical a) call the insurance company and report the accident by phone, b) give written notice to the company, c) ask the nearest policeman to report the accident to the

company, d) take the car to the company immediately so that they can see the damage.

10. In case of coverage C in which medical payments are made, a) the company has the right to require physical examination by a physician whom they select, b) the company has no right to make further examinations if the physician of the insured is willing to provide the company with his records, c) the company cannot make medical payments to the insured person directly but must pay the institution or persons rendering the service, d) proofs of claim for medical payments may be given orally.

11. If the insured cancels this policy, earned premiums will be a) considered null and void, b) computed in accordance with the customary short-rate table, c) pro rated, d) based on depreciation of the car.

Answers: 1)—, 2)—, 3)—, 4)—, 5)—, 6)—, 7)—, 8)—, 9)—, 10)—.

Check your answers by referring to the Answer Key, page 387.

Comprehension Score: _____

Interpreting an Apartment Lease

A recent survey has revealed that 13,000,000 Americans live in apartments, so it seems advisable to discuss a common form of apartment lease.

PARTIES THIS LEASE, made the 20th day of September, 1957, between Washington Heights Corp., 286 E. 148 St., Bronx 55, N.Y. hereinafter referred to as Landlord, and Frank B. Watson hereinafter referred to as Tenant.

PREMISES WITNESSETH, that the Landlord hereby leases to the Tenant, and the Tenant hereby hires and takes from the Landlord, the apartment known as Apartment 3B on the third floor in the building known as 600 W. 180th St. in Manhattan, New York, N.Y. to be used and occupied solely as a strictly private dwelling apartment, by the Tenant and the family of the Tenant,

TERM consisting of 3 persons, and not otherwise, for a term to commence on the 1st day of October 1956, and to end on the 30th day of September 1958.

"Parties" in the left-hand margin of the first section refers to the people who are negotiating the rental agreement. The first word typical of legal language is "hereinafter," which of course means that, after this first mention, in this particular agreement the person who is renting the apartment will be referred to as Landlord.

"Premises" in the next section, of course, means the building in which the apartment is located. "Witnesseth" is a word peculiar to the legal profession and is a short way of saying "It is witnessed."

The next section, identified as "Term," has to do with the length of time the lease is to cover, and the use to which the apartment will be put. The phrase "occupied solely as a strictly private dwelling apartment" would seem to be repetitious in its use of both "solely" and "strictly," but this perhaps is a double protection to the landlord. The phrase "and not otherwise" also appears to the layman to be superfluous following the statement "the family . . . consisting of 3 persons"; but upon careful consideration it is obvious that any four people other than the tenant and his family could live there if the lease didn't state specifically "and not otherwise."

The specific date on which the lease becomes effective and on which it ends are important considerations. Many tenants think that because they move in on the first day of the month, their lease is up on the first. The tenant should read his lease term very carefully, particularly in regard to the ending date. In the case above, if the tenant assumed that his lease ended on October first because it began on October first, he might find another family moving into the apartment on the day he intended to move out, and the movers-in would have a perfect right to the apartment because that is the day on which their rent begins. The former tenant should have moved out on September 30.

> **RENT** unless sooner terminated as hereinafter provided, at the annual rent of Two Thousand One Hundred Seventy-Two ($2,172.00) Dollars due and payable in advance in equal monthly installments of $181.00 each on the first day of each and every month during the term.
>
> **THE TENANT COVENANTS:**
>
> FIRST.—The Tenant will pay the specified rent and any "additional rent" at the time and in the manner herein provided, to the Landlord at the office of the landlord, 286 E. 148 St., Bronx 55, State of New York, or at such other place as the Landlord may designate from time to time hereafter.

In the "Rent" section above, the first clause means that there are different conditions under which this rent may be paid and that these conditions will be stated later on. Look out for them.

If you were signing this lease as a tenant, would you know what you were agreeing to under the caption "The Tenant Covenants"? The word "covenant" when used as a noun means a written agreement entered into by two or more persons or parties under seal. When used as a verb, as in the phrase "the tenant covenants," it means that the tenant promises by covenant, or binds himself by covenant.

> **REPAIRS** SECOND.—That, throughout said term, the Tenant will take good care of the demised premises and appurtenances, and suffer no waste or injury; make, as and when needed, all repairs and replacements in, to and about the demised premises and the fixtures and appurtenances, which repairs shall be in quality and class, equal to the original work; comply with all laws, ordinances and governmental regulations, and the regulations of the New York Board of Fire Underwriters, applicable to the demised premises; suffer the Landlord to make repairs and improvements to the demised premises and to all parts of the building and to comply with all orders and requirements of

ORDINANCES, LAWS, ETC. governmental authority applicable to said demised premises or building or to any occupation thereof, after default by Tenant; throughout said term and forever afterward, indemnify and save harmless the Landlord from and against any and all liability, arising from injury during said term to person or property, occasioned wholly or in part by any act or omission of the Tenant, or of the guests, servants, assigns, under-tenants or sub-tenants of the Tenant; repair at or before the end of the term, all injury done by the installation or removal of furniture and property so as to restore the demised premises to their original state; and, at the end or other expiration of the term, to quit and surrender the demised premises in as good order and con-

MOVING dition as they were at the beginning of the term, reasonable wear excepted.
INJURY If said premises be not surrendered at the end of the term, the Tenant will
SURRENDER make good to the Landlord all of the damage which the Landlord shall suffer
INDEMNIFY by reason thereof, and will indemnify the Landlord against all claims made
LANDLORD by any succeeding tenant against the Landlord founded upon delay by the Landlord in delivering possession of the premises to said succeeding tenant, so far as such delay is occasioned by failure of the Tenant to so surrender the premises.

This section of the lease has to do with repairs and damages and is very important. "Demised premises" means the premises transferred by lease. "Appurtenances" means something belonging to or attached to something else as an accessory or adjunct. You are committing yourself to repair such things as Venetian blinds, broken mirrors in medicine cabinets, loose or detached doorknobs, etc.

As you read the second line you find that you are to make not only repairs but also "replacements," and that all of this applies not only to "appurtenances" but also to "fixtures." This word "fixtures" makes you realize that you are responsible for repairs and replacements made necessary by defects in electric light fixtures, the refrigerator, the gas stove, etc.

As you read on in the third and fourth lines you find that you are not allowed to patch up things yourself as a novice.

You even "suffer the landlord" to do all these things in case you as a tenant "default." "Suffer" as used in this legal document means "permit" and "default" means your failure to meet your obligations in regard to these matters.

"Indemnify" means to compensate for loss or damage. "Liability" means the state of being liable or exposed to some accidental or incidental result or occurrence. In the light of these meanings you realize that as a tenant you will have to pay indemnities for any injuries or accidents resulting wholly or in part from any act or omission of yours, as such happenings may affect anyone at all whom you have in the place. And finally you read that you have to pay the landlord for any claims of the succeeding tenant in case you stay overtime and delay his occupancy.

THIRD.—That the Tenant will not expose or permit any sign, advertisement
NEGATIVE or illumination at any window of the demised premises, or project anything
COVENANTS out of the windows or other openings in the exterior walls of the said

OCCUPANCY building; will not place any pots, plants, boxes or other objects on the window-sills of the building; will not do anything or suffer anything to be done upon the demised premises deemed extra-hazardous on account of fire, or which will increase the rate of fire insurance upon said building; will not permit the accumulation of waste or refuse matter; will not drive nails into, drill into, disfigure or deface any part of the demised premises or building or suffer the same to be done; will not install or cause to be installed any additional electric wiring or outlets; will not use the demised premises or any part thereof or suffer the same to be used for any purpose other than as a private dwelling apartment, nor by any one other than the Tenant and the immediate family of the Tenant consisting of the above designated number of persons. The Tenant and the executors and administrators of the Tenant, will not, without the written consent of the Landlord first obtained in each case, either sell, assign, mortgage, pledge or transfer this lease, underlet or sublet the demised premises or any part thereof or make any alteration, addition or improvement in or to the demised premises. The premises hereby leased shall be used and occupied by the Tenant and the immediate family of the Tenant only as a strictly private dwelling apartment and for no other purpose, and the character of the occupancy of the demised premises as herein expressed, is an especial consideration and inducement for the granting of this lease by the Landlord to the Tenant, and the Landlord shall at all times have the right to an injunction restraining the use of the demised premises by others than the Tenant and the said immediate family of the Tenant. In the event of violation by the Tenant of the restrictions against selling, assigning, mortgaging, pledging or transferring this lease or underletting or subletting the demised premises or any part thereof, or if the Tenant shall cease to occupy the demised premises or permit the same to be occupied by parties other than as aforesaid, or violate any other restrictions or condition herein imposed, this lease may, at the option of the Landlord, or the agents or assigns of the Landlord, be terminated in the manner provided in the first paragraph of section "Seventh" hereof.

This paragraph covers those items which the tenant promises not to do. "Executors and administrators" are those persons who would be handling the business of the tenant in case of his death or incompetency. "Injunction" means a judicial order requiring the party who is served to take or to refrain from taking some specified action. The Landlord may serve an injunction preventing the tenant from letting anyone live in the apartment other than his own family.

Sections Fourth through Sixth are omitted. We'll go on with the Seventh section, presenting you with a different type of reading experience.

Reading in Response to Directions

Section Seventh will be presented together with directions as to what you are to look for as you read.

In reading this next paragraph you will encounter the word *tender* used in a legal sense, to a formal offer of satisfaction. Now, this one legal term out of the way, read the following paragraph to find out:

1. If the landlord terminates a lease because of default of the tenant, is the tenant still liable for damage to the apartment, repairs, replacements, etc?

2. Under what specific conditions can the landlord give the tenant five days' notice to end the term of this lease?

DEFAULTS

FIVE-DAY NOTICE

SEVENTH.—If the Tenant shall default in fulfilling any of the covenants or conditions of this lease (other than the covenant for the payment of rent), or in complying with any of the rules and regulations for said building herein contained or referred to or hereafter established as herein provided, or if the Tenant becomes insolvent or be adjudicated a bankrupt, or applies for or takes the benefit of any bankruptcy or insolvency act or any act of statutory provisions for the relief of debtors, now or hereafter enacted, or makes a general assignment for the benefit of creditors, or if a Receiver or Trustee be appointed for the Tenant's property, or if this lease or the estate of the Tenant hereunder be transferred or pass to or devolve upon any other person or corporation, or if the Landlord, or the assigns of the Landlord, or the agent for the time being of the Landlord or of said assigns in respect to said building, shall deem objectionable or improper any conduct on the part of the Tenant or occupants, the Landlord may give to the Tenant five days' notice of intention to end the term of this lease, and tender the rent paid on account of the unexpired term demised, and thereupon at the expiration of said five days, the term under this lease shall expire as fully and completely as if that day were the date herein definitely fixed for the expiration of the term, and the Tenant will then quit and surrender the demised premises to the Landlord, but the Tenant shall remain liable as hereinafter provided.

In the next paragraph you will meet the phrase "by summary dispossess proceedings"—dispossession without the formality of court proceedings. *Indictment,* when used in regard to legal matters, means a formal charge or accusation.

1. Under what conditions can the landlord re-enter a leased apartment without being liable to indictment, prosecution, or damage?
2. For what amount of damages can the tenant be held, and when must damage payments be made?
3. What other expenses may the landlord demand of the tenant?
4. What rights has the landlord in regard to reletting the apartment?
5. What rights does the tenant waive under these conditions?
6. In what way do statements in this lease cause the use of the words "re-enter" and "re-entry" to include more than that to which they are restricted in their technical legal meaning?

RIGHTS UPON DEFAULTS

If the Tenant shall default in the payment of the rent or "additional rent" reserved hereunder, or any part thereof, or if the notice last above provided for shall have been given and said five days' period shall have elapsed, or if the demised premises become vacant or deserted, the Landlord, by its agents or servants, may immediately, or at any time thereafter, re-enter the demised premises and remove all persons and property therefrom, either by summary dispossess proceedings or by any suitable action or proceeding at law, or by force or otherwise, without being liable to indictment, prosecution or damages therefor, and the Tenant, whether or not the premises be re-let as hereinafter provided, shall remain liable to the Landlord for damages equivalent in amount to all of the rent reserved hereunder to the time when this lease would have expired but for such termination, and the same shall be due and payable by the Tenant to the Landlord on the several rent days above specified, and also in case of any such re-entry, the Tenant shall pay to the

Landlord on demand an amount equal to all legal and other expenses incurred in removing the Tenant, the commissions for re-letting the demised premises and collecting rent, the cost of redecorating, refinishing and repairing the demised premises and such other expenses as the Landlord may incur in connection therewith. Upon any such re-entry, the Landlord, at its

RE-ENTRY option, may re-let the demised premises or any part or parts thereof for the remainder of the demised term or any part or parts thereof or for a period extending beyond the date for the expiration of this lease and receive the rents therefor, it being understood that upon re-letting the Landlord may grant a concession or free rent for a portion of the term, and the rents collected for the balance of the agreed term of the Tenant on any such re-letting may be applied to pay any of the aforesaid items remaining unpaid and to the fulfillment and performance of the other covenants of the Tenant here-

RELETTING under, and the net avails thereof shall be applied by the Landlord on account of any rent unpaid by the Tenant for the remainder of the demised term; but the Tenant, however, shall pay to the Landlord upon each of the rent days the amount of any and all deficiencies then existing. The Tenant hereby expressly waives any and all rights of redemption now or hereafter existing under the Civil Practice Act of the State of New York or any other present or future law, in case the Tenant shall be dispossessed by judgment or warrant of any court or judge; and the Tenant waives any and all rights now or hereafter existing under Real Property Law §227 and §233; and the

WAIVER Tenant waives all rights to trial by jury in any summary proceeding here-
BY TENANT after instituted by the Landlord against the Tenant in respect to the demised premises and in any action hereafter brought to recover rent or "additional rent" becoming due hereunder or in any other proceeding or action or any cause of action directly or indirectly involving the terms, covenants or conditions of this lease or the demised premises. The words "re-enter" and "re-entry" as used in this lease are not restricted to their technical legal meaning. Tenant agrees that the covenants of the Tenant herein contained on the part of the Tenant to be performed, shall be deemed conditional limitations as well as covenants and conditions.

On Your Own

As a result of the guidance which you have had up to this point, you should be able to proceed with competence in analyzing and interpreting any lease you are ever asked to sign.

Don't try to cover the whole thing in one reading until you have acquired greater skill in working with separate paragraphs of this type of material.

1. At the left of each paragraph note the title in boldface type. Make the same use of this that you make of subtitles when previewing an article.

2. Skim through the paragraph to get a general idea of its content.

3. As you skim try to locate clusters of closely-related ideas in the same way you learned to do in reading paragraphs for details.

4. Frame a question which could be answered by each of the clusters.

5. Jot your questions down on a piece of paper as you formulate them.

6. Reread each paragraph for the purpose of finding specific answers to your questions.

Now take out your own legal papers. Read and interpret them just as carefully as you have been doing with the sample legal forms. See if they contain some important points which you never suspected were in them.

In the future whenever and wherever you are confronted with a legal paper to sign, tackle it in the same way that you have been tackling the legal forms with which you have just been working. Don't ever take a chance on signing one of them until you are sure that you understand all its statements.

CHAPTER 14

Installing a Reading

Improvement Program

in Your Company

Reading: An Office Tool

THE modern businessman is enmeshed in a never-ending combat with printed words. There they lie before him in continuing accumulations, and he does not dare ignore them. They are quiet. They don't cry out at him verbally. But mentally they scream at him for attention! He knows that he must give them the consideration they demand, or else he will be unable to dispatch the daily activities in his office with efficiency. Besides, he would like to have a little time evenings and week ends to read for pleasure and general enlightenment—current events, recent novels, or magazine articles which have nothing to do with his work. Instead, he frequently must carry his office reading home in order to cover what he *has* to read to meet the demands of his next day's work.

The opinion of corporation presidents as expressed in a discussion held by American Management Association was that not less than 25 per cent of an executive's time is spent in reading in connection with his business. Sometimes he spends as much as fifty per cent or seventy-five per cent of his time in reading. The consensus was that at other levels business employees spend an average of two hours of each workday in some form of business reading.

Reading is one of a businessman's most important tools. He keeps himself alert to new developments in office equipment. He spares no expense to install gimmicks and gadgets which promise to insure greater speed and accuracy in turning out his products. Does he do anything about installing an improved tool in reading? He can and should.

Many business firms and industrial plants are providing reading improvement programs for their executives and employees. Executives are recognizing more and more the need for and value of increased skill in reading. But the concept of installing a reading improvement program in an office is comparatively new. Executives, training directors, and personnel directors are exploring possibilities, inquiring about results, and requesting help in setting up such programs.

What Are the Values of a Training Program in Reading?

Savings in dollars and cents. The most apparent and perhaps the most convincing value is the saving in dollars and cents. The speeded-up production of an individual means a greater output without a commensurate expenditure in salary and extra working hours.

Take a hypothetical situation: a certain company has ten executives whose salaries average $15,000 per year—a total of $150,000. Let us say that this company also has twenty employees who hold responsible positions involving considerable reading and whose salaries average $6,000 per year—a total of $120,000. Suppose further that all these people work the usual seven hours a day (nine to five with an hour for lunch) five days a week.

If the executives devote twenty-five per cent of their time to reading, then twenty-five per cent of their salary is paid for this type of activity. Twenty-five per cent of their total salary is $37,500. If these men should learn to read even twice as fast as they do (and that's a conservative possibility), their reading time could be reduced to twelve and one-half per cent, saving $18,750. Similarly, the twenty employees who read on an average of two hours per day, if reading twice as fast, could reduce the company's expense by $15,500. The total saving for the executives and the twenty employees together would be $34,250 during the course of a year. The time saved could be devoted to the output of the company.

Savings in errors. Another saving realized would be in the reduction of errors, so costly to every company. In learning to comprehend what they read with greater accuracy, the personnel would make fewer mistakes, and their interpretations and applications would be more clear-cut and to the point.

Savings on the human side. Easier and more efficient reading reduces tension and fatigue. In terms of the physical and mental well-being of employees alone, the acquisition of increased efficiency in reading skills is rewarding.

Who Finances Such a Program?

In the majority of cases the cost of a reading program is borne by the company. Businesswise, the company considers the returns of its investment to be so promising that it does not hesitate to make the comparatively small expenditure for the training of personnel.

Psychologically also it is highly desirable for the company to pay the cost of the training. If a company asks its employees to pay for their own reading training, all or in part, out of their own salaries, resentment often crops up. Under these conditions emotional overtones prevent the trainees from profiting fully from their instruction.

Two instances have come to my attention, however, in which the company has borne half the expense and the employees half. In each of these cases the request came from the employees for reading training, and the company offered to pay half the expense. Such a circumstance is the exception, not the rule.

Length and Time of Course

Length of course. Length of adult Reading Improvement courses varies greatly. Some reading centers offer a course in as few as ten hours. Others vary from twenty to thirty, and some offer a forty-hour course.

In my own experience I have found a course of twenty-eight to thirty hours to be very satisfactory. Those taking the course make about as much improvement as they are going to make in the first twenty hours. An additional eight or ten hours can establish the new skills.

Time in the day. Training in reading for the personnel of a company is practically always given on company time. Some companies prefer having the course conducted the first thing in the morning before employees become involved in their day's work. Such a plan has the advantage of permitting employees to put forth their best efforts in making the most of their training while they are fresh and while their minds are free from partly finished jobs.

Another favored time is the last thing in the afternoon. Many companies have their trainees close up their usual work an hour or so before quitting time, then attend the Reading Improvement class and go home. In one instance, the employees began their training course at 4:30, and stayed until 5:30, thus using one half hour of the company's time and one half hour of their own.

Some companies use the last part of the forenoon, some the first part of the afternoon, some the middle of the forenoon, and some the middle of the afternoon. Either the first hour in the morning or the last hour in the afternoon is recommended, with preference for the morning hour.

Length and frequency of sessions. How much time should be given to one session and how often should the sessions occur? Companies whose programs the writer has supervised have held sessions variously of one half hour, one hour, one and a half hours, and two hours. In my opinion one half hour is too short a time in which to accomplish much skill-building. The other periods are all right under certain conditions. It all depends on their frequency.

How often should a group meet for reading training? This depends upon the convenience of the employer—the frequency with which he can spare his employees from their work. Some have one hour twice a week or one hour three times a week. Others have two hours once a week or two hours twice a week. Two hours twice a week is the most common practice, but one hour two or three times a week or even daily would seem to be the best arrangement, because frequent short periods are more effective in producing results in any learning situation than less frequent long periods. Another very important consideration is the regularity with which the periods are observed. Regardless of the length of the period or its frequency, it is imperative that regularity of time intervals be observed. The class should be held at the same hour every day and on the same days every week.

How to Initiate a Program

In a few cases one or more of the employees became interested in reading improvement and asked the employer if they might have a course in the offices of the firm.

In the great majority of cases, however, the company initiates the training program. Usually this is done by the Personnel Director or the Director of Training. In smaller companies the program is usually initiated by the President or Vice President.

The officer of the company who wishes to generate interest in a training program in reading may use a single approach or a combination of approaches. It usually takes a period of several months to bring the first reading course to fruition. Sometimes considerable tact is necessary. In an occasional situation two or three of the poorest readers in the group either don't want to be "discovered" through the use of a reading program or else they think they have been discovered already and suspect that the boss is moving directly toward their re-education. If some in the group resist the course, it is advisable to move slowly and gradually work up enthusiasm before doing anything definite about installing a program.

The personnel director, president, or other officer in charge usually starts out by telling the group of some talk he has heard, some conversation in which he has engaged, or some article or book he has read which had to do with reading improvement. Others are asked to tell what they have heard or read about the subject. Perhaps this chitchat about happenings in the world of reading improvement may continue incidentally as a part of general meetings for some time before any direct approach is made.

Some firms ask for a volunteer who would like to take a reading improvement course at some clinic or laboratory in the vicinity. The expense, of course, is borne by the company in such a case. The volunteer reports periodically to the group on techniques used and progress made. This usually is a very effective and convincing way of stimulating group interest in reading improvement.

Other employers have used outside speakers with very satisfactory results. A personnel director who has already installed a reading program is asked to come in and tell of his experiences and results. A reading specialist from a nearby university, college, or reading laboratory may be invited to give a talk on some phase of reading and to tell what he knows about adult reading improvement.

How Many in a Class?

This question is asked very frequently: "How many can be trained in one group?"

If a sampling of specialists in the teaching of adult reading were asked this question, a great variety of answers would result, ranging all the way from five to one hundred. In my own experience I find that from ten to twenty who have similar reading needs and are fairly homogeneous in initial ability can be handled very satisfactorily in one group. This assumes that the procedures used are those in which the instructor develops new techniques and gives practice on them with the group as a whole, at the same time permitting each individual to progress at his own rate.

Who Conducts the Course?

There are at least four arrangements which firms in different parts of the country have tried in regard to providing instruction for their groups: (1) employing a reading specialist trained and experienced in reading improvement at the adult level; (2) training someone on the company's own staff to do the job; (3) having someone in the company conduct the course even though he has not had special training; (4) letting the employees work by themselves with no teacher.

Employing a trained specialist. The most effective program is the one in which a fully-qualified reading specialist is employed to instruct the group. The reading process is a complex one. The field of reading improvement is highly specialized, just as the field of law or dentistry is specialized.

The *fully*-qualified reading specialist is one who holds an advanced degree in the field of reading improvement or in psychology or education with special training in reading. If he hasn't the degree in one of these special areas, he should at least have taken several graduate courses in reading, including training in teaching *adult* reading. Not only should he have had courses in reading; he should also have had experience in teaching reading, not to students alone but also to adults in life beyond college.

The teaching of reading to adults beyond college is a new field of endeavor and one in which the demand for instructors is greater than the supply of professional people trained for the job. Consequently, in this rapidly-growing field we find the many rackets and quacks characteristic of all new businesses or professional innovations. Some people decide to offer reading improvement courses for adults largely because they think this is a lucrative field, and they proceed to "set up shop," calling themselves reading specialists, even though they have had no specific preparation in the teaching of reading. They seem to think that the teaching of adult reading is so simple that anyone can do it and, what is even more unfortunate, the people who employ them seem to think so, too. These same people wouldn't employ the services of a lawyer or a dentist unless he had taken special training in his field, yet they often pay anyone who *says* he is a reading specialist.

Before you employ a reading specialist to give courses for your firm, be sure to find out:

How many courses in *reading* has he taken?

At what university or college did he take them?

How much experience has he had in teaching reading improvement to adults beyond school or college age?

What has he achieved with some of the adult groups he has taught —not just group averages, but the gains of each individual in each group?

If these questions reveal that the person under consideration has had adequate training and experience and can get results with adults, you may consider him qualified to do the job.

If you are able to obtain a thoroughly-trained and experienced instructor, your executives or employees will make greater gains and retain them more permanently.

In case a company employs a trained specialist from a university, college, or other type of reading center within the vicinity, this instructor comes to the offices of the company from one to three times a week at a stated hour until the course is finished. Sometimes a company runs parallel courses, having the specialist work with one group the first hour of his visit and with another group the second hour.

However, more frequently the company engages the specialist to give one course; when that course is finished he gives another one, and so on.

If the instructor comes from a reading center which is at a distance from the company's office, he may be employed by the company on a full-time basis for one month, two months, or whatever length of time is necessary. This arrangement works out exceptionally well if there is a large number of employees to be trained, and if the company's work is of such a nature that it is better to release smaller groups at different times throughout the day than to release larger groups at one or two set times during the week.

Here is one example of how such an arrangement actually worked: a company located several thousand miles from New York University requested that a specialist from this institution be sent to work with its groups. Upon arrival the specialist was given a large office for use as his teaching headquarters. He reported there for work at nine o'clock each morning and stayed throughout the day. He made and kept appointments very much as a physician or a dentist might do. One of the executives arranged the appointments as individuals or groups could be released from work. Every effort was made, however, to see that everyone had one hour of training regularly every day. It was necessary also for the members of a particular group to meet together each time, because each group was organized in terms of its special needs as determined by the particular type of reading which its members had to do in their work for the company. Such an arrangement requires very careful organization on the part of an executive.

Most firms consider it to be psychologically desirable to have the first course given to their top executives. This has two advantages: first, the executives who have taken the course can speak with enthusiasm about the results, and their enthusiasm will prove to be impressive and contagious; second, if the executives themselves take the course, then those in the lower echelons won't be apt to complain that the boss wants them to take it because he thinks they are dumb or uneducated.

Training a specialist of your own. Large concerns that have hundreds of employees and a heavy yearly turnover in personnel find it advantageous to train one of their own people to do reading-improvement work. This person then remains with the company as a permanent instructor and usually devotes his full time to giving courses in reading to those who have to read, and training in rapid perception to those who have to deal with figures.

If you decide to train a person in your own company to do this work, be very careful to choose one who has the right qualifications. First of all, he should be a highly intelligent individual, preferably with a college degree. He should have the inclination to teach. He should be broad-minded, patient, understanding, tactful, and certainly he should be enthusiastic about the possibilities of reading improvement. Adults who are taking a reading course are prone to argue over some fine point in the precise sentence which expresses the main idea of a certain paragraph or some other detail. The instructor must be able to disagree with the arguers amiably and take a firm stand of his own when necessary.

The second and equally-important consideration is choice of the institution or center in which the chosen instructor will be trained. Be sure that it is one with an excellent reputation in the specialized field of reading instruction in general, and one that has high standards in regard to reading improvement for adults in particular.

Your trainee needs a very good background of instruction in the psychology and methodology of teaching reading. He needs also to have some practice in standing before a group of adults and actually teaching reading improvement at that level. Therefore, as your first step in preparing him for your work, send him out to the nearest university or teachers college to take some courses in the art of teaching reading. Secondly, see if you can arrange for him to have some "practice teaching" in adult reading improvement under the supervision of some reading specialist who has charge of adult reading in the university or other highly reputable reading center.

An ideal plan is the one that was used by a large engine manufacturing concern with headquarters in New York and branches in other parts of the country. This company decided to put its own program into effect and requested The Reading Institute of New York University to train one of its employees, Mr. M———, to do the work. Mr. M——— had already had college training in psychology. It was recommended that he take three courses of individual instruction in the theory and pedagogy of reading. Each of these courses was twenty hours long. They were taken in successive sessions of one to two hours.

Mr. M———— came to The Reading Institute regularly for this background work. He was assigned considerable outside reading and study to do in addition to the regular instruction during the hours that he worked with the teacher. The class meeting period was given over largely to lecture and discussion. Sometimes, however, it was devoted to such activities as preparing practice materials, learning how to make slides, drafting record forms, etc. Everything that was done in training this individual was pointed directly toward the needs of his particular company, where the employees were practically all engineers with a great deal of technical reading to do. So instruction and experiences provided in the individual instruction courses were designed specifically to get Mr. M———— ready to teach reading improvement in the particular kind of material which these employees had to read.

Following the background instruction, a trained specialist from The Reading Institute gave three courses to groups in the company. They were given for the purpose of completing Mr. M's———— training. Each of these courses was twenty-eight hours in length, one hour twice a week, and the three courses were given in succession, one after the other.

While the specialist from The Reading Institute taught the first group, Mr. M———— took the course along with the other men. Mr. M———— lived through the course as a consumer in the same way others would live through it while taking the course under his direction later on. In the meantime he had an opportunity to observe the techniques of the specialist who was teaching the group throughout an entire series of class meetings.

As the next step, Mr. M———— participated in teaching a course. The specialist did the major work in this second course, but Mr. M———— was given increasing opportunities to work with the group as the course proceeded. In other words he did "practice teaching" in this course under the supervision of the specialist.

Finally, in the third course, Mr. M———— took over the responsibility of teaching the class on his own while the specialist observed and took notes. Following each teaching period the specialist held a conference with Mr. M———— in regard to ways in which he might improve his teaching.

After this third course Mr. M———— began training personnel

in his organization "on his own," and did so with very excellent results.

Another type of training program which has been used with success is one in which the trainee devotes full time, day in and day out, to a highly concentrated period of training. This kind of training program is especially appropriate when the company to be served is located at a great distance from an adult reading-improvement center where instructors are trained.

For example, the Arabian-American Oil Company decided to do reading-improvement work with many of its employees in Arabia. The executives in Arabia selected Mr. B————, a promising young man with the right background training in college, and sent him to America to be trained as an instructor of adult reading improvement for their company.

Mr. B———— took up his residence in New York at a hotel one block from The Reading Institute of New York University and devoted full time to studying. He came to the Institute at nine each morning and stayed until dinnertime and often came back in the evening.

Each day he was required to spend two hours daily with an instructor who lectured on the psychology and pedagogy of reading. He was made acquainted with available materials in the field; and he was also shown how to prepare "homemade" materials and how to operate the instruments. A certain portion of each day was devoted to reading and study of selected references. Another part of each day, and sometimes evening as well, was devoted to observation of the Institute's instructors as they taught reading to groups of adults.

After two weeks of this full-time intensive work, Mr. B———— was given some opportunity to teach a class under the supervision of one of the Institute's specialists. These opportunities increased as Mr. B———— continued to work with us.

Mr. B———— was unusually adept in digesting the background information given to him through lectures and reading, and he demonstrated unusual skill as a teacher. At the end of one month he was pronounced entirely capable of conducting by himself the particular type of adult reading courses needed by his company. He then returned to Arabia and, according to last reports, is distinguishing himself by obtaining unusual results.

Company personnel guiding a course without training. Though the most desirable practice is to have a trained instructor to conduct adult reading courses, in some small companies, which are located at a distance from an adult reading center and which have only ten or twelve people to be trained, either engaging a trained specialist or training an employee is impractical.

In such a situation it is possible to conduct a reading course with the use of this text, under the guidance of some member of the company. The president, or someone whom he may designate, assumes chairmanship of a "self-improvement" group which meets regularly three or four times a week on company time.

After the members of the group receive copies of this book and write their names on them, they are asked to read Chapter One and to take the two tests in this chapter. For time-keeping purposes, each individual should be provided with a stop-watch or a stop-clock. The chairman takes the leadership in telling the group what to do and in keeping activities moving along at a lively tempo.

Records of speed and comprehension should be kept meticulously. The chairman should make sure that each individual records his rate and comprehension score after completing each of the tests in Chapter One and all exercises in successive chapters.

Continue in this same general way until the entire book has been covered. The chairman should at all times keep the meetings moving along with enthusiasm and with expressed recognition of gains reported. Under these conditions reading improvement should result, with very little expenditure of anything other than time on the part of the company.

If the chairman decides to purchase some of the instruments described on pages 367-371 in this chapter, he may do so. It is quite possible, however, to increase speed to a high degree without the use of instruments.

Letting employees work by themselves. Some firms are providing their employees with "kits" to use in improving their reading at home. No doubt some gains can be realized through such an arrangement. It is an unusual individual, however, who, when working on his own, will push himself as hard as an instructor will push him— and one must *force* speed if outstanding gains are to be made.

Another factor to be considered is the adequacy of the reading material in the "kit." Is it broad in scope? Does it undertake to develop all the fundamental reading skills needed by adults? Does it place emphasis on the special skills needed by the individual in his "on-the-job" reading? And does it provide enough practice material really to fix the new skills?

Granting that one has adequate material and the will to drive himself, he can, through his own efforts, improve his reading ability considerably. This book can be used to good advantage in such a situation.

What Skills Should Be Developed?

The complex process of reading doesn't lend itself to teaching as a "lump sum." Reading consists of dozens of different skills, and we use different combinations of these skills as our purposes for reading vary and as we read different kinds of materials.

Most executives and employees in business and industry use certain groups of skills predominantly in their particular kind of on-the-job reading. Of course there are the common skills of recognizing words, abstracting meanings from symbols, moving the eyes from left to right, perceiving words in groups, reading rapidly, etc. Over and above these common skills, however, there are specialized skills. Some of these skills may be used predominantly by a group that does one kind of reading in a firm, and other of the special skills may be used predominantly by another group of employees who work for the same company but who do a different kind of reading.

All groups in business and industry profit by having training in reading to grasp increasingly longer units of thought, the skill which is treated in Chapter Two. All groups need to have training in rapid reading as discussed in Chapter Three. It would be helpful for all groups to have training in sensitizing themselves to the observance of direction words, as shown in Chapter Four.

Specialization in a firm's reading needs begins with preview techniques described in Chapter Five. Some groups engage in a type of reading in which they preview practically all the time. A course for them should devote much time to the development of skills needed in doing previews adeptly.

There are some groups who need particularly to read for main ideas and have no reason for grasping details at all. This group, then, should have a great deal of practice in quickly finding main ideas as developed in Chapter Six.

In other groups, a large number of them, the fundamental purpose for reading is to grasp details in technical, factual material. A course for such a group should devote a major proportion of its time to developing the special skills treated in Chapter Seven, "Mining for Details."

If a group has to do a lot of memory work in connection with reading, then emphasis should be placed upon developing the skills described in Chapter Eight, "Wake Up Your Memory!"

The group confined largely to one pattern of writing should have special practice in using techniques adapted to that particular pattern. The skills needed in identifying and working with different patterns treated in Chapter Nine will offer help in developing particular techniques.

Skimming is another skill which may be very useful for some groups and of no use at all to those who have to grasp all the detailed facts. If the skimming skill serves a particular group more often than any other skill, then much time in the course should be devoted to skimming techniques as described in Chapter Ten.

To sum up, the skills most needed by executives and employees in business firms and industrial plants are those treated in this book. But the same emphasis should not be placed on all of them. The class period should be devoted predominantly to the development of the particular set of skills most needed by members in the group to accomplish their specific purpose.

If a group in a company is mixed and its members do all kinds of reading, then their practice should be about equally distributed on the different skills. In this case each individual should supplement his general practice with additional practice on the particular set of skills he himself needs to use most frequently. The "Follow-Up" suggestions at the end of the chapter which treat the particular set of skills under consideration should be helpful in pointing out ways of obtaining this extra practice.

In conclusion, if a group must read all kinds of materials for all kinds of purposes, they should have a general reading-improvement course such as is offered in this book. If, on the other hand, there are several employees who in their daily work have to read a specific kind of material for a specific purpose, they should have training in the common skills and in addition should concentrate on developing to a high degree those specific skills which they need.

Differentiated Courses

I cannot stress strongly enough the need for differentiated reading courses in business and industry. There is no one blanket course which will best meet the needs of those who have to do a special type of reading peculiar to the work of their company. A course for each company should be specifically tailored for that company, both in regard to techniques and materials.

As an example of a plan used in setting up differentiated courses, the following is the general procedure used by The Reading Institute of New York University[1] in preparation of a course in the office of a company.

1. A business or industry invites The Reading Institute to give a course to a group at its place of business.

2. One of the Institute's adult-reading specialists is sent to the office of the company.

3. This specialist talks with the Training Director about the reading done by the group to be trained.

4. He observes the reading habits of the men at work.

5. He obtains typical samples of the materials which the men have to read in connection with their work.

6. He brings these samples back to the Institute where they are analyzed for specific skills.

7. A program is planned in terms of these specific needs, and additional material is prepared.

8. While the group receives instruction in many skills, a goodly portion of each class period is devoted to work with specialized materials which approximate those with which the group has to work, and with procedures designed specifically to develop the skills most needed in reading that particular type of material.

9. At the end of the course a complete report is sent to the Training Director in which the gains for each individual and for the group as a whole are charted.

Examples of differentiated programs. Perhaps the best way to show how differentiated programs work out is to describe a few which were selected because the groups involved varied widely in the kind of work they had to do and the kind of material they had to read.

The first two examples are concerned with clerical workers who were given courses to improve their skills in two different types of work. The third example describes a course given to executives to improve their ability to do technical reading. The fourth example

[1] The Reading Institute of New York University is one unit in the University's Division of General Education under the Deanship of Paul A. McGhee.

tells about a course given to personnel whose work was largely concerned with the reading of easy, narrative material.

A program for I.B.M. proof-machine operators. One of the Federal Reserve banks asked to have a course given to a group of fifteen proof-machine operators whose work consisted of reading and recording two series of numbers on each of many checks which they processed daily. It was hoped that such a course might step up efficiency, lessen fatigue, help operators to experience more job satisfaction, and increase their pay because of increased production.

A course which would meet the needs of these girls did not require development of all the reading skills. These employees had no occasion in the bank's work to locate the main idea in a paragraph, to grasp details in technical material, to detect patterns of writing, etc. They needed only to increase their ability to locate and to read these numbers quickly and accurately.

A course was tailored to meet the specific needs of this group. The first step in this tailoring process was to have 1,800 photostatic copies of checks reproduced on slides. Some other banks had previously provided training for their I.B.M. proof-machine operators, but such training had consisted mainly of flashing series of numbers of increasing lengths on a screen for decreasing periods of time. Studies have shown repeatedly that transfer of training takes place when the learning elements and situation are identical with those in the real situation. Simply flashing numbers did not duplicate the real situation. These girls needed not only to recognize numbers quickly but also to increase their speed in locating these numbers on different checks, for one of the numbers doesn't always appear in the same place on a check. There was some manual work involved, also —that of punching the key on the machine to record the number.

Because of the need for providing training in the total job, the specially-designed course was not confined to flashing numbers on the screen alone. The instructor flashed duplicates of the checks themselves with the numbers on them; and for a part of the time the operators actually punched the numbers into I.B.M. keyboards just like those they used in their daily work.

The instructor met with this group fifteen minutes daily for five weeks, totalling 6¼ hours. Records were kept of speed and accuracy, and an hourly check was made of each employee's production during the entire training period.

At the end of the training period it was found that the accuracy for the group as a whole increased from 67 per cent to 98 per cent and that their speed of on-the-job production increased 8 per cent. In breaking down production by ability groups, it was found that the experienced operators made a gain of 5 per cent; the average operators a gain of 7.9 per cent; and the below average operators a gain of 12.6 per cent.

A program for adjustors and correspondents. Another course offered for clerical workers involved the development of skills which were entirely different from those needed by the I.B.M. operators. The members of this second group worked with words rather than numbers and needed to be highly trained in specific reading skills.

The reading of this group was concerned largely with letters— letters informing of change of address, changes of orders from regular to *de luxe* form, and inquiries of a great variety. Form letters are available for answering much of this correspondence, but the clerical worker must quickly spot the one phrase or sentence which is the key to the kind of answer to be given. This type of reading requires development of two specific reading skills: ability to find the main idea in a paragraph, and ability to skim.

In this particular situation training in reading improvement was complicated by the fact that the letters were handwritten in many cases; if not handwritten, then typewritten.

An ordinary general course in which these people did exercises in a reading workbook and used one of the gadgets would probably have yielded disappointing returns. But the particular needs of this group were carefully analyzed, and special materials and techniques were devised for use in developing particular skills for their daily work.

One hundred and fifty 3 x 4" slides were prepared from sections of letters representing characteristic difficulties which these mail readers encountered. The slides were used as the basis of instruction in skimming and locating a pertinent phrase or sentence. After spotting the significant item, members of the group selected the appropriate form letter to use in reply and actually engaged in the routing and processing of the letter.

Additional daily practice was afforded in reading real letters received the day previous to the practice. These letters were thrown on a screen with an opaque projector.

Of course this work was supplemented with other reading improvement measures, but the bulk of the time was devoted to the use of special materials to develop specific skills.

At the end of the course the following average gains had been made:

		Initial	Final
Cooperative Reading Test	Speed	47 Percentile	63 Per cent
	Comprehension	33 Percentile	51 Per cent
College Level Material	Speed	280 words per min.	370 w.p.m.
	Comprehension	82 Percentile	88 Per cent

Gains in on-the-job production were very gratifying. The supervisor checked the production of each of these mail readers and correspondents the last of August before their training course began and again in November when the course ended.

Three different types of work were done by the women taking the course. Some of them took dictation and answered correspondence. This group increased their output from 14.6 letters per day before the course to 15.7 letters per day after the course.

The second group which handled the more routine letters not containing payments increased from 83.9 to 98.5 as shown in their production comparisons before and after taking the course.

The third group, answering all mail accompanied by payments, increased its output from 191.9 before the course to 218.5 after the course.

Of special interest are the results of the Minnesota clerical tests independently conducted by the company's own Personnel Department before training was initiated and at the conclusion of training. These tests in turn were compared with the results from another form of the test which had been administered to each of the employees six years previously. The results indicated that greater gains were made during the twenty-eight hours of training than had been made in six years (average for the group) in standard on-the-job practice.

No doubt these fine gains were due in part to the fact that these workers were given a course specifically designed to meet their particular needs.

A program for executives reading technical material. A large pharmaceutical company in New Jersey decided to have a reading improvement course conducted for the benefit of their executives whose reading needs were increasing because of the many new drugs. These executives were having to spend a very large proportion of their time acquainting themselves with studies being made in research laboratories, and learning of new production methods which permit manufacturers profitably to mass-produce drugs which only a short time previously had been limited to small amounts produced in test tubes.

The materials they had to read were technical and filled with factual details. The specific skills which they most needed were those which are necessary in grasping clusters of details as related to larger topics. By far the major proportion of time in their course was devoted to the development of techniques described in Chapter Seven, "Mining for Details."

Special material also was used with this group. Very frequently guided practice was given in reading the actual materials they had to read in connection with their work. Mimeographed material was also prepared for use in developing the special skills they needed. They were given training in the rapid and accurate perception of special pharmacal phrases and complex chemical formulas. Extensive practice was provided in reading supplemental materials in science and technology.

As a motive for continuous improvement in grasping details rapidly and accurately, a daily graph was kept by the class, which convened fourteen times for two hours each. The group started with a median comprehension score of 85 per cent and ended with a median comprehension score of 85 per cent. Their rate increased from a median of 320 words per minute to a median of 780 words per minute. To make such a gain in speed in reading technical material and to hold their comprehension constant was a real achievement.

A program for personnel reading easy, narrative material. A large motion picture studio requested the New York University Reading Institute to send a man to Hollywood to give reading-improvement courses to some of their executives and other personnel. Executives from other studios visited the reading classes at this studio and began asking to have courses given in their own studios. It worked out that the instructor stayed in Hollywood for six months and gave courses not only in this studio, but also in several other studios and allied agencies.

The jobs of the people with whom he worked varied from those of story editors to production chiefs. Some of the lawyers of one company took the course. The first step in organizing the classes was to divide the total participants into groups according to their reading level, and according to the special skills they needed in order to read the material they had to read for the purpose for which they had to read it.

The larger portion of the reading done was concerned with scripts or novels. The people whose work required continuous reading of this material needed a course very different in nature from that given to the lawyers. The content of scripts or novels varies greatly from that found in legal contracts or in the technical literature of the pharmacal company mentioned in the preceding example.

For these people who wanted to read quantities of novels and scripts to evaluate possibilities for picture production, a course had to be specifically devised to develop speed and comprehension when reading for the purpose of following a story plot. Novels, scripts, and specially-prepared mimeographed materials were used, and teaching techniques were employed to develop particular skills for script-readers.

And so with each of the other types of readers in the Hollywood studios. Differentiated courses were given in terms of skills required in reading different types of material for different purposes.

The results were very gratifying. The average beginning rate of the Hollywood people was 250 to 300 words per minute with 75 per cent comprehension. The average rate at the end of each program was somewhat over 800 words per minute with 85 per cent comprehension.

Here are a few examples of benefits derived from this reading-improvement work:

A studio executive increased his reading speed from 300 words per minute to almost 700 words per minute. He recently commented that he now does not have to take his reading home each day as he formerly did.

An actor's agent increased his reading speed from 200 words per minute to over 800, while maintaining his reading comprehension at 95 per cent. He said that his reading time on a standard motion-picture script had formerly been over 2½ hours but now is about 40 minutes. Since he often reads over 10 scripts per week, this is a real saving in time.

A year after the reading course had been completed an executive in one of the studios wrote: "I checked my reading speed the other day and it might interest you to know that I am running about 930 words per minute. The course has been of immeasurable help in my reading activities."

An independent motion-picture producer increased his reading speed from 350 words per minute to 1,200 words per minute and his comprehension from 90 to 95 per cent. He now finds it possible to read an average-length novel in about one hour. This saves him considerable time, because most of his professional reading consists of screening novels for possible motion pictures.

At one studio noted for its strict budgeting practices, the man in charge of production found reading improvement to be of such value that he arranged a second course for those who had not been able to attend the first.

Are Gains in Speed and Comprehension Retained?

Most people are convinced that marked gains in speed and comprehension can result from a reading-improvement course. Questions which frequently follow a statement of such a conviction, however, are "But do those who take a course retain these gains? Do these gains simply spurt up under the stimulation of the course and then recede to the previous normal after the course is over?"

No flat statement can be given in answer, for the retention of reading gains probably varies with individuals and with the kind of instruction they received.

A course which contributes most to permanency in an individual's gains is one which thoroughly establishes fundamental skills and which establishes these skills through situations comparable to those in which the person will make use of them.

Retention also depends to a certain extent upon the individual. To retain the skills permanently he must continue to do considerable reading, and he must continue to apply the techniques he has learned.

For one large institution The Reading Institute of New York University had been giving successive courses from October 1953 to June 1955. This was an excellent setting in which to check the carry-over effects of the courses. On file are the beginning and ending scores of three groups taking the course. One took it from October 1953 to January 1954; one from March 1954 to June 1954; and one from February 1955 to June 1955. Each of these three groups was retested in January 1956. The materials used in the retest were comparable to those used at the beginning and at the conclusion of each course: an informal test of speed and comprehension in reading difficult material, an informal test of speed and comprehension in reading easy material, and one standardized test—the Co-operative Reading Test, C 2.

The average of the three groups in reading difficult material is presented here:

Words Per Minute			Per Cent of Comprehension
Before Training	281	Beginning of Course	83
End of Course	531	End of Course	88
Retest	422	Retest	91

Obviously these people had lost somewhat in speed attained at the end of the course, but they were still reading on an average of 141 more words per minute than they had covered before taking the course. In comprehension they had gained an average of three points above the score made at the end of the course. These gains in comprehension are not sizable, but they do indicate that, in their continued reading, comprehension did not suffer in spite of the accelerated speed with which they read this difficult material.

The averages resulting from the informal retest of easy material are as follows:

Words Per Minute		Per Cent of Comprehension
Before Training	380	83
End of Course	588	87
Retest	705	82

These results show that the groups went right on gaining in speed long after the courses were finished. On the retest they read an average of 325 words per minute faster than they had read before they took the course. Even at an increase of 325 words per minute they had maintained an average comprehension within one per cent of that with which they started.

The results of these informal tests are not entirely reliable because the forms of the material used and the comprehension questions asked had not been standardized. One standardized test, however, had been given before and after training and was given again in the retest. A different but comparable form was used upon each of the three different occasions.

Here are the mean scores of the three groups in terms of percentile ranks on speed rate plus comprehension:

		Retest
Start of Training	*Conclusion of Training*	*Several Months Later*
57th percentile	74th percentile	79th percentile

On this standardized test, which was the most reliable measure used, the group percentiles show that the class members not only maintained their gains in reading but continued to make gains long after the course was over.

Much more research should be conducted to ascertain the permanency of gains made as a result of taking adult reading-improvement courses. At the present time, however, we have reason to believe that a large percentage of gains in speed and in comprehension are retained, and that many people continue to grow both in speed and comprehension after the course is finished.

What About the Gadgets?

Many, but not all, of the professional laboratories which offer speed-reading courses for adults use instruments which pace the eyes. Some believe that these instruments are very beneficial; others think their importance has been overrated. It is possible to develop a high speed in reading without the use of instruments. Most adults are fascinated by these instruments, however, and enjoy using them. Probably the chief value of instruments is two-fold: they motivate attempts to read faster, and they show a person how fast he really can read when he is forced.

If instruments are used, care should be taken to make sure that the speed achieved while reading with the use of the instruments is transferred to natural reading. After the use of an instrument the instructor should give some such directive as this: "You have found out how fast you can read when the instrument is forcing you. Now, do the same thing without the instrument. Force your own eyes along over the next article and see if you can keep up to the instrument speed." Unless by far the larger portion of the speed practice is done while reading material under natural conditions, the speed attained during instrument work is apt not to carry over and remain.

The investigations in regard to eye movements described in Chapter Two provided the impetus which resulted in the different types of speeded-reading instruments now on the market. All of them are based on the principle of "widening the eye span"; that is, training the eye to take in a wider span of print than it has been accustomed to do. Therein lies a danger in the misuse of instruments. If one thinks only of mechanically training the physical capacity of the eye to take in more words at a glance, he is looking upon the reading process in a very superficial way. Reading is a complex *mental* process, and any attempt to speed reading must take into consideration the quickening of mental perception in picking up meanings from printed symbols. It is not just a matter of changing something that one does physically with his eyes. This misinterpretation of the fundamental process of reading is a danger which one must continuously combat when using instruments, lest those in training develop a wrong concept of the reading process.

There are two types of instruments: some are used for diagnostic purposes, others are designed to force speed in reading.

Diagnostic Instruments

Ophthalmograph: Perhaps the most widely used of the diagnostic instruments is the American Optical Company Ophthalmograph. This instrument is used in photographing eye movements while reading. The present-day model of this instrument is an offspring of the bulky and expensive contrivance described in Chapter Two. That first experimental camera was too technical and too cumbersome to lend itself to practical use in schools. Eventually, however, the American Optical Company developed a compact, easily-operated eye-movement camera which it calls the ophthalmograph. With a limited amount of training anyone can make photographic reproductions of the eye movements of a reader with the use of this instrument.

The ophthalmograph is not a speed instrument. Its function is largely diagnostic. By examining the record of an individual's eye movements as revealed by the ophthalmograph, it is possible to tell whether or not he is reading in large or small units, whether or not he is making backward or regressive movements as his eyes move over a line of print, and whether or not he makes an accurate return sweep when he moves his eyes from the end of one line to the beginning of the next. It is also possible to ascertain the length of time for each of the fixation pauses which are made by the reader as his eyes progress along the lines of print.

In addition to its use in diagnosing eye movements, some reading centers use the ophthalmograph records as a measure of progress. A "picture" of the eye movements of each individual is taken at the beginning of a reading-improvement course and again at the end, and the two are compared. Such before-and-after eye-movement pictures usually show considerable improvement in the behavior of the eyes and in the decreasing length of the fixation pauses.

Visual screening instruments: There are two instruments which are widely used for visual-screening purposes. One of these is the Keystone View Company's telebinocular. This instrument is a modified stereoscope through which the person who is being tested views a set of ten cards mounted on stereoscopic slides. On these ten cards are printed the Visual Sensation and Perception Tests of the Bett's *Ready to Read* battery. The tests on these cards are supposed to screen for defects in distance fusion, binocular visual efficiency, left-eye visual efficiency, right-eye visual efficiency, vertical balance or posture, depth perception, lateral balance or posture, reading-distance fusion, and sharpness of image.

With a moderate amount of training a psychologist or teacher can give the telebinocular tests. The results should be used only for rough screening purposes, however, to find out which individuals should be referred to an eye specialist for a thorough and professional examination.

Another instrument which is in wide use for visual-screening purposes is Ortho-Rater. The Bausch and Lomb Occupational Vision Tests are given through the use of this instrument.

These instruments can be procured from the companies listed on the following page:

The Ophthalmograph,
American Optical Company,
302 Hurst Boulevard,
Buffalo, New York

Keystone Visual Survey Telebinocular,
Keystone View Company,
Meadville, Pennsylvania

The Ortho-Rater and Occupational Vision Test,
Bausch and Lomb Optical Company,
Rochester, New York

Corrective Instruments

The tachistoscope: This instrument, commonly called the "tack,"
has in the past been widely used in training for reading improvement. Its use at the present time, however, is highly controversial.
Some studies show that it has little value; others that it is of great
value. Opinions are strongly expressed pro and con this flash-meter
type of reading instrument. One increasingly hears the opinion expressed that speed of reading is dependent upon the rate with which
the brain can assimilate ideas rather than upon the rate with which
the eyes can pick up visual impressions. Others "swear by" the
tachistoscope and claim that it is their most valuable tool in teaching
reading improvement.

The tachistoscope is used in flashing series of figures or phrases on
a screen or blackboard. The sets of figures or phrases are printed on
cards which are inserted in the tachistoscope. The set of cards for
figures contains series of numbers of increasing lengths, likewise the
set of phrase cards contains phrases of increasing length. The instrument is electrically controlled and can be so adjusted as to flash
numbers or phrases in rapid succession and for decreasing lengths
of time.

Tachistoscopes are manufactured and sold by:

Keystone Tachistoscopic Outfit (for group use),
Keystone View Company,
Meadville, Pennsylvania

Renshaw Tachistoscopic Trainer (for individual use),
Stereo Optical Company,
3539 N. Kenton Avenue,
Chicago 41, Illinois

The Tachitron,
Stereo Optical Company,
3539 North Kenton Avenue,
Chicago 41, Illinois

The Timex,
Educational Development Laboratories Inc.,
15 Washington Place,
New York, New York

The PDL Perceptascope (a combined Tachistoscope and 16mm. movie
  projector),
Perceptual Development Laboratories,
115 North Meramec Avenue,
St. Louis 5, Missouri

Reading pacers: Probably the most widely known of the speed-
reading instruments is one which belongs to the family of pacers,
accelerators, rate controllers, and "trainers." These instruments all
operate on the same principle. A platform is provided on which an
open book or article can be placed. A metal lever, wire, or beam of
light is then moved over the page at any rate desired. As the lever
moves along it covers up the lines of print one by one, and the
reader has to hurry along in reading each successive line before the
lever catches up with him and covers up the line.

This instrument has the advantage of permitting the reader to
use directly the types of material that he normally reads.

The following companies sell reading pacers:

A.V.R. Rateometer,
Audio Visual Research,
531 S. Plymouth Court,
Chicago 5, Illinois

Keystone Reading Pacer,
Keystone View Company,
Meadville, Pennsylvania

Reading Rate Controller,
Three Dimension Company,
3512 N. Kostner,
Chicago, Illinois

Reading Rate Controller, Model SO-2,
Stereo Optical Company,
8539 North Kenton Avenue,
Chicago 14, Illinois

Shadowscope Reading Pacer,
Lafayette Instrument Company,
Lafayette, Indiana

S.R.A. Reading Accelerator,
Science Research Associates,
57 W. Grand Avenue,
Chicago 10, Illinois

Reading films: Another popular speed device consists of films which are shown with the use of a 16-millimeter moving-picture projector. The films consist of several complete selections. Each selection is flashed on the screen a section at a time. While all the words on the screen are visible, successive phrases stand out more prominently as they are flashed from left to right across the lines until the section is completed. The rate of flashing these phrases can be controlled and varied from slow to high speeds.

These films can be procured as indicated below:

Harvard Reading Films,
Harvard University Press,
Cambridge, Massachusetts

Iowa Reading Training Films (Easy, designed primarily for high school
  use)
University of Iowa, Iowa City, Iowa

The Controlled Reader (This title includes both the instrument and its
  accompanying film materials),
Educational Development Laboratory,
15 Washington Place,
New York 3, New York

Instructional Materials

Since the teaching of reading improvement for adults is still somewhat of an innovation, not too many instructional books on this subject have yet appeared. Up to this time instructors of adult courses have had to depend largely upon workbooks designed for use at the college level. However, special books and workbooks for adults interested in the types of life-reading done outside of or beyond college are now beginning to appear. The availability of materials designed for adults will no doubt improve rapidly.

Bound Books

Judson, H., and Baldridge, G., *The Techniques of Reading*. Harcourt, Brace & Company, New York, 1956

Leedy, Paul D., *Reading Improvement for Adults*. McGraw-Hill Book Company, Inc., New York, 1956.

Lewis, Norman, *How to Read Better and Faster*. Thomas Y. Crowell Co., New York, 1951

Witty, Paul, *How to Become a Better Reader*. Science Research Associates, Chicago, 1953 (Intended for college use, also)

Paper-Covered Workbooks

Baker, William D., *Reading Skills*. Prentice-Hall, Inc., New York, 1954

Brown, I. I., *Efficient Reading*. D. C. Heath & Company, Boston, 1952

Casper R., and Griffin, E. G., *Toward Better Reading Skill*. Appleton-Century-Crofts, Inc., New York, 1949

Glack, M. D., *The Improvement of College Reading*. Houghton Mifflin Co., New York, 1954

Herr, S. E., *Effective Reading*. Tulane University, New Orleans, Louisiana, 1954

Lewis, Norman, *How to Read Better and Faster*. Thomas Y. Crowell Co., New York, 1951

Miller, Lyle L., *Increasing Reading Efficiency*. Henry Holt & Co., Inc., New York, 1956

Perry, W. E., Jr., and Whitlock, C. P., *Selections for Improving Speed of Comprehension*. Harvard University Press, Cambridge, Massachusetts, 1948

Spache, George D., and Berg, Paul C., *The Art of Efficient Reading*. The Macmillan Company, New York, 1955.

Tests

Tests specifically designed for use with adult readers are very scarce, and instructors of adult classes have been forced to use tests originally prepared for college use.

For Adult Readers

One test has now been published which was prepared especially to check reading skills of *adults:*

Spache, George, *Test of Reading Flexibility*. University of Florida, Gainesville, Florida, 1956

This test measures (1) reading of easy material, (2) reading of difficult material, (3) skimming.

College-Level

Davis, Frederick B., and King, Harold U., *Co-operative English Test, Test C 2: Reading Comprehension, Higher Level*. Co-operative Test Division, Educational Testing Service, 20 Nassau St., Princeton, New Jersey, 1940-51

This test measures speed, comprehension, and vocabulary; it has three forms, R, S, and T, and provides college norms.

Nelson, M. J., and Denney, E. C., *Nelson-Denney Reading Test*. Psychological Corporation, New York, 1929, rev. 1938

This test measures speed, comprehension, and vocabulary. It has two forms, A and B, and provides college norms.

Answer Keys

Chapter One

Selection 1, pages 4-9:

1) d   2) c   3) c   4) b   5) c   6) d   7) b   8) a   9) d
10) c

Selection 2, pages 10-13:

1) d   2) c   3) c   4) b   5) d   6) c   7) c   8) c   9) c
10) d

Chapter Two

Selection 1, pages 23-24:

1) c   2) d   3) c   4) b   5) d

Selection 2, pages 24-25:

1) d   2) a   3) c   4) b   5) c

Selection 3, pages 25-28:

1) b   2) c   3) a   4) d   5) d

Selection 4, pages 27-28:

1) c   2) b   3) a   4) d   5) b

Selection 6, pages 29-32:

1) a   2) c   3) d   4) b   5) a   6) a   7) c   8) b   9) a
10) d

Chapter Three

Selection 1, pages 37-39:

1) c   2) b   3) a   4) c   5) d   6) d   7) b   8) d   9) d
10) b

Selection 2, pages 40-42:

1) d   2) b   3) d   4) b   5) a   6) d   7) c   8) c   9) b
10) d

Selection 3, pages 42-46:

1) d   2) c   3) d   4) b   5) a   6) d   7) d   8) b   9) c
10) c

Vocabulary Test, pages 46-48:

1) disintegrating, 2) collateral, 3) horticulture, 4) obsolete, 5) progeny,
6) agenda, 7) derelict, 8) distaff, 9) decrepit, 10) burgeon.

Chapter Four

Selection 1, pages 56-57:

Go-ahead Words		Turn-about Words
and	moreover	nor
and	consequently	rather
and	and	not
and	and	but
and	and so	but
and	and	even though
and	and	not
and	and	on the other hand
and	and	but
therefore		

Selection 2, pages 57-61:

1) c   2) d   3) b   4) a   5) c   6) b   7) d   8) b   9) c
10) f

Selection 3, pages 61-64:

1) c   2) c   3) b   4) c   5) b   6) d   7) a   8) b   9) d
10) c

Vocabulary Test, pages 64-65:

1) reinvigoration, 2) artisans, 3) several, 4) honesty, 5) convincing, 6) flippantly, 7) resource, 8) exclusion, 9) associates, 10) insecure.

Chapter Five

Selection 1, pages 69-76:

1) d   2) d   3) c   4) b   5) c   6) a   7) b   8) c   9) d
10) b

Selection 2, pages 77-83:

1) d   2) c   3) d   4) c   5) b   6) d   7) c   8) a   9) b
10) d

Vocabulary Test, pages 84-85:

1) shoals, 2) lichen, 3) myriad, 4) fecund, 5) bushwhack, 6) vindication, 7) encompass, 8) wraith, 9) chute, 10) bend, 11) estuary, 12) vulnerable, 13) escarpment, 14) spate, 15) veritable, 16) muskeg, 17) tributary, 18) domain, 19) pessimistic, 20) portage

Chapter Six

Exercise 1, pages 91-93:

Paragraph 1) a   Paragraph 2) b   Paragraph 3) c

Exercise 2, pages 93-97:

Paragraph 1) b   Paragraph 2) c   Paragraph 3) c   Paragraph 4) d   Paragraph 5) d

Selection 1, pages 99-105:

1) a   2) d   3) c   4) a   5) b   6) d   7) d   8) b   9) c
10) a

Vocabulary Test, page 105:

1) enhances, 2) dynamic, 3) ethereal, 4) incendiary, 5) accentuated, 6) permeates, 7) animosities, 8) therapeutic, 9) regeneration, 10) consonance

Chapter Seven

Paragraph 1, Pages 110-111

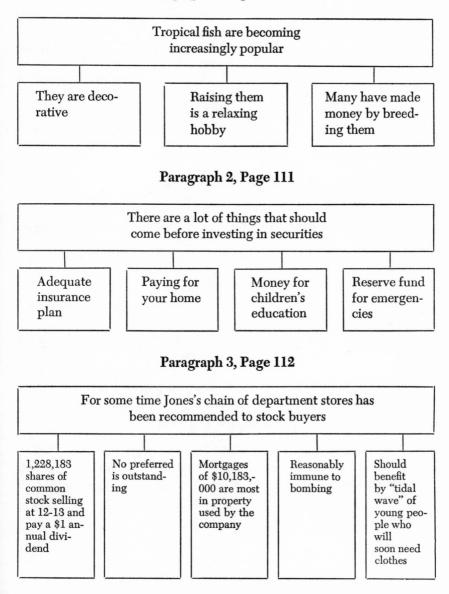

Tropical fish are becoming increasingly popular

| They are decorative | Raising them is a relaxing hobby | Many have made money by breeding them |

Paragraph 2, Page 111

There are a lot of things that should come before investing in securities

| Adequate insurance plan | Paying for your home | Money for children's education | Reserve fund for emergencies |

Paragraph 3, Page 112

For some time Jones's chain of department stores has been recommended to stock buyers

| 1,228,183 shares of common stock selling at 12-13 and pay a $1 annual dividend | No preferred is outstanding | Mortgages of $10,183,-000 are most in property used by the company | Reasonably immune to bombing | Should benefit by "tidal wave" of young people who will soon need clothes |

Paragraph 4, Pages 112-113

Main Idea	Major Details
A leather sole has been developed which possesses qualities of composition soles.	Developed by shoe manufacturer rather than tanner.
	Contains all desirable features of orthodox leather sole.
	Has the comfortable "cushiony" characteristics of synthetic soles.
	Ordinary chrome-tanned leather is used.
	Pumped to loosen fibers and create air cells.
	Claimed that it is strengthened by this process.
	Tests indicate it wears better.
	About half the weight of ordinary sole.

Paragraph 5, Page 113

Main Idea	Major Details
The history of production is easily sketched.	Early primitive man merely appropriated what nature provided.
	Through the centuries man learned to work over the products of nature more and more.
	Later the use of animals caused great expansion.
	Later natural forces were harnessed to production.
	At present U.S. has more than a billion horsepower of energy.

Paragraph 6, Page 114

Main Idea	Major Details
I. The essence of Cambridge is in its surroundings.	A. It is in the crocuses and daffodils
	B. It is in the roses and lupines
	C. It is in the sounds of the bells of the church
	D. It is in the swifts
	E. It is in the meadows

Paragraph 8, Pages 115-116

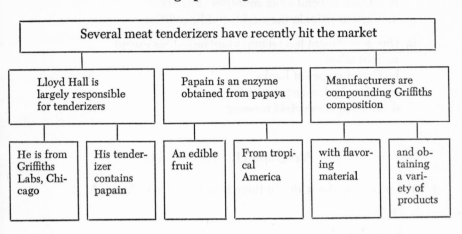

Several meat tenderizers have recently hit the market

Lloyd Hall is largely responsible for tenderizers	Papain is an enzyme obtained from papaya	Manufacturers are compounding Griffiths composition

He is from Griffiths Labs, Chicago	His tenderizer contains papain	An edible fruit	From tropical America	with flavoring material	and obtaining a variety of products

Paragraph 9, Pages 116-117

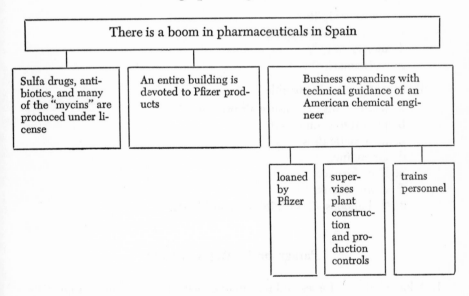

There is a boom in pharmaceuticals in Spain

Sulfa drugs, antibiotics, and many of the "mycins" are produced under license	An entire building is devoted to Pfizer products	Business expanding with technical guidance of an American chemical engineer

loaned by Pfizer	supervises plant construction and production controls	trains personnel

Paragraph 10, Pages 117-118

I. Public industries are less important in the United States than in some other countries.

II. What are the two major sub-topics and details belonging under each?

   A. European countries and public industries controlled by the government

    a. Australia, New Zealand, Canada—railroads
    b. France, several other countries—tobacco
    c. Various cities in the world—public utilities

B. Our government has no important industries except:
    a. Post office
    b. Certain types of banks
    c. A few hydroelectric plants
    d. None of these yield revenue

Paragraph 11, Pages 118-119

1. We know a lot about air but there is still more to be learned.

A. Properties
    a. substance
    b. weight
    c. pressure
    d. compressibility
    e. expands and contracts
    f. inertia
    g. resistance

B. Inventions made possible
    a. instruments to measure air pressure
    b. pumps to compress it
    c. pneumatic tires
    d. air engines
    e. blast furnaces
    f. vacuum tanks
    g. (1) balloons, (2) dirigibles, (3) airplanes.

Paragraph 12, Pages 119-120

1. A knowledge of forces and resources of nature enables us to appreciate and understand our environment.

A. Science has:
    a. changed waste places into gardens
    b. conquered germ diseases
    c. controlled sources of power in nature
    d. promoted travel under water and through air
    e. illuminated cities
    f. improved fruits, root crops, cattle, horses and sheep.

Paragraph 14, Page 121

I. Characteristics which make automobiles the generally comfortable, smooth-running vehicles they are—(as distinct from simple conveyances providing places to sit and engines to move them around)—are built into every American passenger car today in varying degrees.

A. They are the end-products of
(1) A great amount of research
(2) expert guidance
(3) technological know-how
(4) management prejudices
(5) consumer studies
(6) dumb luck, and
(7) shrewd guesswork.

B. As a result, the various brands of cars are notably unlike each other
(1) in handling
(2) economy
(3) ease of repair
(4) power and speed
(5) riding qualities
(6) noise level
(7) driver vision and safety

Paragraph 16, Page 122

In the Hudson, opposite West Point, is a famous little island that recalls heroic days of the Revolutionary War. From one end of the island a great chain was stretched across the river to the cliffs below West Point, to keep back the British fleet. The links of the chain were forged in a blacksmith shop at New Windsor, New York, and were carried down the river on a log boom. A part of the chain is today on view at Washington's headquarters, Newburg, New York. Another section of the chain is to be seen at West Point.

Paragraph 19, Pages 124-125

1. Plastics
2. (a) molded (b) bent (c) carved
3. (a) rubber (b) resin
4. (a) 1. carbolic acid, (2) formaldehyde
   (b) 1. phenals, (2) aldehydes

Selection 1, pages 126-128:

1. (a), (b), (c) Any three of these: weaving, embroidering, making furniture, carving wood, building houses.
2. (a) London, (b) Paris, (c) Rome
3. (a) Architecture: made more progress than in others, (b) Painting: still dependent on Parisian influences, (c) Music: contributed new motifs, but not a composer of first rank, (d) Drama: achieved some individuality, (e) Motion pictures: set world standards but not high.
4. (a) art education, (b) advertising, (c) higher incomes, (d) shorter working days, (e) need for leisure time activities
5. (a) Yes, (b) No
6. (a) commercial, (b) industrial

Selection 2, pages 129-134:

1) c   2) c   3) b   4) c   5) b   6) d   7) a   8) b   9) c
10) b

Selection 3, pages 135-138:

1) c   2) d   3) d   4) a   5) d   6) b   7) d   8) b   9) b
10) b

Vocabulary Test, pages 138-139:

1) c   2) b   3) b   4) b   5) c   6) b   7) a   8) c   9) c
10) c   11) b   12) c   13) b   14) b   15) a   16) b   17) a
18) c   19) a   20) b

Chapter Eight

Selection 2, pages 160-164:

1) yes   2) yes   3) yes   4) yes   5) no   6) no   7) no   8) yes   9) no   10) yes

Selection 4, pages 168-173:

1) lumbago, 2) lumbo-sacral, 3) posture, 4) muscles, 5) middle-age, 6) lower back, 7) avoided, 8) aspirin, 9) proper use of the body, 10) symptom

Exercise 1, pages 175-176:

I. Technical division of labor developed with the growth of the factory system.

II. A. Cause of the use of machinery

    a. When tasks reduced to simple repetitive actions they can be done more cheaply by machines.

    b. Machines are more regular and accurate and they do not tire.

  B. Result of use of machines

    a. New types of labor needed to design, set up, and attend the machines.

    b. Others needed to take charge of management.

    c. Others to sell product.

    d. Others to feed machines and take away materials.

Exercise 2, pages 176-177:

1) radiators, 2) air valves, 3) air is allowed to escape, 4) attic, 5) and 6) a) overflow, b) freeze, 7) basement, 8) compressed, 9) forces the water back, 10) valves

Exercise 4, pages 180-181:

1) 2 hours a day for 3 years, 2) $1,500, 3) $15,000, 4) ⅓ of total amount collected, or $5,000, 5) $3,500

Selection 1, pages 182-184:

1) $53.00, 2) 58 percent, 3) $375.00, 4) 10 percent, 5) 17 percent, 6) one-third, 7) Midwest, 8) Midwest, 9) 63 percent, 10) 41 percent

Selection 2, pages 184-189:

1) c   2) b   3) a   4) d   5) d   6) c   7) a   8) b   9) d
10) b

Selection 3, pages 189-196:

1) a   2) a   3) d   4) c   5) c   6) d   7) c   8) c   9) b
10) b

Selection 4, pages 196-201:

1) c   2) c   3) d   4) d   5) c   6) c   7) b   8) b   9) a
10) d

Vocabulary Test, page 202:

1) l   2) h   3) a   4) p   5) j   6) q   7) n   8) e   9) f
10) d   11) c   12) k   13) r   14) s   15) i   16) t   17) b
18) g   19) o   20) m

Chapter Nine

Practice Section I, pages 209-212:

1) Sharing experience, 2) Question-answer, 3) Sharing experience, 4) Question-answer, 5) Question-answer, 6) The Great Plains or remote sections of the West, 7) Baby food formulas, 8) A man lying in the bottom of a pitpan, or dugout canoe, 9) Emotional stress, 10) Heavy snowfall

Practice Section II, pages 213-216:

1) Substantiated fact, 2) Opinion-reason, 3) Information, 4) Substantiated fact, 5) Opinion-reason, 6) 5,000, 7) Rise of Soviet-Union, 8) 1913 Liberty Nickel, 9) The Cradle Society, Evanston, Illinois, 10) secure

Practice Section III, pages 216-237:

Selection 1, pages 217-221:

1) d   2) c   3 d   4) b   5) c   6) d   7) a   8) b   9) d
10) d

Selection 2, pages 221-227:

1) d   2) a   3) c   4) d   5) b   6) b   7) a   8) b   9) c
10) c

Selection 3, pages 227-230:

1) b   2) b   3) a   4) c   5) c   6) d   7) b   8) a   9) b
10) c

Selection 4, pages 230-234:

1) a   2) d   3) c   4) c   5) d   6) d   7) d   8) a   9) b
10) c

Selection 5, pages 234-237:

1) d   2) c   3) a   4) b   5) c   6) d   7) a   8) d   9) a
10) d

Vocabulary Test, page 237:

1) unpremeditated, 2) commotion, 3) marvel, 4) incongruity, 5) examiner, 6) terminology, 7) ingenious, 8) discerned, 9) dominantly, 10) insertion, 11) pine, 12) provisional, 13) puissance, 14) encroach, 15) surpassing

Chapter Ten

Selection 1, pages 245-248:

1) b   2) b   3) d   4) c   5) b   6) c   7) a   8) a   9) c
10) c

Selection 2, pages 249-252:

1) c   2) a   3) d   4) d   5) a   6) c   7) d   8) d   9) c
10) d

Selection 3, pages 253-256:

1) b   2) a   3) a   4) d   5) a   6) c   7) d   8) a   9) c
10) a

Selection 4, pages 256-260:

1) a   2) c   3) c   4) c   5) c   6) b   7) b   8) c   9) b
10) d

Selection 5, pages 268-270:

1) true, 2) false, 3) true, 4) false, 5) false, 6) true, 7) true, 8) true, 9) false, 10) true

Selection 6, pages 271-273:

1) The gardener, 2) The gardener suggested it to the lady of the house, 3) It was beginning to look not like a petunia at all, 4) He didn't know what the plant was, 5) Gardener's tentative conclusion was that it was Nicotiana

Selection 7, pages 273-276:

1) c   2) d   3) d   4) c   5) c   6) c   7) c   8) b   9) c
10) d

Selection 8, pages 276-280:

1) a   2) b   3) a   4) b   5) d   6) c   7) c   8) d   9) b
10) c

Vocabulary Test, pages 280-281:

1) a   2) c   3) b   4) a   5) c   6) b   7) c   8) c   9) a
10) c   11) c   12) b   13) c   14) c   15) b

Chapter Eleven

Vocabulary Test, pages 289-291:

a) blotter, b) facsimile, c) newsprint, d) upper case, e) banner line, f) bold face, g) caption, h) dummy, i) dogwatch, j) breakover, k) feature, l) filler, m) lead, n) masthead, o) linotype, p) lower case, q) morgue, r) kill, s) copy, t) scoop

Selection 1, pages 291-297:

1) c   2) d   3) b   4) d   5) a   6) d   7) d   8) d   9) c
10) b

Selection 2, pages 298-303:

1) c   2) d   3) b   4) c   5) b   6) d   7) c   8) d   9) a
10) c

Selection 3, pages 303-305:

1) c   2) b   3) d   4) d   5) a   6) d   7) a   8) c   9) d
10) b

Chapter Twelve

Exercise 1, page 318:

1) the writer, 2) the manufacturers of the toothpaste, 3) to persuade

you to buy the paste, 4) to be admired, 5) glad words, 6) your own decision

Exercise 2, pages 318-319:

1) the Communist leader, 2) Soviet Union, 3) to bolster the influence of the Soviet Union with peoples of Eastern Europe, 4) fear, 5) stacking the cards, 6) your decision

Exercise 3, page 319:

1) Krushchev, 2) Soviet Union, 3) to strengthen the estimate of the Soviet's power, 4) fear of death by bombs, 5) stack the cards, 6) your decision

Exercise 4, page 319:

1) the writer, 2) the one who wants to sell the information, 3) to sell the information, 4) desire to be powerful, 5) glad words, 6) your decision

Selection 1, pages 320-324:

1) d   2) b   3) d   4) a   5) c   6) d   7) c   8) a   9) b
10) d

Chapter Thirteen

Reading an Automobile Insurance Policy, pages 329-337:

1) d   2) d   3) d   4) c   5) d   6) a   7) d   8) d   9) b
10) a

Index